Arjuna in the *Mahabharata*

Vittorio (appropriately named) Mezzogiorno as Arjuna and Bruce Myers as Krishna on the battlefield at Kurukshetra, in the *Bhagavadgita* scene from Peter Brook's production of *The Mahabharata.* Photograph © 1987 Martha Swope.

Arjuna
in the
Mahabharata:

Where Krishna Is, There Is Victory

by Ruth Cecily Katz
Foreword by
Daniel H. H. Ingalls

MOTILAL BANARSIDASS PUBLISHERS
PRIVATE LIMITED • DELHI

First Published : Columbia, U.S.A., 1989
First Indian Edition : Delhi, 1990

ISBN: 978-81-2080-744-0

Also available at:

MOTILAL BANARSIDASS
41 U.A. Bungalow Road, Jawahar Nagar, Delhi 110 007
8 Mahalaxmi Chamber, Warden Road, Mumbai 400 026
120 Royapettah High Road, Mylapore, Chennai 600 004
Sanas Plaza, Subhash Nagar, Pune 411 002
16 St. Mark's Road, Bangalore 560 001
8 Camac Street, Calcutta 700 017
Ashok Rajpath, Patna 800 004
Chowk, Varanasi 221 0011

PRINTED IN INDIA
BY JAINENDRA PRAKASH JAIN AT SHRI JAINENDRA PRESS,
A-45 NARAINA, PHASE I, NEW DELHI 110 028
AND PUBLISHED BY NARENDRA PRAKASH JAIN FOR
MOTILAL BANARSIDASS PUBLISHERS PRIVATE LIMITED,
BUNGALOW ROAD, DELHI 110 007

To my parents,
and to the Honorable C. V. Narasimhan

Heroes of many kinds are proclaimed; hear from me, then, their goals. Rewards are assigned to the families of heroes and also to the hero himself. Heroes of sacrifice, heroes of self-control; others who are heroes of truth; heroes of battle are also proclaimed, and men who are heroes of giving. Others are heroes of intellect, and heroes of patience are others; and also heroes of honesty, and men who live in tranquillity. But there are many other heroes by various disciplines. There are heroes of Vedic study, and heroes who delight in teaching. There are heroes in obedience to teachers, and others in obedience to fathers. There are heroes in obedience to mothers, and others are heroes in alms. And many are heroes of *samkhya*, and others are heroes of *yoga*. There are forest-dwelling heroes, and householder heroes, and heroes in the honoring of guests. All go to heavens won as fruit of their own acts.

Mahabharata XIII.74.22–27

CONTENTS

Contents

EDITOR'S PREFACE

Studies in Comparative Religion is a series of books dedicated to providing specialist treatments of a wide variety of traditions and theoretical topics. Each project is a result of original scholarship, but aimed at a wide educated audience interested in current research in comparative religion as a human science that incorporates a variety of related disciplines. The series will eventually embrace studies of aspects of the religions of Native America, Europe, the Near East, Africa, and Asia.

Ruth C. Katz's *Arjuna in the Mahabharata* is a work of unusual breadth and depth that will attract readers in religious studies, comparative literature, Sanskrit, Asian studies, and the humanities in general. A thorough analysis of the monumental text of the *Mahabharata* in its complex and many-layered contexts of classical Indian culture, literature, religious doctrine and ritual, and historical development shows the epic figure Arjuna to be a religious role model for Hinduism, on the one hand, and perhaps the most fully realized example of the Indo-European/Semitic hero, on the other. The author has provided an illuminating discussion of the history of the text of the *Mahabharata,* showing its stages of composition and compilation, and an equally absorbing and carefully considered review of modern theories both of the complex text and its interpretation.

But with all of this book's valuable and accessible scholarly grounding, which specialists in comparative literature will find appealing, the author's fundamental contribution is a portrait of Arjuna that focuses finally on his profound spiritual meaning for Hindus, and by fortunate extension through works of interpretation such as this book, for any human being who ponders the great story of this complete person.

Frederick M. Denny

FOREWORD

It is difficult to characterize the *Mahābhārata*. One can say that it is probably the longest poem ever written: roughly 200,000 lines, most of them of sixteen syllables each. One can say that it was composed in the Sanskrit language, in northern India, over a period probably extending from 400 B.C. to A.D. 200. Its main story line constitutes an epic of the rivalry and war between two families of cousins. But hundreds of minor stories are told along the way. And not only stories are told. Prayers and hymns are recited. Long passages of advice are given on ethics and on royal administration. Virtually all the places of pilgrimage in northern India are described and their marvels recounted. Systems of philosophy and asceticism are summarized. In one famous section, the *Bhagavadgītā*, Krishna, as God incarnate, advises the hero Arjuna on how to attain salvation.

Obviously, in a poem of such diverse character different readers will be attracted by different constituents. To speak of myself, the chief delight that I have found in reading the poem comes from the interplay of its epic characters. A pious Hindu may set above this pleasure the solace which the poem gives him of communing with God. But Hindus no less than the few Westerners who have read the poem have taken joy and instruction from the portrayal of the Pāṇḍava brothers of the ancient epic and of their allies and enemies. To all the situations that arise in the story we are given the reactions of the three oldest Pāṇḍavas and, what is more, the response of others to their reaction. These characters are thus presented in greater breadth than those of any other epic which I have read. We know, for example, what Achilles felt about Briseis, but we are never told what she may have felt about him. Or how did his Myrmidons regard him? In the Indian epic, Draupadī is given a chance to speak about her husbands. And although the common man figures little in any epic literature, we are given in the *Mahābhārata* the remarks of the half-caste Vidura. His remarks are informed with a common humanity trimmed of the prejudice of any particular class.

Of the Pāṇḍava brothers, the reaction to events that we find in Yudhiṣṭhira is primarily that of piety and religion. Of Bhīma it is the reaction of brute strength. Arjuna, the subject of this monograph, is the youngest of the three full brothers—there are also two half-brothers, to make five Pāṇḍavas in all. Arjuna contains traits of his older brothers, but with them is still very much himself. He kills more enemies than Bhīma, but he has feelings of compassion and remorse which Bhīma lacks. He does not preach morality, as does Yudhiṣṭhira; and yet, when God speaks to man in the *Mahābhārata*, it is to Arjuna that he speaks, not to his pious older brother.

An analysis of the character of Arjuna cannot fail to enlighten the reader on the nature of early Hindu culture from which the picture of this hero arose. At the same time it will reveal some of the beauties and truths which remain in the *Mahābhārata* for the modern reader to savor, if his eyes are opened.

This book on Arjuna grew out of a doctoral thesis which Ruth Katz completed at Harvard University in 1980. As her teacher in Sanskrit and her thesis adviser, I had the duty of reading the thesis and the pleasure of talking with her frequently about it. The work has grown in several respects since that time, but its approach to its subject is still the same. It is an approach that strikes me as admirable in regard to both the selection of fact which it embodies and the aim which it achieves.

Ruth Katz's interest in the subject began from her first readings in the *Mahābhārata*, with Whitney's grammar on the right of the page and Apte's dictionary on the left. As she progressed to a more rapid reading of Sanskrit and to a complete survey of the poem, she gathered the traits of Arjuna into three compartments, or levels, which serve as the framework for this book: Arjuna as hero, Arjuna as human, and Arjuna as religious devotee. Professor Katz has taken all her basic material from the source itself. She has not superimposed traits on Arjuna from the heroes of other epics, as not a few comparativists have done. She compares him with other heroes, however, and many of her comparisons are enlightening, not only for the study of the *Mahābhārata* but for the study of other epic and religious literature as well. She reports conscientiously what other scholars have said of her hero. But the picture of Arjuna that emerges from this study is faithful to the *Mahābhārata* text.

Foreword

The *Mahābhārata* itself, of course, does not tell us in so many words that Arjuna was a three-stranded or three-leveled being. His actions and emotions are portrayed as the story gives rise to them. The contradictions that appear in his character, as they do in life itself, are left to the reader to explain as he sees fit. Ruth Katz notes, only to reject it, the theory that the complication of Arjuna's character arises from the superimposition on one another of successive historical layers of composition. In regard to this matter, which has long been a subject of debate, I may state my own opinion. I do believe that there are older and younger parts of the *Mahābhārata* and that these parts can eventually be identified by linguistic analysis. One may thus come to discover changes of custom, changes of geographical knowledge, changes in the art of warfare from passages of earlier to those of later composition. But I see in the text no reason to suppose that any great change occurred, despite the long period of composition, in the main story line or in the characters who act out the story. I agree with Ruth Katz that the complex character of Arjuna is essential to the poem in any form which we shall be able justly to hypothesize of it.

Ruth Katz's three-layer framework has much to recommend it, not only for the convenience of description but for an understanding of Arjuna's ultimate value as a literary creation. It serves to point out the areas of tragedy in the epic, which arises usually from conflicts of the heroic and the human. Such are Arjuna's initial horror at the onset of the war and later his uncontrollable grief over the death of his son, Abhimanyu. The framework emphasizes, by giving it a separate level, Arjuna's religious striving. The religious dimension is necessary for the solution of the tragic tensions. It is also the element of the *Mahābhārata* that has been most prized by Indians and that is doubtless responsible for the preservation of the text through so many centuries to our own time.

This is a book of careful and accurate research and of illuminating analysis.

Daniel H. H. Ingalls
Wales Professor of Sanskrit, Emeritus
Harvard University

Hot Springs, Virginia
October 28, 1988

NOTE ON TRANSLITERATION AND TRANSLATION

A few words must be said regarding the transliteration of Sanskrit names and technical terms in the present study, as follows. In the interest of accessibility, the decision has been made to employ a simplified transliteration throughout the main body of the text, including all of the author's own translations from the Sanskrit:

1. Omitting all diacritical marks generally employed in standard transliteration, except insofar as they are required in order to distinguish between two otherwise identical words: namely, in the cases of Bharata/Bhārata—only where these two appear in juxtaposition—and Vasudeva/Vāsudeva (the latter member of each pair being a patronymic), Uttara/Uttarā, Vidura/Vidurā, and Krishna/Krishnā (the latter, an epithet of Draupadi; the long *a* at the end of the name makes it into a feminine here, as in the two preceding pairs), Krpa/*krpā*.

2. Making some concessions to pronunciation: namely, what appears in the standard transliteration as *c* appears in the simplified transliteration as *ch*, pronounced as in English ("child"); and standard transliteration *ś* (formerly *ç*) and *ṣ* both appear in simplified form as *sh* in order to suggest the proper pronunciation—although the former is a palatal, the latter a lingual.

3. For familiarity's sake, rendering the standard transliteration "Kṛṣṇa" as "Krishna" throughout; likewise, "Krishnadvaipayana" (another name for Vyasa), "Krishnasarathi" (Arjuna), "Krishnā" (Draupadi), and the phrase *krishnavadatasya*.

On the other hand, diacritics are maintained in all bibliographic citations (in text, notes, and Bibliography) and all direct quotations in English and French; spellings of Sanskrit words included in these precisely duplicate those of the cited or quoted source, whether standard (as is generally the case) or idiosyncratic. Bracketed insertions into quotations, adhering, as they do, to the main body of the text, revert, however, to simplified transliteration, as do all Sanskrit quotations. The inevitable decision to maintain the original spelling in citations and quotations makes for some inconsistency between these and the main body of the text, but not enough, it is believed, to cause confusion. Lest there be doubt, the index of this study gives the standard form along with the simplified form of many important Sanskrit names and terms.

The reader will note, in particular, inconsistency in spelling between passages taken from the first few books of the *Mahabharata* and those taken from the remainder of the text. This is because passages from *Mahabharata* I–V are quoted from J. A. B. van Buitenen's translation of those books (Critical Edition),[1] which employs standard transliteration. Passages from *Mahabharata* VI–XVIII (including the *Bhagavadgita* [early Book VI], which van Buitenen had translated before his death,[2] but which most Sanskritists prefer to tackle alone) appear as translated by the present author; in these, thus, the simplified transliteration is employed.

Notes

1. J. A. B. van Buitenen, trans. and ed., *The Mahābhārata*, Books I–V, 3 vols. (Chicago: University of Chicago Press, 1973–78). With kind permission of the University of Chicago Press.
2. J. A. B. van Buitenen, trans. and ed., *The Bhagavadgītā in the Mahābhārata: Text and Translation* (Chicago: University of Chicago Press, 1981).

ACKNOWLEDGMENTS

With warmest thanks to the committee that guided this work when it was still in the form of a doctoral dissertation: John B. Carman, Diana Eck, Daniel H. H. Ingalls, and Gary Tubb; to my colleagues at that time at Harvard University's Center for the Study of World Religions, and to many wonderful Harvard professors; to those with whom I studied earlier, at Barnard College, especially Theodor H. Gaster, Anne Prescott, and Barry Ulanov; to my very supportive colleagues, presently, at Florida State University, including Mrs. Maureen Jackson—and to my excellent students; to the staff of the Oriental Division of the New York Public Library, especially Usha Bhasker, Massoud Pourfarrokh, and Sunita Vaze; to Kate Bemis, Alena Beničkova, Cathy Benton, Sidney Brown, James Doan, Alf Hiltebeitel, Wendy Johnson, Jon Marin, Karen Osborne, Richard Peters, Carla Reid, Robin Rhodes, Holly Seeling, Arvind Sharma, and Deva Williams; to several loving and cheerful friends and relatives; to Frederick M. Denny and Kenneth Scott, for their faith in my work; to the University of South Carolina Press, headed by Ken Scott. Special thanks to the University of Chicago Press, for permission to quote extensively from J. A. B. van Buitenen's *The Mahābhārata*, Vols. I–III, © 1973, 1975, 1978, by The University of Chicago. Thanks also to the *Journal of Studies in the Bhagavadgītā* for permission to reuse material first published in my article "Human and Divine Time in the Bhagavadgītā" (1981) and to the *Journal of South Asian Literature* for permission to reuse material first published in my article "The *Sauptika* Episode in the Structure of the *Mahābhārata*" (1985).

It was not until I was already proofreading the present work that I was able to attend a performance of Peter Brook's long-awaited production of *The Mahabharata,* playing, remarkably, just a few blocks away from my New York "second home," at the Brooklyn Academy of Music. I joyfully thank Mr. Brook and playwright Jean-Claude Carrière for their effort—the humor of "Book IV" was particularly appreciated—and I am most pleased to be able to present a scene from the production as my frontispiece.

Only while indexing—a process unexpectedly prolonged by a four-month trip to South Asia—did I learn of the appearance of the first volume of Alf Hiltebeitel's awaited work *The Cult of Draupadī* (for full reference, see below, chap IB, n. 48). Although Hiltebeitel has now moved beyond simple study of the Sanskrit *Mahabharata* and into the realm of Tamil folk cult (and its use of *Mahabharata* themes), his work touches mine at many points. And since the appearance of an important new work relating to one's area of research demands a certain amount of fine tuning of one's own understanding—and writing—I would have liked to have been able to bring Hiltebeitel's new insights into the present work, if only in a small way, around such pertinent themes as fish symbolism in the epic (Hiltebeitel, pp. 202–11, etc.); comparison/contrast of Draupadi and Subhadra (pp. 218–22); *brahmashiras* and its relationship to Shiva and various epic characters (pp. 372–79, 424–31, etc.). It would also have been appropriate to update some of my endnotes with new references to certain of Hiltebeitel's ideas already cited on the basis of his previous articles, in which they were first developed: for instance, his interpretation of Arjuna Savyasachin (in the context of the Draupadi cult) as he who "knows how to unite the left (the female side) with the right (the male side)," thus, one with " 'left-handed' knowledge" (pp. 207–8, to supplement my Appendix, n. 65); or his interpretation of Arjuna as eunuch as Ardhanarishvara (p. 296, to supplement my chap. ID, n. 40—although I would have had to argue that "blue facial coloring . . . and a peacock crown" do not strike me as particularly Shiva-like). Notes featuring Biardeau's ideas could also have been updated with Hiltebeitel's favorable comments, and my all too brief mention of Pandava cults (chap. IA, n. 7) could have been enhanced considerably with information nicely summarized by Hiltebeitel on his pp. 131–35; likewise, my discussion of Arjuna's fertility persona (chap. IB), with reference to his seven (or so) extra wives, à la the Draupadi cult. And so much more. I was, however, spared the temptation of engaging in yet another set of revisions, as just outlined, by the fact that the present work was already in the form of page proofs, so that no substantive changes could be made. (Perhaps it is just as well, insofar as ongoing scholarly discussion could make such revision an endless task!) But I am most pleased at least to have the opportunity now to thank Hiltebeitel for his new work, which so greatly broadens the boundaries of *Mahabharata* scholarship, and to acknowledge my debt to him once again. I will look forward to his two projected additional volumes of *The Cult of Draupadī*, particularly his "*Mahābhārata* interpreted through the centrality of the goddess" (p. xviii), which I anticipate in part as a fascinating retrieval of such pre-/non-Indo-European materials as the pre-Sovereignty Goddess figure and the Goddess-Arjuna/Shiva (see my chap. IIIA, n. 26) sacred marriage, out from under the Indo-European overlay featured (in all its strengths and weaknesses) in the work I here present.

Arjuna in the *Mahabharata*

INTRODUCTION

Janamejaya, king at Hastinapura, decided to hold a snake sacrifice to avenge the death of his father, Parikshit, by snakebite:

> *The snakes began to drop into the blazing flames, writhing and wretched and crying out to one another. They darted and hissed and wildly coiled about with tails and heads as they fell into the radiant fire—white, black, blue, old, and young—screeching terrifying screams, they fell into the high blazing flames, hundreds of thousands and millions and tens of millions of the Snakes died powerless . . . some tiny like mice, others fat like elephant trunks, or huge and strong like rutting bull elephants, all sorts of them in vast numbers, manycolored, poisonous, and loathsome, mordacious and powerful, they fell into the fire.* [Mahabharata *I.47.20–25*][1]

Among the many guests entertained by Janamejaya on this occasion was the brahmin Vaishampayana, a student of the famous sage Vyasa, editor of the Vedas and the Puranas. Knowing by reputation the narrative skill of this illustrious visitor, Janamejaya importuned him:

> *Sir, . . . you have been a witness to the deeds of the Kurus and the Pāṇḍavas. I want you to tell me about their acts, brahmin. How did that Breach arise between these men of untroubled deeds, and how did that great War come about, which was to be the destruction of the creatures, between all my grandfathers [ancestors] whose minds were smitten by fate?* [Mahabharata *I.54.18–20*]

Then, in couplets first composed by Vyasa himself, Vaishampayana related to Janamejaya the epic poem Mahabharata,[2] *the story of the great war fought at Kurukshetra by the Pandavas against the Kauravas (the sons of Dhrtarashtra), to avenge the humiliation of Draupadi and the theft of the kingdom, along with the events that led up to and followed the war. The bard Ugrashravas heard Vaishampayana's recitation and carried the epic tale of the Pandavas and the Kauravas to the hermitage of the sage Shaunaka; later it was conveyed to the world.*

Janamejaya's immediate ancestors, the Pandavas, were five brothers, Yudhishthira, Bhimasena (Bhima), Arjuna, and the twins, Nakula and Sahadeva, Draupadi being their common wife. Their enemies, the Kauravas, were their first cousins. The pivotal member of the Pandava family—the middle brother—was Janamejaya's great-grandfather, Arjuna, the subject of the present study.

Introduction to the *Mahabharata*

The *Mahabharata*, generally referred to as the Great Epic of India (as opposed to the other major pan-Indian epic, *Ramayana*, the story of the hero Rama Dasharathi), is an epic poem in the ancient language Sanskrit, the title of which means, literally, "the great [story of the war of the] descendants of Bharata [that is, the Pandavas and the Kauravas]." It appears to have been composed between the fourth century B.C. and the fourth century A.D. (see below). (The dates of the *Ramayana* are c. 200 B.C. to A.D. 200.)[3] As a piece of literature, the *Mahabharata* in many ways resembles, and shows family ties with and parallels to, similar products of the "heroic age"[4] worldwide, particularly Indo-European products (epics and sagas)[5]—for the Sanskrit language and the literature composed in it belong to the Indo-European linguistic group. Therefore, to gain a certain conception of the *Mahabharata*'s format and ambiance, one need only think, for example, of the Greek epic the *Iliad*, with its many reminders of oral composition (simple metrical structure, traditional themes and, outstandingly, formulaic building blocks),[6] replete with chariot warfare, violent action, and heroic sentiments.

On the other hand, the *Mahabharata* also has what might be considered typically Indian features, as suggested by its length, unmatched in other epic literatures: approximately 100,000 couplets (though reduced by a quarter in the Critical Edition), eight times the size of the *Iliad* and the *Odyssey* combined. According to the *Mahabharata*'s own well-known words (I.56.33* and XVIII.5.38): "Whatever is here . . . is found elsewhere. But what is not here is nowhere else." Shaped by the epic

*Throughout text and notes, references of the form I.56.33 indicate those stanzas in the *Mahabarata*, unless otherwise specified.

story line, the *Mahabharata* is yet an unevenly textured repository for all manner of mythic, legendary, didactic, and folkloric material, including many subordinate tales. The oftentimes baroque nature of this accretion may be judged from the description of the snake sacrifice with which this introduction opens—particularly when it is realized that no such sacrifice seems ever to have existed historically; it probably represents something else (see chap. IC, below).* The characters and situations represented in the *Mahabharata* narrative can be rather baroque as well; but perhaps this is just a veneer. Their human side is equally prominent, as the present study will indicate. Overall, the *Mahabharata* may be said to embody the abundance of India, a nation that has been, through the centuries, uniquely capable of living with untrammeled growth, even contradictions. To this day, "Bhārata" ("the family of Bharata") is the name for India in the modern Indian languages, with the implication that Bharata, besides simply having been a distant ancestor of the Pandavas and the Kauravas, was somehow the forerunner of all Indian culture.

Indian society was and still is apportioned into an ideal four-tiered hierarchical class structure, comprising, from highest to lowest, brahmins (priests), *kshatriya*s (warriors), *vaishya*s (farmers and artisans), and *shudra*s (servants to the other classes). Under this categorization, the infinitely more complex caste system of India was and is subsumed. As might be expected, the characters in the *Mahabharata* chiefly represent the two upper of these four classes, with a few exceptions, including several members of the *suta* (charioteer and bard) caste (also mentioned as reciters of the epic, including Ugrashravas), and one character, the wise and virtuous Vidura, of mixed brahmin/"slave" (I.100.23ff.) descent.[7] Although the didactic sections of the epic have come to include substantial instruction for common people (see chaps. IIA1, IIA3, etc.), the epic narrative itself depicts them, for the most part, only en masse, reacting undimensionally to the deeds of their rulers, performed upon the epic stage.

Traditionally, brahmins and *kshatriya*s have had a complex, symbiotic relationship: brahmins controlled the spiritual power in Indian society, while *kshatriya*s, as a rule (or ideally), controlled the material power.

*Referrals in text and notes to Introduction, chaps. IA–IE, IIA1–IIA3, IIB–IIC, IIIA, IIIB1–IIIB2, IIIC–IIID, Conclusion, and Appendix indicate those sections in the present study.

In the *Mahabharata*, the two groups often cooperate, and as often clash. Just so, what might be called the brahmanic and *kshatriya* strands of the *Mahabharata* overlap and intertwine, yet are sometimes strikingly separate. In brief, the *kshatriya* strand supplies the basic heroic story. Some didactic passages attached to the epic, outstandingly the teaching of Vidurā (not to be confused with Vidura, above) (V.131ff.) also reflect primarily the issues and ideals of the *kshatriya* class. The brahmanic strand accounts for the material of a large portion of the didactic books of the *Mahabharata* (Books XII–XIII) and other didactic passages dispersed throughout the epic; it advocates brahmanic philosophies and, in a heavy-handed manner, glorifies brahmins, even as it preaches to *kshatriya*s.

But there is a third strand in the *Mahabharata*, which passes beyond the class/caste system: this is the strand of *bhakti*, religious devotion. Of all texts in the Indian heritage, it is the *Mahabharata* that is considered to have first brought the concept of *bhakti* to the fore.

Bhakti is devotion to God, conceived of as a means to religious salvation. Although the Indian—Hindu—tradition recognizes a large number of gods and goddesses, of greater or less importance, it is not inappropriate for a Westerner to gain a preliminary understanding of *bhakti* in Judeo-Christian (monotheistic) terms; for the *bhakta* (devotee) generally chooses one god or goddess as his or her special object of attention. Furthermore, there is a well-developed sense in the Hindu religious consciousness that all gods and goddesses are actually manifestations of the One, complementary, if not identical. Thus one finds three of the major deities, Brahma, Vishnu, and Shiva, combined in the so-called Hindu Trinity, as creator, preserver, and destroyer of the universe, respectively, each being, at the same time, creator, preserver, and destroyer together, in his own right. In the *Mahabharata*, the particular focus of *bhakti* is Vishnu, incarnate in Krishna. The *bhakti* strand of the text is that which concentrates upon devotion to Vishnu/Krishna as the major goal and guiding force of life; it may be located in the didactic books and, especially, in association with the character Krishna, participating in the epic narrative as a staunch Pandava ally. Of outstanding importance here is the *Bhagavadgita* ("The Song of God") (*Mahabharata* VI.23–40), a lecture delivered by Krishna to Arjuna on the battlefield, just before the start of the Kurukshetra War, advocating, among other things, devotion to Krishna. Through the centuries, the *Bhagavadgita* has become, independent of the rest of the epic, a most important devotional text of Hinduism. The god Shiva also plays a role in the *bhakti* strand of the *Mahabharata*,[8] as does the Hindu goddess Shri, or Lakshmi. (Brahma, insofar as he is merely a personification of the concept *brahman* [see, especially, chap. IIIB1], is not an important devotional figure; he tends to move above the epic action, functioning as an elder statesman of the pantheon.)

Devotion to gods and goddesses was surely a very ancient Indian practice, going back, perhaps, to the dawn of civilization, but *bhakti* per se is not reflected clearly in religious literature until the time of the *Mahabharata*. The earliest extant proto-Hindu texts, the Vedas (c. 1200–900 B.C.), supplemented by the Brahmanas (c. 900–700 B.C.), do introduce a pantheon of deities, featuring the warrior/storm god Indra (also Agni, Soma, Varuna, etc.). But not only does the shift to *bhakti* entail a complete reshuffling of the pantheon, with the relatively minor Vedic deities Vishnu and Rudra/Siva being promoted and the other deities (even Indra) relegated to a secondary position; in addition, the goal of worship changes, from the Vedic emphasis on worldly prosperity to ultimate salvation, which is *bhakti*'s goal. Furthermore, the Vedic deities are to be worshiped by large-scale sacrifice—the accompanying hymns of which constitute the Vedas—as opposed to the simple, lovingly given offerings (*puja*) characteristic of *bhakti*. Later supplementary texts, the Upanishads (c. 700 B.C.), introduce the concepts of *samsara* (transmigration—the round of birth, death, and rebirth), *karma* (literally, "action," past actions determining future births), and *moksha* ("release" from this cycle, to ultimate salvation), which will come to characterize classical Hinduism; but they, for the most part, advocate meditation, leading to *jnana* ("knowledge"), as the means to *moksha*. In this textual progression, the *Mahabharata*, with its advocacy of *bhakti*, marks the next step, which is, strikingly, the final step into fully developed Hinduism. The *Ramayana*, composed, as mentioned above, at approximately the same time, shows a similar development, featuring Vishnu incarnate in Rama.

Heroic literature always reflects the religious milieu of the society that has produced it. It may be argued, although this is a matter of scholarly debate (see below), that the *Mahabharata* looks backward toward the Vedas and forward toward the Puranas (third/fourth century A.D., and for a number of centuries following), those Hindu texts that delineate fully the mythologies of the gods and goddesses of *bhakti*. This suggestion is particularly interesting in that the Vedas are archetypically Indo-European, and would thus define what is characteristically Indo-European in the epic text; while the Puranas are archetypically Hindu. That the *Mahabharata* does indeed combine these two influences is the position taken by the present study.

That the material of the Vedas would be retained and utilized even as the material of the Puranas supersedes it is very much as one might expect: the Hindu tradition never loses any of its strata from the past. Indeed, India continues to the present day to accord highest honor to the Vedas, which are even referred to as *shruti* ("what is heard—revealed") as opposed to the less authoritative *smrti* ("what is remembered," traditional lore), including the epics and Puranas, and even the *Bhagavadgita* itself.

Why Study Arjuna?

It will be clear from the preceding discussion that the *Mahabharata* is well worth study both as a classic of world literature and as an entrée into Indian culture. Why, then, study Arjuna in particular? First, because Arjuna is a great heroic figure of India, the Indian Achilles, about whom one must learn if one is to know anything about India (especially since the Indian epics are far better known and more influential in their own cultural milieu than are the *Iliad* and the *Odyssey* in the West). As the *Mahabharata* is an entrée into Indian culture, so Arjuna is an entrée into the *Mahabharata*—in many ways more central to the epic than his brothers (although this too is controversial), as his relationship to Janamejaya implies. Second, Arjuna is an extremely important figure for the Hindu religious tradition: as the hero to whom the *Bhagavadgita* was recited by Krishna, Arjuna becomes a religious role model, an "everyman" struggling for truth. This side of Arjuna's character is well known even to many Westerners, who have read the *Bhagavadgita* for religious inspiration. To study Arjuna, and further to study him within the context of the *Mahabharata* as a whole, significantly enhances one's understanding of Hinduism. Third, and most important to non-Indologists, the study of Arjuna provides a unique opportunity to consider the figure of the Indo-European/Semitic[9] hero in all its aspects, for what is implicit in other such heroes (Achilles, Aeneas, Arthur, Beowulf, the

Buddha, Cuchulainn, Gilgamesh, Herakles, Isfandiyar, Jacob, Jesus, Moses, Odysseus, Rama, Roland, and Rustam, among others) is explicit in Arjuna. Whereas the others operate against fixed religious backgrounds, Arjuna incorporates and grows with his religious context, clearly reflecting its development over time. In short, Arjuna is "hero unedited"—although it must be pointed out immediately that his disparate aspects hang together surprisingly well, displaying unity even in their diversity.

The Approach

The aim of the present study will be to provide a complete and coherent portrait of this complex figure. This task will be undertaken in three parts, each being a discussion of one vital level of Arjuna's personality: Arjuna as epic hero; as human being; and as religious devotee or hero of religion. As the discussion progresses, interconnections between the three levels will also be indicated. Comparative materials from Indo-European and Semitic sources will be introduced as pertinent, including brief reference to Christianity, primarily in the conclusion. An appendix dealing with the epithets of Arjuna will include material relevant to all three levels of his character.

The subdivisions employed here are an outgrowth of years of living with the *Mahabharata* text and attempting to enter into its spirit. As will become evident, similar or parallel levels may be discovered in the other major *Mahabharata* characters and the story as a whole, and these will be referred to frequently. But the contrast between the levels is clearest in, and most basic to, the character of Arjuna; this fact, along with Arjuna's central role in the epic, and the various arguments adduced above, justifies concentration on him.[10]

Details of the *Mahabharata* plot will be unfolded as the discussion progresses, to provide all necessary background and, by the end of this study, retell the entire tale. What follows, however, is a list of the eighteen books into which the epic is divided, with a brief summary of the contents of each, for the reader's convenience.

Outline of the *Mahabharata*

BOOK I. *Adiparvan* ("Book of the Beginning"): Offers background material, and the early lives of the Pandavas and the Kauravas.

Book II. *Sabhaparvan* ("Book of the Assembly Hall"): Recounts the jealousy of the eldest Kaurava, Duryodhana, at the prosperity of the Pandavas, as evidenced, for example, by their newly built assembly hall. Duryodhana responds by challenging the Pandavas to a dice game, held in the Kauravas' assembly hall; the Pandavas lose everything, are reprieved and lose again, and are sent into temporary exile in the forest.
Book III. *Aranyakaparvan* ("Book of the Forest"): The Pandavas spend twelve years in the forest, having many adventures and hearing many tales.
Book IV. *Virataparvan* ("Book of Virata"): The Pandavas pass a thirteenth year of exile, incognito, in the Matsya kingdom, ruled by King Virata.
Book V. *Udyogaparvan* ("Book of the Effort"): All peace missions failing, the Pandavas and the Kauravas prepare for war.
Books VI–IX. *Bhishmaparvan, Dronaparvan, Karnaparvan,* and *Shalyaparvan* ("Book of Bhishma," "Book of Drona," "Book of Karna," and "Book of Shalya"): The Kurukshetra War is fought, with the Pandavas finally emerging victorious. The names of these four books are the names of the four generals who lead the Kaurava forces—and are killed—in succession.
Book X. *Sauptikaparvan* ("Book of the Night Attack"): The surviving Pandava allies are killed off by the few surviving Kaurava partisans. The five Pandava brothers themselves remain alive, along with Krishna and his compatriot, Satyaki; and the Pandava heir, Parikshit (father of Janamejaya), killed in his mother's womb, is promised revival by Krishna.
Book XI. *Striparvan* ("Book of the Women"): The women mourn, and funeral rites are observed.
Books XII–XIII. *Shantiparvan* and *Anushasanaparvan* ("Book of Peace" and "Book of Instruction"): The didactic books of the epic. The teachings offered are, for the most part, placed in the mouth of Bhishma, who lies on his deathbed. (Mortally wounded long before, he has postponed his actual demise for an auspicious moment.)
Book XIV. *Ashvamedhikaparvan* ("Book of the Horse Sacrifice"): Describes Yudhishthira's great horse sacrifice (*ashvamedha*), by which he legitimates the Pandava rule.
Book XV. *Ashramavasikaparvan* ("Book of Hermitage Dwelling"): The surviving parents of the Pandavas and the Kauravas retire to the forest in their old age, and eventually die in a forest fire.

BOOK XVI. *Mausalaparvan* ("Book of the Club Fight"): The Vrshnis, Krishna's people, kill themselves off in a fateful club fight. The Krishna incarnation itself comes to an end.
BOOK XVII. *Mahaprasthanikaparvan* ("Book of the Great Journey"): The Pandava brothers and Draupadi retire from the world.
BOOK XVIII. *Svargarohanaparvan* ("Book of the Ascent to Heaven"): Yudhishthira ascends to heaven and is permitted to observe the ultimate fates of his brothers, the Kauravas, and others.

The Epic Text: Consistency and Inconsistency

If Arjuna is hero unedited, it is because the *Mahabharata* is epic unedited; not completely unedited, of course—how could one accuse Vyasa, whose very name means, literally, "editor," of such negligence?—but in some sense more like an encyclopedia than an epic at all. One's understanding of the nature of the text determines one's understanding of Arjuna.

The two most frequently cited views regarding the process of composition that made the *Mahabharata* what it is today are generally considered contradictory. The first is the traditional Indian view, just referred to, presented by the epic itself (I.1.9, etc.) and offered at the start of this introduction: the *Mahabharata* had a single composer, Vyasa, who also appears as a character in the epic action, a progenitor and adviser of the central participants. For Hindus, this assertion may take on the force of religious conviction, when they regard the *Mahabharata* composer Vyasa as identical with that seer (sage), also called Vyasa, to whom the compilation of the Vedas and the Puranas is attributed traditionally.[11] Similar to the traditional view, minus its religious overtones, is the idea of the *Mahabharata*'s composition by a single editor, advanced in the West in the late nineteenth century by Joseph Dahlmann; this editor, Dahlmann asserted, had devised the epic as a legal textbook, combining didactic statements with illustrative heroic tales.[12] Soon after it appeared, Dahlmann's view (and thus, by implication, the traditional view) was challenged by E. Washburn Hopkins.[13] In *The Great Epic of India: Its Character and Origin*,[14] a book that is still well regarded, Hopkins stressed the inconsistencies to be found in the epic, viewing them as the result of eight hundred years of interpolation of an original core, which was very different from the final product. Hopkins also referred to the oral transmission of the work,[15] but was not able to extend his study in that direction, since the nature of oral composition was not well understood at the time he wrote. His summary of the stages in the epic's development reads as follows:

> . . . Bhārata (Kuru) lays, perhaps combined into one, but with no evidence of an epic before 400 B.C. A Mahābhārata tale with Pandu heroes, lays and legends combined by the Puranic diaskeuasts, Krishna as a demigod (no evidence of didactic form or of Krishna's divine supremacy), 400–200 B.C. Remaking of the epic with Krishna as all-god, intrusion of masses of didactic matter, addition of Puranic material old and new; multiplication of exploits, 200 B.C. to 100–200 A.D. The last books added with the introduction to the first book, the swollen Anuçāsana separated from Çānti and recognized as a separate book, 200 to 400 A.D.; and finally 400 A.D. + : occasional amplifications.[16]

Indian scholars, understandably, tend to comment favorably on Dahlmann's approach, but are far more critical of the work of Hopkins. Many Western scholars, on the other hand, have preferred the approach of Hopkins; to them, "Vyasa" is purely mythic.[17] To the author of the present study, however, the epic has always appeared both consistent and inconsistent: although it is clearly not a uniform work, the product of one composer or even one period of time (its style and diction are uneven, it contains seeming contradictions and repetitions, and not all of its symbolism is carried through with regularity), it does seem to have a central guiding force. An Indian scholar, Vishnu Sitaram Sukthankar, the first editor of the Critical Edition of the *Mahabharata*, points to this situation with great forcefulness. One should, Sukthankar writes, "bear in mind that however much the textual critic might peel off from the external trappings of the Great Epic, its Gestalt remains absolutely unaltered."[18] J. A. B. van Buitenen, a great translator of the epic, apparently agrees, although his statement is more reserved than that of Sukthankar:

> I should like to believe that there is *organic* growth in the *Mahābhārata*, in the sense that an interpolation was not extraneous to the text but was attracted, even at times provoked, by an incident in the "original."[19]

Evidently, an approach between the traditional Indian view and the view of Hopkins is called for.

The present study would propose the following picture of *Mahabharata* evolution in three stages. First, the poetry existed as heroic epic in a fluid, oral state, as individual tales and cycles of tales, recited primarily by members of the *suta* caste. (It seems that *sūta*s became bards for the very reason that they served as charioteers in battle, and as such could observe the fighting without actually participating; that is, although many charioteers were certainly killed in battle, they were not the central combatants—in fact, the official rules of battle, at least insofar as the epic text preserves them, declare charioteers inviolable.[20] After the battle was over, the *suta* could report on the heroic feats he had observed.) Later, the material was collected and reworked, at a definite, though indeterminate, historical moment. (In interpreting oral literature, there is every reason to posit such a moment, to explain how a loose oral format eventually turned into the poem we now possess.)[21] It seems probable that this second stage took place in a royal court, and that its product, in contradiction to Hopkins's reconstruction, included didactic and devotional elements. Lastly—and here the *Mahabharata* differs from many other works of epic literature, including those attributed to Homer—the epic continued to be transmitted in a loose form, oral or written (or, most likely, both). That is, the basic work was no longer altered (if passed down orally, it was now memorized, more or less accurately); since, however, there was no interdiction on interpolations, poets of various schools of thought could add what they wished to it—and they did so, in huge amounts. One such group, which appears to have taken over and reedited the epic early in this third stage, was a family of brahmins known as the Bhargavas; they added Bhargava stories with Bhargava characters to the epic, and they, or others like them, must also have been responsible for much of the epic's didactic accretion.[22] Devotional groups also interpolated the epic at this time. Later in the third stage, as the *Mahabharata* spread throughout India, regional variations became the rule. Eventually, separate manuscript traditions crystallized.

Some complications, even contradictions, would have entered the epic as early as the first stage, by way of the oral composers' characteristic use of formulas without regard to contextual details and stringing together of traditional themes according to traditional story patterns.[23] Indeed, formulas would still have been employed at later stages, in imitation of the ancient style. Much more serious complications would have arisen during the third stage, the stage of transmission, to account for the epic's "unedited" and "Indian" flavor. (Indians evidently considered the *Mahabharata* to have been edited quite enough; thus their conception of a single composer, Vyasa.) On the other hand, those who oversaw the epic in the intermediate period of collection and reworking, while not obliterating diversity within and among the traditional stories brought into it, would have given the whole its basic shape. What they produced would have been the often sought epic "core," and it is here that the work's ultimate unity would have been forged.

The picture proposed here has the advantage of combining the traditional Indian view of the epic's origin with certain suggestions advanced by Western scholarship, particularly the theory of oral composition. Besides being appropriate to a student who, while a Westerner herself, strongly desires to be true to the Indian spirit of the text under consideration, such a view is satisfying in that it stands up to the test of the epic as neither Hopkins's view alone nor the traditional view alone can.

The *Mahabharata* itself offers an account of its own early history, which seems to reflect, in outline, the hypothesized developmental process just presented. After Vyasa composed the *Mahabharata*, the epic states, he taught it to five disciples, through whom it later spread to the world at large (I.57.74–75).[24] The one of these five who is said specifically to have imparted the epic to the human world, Vaishampayana (XIII.5.42),[25] did so by reciting it at the snake sacrifice of King Janamejaya (I.1.8, etc.). There the *suta* Ugrashravas heard Vaishampayana's recitation, and he in turn recited the epic to a group of brahmins led by the Bhargava Shaunaka, during a sacrifice they were performing at the Naimisha Forest (I.1ff.). Most of the epic is presented in what purport to be the words of Vaishampayana to Janamejaya, as reported by Ugrashravas to Shaunaka. Another *suta* is also mentioned as having reported some of the epic action; this is Samjaya, in whose words is described most of the actual fighting of the Kurukshetra War, that is, the main body of material included in Books VI through IX (and part of X) of the extant text. Samjaya, we are told, had been given divine sight by Vyasa, so that he could report on the war to the blind king Dhrtarashtra, the father of the Kauravas, whom he served as charioteer (VI.2.8ff.). In the extant epic, Dhrtarashtra's questions and Samjaya's answers are reported by Vaishampayana. In sum, three recitations of all or part of the epic material are mentioned after its original composition by Vyasa, whose own recitation of the material is not detailed. It is possible to correlate these three recitations with the three stages of epic development outlined above, taking each recitation as representative of one stage. The early period of oral composition is represented by Samjaya's reporting to Dhrtarashtra. The period of late transmission is embodied in Ugrashravas's recitation to Shaunaka. Vaishampayana's recitation to Janamejaya is, thus, left to represent the intermediate stage of epic development, the period of collection and reworking.[26]

What was the nature of the collection made for the king whom the epic calls Janamejaya? On the basis of clues in the text itself, one may surmise that it would have contained, in reduced form, all three strands of the epic delineated above: it would have been a story of warrior heroism (for Janamejaya was a *kshatriya*, who had asked to hear about his ancestors), replete with priestly instruction from a brahmin reciter (credible historically, since Indian kings did have brahmin advisers), with strong devotional content, since this Janamejaya appears to have been one of a line of Vishnu/Krishna devotees (see chap. IIIC). Even if no such historical Janamejaya ever existed, or if the Janamejaya of the epic represents a line of kings instead of an identifiable individual,[27] the preceding analysis brings us, perhaps, as close to the epic core as we can presently come.[28]

One may best understand certain aspects of the epic's characterization of Arjuna by realizing that they must have been included to please those who called themselves his descendants or to legitimate their kingship. It has been suggested, on the basis of the Himalayan birth and polyandrous marriage of the Pandavas, and because their name does not occur in the pre-epic (Vedic and Upanishadic) literature of India, that they represent some foreign group that had, historically, invaded the Indian subcontinent, probably from the north;[29] legitimation would have been particularly necessary for the descendants of such a group. In any case, all levels of Arjuna's character may be viewed from the perspective of his "descendants": Arjuna is called a great hero for purposes of glorification (with much of the heroic material being derived from the ancient poetic tradition); he is presented as human so as to mirror the problems of a real king; he is shown as a devotee so as to indicate how these problems may be overcome, probably in reflection of his "descendants' " own solution to their moral dilemmas. Because Arjuna's human component was the source of his troubles, it was easy for others besides his own "descendants" to relate to these troubles as time passed. The extant (interpolated) *Mahabharata* came, therefore, to include discussion of Arjuna's difficulties by a number of poets over a long period of time, and their offering of various solutions to these difficulties. The unity in diversity of Arjuna's characterization in the extant epic is based upon its completeness in the original "core."

How will this view influence the treatment of Arjuna in the present study? Naturally, it will mean that Arjuna's various aspects can and will be looked at as they exist in the extant epic, with awareness of their historical antecedents, but with no attempt to order them chronologically. These aspects will be separated from one another so as to provide a better understanding of Arjuna, but connections between them will also be sought. It will be noted in particular how the devotional level of Arjuna's character relates to its heroic level through the mediation of its human level; that is, how devotion restores Arjuna's heroism, which is threatened by his humanity. In this manner, a deep and complete view of Arjuna will be attempted, a view that reflects the way in which a Hindu, involved in Hindu culture, might see or have seen him on the basis of the epic as passed down through the centuries more or less in its current form.

The epic grows as it is recited again and again, but its basic message remains intact: Arjuna is *the* great hero. Finally, the epic becomes a complete mythic corpus in the Lévi-Straussian sense: an effort (partly unconscious) to convey a chosen message in as convincing a manner as possible, by means of repetition, permutation, transformation, and multivalent symbols.[30] Arjuna is seen to be all the sorts of hero mentioned in the opening quotation of this study, on the basis of his innate prowess supported ultimately by his religious devotion.

On the other hand, inconsistencies are fully to be expected in the extant epic. Some of these inconsistencies may, as mentioned above, be attributed to the oral composition of much of the poetry; the rest have to do with the late process of interpolation. The words of Sukthankar, quoted above, seem to exaggerate; those of van Buitenen are truer. That is, although the *Mahabharata* does, indeed, suggest organic growth, its "Gestalt" would seem to have undulated somewhat over time. The present study will note inconsistency where pertinent, and make no attempt to force the material. The most important inconsistency to be dealt with results from the exaltation of Yudhishthira by certain elements among the epic poets, as an alternative to the ideal represented by Arjuna (see chap. IIID).

A final note: the view of epic development just outlined is one that allows for the validity of critically editing the *Mahabharata* text; a collation of the various manuscript traditions, the Critical Edition, although it certainly includes much later material (for instance, brahmanic and many devotional additions), may be viewed as a version of the epic that more closely approaches the earliest *Mahabharata* collection than do the locally differentiated manuscripts accounted for in its appendices. Furthermore, with regard to Arjuna, at least, the basic structure would seem to hold firm despite any number of interpolations. On this basis, the Critical Edition of the *Mahabharata* is the edition utilized by the present study.

The Scholarly Context

Since the *Bhagavadgita* is widely read apart from its epic context both in India and in the West, a number of inquiries into Arjuna's character have been undertaken as parts of studies of that text alone. In such studies, which have often been of the nature of commentary (that is, representations of particular religious and philosophical positions), Arjuna has generally been treated as an "everyman" figure, listening to the preaching of the Lord, with whom he—like all men—is intimately connected. Sri Aurobindo Ghose, for example, wrote of him:

> Arjuna, the disciple who receives his initiation on the battlefield . . . is the type of the struggling human soul who has not yet received the knowledge, but has grown fit to receive it by action in the world in a close companionship and an increasing nearness to the higher and divine Self in humanity.[31]

Sarvepalli Radhakrishnan wrote:

> The pupil, Arjuna, is the type of the struggling soul who has not yet received the saving truth. He is fighting with the forces of darkness, falsehood, limitation, and mortality which bar the way to the higher world. When his whole being is bewildered, when he does not know the valid law of action, he takes refuge in his higher self, typified as Kṛṣṇa.[32]

A non-Hindu scholar, Sylvain Lévi, who saw the *Bhagavadgita* as the core of the *Mahabharata*, characterized Arjuna as "the perfect chevalier . . . also the perfect devotee."[33] These statements are all valid as far as they go, yet there is much more to Arjuna, which can be understood only by examining his role in the epic as a whole, rather than the *Bhagavadgita* alone.

A tradition of Sanskrit commentary on the body of the *Mahabharata* exists,[34] but it has been beyond the scope of the present study to explore it. As illustrated by the commentary of Nilakantha (seventeenth century),[35] which has been consulted on some points, Sanskrit literary commentaries generally gloss line by line, briefly treating difficult passages rather than providing an extended treatment of any single issue. For the present, therefore, it has been judged most practical and illuminating to concentrate directly upon the Sanskrit text of the epic, in its critical version, in order to look precisely at what this text says about Arjuna.

The study undertaken here is thus in the province of modern scholarship rather than traditional commentary. Yet the work of modern predecessors is of only limited applicability. Modern studies of Arjuna in the context of the epic are few, and those that one finds are largely unsatisfactory; for much like commentators, modern scholars have tended to impose individual biases upon the figure of Arjuna and the epic text as a whole.

The best—or worst—illustration of this limitation is the one published full-length monograph on Arjuna to date (all other studies of Arjuna being at most sections of larger works), *Arjuna: Ein Beitrag zur Reconstruction des Mahābhārata*, by Adolf Holtzmann the younger.[36] This work was an outgrowth of Western discomfort with certain seemingly unheroic behavior engaged in by the Pandava brothers during the Kurukshetra War, namely, the fact that they resort to trickery to gain their victories. To deal with this contradiction in heroic terms, Holtzmann propounded a theory of "inversion," which had first been suggested by his uncle, Adolf Holtzmann (elder), stating that the Pandavas, including Arjuna, were the villains of an original version of the epic, rather than its heroes, as they are in the extant epic.[37] This theory caused Holtzmann to view Arjuna with great sarcasm, treating many of Arjuna's actions as hints of his former villainous role.

But Holtzmann has not been the only scholar to try to "reduce" the *Mahabharata*, and Arjuna with it; this has been done since the earliest days of modern *Mahabharata* scholarship, beginning in the nineteenth century, when Monier Monier-Williams, contrasting the *Mahabharata* with the Greek epics, referred to its characters as one-sided and lacking in depth[38] (a notion that in fact could not be further from the truth). In line with his effort to understand the origins of the epic story in terms of nature-mythology theories prevalent in the nineteenth century, Alfred Ludwig saw Arjuna as a personification of one of the five seasons.[39] Joseph Dahlmann, attempting to explain why the epic combines a central story with huge amounts of didactic material, viewed Arjuna and his brothers as righteous victors in a war against evil, who had been used, at the same time, as legal case studies by the *Mahabharata* redactor.[40] E. Washburn Hopkins treated the trickery perpetrated by Arjuna in the Kurukshetra War simply as an example of early morality, a vestige of the epic's historical development as he had reconstructed it.[41] Later, Gerrit Jan Held characterized Arjuna as the "ideal initiate," without attempting to delve further into his personality.[42]

The practice of forcing the *Mahabharata*, and Arjuna, into constrictive frameworks persists. Even in recent times the tendency has been to focus sharply upon one's own preoccupation, implying—tacitly, at least—that other sides of the epic are unimportant. Heino Gehrts, for example, argues that the epic story is tightly modeled upon the ancient royal consecration ritual, every epic event being an elaboration of some occurrence in that rite. The epic's purpose, he asserts, is to criticize the ritual by showing how it can go wrong.[43] Many of Gehrts's observations are fascinating, but his overall interpretation is one-sided, and his Arjuna is no more than a symbolic sacrificer.

Georges Dumézil sees the entire *Mahabharata* as a *transposition* of Indo-European (Vedic) mythology, and emphasizes the connection of each epic character with his progenitor deity, including Arjuna's connection with Indra. The epic plot is viewed by Dumézil as a transposition of the prototypical Indo-European war between gods and demons, or their equivalents. All along, Dumézil insists upon his own view that the epic cast of characters, as a product of Indo-European thought, is tripartite in structure, a view that in itself may be justifiable, but not to the exclusion of all else.[44]

One scholar whose work on the *Mahabharata* has been particularly useful and inspirational is Madeleine Biardeau. In view of the importance of her major article on Arjuna, part of her much longer serial study of the epic as a whole[45] (and in view of the impressive recent work of her disciple Jacques Scheuer),[46] it is necessary to specify the ways in which her approach compares with that of the present study.

Biardeau's work on the epic is often contrasted specifically with Dumézil's, in that Biardeau bypasses the Indo-European connections of the epic story in favor of later, Hindu connections.[47] That is, Biardeau concentrates on the devotional Puranic milieu of the epic, rather than the Vedic antecedents, treating the epic story as a tale of restoration of the *dharma* ("law") (see chap. IA, etc.) by the *avatara* (incarnation of God), such as is to be found in the Puranas, but somewhat transformed; behind this version of the story, she says, is the intention of sanctifying kingly duties by connecting them with the deeds of the *avatara*.[48] In Biardeau's study, repeated emphasis upon the mythic pattern of *pralaya* (periodic dissolution of the universe) as the structural basis of the epic story replaces Dumézil's emphasis upon the Indo-European cosmic battle.

The approach of the present study lies between Dumézil's and Biardeau's,[49] and takes suggestions from both, with the attitude that both the Indo-European background and the Indian context must figure into successful *Mahabharata* interpretation at all levels. Dumézil's approach has particularly influenced the presentation of Arjuna's heroic aspect; the influence of Biardeau may be noted somewhat here (with regard to the specifically Indian aspects of the hero), and very much more in the presentation of Arjuna's devotional aspect, where the focus is upon his relationship with Krishna as *avatara*.

But what of the human aspect? Extensive development of this side of Arjuna's character is unique to the present study.

The "everyman" interpretation of Arjuna based on the *Bhagavadgita* sees Arjuna's humanity, but not to the fullest extent, since it tends to ignore his individuality. On the other hand, most studies of the epic as a whole, including Dumézil's and Biardeau's, ignore Arjuna's humanity entirely. It appears that the only scholarly study of the full *Mahabharata* that places due emphasis upon the human side of the epic characters is Alf Hiltebeitel's *The Ritual of Battle: Krishna in the Mahābhārata*,[50] which, in chapter 1, notes that the difference between epic and myth is primarily a function of the human consequences that epic heroes, unlike gods, face as a result of their actions. Hiltebeitel does not, however, concentrate on the human side of the *Mahabharata* figures; in *The Ritual of Battle* he too proves ultimately to be more interested in those features of the epic that correspond to mythic models than those that diverge from them. Hiltebeitel has nonetheless provided direction for further study.

Hiltebeitel feels that all epics include by definition a certain human dimension; therefore he does not treat the heroic and human aspects separately.[51] The present study agrees that the heroic always includes something of the human, but asserts that the human dimension is particularly pronounced in the great Indian epic—which is perhaps surprising, since Indian thought is generally stereotyped as extremely abstract. The present author was prepared to proceed beyond that stereotype in the course of her studies with Daniel H. H. Ingalls, of Harvard University, who always emphasized the human depth of the *Mahabharata* characters.

The hint has also come from other quarters. Van Buitenen, for example, suggests that attention ought to be paid to the individuality and "quirks" of the *Mahabharata* characters, over and above their symbolic or typical roles.[52] Also influential has been the present author's good friend C. V. Narasimhan, who writes in the introduction to his translation of excerpts from the epic:

> The perennial appeal of the *Mahābhārata* consists, I believe, mainly in the fact that, although it is an epic of the exploits of heroes, it also reveals a very human story. The human beings who pass through its pages display fraility as well as greatness. Even Lord Kṛṣṇa, who is believed to be one of the incarnations of Viṣṇu himself, behaves as a human being.[53]

R. C. Zaehner's emphasis, in his classic introduction to Hinduism, on Yudhishthira's (human) moral consciousness[54] recently blossomed into a complete monograph by Norbert Klaes.[55] It is in detailed application of such a perspective to the figure of Arjuna, and thence to the epic as a whole, that the present work differs most from Dumézil's, Biardeau's, and others.

Regarding the potential advantage of such a perspective, the following may be said. Because of its intentionally one-sided stance, Dumézil's approach does not miss the human component as much as Biardeau's does. Biardeau aims at producing a broad, coherent, and value-oriented picture[56] of the epic hero. Ignoring the human side, she tends to idealize the hero and his task, which leads to at least one seeming distortion in her interpretation: the Kurukshetra War, she says, ends in a complete victory of good over evil, inaugurating a Krtayuga, or golden age; the trickery committed in the course of the war is passed over quickly as necessary to save the greater *dharma*.[57] In the opinion of the present author, however, the victory of the good is apparent at the heroic and devotional levels of the epic text, but not at its human level.[58]

Notes

1. Unless otherwise specified, all *Mahabharata* references are from the critical text, as presented in the Critical Edition, 19 vols. plus 6 vols. of indexes, ed. Vishnu S. Sukthankar, S. K. Belvalkar, P. L. Vaidya, et al. (Poona: Bhandarkar Oriental Research Institute, 1933–72). In referring to the apparatus and appendices to the critical text, the entire work has been designated as the Poona Edition. Unless otherwise specified (in rare instances), all translations from Books I–V of the *Mahabharata*, including the preceding, are quoted from van Buitenen, *Mahābhārata* (for reference, see Note on Transliteration and Translation, n. 1, above). Translations from Books VI–XVIII of the *Mahabharata* are the present author's own.
2. Or perhaps, *Bharata*. On the basis of *Mahabharata* I.1.61 and later evidence, the name *Bharata* has sometimes been applied to the epic without its subordinate materials, that is, presumably, the epic before it was interpolated to become the full *Mahabharata*; see, e.g., Chintaman Vinayak Vaidya, *The Mahābhārata: A Criticism* (Delhi: Mehar Chand Lachhman Das, 1966), pp. 3f.
3. This and the other dates of texts (besides the *Mahabharata* itself) offered in this section have been quoted from the convenient compendium on pp. 17–18 of Wendy Doniger O'Flaherty, *Hindu Myths: A Sourcebook Translated from the Sanskrit* (Harmondsworth: Penguin, 1975).
4. A phrase and concept popularized by H. Munro Chadwick and N. Kershaw Chadwick (see, e.g., H. Munro Chadwick, *The Heroic Age* [Cambridge, Eng.: Cambridge University Press, 1912]), widely adopted but also much criticized, as, e.g., by Ruth Finnegan (*Oral Poetry: Its Nature, Significance and Social Context* [Cambridge, Eng.: Cambridge University Press, 1977], pp. 247–48): "For the Chadwicks, the primary evidence on which this theory rested was to be found in the poems themselves. It is significant that it is often unclear in their discussion of the 'heroic age' whether this term refers to the period in which the poems were composed, or to the society actually depicted in the poems. The reason for this is that though they occasionally distinguish between them, the Chadwicks regard them as basically one and the same. Their view is that the poems were primarily composed as celebratory accounts of the deeds of contemporary warrior princes and heroes: as such, they assume, the poems give a more or less exact picture of current conditions. . . .

   "The . . . difficulty lies in the Chadwicks' implicit acceptance of the reflection theory of literature—the idea that the minstrel gives an accurate picture of the world around him."

5. Following the terminology used by H. Munro Chadwick and N. Kershaw Chadwick in *The Growth of Literature*, 3 vols. (1932–40; rpt. Cambridge. Eng.: Cambridge University Press, 1968), where the term "epic" refers to heroic poetry and "saga" to heroic literature in prose.
6. Regarding these characteristics of oral epic, see Albert B. Lord, *The Singer of Tales*, Harvard Studies in Comparative Literature, 24 (Cambridge, Mass.: Harvard University Press, 1960), especially chaps. 3–5. A definition of the important technical term "formula," as offered by Lord (quoting Milman Parry), is appended here for the reader's convenience: "A group of words which is regularly employed under the same metrical conditions to express a given essential idea" (Lord, p. 30).
7. Also to be mentioned in the present study: Ekalavya (see especially chap. IA, n. 93); the family burned in the lacquer house (see chap. IB); and Yuyutsu (see chap. IIA3, n. 57).
8. For thorough discussion of Shiva's role in the epic, see Jacques Scheuer, *Śiva dans le Mahābhārata*, Bibliothèque de l'Ecole des Hautes Etudes, Section des Sciences Religieuses, vol. 84 (Paris: Presses Universitaires de France, 1982).
9. These two groups being, perhaps, more closely connected than their separate designations would lead one to surmise; see, e.g., the Indra-Marduk similarity referred to on p. 80, below.
10. The three levels of Arjuna's personality hereby revealed correspond in part to those noted by Vishnu Sitaram Sukthankar as running through the epic as a whole; he calls them "planes": the "mundane," the "ethical," and the "metaphysical" (*On the Meaning of the Mahābhārata*, Society's Monograph, no. 4 [Bombay: Asiatic Society of Bombay, 1957]; these planes provide the titles for the various sections of the study). Using the example of Anandatirtha (Madhvacharya) (thirteenth century A.D.), Sukthankar (p. 120) points out that his conception, particularly that of a metaphysical plane over and above the obvious story line, has precedents in early Indian thought. There are differences between the present view and Sukthankar's, however. Sukthankar is less concerned with the connections between "planes" than is the present study with those between "levels." Also, on the metaphysical plane he emphasizes philosophical concepts rather than, as in Part III of the present study, religious (devotional) elements: the Kurukshetra War becomes, for him, a battle against the passions of the lower self, with Arjuna representing a man who has overcome the lower self (Sukthankar, *Meaning*, pp. 101ff.). In the present treatment of Arjuna, Sukthankar's metaphysical plane has been replaced by the "devotional" level, because it is felt that Arjuna is never strictly a philosopher in the epic: he is permeated with religious devotion throughout. A "metaphysical" interpretation is, in the present author's opinion, more appropriately applied to the character of Yudhishthira; and those who are more concerned with the metaphysical than the devotional aspects of the *Mahabharata* are undoubtedly more taken with Yudhishthira's message than with Arjuna's. (These issues are discussed further in Part III, particularly chaps. IIIB1 and IIID.)
11. On Vyasa as the arranger of the Vedas, see *Mahabharata* I.54.5 and I.57.73. On Vyasa as the author of the Puranas, not mentioned in the *Mahabharata*, see Moriz

Winternitz, *A History of Indian Literature*, I, trans. S. Ketkar, 2nd ed. (1927; rpt. New Delhi: Oriental Books Reprint Corporation, 1972), 322, etc.

12. See, especially, Joseph Dahlmann, *Das Mahābhārata als Epos und Rechtsbuch: Ein Problem aus Altindiens Cultur- und Literaturgeschichte* (Berlin: Felix L. Dames, 1895), pp. 280ff., and *Genesis des Mahābhārata*, vol. I of *Mahābhārata-Studien: Abhandlungen zur altindischen Literatur und Culturkunde* (Berlin: Felix L. Dames, 1899), pp. 168ff.
13. See E. Washburn Hopkins, "The Bhārata and the Great Bhārata," *American Journal of Philology* 19 (1898): 1–24, and *The Great Epic of India: Its Character and Origin* (New York: Scribner, 1901), pp. ix f.
14. For reference, see preceding note.
15. Hopkins, *Great Epic*, p. 60.
16. Hopkins, *Great Epic*, pp. 397–98.
17. With regard to Indian scholars' favorable view of Dahlmann, see, e.g., Sukthankar, *Meaning*. Although critical of many of Dahlmann's findings, Sukthankar writes (p. 19): "A certain underlying unity of aim and plan in this gigantic work was postulated and dogmatically emphasized by this great Jesuit scholar, who of all foreign critics of the *Mahābhārata* may be said to approach nearest to any real understanding of the Great Epic of India." On the other hand, Sukthankar writes very sarcastically about Hopkins "who, as a result of an intensive study of the epic extending over many years, made the interesting discovery that there was no text there at all. He could see only a nebulous mass of incongruities, absurdities, contradictions, anachronisms, accretions and interpolations!" (pp. 7–8). Regarding Western scholars' favorable view of Hopkins, see van Buitenen, *Mahābhārata*, I, xxxiii. For an exception to this rule, however, see below, n. 58, complemented by chap. IIA3, n. 93.
18. Sukthankar, *Meaning*, p. 23.
19. Van Buitenen. *Mahābhārata*, III, 19.
20. See chap. IIA3, n. 1.
21. See Lord, pp. 141ff., on the Homeric epics.
22. See Vishnu Sitaram Sukthankar's seminal article entitled "The Bhrgus and the Bharata: A Text-Historical Study," in his *Critical Studies in the Mahābhārata*, vol. I of *Sukthankar Memorial Edition*, ed. P. K. Gode (Bombay: Karnatak Publishing House, 1944), pp. 278–337; also, Robert P. Goldman, *Gods, Priests, and Warriors: The Bhṛgus of the Mahābhārata*, Studies in Oriental Culture, Columbia University, no. 12 (New York: Columbia University Press, 1977).
23. Such aspects of oral poetry in the extant *Mahabharata* have been discussed by the Russian scholar Pavel A. Grintser, in his *Drevneindiiskii epos: genezis i tipologiia* (Moscow: Nauka, 1974).
24. Cf. I.1.64, etc.
25. Cf. I.1.56f.
26. Strikingly, a most important attempt to isolate the epic core selects a body of stanzas (those of the irregular *trishtubh* variety) which, in Book I, features Janamejaya's snake sacrifice; see Mary Carroll Smith, "The Core of India's Great Epic," Dissertation, Harvard 1972, p. 10.

27. As the name "Janamejaya" is applied to a number of different figures, in the epic and elsewhere, including some from much earlier generations (*Mahabharata* I.89.44, 47; I.90.11; etc.; see also II.8.21, "the eighty Janamejayas"), and so might have been borrowed as prestigious, it cannot be assumed to have been the real name of a historical individual who was Arjuna's great-grandson. Nonetheless, this Janamejaya seems to represent a king or group of kings who existed historically. A King Janamejaya, descendant of Parikshit, is known to Indian texts as early as the Brahmanas.
28. This is not to say that, e.g., heroic poetry without the devotional element never existed in India. Such poetry, corresponding to the first two phases of Hopkins's developmental schema cited above (with Krishna either absent or not yet divinized fully) probably did exist at one time. Jan Gonda thus suggests, agreeing with the earlier work of Walter Ruben, that Krishna was once a hero, not a god; see his *Aspects of Early Viṣṇuism*, 2nd ed. (Delhi: Motilal Banarsidass, 1969), pp. 154–55. What is meant, rather, is that poetry without all three strands would not have qualified as *Mahabharata*, or even *Bharata* (see above, n. 2). The "core" located by M. C. Smith (see above, n. 26) includes all the elements mentioned here.
29. See, e.g., E. Washburn Hopkins, "The Social and Military Position of the Ruling Caste in Ancient India, as Represented by the Sanskrit Epic," *Journal of the American Oriental Society* 13 (1889): 64, and *Great Epic*, pp. 376, 400; also, *The Cambridge History of India*, I, ed. E. J. Rapson (New York: Macmillan, 1922), 258, and Johann Jakob Meyer, *Sexual Life in Ancient India: A Study in the Comparative History of Indian Culture* (Delhi: Motilal Banarsidass, 1971), p. 108.
30. See Edmund Leach, *Claude Lévi-Strauss* (New York: Viking, 1970), pp. 58ff., for a helpful summary of this aspect of Lévi-Strauss's thought, based on "general information theory." This conception provides the organizing principle behind Lévi-Strauss's *Mythologiques* trilogy.
31. Aurobindo Ghose, *Essays on the Gita*, Sri Aurobindo International Centre of Education Collection, vol. 8 (1922; rpt. Pondicherry: Sri Aurobindo Ashram, 1966), p. 17.
32. Sarvepalli Radhakrishnan, *The Bhagavadgītā: With an Introductory Essay, Sanskrit Text, English Translation and Notes* (1948; rpt. New York: Harper Torchbooks, 1973), pp. 36–37.
33. Sylvain Lévi, "*Tato jayam udirayet*," trans. L. G. Khare, *Annals of the Bhandarkar Institute* 1 (1918–19): 16.
34. On *Mahabharata* commentary, see Sukthankar, "Notes on Mahabharata Commentators," in *Critical Studies in the Mahābhārata*, pp. 263–77.
35. See *Mahābhārata* with the commentary *Bhāratabhāvadīpa* of Nīlakaṇṭha, 18 books (Bombay: Gaṇpat Kṛṣṇājī, 1885–88), or *The Mahābhāratam with the Bharata Bhawadeepa Commentary of Nīlkaṇṭha*, ed. Ramchandrashastri Kinjawadekar, 2nd ed., 6 vols. (New Delhi: Oriental Books Reprint Corporation, 1979).
36. Adolf Holtzmann (younger), *Arjuna: Ein Beitrag zur Reconstruction des Mahābhārata* (Strassburg: Karl J. Trübner, 1879).
37. The name "inversion-theory" was applied to the Holtzmanns' view by Hopkins; see, e.g., "Position," pp. 60f. For the Holtzmann theory, see Adolf Holtzmann

(elder), *Indische Sagen* (Stuttgart: Adolph Krabbe, 1854), I, viii f., and many later works.

38. Monier Monier-Williams, *Indian Epic Poetry: Being the Substance of Lectures Recently Given at Oxford: With a Full Analysis of the Rámáyaṇa and of the Leading Story of the Mahá-Bhárata* (London: Williams and Norgate, 1863), p. 54.
39. Alfred Ludwig, *Über das Verhältnis des mythischen Elementes zu der historischen Grundlage des Mahâbhârata*, Abhandlungen, 6th Series, vol. 12, Classe für Philosophie, Geschichte und Philologie, no. 5 (Prague: Verlag der königlichen böhmischen Gesellschaft der Wissenschaften, 1884), p. 14.
40. Dahlmann, *Epos und Rechtsbuch*, Part I, and *Genesis*, passim.
41. Hopkins, "Position," pp. 62ff., etc.
42. Gerrit Jan Held, *The Mahābhārata: An Ethnological Study* (London: Kegan Paul, Trench, Trubner and Co.; Amsterdam: Uitgeversmaatschappij Holland, 1935), p. 186.
43. Heino Gehrts, *Mahābhārata: Das Geschehen und seine Bedeutung*, Abhandlungen zur Kunst-, Musik- und Literaturwissenschaft, vol. 178 (Bonn: Bouvier, 1975).
44. Dumézil's major study of the epic, entitled "La terre soulagée," appears as Part I of his *Mythe et épopée: L'idéologie des trois fonctions dans les épopées des peuples indo-européens* (Paris: Gallimard, 1968) (to be referred to as *Mythe et epopee* I, because supplementary volumes by the same name have since appeared), pp. 33ff.
45. Madeleine Biardeau, "Etudes de mythologie hindoue," I–V, in *Bulletin de l'Ecole Française d'Extrême Orient* 54, 55, 58, 63, 65 (1968, 1969, 1971, 1976, 1978); hereafter cited as "Etudes." The section on Arjuna appears in "Etudes" V, pp. 87–204. The first three parts of "Etudes" have been reprinted, with slight modifications, including omission of Biardeau's preliminary "Contribution à l'étude du mythe-cadre du *Mahābhārata*," which had originally appeared as the appendix to "Etudes" II, as *Cosmogonies purāṇiques*, vol. I of *Etudes de mythologie hindoue*, Publications de l'Ecole Française d'Extrême Orient, vol. 128 (Paris: Ecole Française d'Extrême Orient, 1981).
46. For reference, see above, n. 8.
47. See Alf Hiltebeitel, *The Ritual of Battle: Krishna in the Mahābhārata* (Ithaca: Cornell University Press, 1976), p. 15, and van Buitenen, *Mahābhārata*, III, 163. Biardeau herself comments on Dumézil's work on the *Mahabharata* in "Etudes" II, p. 98, where she rejects the Indo-European connection for the Hindu connection; "Etudes" IV, p. 218, n. 1, where she voices her hope for a future reconciliation of the two approaches; etc. She expresses her great intellectual debt to Dumézil in "Conférence de Mlle. Madeleine Biardeau," *Annuaire de l'Ecole Pratique des Hautes Etudes, v^e Section (Sciences Religieuses)* 77 (1969–70): 172. (This article is part of a series of short reports by Biardeau on the preceding years' work of her "Religions de l'Inde" seminar at the EPHE, which conducted a continuing discussion of the *Mahabharata*. In view of discrepancy in the manner of dating the volumes through the years, articles from this series are cited hereafter [as "Conférence"] with volume number and page.)

48. Biardeau, "Etudes" V, pp. 162, 195.
49. Hiltebeitel also stresses the fact that his approach combines Dumézil's and Biardeau's; see *Ritual*, p. 15. Van Buitenen states that his view lies between Dumézil's and Biardeau's; *Mahābhārata*, III, 163.
50. For reference, see above, n. 47.
51. See, e.g., Hiltebeitel, *Ritual*, p. 146.
52. Van Buitenen, *Mahābhārata*, III, 163ff.
53. Chakravarthi V. Narasimhan, *The Mahābhārata: An English Version Based on Selected Verses*, Records of Civilization, Sources and Studies, 71 (New York: Columbia University Press, 1965), p. xx.
54. R. C. Zaehner, *Hinduism* (1962; rpt. London: Oxford University Press, 1971), pp. 115ff., etc.
55. Norbert Klaes, *Conscience and Consciousness: Ethical Problems of Mahabharata* (Bangalore: Dharmaram College, 1975).
56. Biardeau, "Etudes" II, pp. 67f., n. 2; 97f.
57. For references, see chap. IIA3, n. 87.
58. One further difference between the present study and the work of Biardeau ought to be mentioned here, for the reader's full information, namely, that Biardeau does not rely upon the Critical Edition of the *Mahabharata*; in fact, she opposes its very existence, arguing that all historical study of the *Mahabharata* text as part of a search for coherent meaning is excluded automatically by recognition of the epic's orally composed fluidity. Any attempt to peel off outer layers of the epic to approach an original version is futile, she asserts, since such a version simply could not exist in a piece of oral poetry. (See Madeleine Biardeau, "Some More Considerations about Textual Criticism," *Purāṇa* 10 [1968]: 115–23, and "The Story of Arjuna Kārtavīrya without Reconstruction," *Purāṇa* 12 [1970]: 301f; see also "Etudes" IV, p. 196, n. 2; "Etudes" V, p. 137, n. 1; etc.) It seems, however, that Biardeau contradicts her own theoretical stance, since she often appears to search for as much consistency in the epic as one would in a work that is written, not oral. Part of Biardeau's search for consistency has been conducted on the basis of a Lévi-Straussian structuralist approach, which takes all versions of a story to be equally valid, and locates the repeated pattern buried in their depths. (For Biardeau's comments on structuralism and its application to *Mahabharata* interpretation, see "Etudes" I, p. 19; "Etudes" II, pp. 67f., n. 2; 98, n. 1; "Etudes" V, p. 137, n. 1. On the equal validity of all versions, see her article "Kārtavīrya.") The structuralist approach suits oral literature very well, perhaps better than it does written literature. Biardeau's search for consistency, however, passes beyond structure to, e.g., specific points of phraseology. Sometimes too she will emphasize a favored version of an episode at the expense of other versions (such, e.g., is her discussion of the burning of the Khandava Forest [see chap. IC of the present study]); enough so that some of her views may strike one as exaggerated (for instance, that she finds the imagery of *pralaya* everywhere, and insists upon the absolute victory of good in the Kurukshetra War). In sum, Biardeau's work seems to reflect an underlying assump-

tion that the epic is, after all, a unity; and see, more recently, "Conférence," vol. 91, pp. 153ff., 173. If this reading of Biardeau's meaning is correct, then the approach taken by the present study lies between her theory and her practice. Her work has been, meanwhile, of great help in drawing attention to certain passages excluded from the critical text.

PART I: HERO

IA. BIRTH AND CHILDHOOD

Heroism Defined: Semidivinity and Positive, Effective Action in Support of World Order (*Dharma*)

Arjuna is the third of five *kshatriya* brothers born in the royal family of the Kuru people (the descendants of the legendary ancestor Kuru), the Pandavas ("sons of Pandu"), who will be the major figures of the "good" side in the Kurukshetra War. (Their cousins the Kauravas are another branch of the same Kuru family.) Although the birth stories of all the Pandava brothers are told in sequence and follow an identical pattern of divine fathering in the Himalaya by means of a magic charm (I.114f.), Arjuna's birth is outstanding in that it is attended with far more celestial clamor than are the births of his brothers; this includes a prophecy by a disembodied voice of the heroic deeds he will perform, and tremendous divine celebration (I.114.28ff.). The disembodied voice also speaks at the births of the other Pandavas, predicting the future characteristics of the newborn children, but with regard to Arjuna the statement is most detailed; replete with mythic and "historical" references, it is addressed to Arjuna's mother, Kunti, as follows:

> In prowess the match of Kārtavīrya, in puissance Śibi's peer, invincible like Indra, he shall broadcast, Kuntī, your glory! Just as Aditi's joy was increased by Viṣṇu [her son], so Arjuna, the like of Viṣṇu, shall increase your joy. He shall bring the Madras under his sway, the Kurus with the Kaikeyas, the Cedis, Kāśis, and Karūṣas, and firmly plant the Fortune of the Kurus. By the prowess of his arms he shall sate the Fire of Sacrifice in the Khāṇḍava Forest with the fat of all creatures. The mighty leader of his people shall vanquish the barons,[1] and with his brothers the hero shall offer up the three sacrifices. Equal to Rāma Jāmadagnya, in puissance the peer of

> Viṣṇu, greatest of heroes, he shall remain undefeated. All celestial weapons he shall obtain, and, a bull among men, rescue the lost fortune. [I.114.29–35][2]

That Arjuna is intended by Pandu to be his "choicest" son (I.114.18) and is obtained only after great austerities (I.114.18ff.) tallies well with the fact that his true father is Indra, the Vedic warrior god and epic "king of the gods" (I.114.21ff.). (His brothers, Yudhishthira, Bhima, and the twins, Nakula and Sahadeva, are sons, respectively, of the gods Dharma, Vayu, and the Ashvins.) Arjuna becomes the mainstay of the Pandavas, and performs the outstanding actions of the *Mahabharata* story: wife winning, weapon winning, decisive victory in the war, protection of the horse in the horse sacrifice performed after the war, engendering the line of royal succession.

If heroism is defined as a peculiar cross between divinity and humanity, as it appears to be in the Greek context and others,[3] then the term "hero" may be applied to all the Pandavas: all of them have divine fathers over and above their nominal father, Pandu.[4] In the case of each Pandava, the divine father's traits pass over to the son,[5] and in another sense the son is seen as identical to the father,[6] or yet again as his partial incarnation (I.61.84f.). The local cults of Pandava worship frequently reported throughout India[7] are undoubtedly related to the semidivinity of these figures, although, as in Greece, the connection between epic literature and hero cult is obscure.[8]

There is, however, another aspect of traditional heroism, broadly defined, which makes Arjuna the preeminent hero even among the Pandavas as a group, explaining, for example, why only he is referred to as "hero" (*vira*) in the birth prophecies: a hero is a figure of positive and effective action,[9] that is—in Indian terminology—action in support of *dharma* ("law" or "world order"; also "virtue," "duty," "right," a connected concept being "truth," in a cosmic sense of the word). The *Mahabharata* states:

> This world always clings to the arms of heroes, like a son. A hero, therefore, deserves respect in all circumstances. Nothing higher than heroism is found in the three worlds [the entire universe]. The hero protects all. All depends on the hero. [XII.100.17–18]

Among the Vedic gods, Indra fulfills this "heroic" role; among the Pandavas, Indra's son, Arjuna. In contemplating the birth of Arjuna, Pandu wishes that he may be "great spirited, wise in policy, sunlike in luster, unassailable, vigorous in action, of the most wondrous aspect" (I.114.25). This, then, will be the present study's definition of Arjuna as hero: semidivinity and positive, effective action.

The Son of Indra: Storm God, Warrior, and Archetypical King

In the *Mahabharata* as a whole, the Sanskrit terms *vira* (cognate with English, "virile") and *shura*, which are generally translated as "hero," are applied rather freely to all the fighters, with reference to the warrior ideal of the *kshatriya* class, that is the *kshatriya-* (or *kshatra-*) *dharma.* It is this ideal, first of all, that is glorified in the figure of Arjuna as hero par excellence. Also glorified in Arjuna is the ideal of the apex of *kshatriya* activity, that is, kingly activity in support of world order: Arjuna is the earthly incarnation of his father, Indra, the archetypical king, with whom Indian kings are often identified or compared.[10] Note how in tracing his ancestry through Arjuna, King Janamejaya is legitimating his rule doubly: he is a descendant of the greatest hero and also of the royal god.

When *dharma* is supported, the result is the successful operation of the whole world, natural as well as human, illustrated, in particular, by the timely fall of rain, that is, fertility. Throughout Indian thought, Indra symbolizes this fertility, on the basis of his Vedic role of storm god and liberator of the waters.[11] Correspondingly, the fertility of a country has frequently, in ancient belief, been viewed as dependent upon the well-being of its king. Arjuna, as Indra's son, takes on the fertility dimension of his divine father. Arjuna's handsomeness, the "wondrous aspect" envisioned for his third son by Pandu when he contemplates calling upon Indra to father him, is at least in part an indication of Arjuna's potency, which continues to be emphasized throughout his story; see, for example, VII.85.80, where Arjuna is described as "dark, youthful, curly-haired [*gudakeshah*], and handsome." Beauty, of course, is a standard component of heroism; thus, in Arjuna's case one may find descriptions that emphasize his good looks along with his strength, as, for example:

> . . . dark, youthful, curly-haired [*gudakeshah*], handsome, great armed, broad chested, great shouldered, striding like an intoxicated

> elephant, with eyes of a chakora bird, copper-eyed, increasing the pain of his enemies. [VII.102.35–36]

And:

> . . . having a great bow, dark, youthful, resembling the leader of an elephant herd, with shoulders prominent as a lion's, with the swaying gait of an elephant, with eyes as wide as lotus blossoms. [XV.32.7]

(Discussion of Arjuna's fertility dimension continues in chap. IB.)

Besides the fact that Arjuna's personality resembles that of his divine father in broad outline, more specific resemblances may also be noted. Even the name "Arjuna" seems to be borrowed from an epithet of Indra (see Appendix). Both Indra and Arjuna are chariot warriors, both are diadem wearers (see Appendix, under Kiritin), and Arjuna's most characteristic weapon, his bow Gandiva, is compared to Indra's thunderbolt (*vajra*, etc.);[12] both Indra and Arjuna are characterized by the scars on their arms caused by the pulling of bowstrings.[13] Indra sometimes helps Arjuna, particularly by tricking Karna (see below and chap. IIA3), or watches over him in combat, as the Greek gods watch over their sons in the *Iliad* (see below).

Most important, the major event of Arjuna's career, his participation in the great war, is to some extent transposed from (Dumézil's term)[14] or modeled after the mythology of Indra. In fact, the story of the war is clearly based upon the Indian myth of the continuing conflict between the gods (*deva*s) and the demons (*asura*s), in which Indra is the gods' champion, and the gods always win in the end,[15] found at all stages of Indian literature, including versions of several episodes in the epic itself (outstandingly, the story of Indra's slaying of the serpent demon Vrtra or Vrtra's double, Namuchi;[16] and compare the story of the churning of the ocean [I.15ff.]). The sides are drawn accordingly: the Pandavas are said to incarnate gods while their enemies, their cousins the Kauravas, incarnate demons, cousins and enemies of the gods, forces of chaos.[17] (Many other *Mahabharata* characters are also said to incarnate supernatural beings; see further, especially, chap. IIIB2.) The decisive alliance of Arjuna and Ķrishna is based upon that of Indra and Vishnu in the mythology (see chap. IE). If there is any historical core to the story, it has been largely subordinated to this mythic model, which evidently goes back to Indo-European antecedents.[18]

However, the fact that Arjuna is Indra's son, who takes after him as warrior-king and borrows much of his mythology, in no way guarantees that Indra imagery will be carried consistently through the epic with reference to Arjuna. One finds that in the main body of the text, especially in the description of battles, formulaic use of the name and image of Indra is applied approximately equally to all the warriors (see chap. IE): comparison with Indra underscores the greatness of a warrior at a particular point in the battle. When the standard formulas which state that even the gods (or gods and demons) with Indra at their head could not defeat a given warrior are applied to Arjuna,[19] they may seem to set Arjuna against his father; one must, however, bear in mind that this is primarily a formulaic manner of speaking. Although the *aindra* (Indra) weapon is primarily Arjuna's, it is sometimes included on lists of his opponents' weapons, as meter permits (IV.53.48; VII.163.27f.; VII.166.2). Even in the prophecy at Arjuna's birth, the comparison with Indra is primarily formulaic, and just one comparison among many.

In short, one may see in Arjuna's connection with Indra both a transposition of mythology, with profound meaning for defining Arjuna's characteristic traits, and a looser, formulaic linkage, which applies also to other warriors. The resonance of any given formulaic description with its mythic background may vary from usage to usage. The same reservation may be applied to formulaic comparison of Arjuna with the natural phenomenon of the storm (see chap. IE).

The Three Oldest Pandavas: Royal and Priestly Dimensions

It has been suggested in the preceding section that Arjuna incarnates the kingly virtues. Arjuna is not, however, the literal king among the Pandava brothers: according to the epic, his brother Yudhishthira becomes, as eldest, the anointed ruler. Yet Yudhishthira frequently seems to be only a figurehead, and it is seen that Arjuna, along with the second Pandava, Bhima, incarnates the power behind the kingly office.

The figure of a relatively passive king who rules with the support of a more active hero or group of heroes is found frequently in Indo-European epic and saga, and one may speculate that the grouping of Yudhishthira and his two oldest brothers derives from Indo-European antecedents. Parallels may, for example, be seen in the cases of Kaykhusraw and Rustam in the Persian *Shahnamah*, Conchobor and Cuchulainn in the Irish *Tain Bo Cuailnge*, Charlemagne and Roland (with the peers) in the *Song of Roland*,[20] and even Agamemnon and Achilles in the *Iliad*.[21] A few statements in the *Mahabharata* imply that a king is not supposed to fight; see, for example, VII.134.66: "I regard it as improper . . . that the king, who has allies, should himself go against the son of Prtha ["son of Kunti"; here, Arjuna][22] for battle, when we are standing here."[23] Yudhishthira does fight sometimes[24]—and his name means "firm in battle"—but most often he wishes to withdraw.

Several episodes of the *Mahabharata* imply that Yudhishthira has a different type of power, a magic, which exists over and above the power derived from his brothers' military support. It is, for example, stated that when Yudhishthira went forth with his brothers into exile, he covered his eyes "lest I burn these folk down to the ground if I look at them with my evil eye" (II.71.11).[25] In Book IV, when King Virata strikes Yudhishthira in unthinking anger, Yudhishthira's blood must be caught in a golden bowl (IV.63.47),[26] since, as Yudhishthira himself states, "if that blood from my nose had fallen on the ground, you would for a certainty have perished with your kingdom, great king" (IV.64.8).[27] In V.140.8–9, just prior to the war, Krishna threatens the enemy with the image of "Yudhiṣṭhira on the battlefield, protecting his grand-army with spells and oblations, unassailable like the sun burning the host of the enemy." Less obviously magical in origin, yet seemingly reflecting a related line of thought, is the idea expressed by Vyasa in VII.158.62 when, trying to stop Yudhishthira from running into the fray, he assures him of impending victory with the words "yato dharmas tato jayah" ("Where *dharma* is, there is victory").

As was stated above, Yudhishthira's divine father is the god Dharma, and thus Yudhishthira incarnates *dharma* in himself, as is appropriate to a king:[28] he is called "King Dharma"[29] (Dharmaraja). The idea that where *dharma* is, victory must follow automatically, is repeated frequently throughout the *Mahabharata*, and becomes a commonplace of epic thought;[30] related to it is a group of formulas that may be interpreted as equating strength with truth, applied to the three oldest Pandava brothers and various warriors.[31] Yet if this idea reflects a certain magical notion of the inviolability and passive power of the king, or of righteousness,[32] that notion is subordinated throughout most of the epic to the idea that the king and the *dharma* rule only by virtue of warrior support. Yudhishthira is not a hero in the traditional sense. His inclination to passivity is often ridiculed by other characters, and he is said to behave more like a brahmin than like the *kshatriya* he really is.[33] (A brahmanic disguise, worn through Book IV, emphasizes this aspect of his character.) He is even called a "eunuch" (*kliba*) (III.34.13, etc.), which in the parlance of the epic means precisely the opposite of a hero, that is, the opposite of one who is a man (*vira*)[34] (see chap. ID for further discussion). Nonetheless, Yudhishthira's "brahmanic" behavior is admired by certain layers of epic thought such as favor nonviolence (*ahimsa*),[35] and his identity as *dharma* incarnate makes him primarily an object of admiration for the epic as a whole. He is seen as particularly wise, on the basis of his innate knowledge of *dharma*,[36] and powerful despite appearances.

Since, however, the dominant trend of *Mahabharata* thought seems to accept the necessity of supporting the king by force, it may be said that force is a component of the royal ideology of the epic as a whole. Indra, as warrior-king in both Vedic and epic mythology, represents the acquisition of kingly power by force. Not Yudhishthira alone, but Yudhishthira, Bhima, and Arjuna together constitute the totality of Pandava kingship: Yudhishthira supplies the *dharma*, Bhima and Arjuna, the supporting power. As pointed out most clearly by Dumézil in *The Destiny of the Warrior*, Bhima and Arjuna are two different types of warrior. The different manners in which they fight reflect the manners of their divine fathers, Vayu, the Vedic wind god, and Indra. Dumézil traces this division back to the hypothetical Indo-European prototype also reflected, for example, in the Greek distinction between Herakles and Achilles.[37] The Vayu/Bhima type of warrior is, according to Dumézil, brutal and not particularly intelligent. The Indra/Arjuna type is, rather, a warrior knight, chivalrous and a master of weapon usage.[38] At times in the epic, Bhima's and Arjuna's personalities clearly evade Dumézil's stereotyping,[39] but the distinction is broadly applicable. That the dominant traits of the three oldest Pandava brothers were perceived as complementary, together creating a unity which presumably represented the requisites of good government, is suggested by the fact that these traits also appear as a triad in the epic in another connection: with regard to the human father and the paternal uncles of the Pandavas, we are told in I.102.19–20 that "wide-striding Pāṇḍu outmatched all men on the bow, Prince Dhṛtarāṣṭra was strong beyond any, while no one in all three worlds was Vidura's equal in his perseverance in the Law and his command of the Laws of the Kings."[40]

The strictly Vayu/Bhima type of hero is, as Dumézil indicates, amoral in behavior (though presumably generally right-hearted). The Indra/Arjuna type, on the other hand, is caught up in a web of moral issues because he lives according to certain rules and regulations.[41] In the Yudhishthira-Bhima-Arjuna triad, then, it will be noted that Arjuna serves as a mediator, incorporating, as he does, awareness of law, as well as elements of the force behind it.[42] In this sense, Arjuna displays a more well-rounded character than either Yudhishthira or Bhima: he takes the best from the ideal extremes presented by the epic in the persons of his older brothers. The fact that Arjuna unites in himself all aspects of kingship explains why he, of all the Pandavas, is said to have been fathered by Indra. Although he is not actually king, Arjuna serves as a model for kingship, the kingly role of support of *dharma* and Arjuna's heroic role being one and the same.

In another way, too, Arjuna as Indra's son is a cross between his two older brothers. While Yudhishthira's controlled behavior is often seen as that which might be expected rather of a brahmin than a *kshatriya*, Bhima's behavior is, by contrast, overwhelmingly that of a warrior. Arjuna's behavior, however, like Indra's, combines both elements. In the *Mahabharata*, Indra, although a warrior, is sometimes shown to have brahmanic traits, or even said to be a brahmin (XII.22.11).[43] In the course of the epic, he appears several times disguised as a brahmin, as, for example, when he comes to beg the earrings and armor of the Pandavas' illegitimate brother, Karna.[44] It has been pointed out above that Yudhishthira also assumes a brahmanic disguise at a crucial point in the epic, as is in character for him. Arjuna too assumes such a disguise, in the scenes of Draupadi's *svayamvara* (I.175ff.) (see chap. IB) and the slaying of Jarasamdha (II.18ff.); in his case, however, the disguise is worn expressly to enable him to perform warrior feats. Although other Pandavas also don brahmanic garb in these scenes, in the first the disguise, like the scene itself, is predominantly Arjuna's. In the second scene, Bhima is the central figure who uses his brahmanic disguise to warrior ends. In Bhima's case, however, there is no further emphasis on brahmanic connections, while for Arjuna a continuing emphasis is apparent. For example, that Arjuna's education in the warrior skills which will come to characterize him is provided by a brahmin, Drona (after an earlier teacher, also a brahmin, Krpa [I.120]), is another indication of his mixed heritage. The other Pandavas—and, indeed, the Kauravas—learn from Drona (and Krpa) also, but Arjuna is preeminently his protégé.[45] Arjuna's great capacity in the realm of ascetic control is an important part of his total character, providing him with a power that parallels the magic residing in Yudhishthira. Such ascetic power is, however, often considered the province of brahmins, not warriors. (See chap. ID for further discussion of this issue.)

Several of the preceding examples suggest that, according to the Indian view, brahmanic qualities often underlie warrior success. In a broader sense, brahmanic support upholds the *dharma*, and the king himself incorporates brahmanic as well as warrior traits.[46] (Peculiarly socially, but appropriately symbolically, the Pandavas and the Kauravas have brahmin antecedents on their human side, through Vyasa, who fathered Dhrtarashtra and Pandu [I.99f.].) Arjuna in particular incarnates the warrior-brahmin combination, and thus his birth prophecy compares him both with the legendary king Arjuna Kartavirya and that *kshatriya*'s archenemy, the Bhargava brahmin Rama Jamadagnya.

The Pandava Family: Unity and Completeness

The next issue to be considered is Arjuna's position in his family as a whole, and the question that arises immediately is why, short of mere chance, are there five Pandavas? The number of Pandavas gives the impression of being an artificial construct, particularly because the two younger brothers, the twins, are separated from the older ones by having a separate mother, Madri.[47] It has already been suggested that the three oldest Pandavas constitute a political entity complete in itself, each making a characteristic contribution to the whole. In contrast, the twins look as though they have been added as an afterthought, for they have less clearly and consistently defined characteristics than their older brothers, and it is hard to say what their distinctive qualities really are.[48] If, then, the fivefold grouping is possibly artificial and intentional, what would be its basis?

Before attempting a detailed answer to this question, an interesting tangential point must be noted: a number of *Mahabharata* scholars of the past have felt that the Pandavas were not characters in the ancient heroic tales on which the extant epic is apparently based. Rather, they have maintained, the original tales detailed a conflict between the Kurus and the Panchala people, and it is the place of the Panchalas that the Pandavas, as newcomers, took over.[49] This theory appears to have some merit, insofar as there is a continuous parallelism in the epic between Panchala themes and the central Pandava story: for example, in the double leadership of the Pandava army by Dhrshtadyumna, a Panchala, and Arjuna (see chap. IE). Similarly, the fact that the elders Bhishma and Drona, both of whom incarnate gods, fight on the Kaurava side in the war can be attributed in part (although the extant epic does not stress this explanation) to their earlier enmity with Panchala figures, Shikhandin and Drupada (succeeded by Dhrshtadyumna). (For more on the elders' position, see, especially, chap. IIA3.) Furthermore, a continuing attempt is made throughout the epic to connect the Pandavas and the Panchalas.[50] (On the Panchalas, see further chap. IIIC.) Here it is most important to point out that the name "Panchala" includes the element *pancha-* ("five"), and may be derived from the fact that this nation was constituted of five tribes that joined together to form it.[51] The fivefold count of the Pandavas may then have originated in an attempt to tie them to the Panchalas.[52] This suggestion, however, is purely hypothetical, and the question "Why five?" still remains, since even the fivefold count of the Panchala tribes would most probably have been based on ideology rather than a truly historical state of affairs.

The grouping of the five brothers has Indo-European parallels, as may be seen by comparison with Celtic materials. The resemblance between the Irish stories of the forest encounters of Niall and his brothers and the sons of Daire with personified Sovereignty (the "loathly bride") and the Indian story of the Pandavas' encounter with Dharma in a similar setting is striking enough to suggest a common source.[53] Furthermore, the grouping of the brothers around Sovereignty in the Irish stories closely resembles the grouping of the Pandavas around the apparently related [54] figure of Draupadi. And most pertinent to the present discussion is the fact that the brothers are five in number in both the Irish stories and the Indian one.

In *Celtic Heritage: Ancient Tradition in Ireland and Wales*, Alwyn Rees and Brinley Rees suggest that in the Celtic tradition the number five symbolizes totality.[55] This symbolism, they imply in their discussion of the five provinces of Ireland, may have been directional in origin: the four directions plus the "elusive fifth," which represents either the center or the whole.[56] Citing their work, Dumézil similarly emphasizes the directional component in the fivefold cosmogonic division of the earth by the "first king," which he takes to be an Indo-European concept.[57] To seek this directional orientation in the *Mahabharata* raises some difficulties, since directions are generally referred to in the epic as four in number (that is, north, south, east, and west) or ten in number (the four primary directions, the intermediary directions, the zenith, and the nadir). Nonetheless, the older Indian materials occasionally describe the directions as fivefold,[58] so the number ten may be seen as a mere doubling of an earlier count. The Pandavas themselves are sometimes correlated with the various cardinal points, paradigmatically in the "Digvijaya" ("Conquest of the World")[59] section of Book II of the *Mahabharata* (II.23ff.), where their military expeditions prior to Yudhishthira's consecration as king are outlined: Arjuna wins the north, Bhima the east, Sahadeva the south, and Nakula the west, while Yudhishthira waits in the center.[60] Even if the directional component is discounted, however, one may observe that the number five is extremely popular in Indian classificatory systems; many sets, that is, are seen as being complete in five members.[61]

The extant *Mahabharata* leaves no doubt that the structure of the Pandava family is based upon unity and completeness. Unity is clearly shown by the fact that the Pandavas share one wife, Draupadi, a complicated and unusual arrangement that they work out with both dignity and organization (for further discussion, see chap. IB).[62] In this regard, as in all others, the Pandavas are mutually supportive and respectful, illustrating such kinship loyalty as is universal to the code of epic heroes. By contrast, the Kauravas, one hundred strong, although they fight for a common cause, often seem to be a disorganized mass, as witness, especially, their manner of birth from a "mass of flesh" (I.107.12ff.).[63] The Pandavas function as a single organism: in one image, a well-rooted tree, the Kauravas being, by contrast, a tree to all intents and purposes rootless (see chap. IIIB1). One may surmise that the fivefold constitution of the Pandava group has entered the epic from an Indo-European source, to complement the picture of unity.

What is the meaning of Pandava unity and completeness? To begin with, these are the unity and completeness of a joint family. As noted above, the symbolism of the number five seems to have been applied in a number of Indo-European cases to groups of brothers. To the Celtic examples may be added many examples from Indian literature, besides that of the Pandavas.[64] In almost all these cases, however, something more seems to be at issue: the families are royal, and their unity and completeness represent their sovereign role.[65] In the case of the Pandavas, fivefold unity requires that the twins be incorporated into the royal ideology, which is otherwise embodied primarily in the figures of the three oldest brothers.

In this connection, it is necessary to refer briefly to the ideas of Stig Wikander, followed by Dumézil, regarding the Pandava hierarchy, which he understands in terms of the Dumézilian "trifunctional" view of Indo-European social structure: on the basis of paternity, Yudhishthira is representative of the so-called first function, that of the priests; Bhima and Arjuna represent the warrior function; and the twins represent the third function, that of peasants and farmers.[66] Indo-European ideology, as Dumézil interprets it, required that the king embody the virtues of all the functions;[67] thus the Pandavas together may be seen as constituting a unified royal group.[68] With regard to Arjuna as an individual, the Wikander-Dumézil view clearly emphasizes a warrior role at the expense of a kingly role: he is modeled after the Vedic Indra as warrior, not the epic Indra as king.[69] Otherwise, the view is in basic agreement with the views presented in this chapter, with one exception: it places undue emphasis on the consistency of the twins' role and thus on the fundamental importance of the fivefold unit as opposed to the threefold one. This point the present study is not willing to concede, since it undermines the uniqueness of Arjuna's position in the family. That is, by recognizing both the threefold and the fivefold structures of the Pandava grouping, it is possible to recognize Arjuna both as youngest and as middle son.

As the youngest son, Arjuna joins a long folkloric tradition in which the youngest (often of three)[70] is the victor among his or her siblings.[71] Meanwhile, as the middle one of the five Pandavas, Arjuna is the mainstay and representative of the group and at the same time its average member: he incorporates all the virtues of his brothers, trifunctional or otherwise, and the entire kingship.[72]

It was mentioned above that Indian thought often identifies or compares the king with Indra. In juxtaposition with this tendency, however, another is often seen: equation or comparison of the king with several gods grouped together, apparently on the basis of his diverse roles and cosmic importance. Classic statements to be found in the *Laws of Manu* (*Manava Dharmashastra*) V.96 and VII.3–8 treat the king as the incarnation of a fairly standard group of "World Guardians" (*lokapalas*), or a composite of particles of these deities: Soma, Agni, Arka, Vayu, Indra, Kubera, Varuna, and Yama. Manu IX.303–11, on the other hand, explains how the role of the king resembles, respectively, the roles of Indra (storm), Arka (sun), Vayu (wind), Yama (death), Varuna (chastiser), Chandra (Soma) (moon), Agni (fire), and Prthivi (earth). A number of similar statements are to be found in the *Mahabharata*, one of which cites five gods as the five forms taken by a ruler: Agni, Aditya, Death, Vaishravana (Kubera), Yama (XII.68.41ff.).[73] In view of the divine affiliation of its members, the composition of the Pandava family in its fivefold form appears to provide another version of such lists. (Although it is noteworthy that the Ashvins are not generally taken to be components of kingship in the later texts, the Vedas do view them as allies of Indra.)[74] Meanwhile, in support of the contention that Arjuna is the representative figure of the whole family, one may refer to the fact that the Pandavas are occasionally viewed by the epic as "five Indras,"[75] multiplications of Indra par excellence, that is, the king par excellence: here, Arjuna. This point may likewise be cited in support of the idea that the significance of the Pandava family resides primarily in its kingly role.

The Heroic Childhood in Its Indian Version

Having discussed Arjuna's birth and his innate position and qualities, it is now appropriate to turn to the epic's treatment of his childhood. It has frequently been maintained that traditional heroes throughout world literature follow very similar life patterns, which are primarily initiatory in nature, but also include characteristic births, childhoods, and deaths.[76] This contention may be accepted here in broad outline, but it must also be noted that, with regard to details, the models vary greatly from culture to culture. In Indian epic literature, a typical heroic childhood may be distinguished, which includes such stock elements as comparison with natural phenomena and animals, discussion of the naming of the hero and the performance of his childhood rites of passage (*samskaras*), mention of his special marks and emphasis on his godlike nature—all seemingly components of a standard, probably oral, genre of praise of royal ancestors or patrons.[77] For example, it is stated of Bharata, an archetypical hero insofar as he is "principal dynast and eponym of the Bhāratas":[78]

> When Duḥṣanta had returned to his seat after making his promises to Śakuntalā, the woman with the lovely thighs gave birth to a son of boundless might, after bearing him for a full three years . . . a son radiant like a blazing fire, enriched with all the virtues of beauty and generosity, true scion of Duḥṣanta. Kaṇva, best minister to the sacred, administered solemnly upon him the sacraments of birth, and others, as he grew in wisdom. He was a large child, with shining and pointed teeth, solid like a lion, wearing on his palm the sign of the wheel,[79] and illustrious, large-headed, and strong. The boy, who appeared like the child of a God, grew up rapidly there. When he was six years old, the child in Kaṇva's hermitage would fetter lions and tigers, boars, buffaloes, and elephants to the trees around the hermitage and run about playing and riding and taming them. Hence the hermits who dwelled in Kaṇva's hermitage gave him a nickname: "He shall be Sarvadamana, for he tames everything!" So the boy became known as Sarvadamana, and he was endowed with prowess, might, and strength. [I.68.1–8][80]

Examples could be multiplied.

A similar statement is made regarding the Pandavas as a group, in the course of three short passages in *Mahabharata* I:

> Then the seers who lived on the Hundred-Peak Mountains gave them all names, with love and ritual and benedictions. . . . The eldest they addressed as Yudhiṣṭhira, the middle one as Bhīmasena, the third as Arjuna—thus they named the three sons of Kuntī. Then the affectionate brahmins named the two sons of Mādrī—the elder of the twins Nakula, the other Sahadeva. All these chiefs of the Kurus were born one year apart. [I.115.19–21]

> So five God-given powerful sons were born to Pāṇḍu, glorious furtherers of the dynasty of Kuru. They bore the marks of greatness, their aspect was benign as the moon's, their pride like a lion's, great archers all, who strode wide like the lion—lion-necked lords of men who grew up with the might of Gods. And as they grew up on the holy Mount Himālaya they astonished the great seers that had foregathered there. These five, and the other hundred, all scions of the dynasty of Kuru, grew up quickly like lotuses in a pond. [I.115.25–28]

> The Pāṇḍavas received the sacraments that the *Veda* prescribes and grew up in their father's house, enjoying the pleasures of life. [I.119.13][81]

Although Arjuna is grouped with his brothers with regard to the general outlines of his early childhood history, only he of all the brothers is said to have special marks on his body, similar to the sign of the wheel mentioned in the description of Bharata, above. These marks are not mentioned in the Book I account, however, but only later. In V.58.9 Samjaya notes that Arjuna has on the soles of his feet "straight lines that [run] upward." In VIII.49.95 Arjuna himself states, in the course of a boast that is unusually strong for his character:[82] "On my two hands these arrows are inscribed, and a bow with arrows, extended in battle. And my two feet have arrows and standards."[83]

As his childhood continues, Arjuna stands out among his brothers and all his peers, as the most skillful fighter. The major portion of the epic's account of the Pandavas' childhood (I.119.13ff.) has to do with Arjuna's instruction in the use of weapons. (In addition, something is said about Bhima's childhood strength, particularly in the context of his early enmity with the Kauravas,[84] but little is said of Yudhishthira's early education.) Both the Pandavas and the Kauravas are taught by Drona, but Arjuna is by far the best student, and he becomes Drona's favorite, surpassing even Drona's son, Ashvatthaman, in this regard.[85] The culmination of Drona's favoritism comes when Drona presents Arjuna with the *brahmashiras* ("Brahma's Head")[86] weapon (I.123.74ff.) while, as is later told, at first withholding this weapon from Ashvatthaman (see chap. IIIC).

A number of incidents that take place in the course of Arjuna's education indicate his superior talent for mastery of weapons,[87] which, combined with superior devotion to his teacher, assures his success, summarized as follows:

> Of the Kurus who studied with Droṇa, Duryodhana and Bhīma excelled in combat with clubs. Aśvatthāman surpassed all in all the esoteric arts. The twins were masters on the sword hilt, beyond all other men. Yudhiṣṭhira was the best on chariots. But Arjuna was the best on every weapon. The Pāṇḍava, chief of the chiefs of warriors, was renowned on earth as far as the ocean for his insight, application, strength, and enterprise in all weapons. Both in weaponry and devotion to his guru, the mighty Arjuna was distinguished by his excellence, even though the arms drills were the same for all;

> among all the princes he was the outstanding warrior. [I.123.40–43]

Arjuna's predominant skill is in archery and is based on his absolute power of concentration upon his target, to the exclusion of all surroundings, as demonstrated during the final examination administered by Drona to his pupils at the conclusion of their studies (I.123.45ff.). It is peerlessness in archery that Drona foresees for his favorite and maintains as the goal of his instruction (I.123.6, 78).

Arjuna's education culminates in his fine performance at a tournament arranged by Drona for his pupils. The following is the epic's account of his feats, as he displays the various weapons he has mastered under Drona's tutelage:

> With the *āgneya* he created fire, with the *vāruṇa* water, with the *vāyavya* wind, with the *pārjanya* rain; with the *bhauma* he entered earth, with the *pārvata* he brought forth mountains. With the disappearing weapon he made it all vanish again. One instant he stood tall, the next squat, then was up in front on the chariot yoke, then again in the middle of the chariot, and the next instant had jumped to the ground. Trained to high excellence, the favorite of his guru hit and shot through fragile targets, and tiny ones, and hard ones, with different makes of arrows. While an iron boar was moved about, he loosed into its snout five continuous arrows[88] as though they were one single one. The mighty archer buried twenty-one arrows in a cow's hollow horn that was swaying on a rope. And in this and other fashions he gave an exhibition of his dexterity with the long sword as well as the bow and the club. [I.125.19–25]

This account shows clearly that Arjuna's powers extend to the near-cosmic; for the weapons listed at the start are, like so many magical weapons in the Indian epics, named after deities (here, personified natural phenomena), whose particular powers they reflect. It is primarily by weapon usage that Arjuna incorporates into himself the various divine powers that, as discussed above, are considered essential to kingship.[89] In the account above one sees that Arjuna's semidivine birth is matched by his accomplishments. His magical powers remind one of Yudhishthira's, yet are very differently exercised.

During the tournament scene another theme is brought into the epic, which will be most important both for Arjuna as hero and for Arjuna as human. This theme is that of Arjuna's competition with Karna, the illegitimate brother of the Pandavas, fathered by the sun god, Surya, and born to Kunti prior to her marriage to Pandu; it is mentioned briefly during the account of the Pandavas' and Kauravas' education (I.122.47), but not developed fully until the tournament. Karna has been raised outside the court by a charioteer, and does not know his true parentage;[90] but he too has been instructed by Drona (I.122.47), and toward the end of the tournament he suddenly enters the arena and accomplishes, as is stated simply, "every feat that the Pārtha ['son of Pṛtha'][91] had achieved" (I.126.12). It is noteworthy that Arjuna takes Karna's performance as a personal insult or challenge: he cannot stand to be matched, for he has already developed that pride which is essential to heroes (I.126.17).[92] A battle begins between Arjuna and Karna, but is stopped when it is discovered that Karna cannot claim a noble lineage: he is not considered heroic material by the members of the court.[93] Duryodhana responds by crowning Karna king of Anga, setting him up against the Pandavas, and creating with him a friendship and alliance that is to endure throughout the epic. The epic is probably referring to this episode when it states, regarding Karna: "He always competed with Arjuna . . . and Arjuna with him, from their first meeting onward" (III.293.19). This opposition reflects the natural opposition between sun and storm, as is emphasized by the fact that Karna's and Arjuna's respective fathers encourage and support them during their encounter at the tournament (I.126.23ff.).[94] The Arjuna-Karna (storm-sun) opposition continues to be superimposed on the epic's more central Pandava-Kaurava (god-demon) opposition, so that Karna becomes a convinced Kaurava supporter in the war, and is himself, at one point, said to be the embodiment of (or possessed by) a demon, Naraka (III.240.19, 32).

The final act of Arjuna's education is his payment of the teacher's requested fee (*gurudakshina*), required according to Indian custom. The fee that Drona requests is the defeat of his archenemy, King Drupada of Panchala. This feat is accomplished by the Pandavas as a group (alternatively, by all of Drona's pupils) (I.128; I.154.22), but that Arjuna is supremely behind the effort is suggested by the epic's statement that Arjuna of all Drona's pupils was the only one to promise the fee in advance (I.122.42ff.). This emphasis on payment of the teacher's fee is a typically Indian aspect of the account of the hero, emphasizing that devotion to elders which is evidently considered essential in a truly admirable figure. By contrast, the evil Duryodhana is said to lack such devotion.[95]

Immediately following the victory over Drupada, the epic relates the story of "The Fire in the Lacquer House" (I.129ff.), the culmination of several Book I attempts by the Kauravas to rid themselves of the cousins whom they envy for their skill and strength.[96] Here Yudhishthira and Bhima manage to save the other Pandavas, Yudhishthira by comprehending a secret message from Vidura, warning him of the danger, Bhima by carrying his brothers away from the burning house. Arjuna himself has no special role in this episode; nevertheless it prepares the way for his feats of wife winning, which will dominate much of the remainder of Book I. For the Pandavas go into hiding after the incident of the lacquer house, and it is from their retreat in the city of Varanavata that Arjuna, already an accomplished hero, disguised as a brahmin, sets out to win Draupadi.

Notes

1. Here translating *mahipalan*, the word "barons" (likewise, "baronage") means, in van Buitenen's translation, the *kshatriya* class.
2. Short versions of the prophecy appear at V.88.64f. and V.135.2ff. These two versions, like that of Book I, state that Arjuna will perform three sacrifices. To try to figure out precisely which acts of Arjuna that statement refers to, as does Biardeau ("Etudes" V, pp. 113f., etc.), is a futile task. Nilakantha glosses all three times as follows: "medhan ashvamedhan" ("The sacrifices are horse sacrifices"). Could Nilakantha have derived his interpretation from the frequent epic usage that measures merit in terms of numbers of horse sacrifices performed (as, e.g., in III.80ff., passim)? In any case, Arjuna participates in only one horse sacrifice in the *Mahabharata* (see, especially, chap. IIB); though cf. chap. IE, n. 46. Another version of the birth prophecy appears in *trishtubh* stanzas VIII.48.6ff. Here Yudhishthira reminds Arjuna of the predictions that were made for him at his birth, in an attempt to stir him to greater feats in battle. The points made are basically the same as those in the Book I version, except that the idea of the three sacrifices is omitted, and Yudhishthira stresses such aspects of Arjuna's character as his knowledge, ascetic power, and beauty, as well as his prowess. According to the words of the prophecy, Arjuna, Yudhishthira says, will never be conquered by any creature and will be the progenitor of a race.
3. See Cecil Maurice Bowra, *Heroic Poetry* (London: Macmillan, 1952), p. 94. Along with Achilles, Herakles, etc., he gives the essentially Sumerian/Semitic example of Gilgamesh. With regard to the Greek epics, Cedric H. Whitman speaks of "that mysterious union of divine and human which is the essence of heroism"; see his *Homer and the Heroic Tradition* (1958; rpt. New York: Norton, 1965), p. 243.
4. Double fathering is common to a number of heroes, e.g., Cuchulainn, Herakles, and Jesus. One purported father is divine, one human in each of these cases, as in the

cases of the Pandavas. See *The Tain: Translated from the Irish Epic Tain Bo Cuailnge*, trans. Thomas Kinsella (London: Oxford University Press, 1969), pp. 21ff., on the birth of Cuchulainn. Herakles was called the son of Amphitryon, as in *Iliad* V.392, although his father was really Zeus.

5. This fact is stressed by Dumézil throughout "La terre soulagee" (see Introduction, n. 44).
6. Father and son are often identified with one another in the Indian epic tradition. Several statements of this identity may be found in the *Mahabharata*, for instance, in the story of Shakuntala; see I.68.47, etc. See below, p. 199, for another example.
7. E.g., in W. Crooke, *The Popular Religion and Folk-lore of Northern India*, 2nd ed. (1896; rpt. Delhi: Munshiram Manoharlal, 1968), I, 206, where, however, Pandava worship is reported to be a dying religion. "Bhîmsen" was still worshiped, according to Crooke, I, 89ff., but this local "godling" was quite different from his *Mahabharata* namesake. Cf. Gerald D. Berreman's detailed discussion of the popular Pandava cult in *Hindus of the Himalayas* (Berkeley: University of California Press, 1963), pp. 101f., 178, 381ff. (This is the first edition. The second edition omits much of the material on Pandava worship.) The Pandavas are also worshiped in the context of the Draupadi cult (see chap. IB).
8. For important work on this subject in the Greek context, see Gregory Nagy, *The Best of the Achaeans: Concepts of the Hero in Archaic Greek Poetry* (Baltimore: Johns Hopkins University Press, 1979). See further, Nagy, "On the Death of Sarpedon," in *Approaches to Homer*, ed. Carl A. Rubino and Cynthia W. Shelmerdine (Austin: University of Texas Press, 1983), pp. 189–217.
9. Bowra, *Heroic Poetry*, chaps. 2–3, especially p. 105.
10. On that aspect of divine kingship in India in which the king was identified with Indra, see Gonda, *Aspects*, pp. 166f. See also E. Washburn Hopkins, "The Divinity of Kings," *Journal of the American Oriental Society* 51 (1931): 309ff. This and other studies of Indian kingship indicate, however, that the idea of royal divinity was not constant; see, e.g., Jan Gonda, *Ancient Indian Kingship from the Religious Point of View* (Leiden: Brill, 1966), p. 35. The king, thus, might as well be compared to Indra as identified with him. The main comparison of the king and Indra in the *Mahabharata* itself is to be found in XII.67.4: "According to the sacred texts, when a king is chosen, he is Indra. Like Indra should the king be honored by one desiring well-being." The issue is complicated further by the fact that Indra often seems to represent only one aspect of kingship, so that the king is seen as a combination of a number of divinities. Nonetheless, the comparison between the king and Indra has become formulaic, and is often repeated, on the basis of the fact that Indra is the king of the gods.
11. On Indra's connection with fertility, see E. Washburn Hopkins, "Indra as God of Fertility," *Journal of the American Oriental Society* 36 (1916): 242–68; Johann Jakob Meyer, *Trilogie altindischer Mächte und Feste der Vegetation: Ein Beitrag zur vergleichenden Religions- und Kulturgeschichte, Fest- und Volkskunde* (Zurich: Max Niehans, 1937), Part III; and Gonda, *Kingship*, pp. 28f. For an explicit *Mahabharata* reference, see XII.207.23.

12. See, e.g., III.48.9; cf. III.46.15 and V.51.13.
13. See, especially, III.44.24f. This sort of scar is considered to be a typical mark of the warrior, as in II.19.39.
14. Dumézil, *Mythe et épopée* I, p. 21, etc.
15. See Wendy Doniger O'Flaherty, *The Origins of Evil in Hindu Mythology* (Berkeley: University of California Press, 1976), pp. 58f.
16. For some references, see p. 170.
17. See, especially, III.240. According to I.61.80ff. Duryodhana incarnates Kali, a demon, but his brothers incarnate *rakshasa*s ("ogres")—specifically, those called *paulastya*s (cf. XVIII.5.19: *yatudhana*s). On the relative goodness and evil of gods and demons, see O'Flaherty, *Origins of Evil*, pp. 57ff. She argues that the gods and the demons are consanguine, and the distinction between them, especially in the early texts, not clear-cut. Later, however, their quarrel is ethicized as a struggle between good and evil (p. 61). To the present author, the god-demon conflict seems generally to be a conflict of order against chaos, if only because the gods' victory is necessary for world order.
18. The question of the historicity of the epic story has been much debated. Both sides are represented, e.g., among the articles in *The Bhārata War and Purāṇic Genealogies*, ed. D. C. Sircar (Calcutta: University of Calcutta, 1969); see, more recently, *Mahābhārata: Myth and Reality: Differing Views*, ed. S. P. Gupta and K. S. Ramachandran (Delhi: Agam Prakashan, 1976), and Ram Chandra Jain, *Jaya: The Original Nucleus of Mahabharata* (Delhi: Agam Kala Prakashan, 1979). The epic itself claims to be *itihasa* (approximately, "history") (I.56.16ff., etc.). The present author's view of the matter is based squarely on the statements of Mircea Eliade in *The Myth of the Eternal Return or Cosmos and History*, trans. Willard R. Trask, Bollingen Series, 46 (1954; rpt. Princeton: Princeton University Press, 1974), as summarized in the following passage from p. 42: "The historical character of the persons celebrated in epic poetry is not in question. But their historicity does not long resist the corrosive action of mythicization. The historical event in itself, however important, does not remain in the popular memory, nor does its recollection kindle the poetic imagination save insofar as the particular historical event closely approaches a mythical model." From this perspective, the present study is not concerned with whether the Kurukshetra War was, historically, a great war, a small war, or no war at all. With regard to the conflict's broad Indo-European mythic parallels, see Dumézil, *Mythe et épopée* I, pp. 222ff., and Hiltebeitel, *Ritual*, chaps. 12–13.
19. As, e.g., in VIII.31.59.
20. A medieval *chanson de geste*, but continuous with the older Indo-European traditions.
21. See Bowra, *Heroic Poetry*, p.105, for further examples and discussion.
22. Partha ("son of Prtha") is a name given to Yudhishthira, Bhima, or Arjuna. In his translation, van Buitenen usually maintains the Sanskrit form of the metronymic, "Pārtha." On this name of Arjuna, see Appendix.
23. The king in question is Duryodhana. The passage is addressed by Krpa to Ashvatthaman.

24. Particularly against Shalya, whom he kills eventually (see chap. IIA3).
25. That the Pandavas' wife, Draupadi, also had the "evil eye" is suggested in such stanzas as I.56.7.
26. Suggestions of fertility ritual, and even Grail imagery, may be seen in this event.
27. Clearly related is a statement made earlier in the same book, at IV.27.12ff., to the effect that any country where Yudhishthira is staying must be enjoying the greatest prosperity.
28. On the king as the embodiment of *dharma*, see Gonda, *Kingship*, p. 68.
29. Van Buitenen's translation; see, e.g., chap. IC, n. 53.
30. Besides the example just quoted, see V.39.7; V.141.33; V.146.16 (van Buitenen translates variously); VI.2.14; VI.21.11; VI.61.16; VI.117.33; IX.62.58; XI.13.9; XI.17.6. Cf. XIII.150.8.
31. This, anyway, is how they are always translated by van Buitenen. For examples of such a formula, *satyavikrama* ("whose valor is truth"), applied to Satyaki, see VII.116.33 and VII.117.55–56, quoted on p. 146 (and chap. IIA2, n. 35).
32. See, e.g., IV.27.12ff.
33. E.g., by Bhima in III.36.19 and XII.76.19 and by Karna in VIII.33.37ff.
34. See, e.g., I.122.7; V.3.3; V.73.17; V.131.5 (where eunuchlike behavior is contrasted explicitly with *kshatriya* behavior); VI.24.3; VI.41, passim; IX.4.25.
35. On nonviolence, see, e.g., the Tuladhara-Jajali conversation of XII.153.ff. XIII.117.37f. is a litany of praise for nonviolence, calling it the highest *dharma*, the highest self-control, the highest gift, the highest austerity, the highest sacrifice, etc. Many other references might also be cited.
36. His knowledge is tested twice by questioning, in III.177 and III.297f., the latter time by Dharma himself.
37. Georges Dumézil, *The Destiny of the Warrior*, trans. Alf Hiltebeitel (Chicago: University of Chicago Press, 1970), pp. 59, 82. Note, however, that C. Scott Littleton prefers to see Achilles as a cross between the Vayu and Indra types ("Some Possible Indo-European Themes in the 'Iliad,' " in *Myth and Law among the Indo-Europeans: Studies in Indo-European Comparative Mythology*, ed. Jaan Puhvel, Publications of the UCLA Center for the Study of Comparative Folklore and Mythology, 1 [Berkeley: University of California Press, 1970], p. 241).
38. Dumézil, *Warrior*, p. 73.
39. For an example regarding Bhima, see chap. IIA1, n. 9. Regarding Arjuna, see chap. IC.
40. Note the inverted order: *dharma* belongs to the youngest brother who, in addition, is also of lower caste than his brothers (see Introduction).
41. Specified in Dumézil, *Mythe et épopée* I, p. 57.
42. Here the present study agrees with Biardeau, who states in "Etudes" IV, pp. 236f., that Arjuna's character is a cross between Yudhishthira's and Bhima's. The Yudhishthira-Bhima-Arjuna dialectic runs through the entire *Mahabharata*. See chap. IIA1, n. 8, for a concrete example.
43. Although Indra is generally known as a *kshatriya*, and even in XII.22.11 is said to have become a *kshatriya*.

44. The fullest version of this story is told in III.293.23ff.; see also I.104.18. The stories of Indra's brahmanic disguise go back to the Brahmanas; see G. V. Devasthali, *Religion and Mythology of the Brāhmaṇas with Particular Reference to the Śatapatha-Brāhmaṇa*, Bhau Vishnu Ashtekar Vedic Research Series, vol. 1 (Poona: University of Poona, 1965), p. 24.
45. The story of this education is told in I.121ff.
46. In fact, throughout the *Mahabharata* various kings, including Arjuna, tend to be praised as *brahmanya*, which means either "brahmanic" or "friendly to brahmins." For Arjuna as *brahmanya*, see III.165.4. Biardeau ("Etudes" V, pp. 120ff., etc.) stresses the brahmanic aspect of kingship.
47. In I.114.65f. Kunti expresses her refusal to have more than three sons. In I.115 she passes her charm on to Pandu's second wife, Madri, who calls upon the divine twins, the Ashvins, with it, enabling her to bear two children with only one use of the charm. The title of a play attributed to the early Indian playwright Bhasa, *Madhyamavyayoga* ("The Middle One"), referring to Bhima, provides one example of the treatment of the sons of Kunti as an entity complete in itself, without the twins. See too Bhasa's play *Pancharatram* ("The Five Nights") II.56.
48. Dumézil stresses the fertility and agricultural aspects of the twins' role, as representatives of the third function (see p. 40), and indeed the divine voice that speaks at their birth stresses their beauty and wealth, but these are not important consistently for their later adventures. Lists that attribute special traits to the individual Pandavas often seem to have chosen the traits of the twins randomly (or, at least, idiosyncratically); see, e.g., the quotation from I.123.40–43 on pp. 43–44, in which all the other characterizations make sense for the epic as a whole, but the point regarding the twins seems randomly chosen because it is not stressed consistently throughout the epic. (Dumézil [*Myth et épopée* I, pp. 98ff.] argues, however, that the sword is also part of the twins' functional identity.) Another point noticeable in this quotation and elsewhere is that although there are five Pandavas, other characters may be included on lists to make up groups of sixes, sevens, or more; and at other times lists may be shorter, all this being suggestive of oral composition. Although this point will not be pursued here, one may at least note that the number six is particularly in evidence with regard to the Pandava family: there are really six brothers, if Karna is included; and six go into exile in the forest, the five Pandavas with Draupadi as sixth.

    Another argument for the secondary inclusion of the twins in the Pandava group might derive from the observation that Nakula and Sahadeva in a sense reduplicate another set of twins, which is far more integral to the structure of the epic cast of characters: namely, Arjuna and Krishna, insofar as they may be taken as a twinlike pair (see chaps. IC and IIIA). In fact, at at least one point (XIV.15.4), Arjuna and Krishna are compared specifically to the Ashvins, that is, the divine twins who were the progenitors of Nakula and Sahadeva.
49. In this regard, a most useful, though brief, article is B. C. Mazumdar's comment on *Mahabharata* I.94 (Critical Edition I.89), in *Journal of the Royal Asiatic Society of Great Britain and Ireland* (1906): 225–26. Mazumdar finds in this chapter remnants of an independent Kuru-Panchala struggle, onto which the Pandava story, he

feels, has been grafted "for conferring dignity upon the heroes of the new story" (p. 225). The many arguments in favor of an original Kuru-Panchala conflict are summarized by N. N. Bhattacharya in his paper entitled "The Kurukṣetra War and the Pāṇḍavas," in Sircar, p. 37. The theory has also been criticized most strongly, however, on the grounds that the Vedic literature (precisely, the Brahmanas and the Upanishads) consistently portrays the Kurus and the Panchalas as friends, not enemies; see, e.g., the comment by Ram Gopal in Gupta and Ramachandran, p. 201.

50. A large part of this is the Draupadi-Pandava marriage (see chap. IB). Note too the recurrent phrase "Pandavas and Panchalas" (*pandupanchala*) and the frequent appearance of the Panchala pair, Yudhamanyu and Uttamaujas, as the protectors of the wheels of Arjuna's chariot (VI.16.19, etc.). With regard to the Panchala generalship of the Pandava army, note that XIV.59.9ff. seems to specify that Shikhandin was the first general, Dhrshtadyumna the second. Arjuna protected Shikhandin, it is stated (XIV.59.9), Bhima protected Dhrshtadyumna (XIV.59.15). Contrast V.149.18ff., in which Arjuna nominates Dhrshtadyumna for general, while Bhima favors Shikhandin.
51. See Hemchandra Raychaudhuri, *Political History of Ancient India*, 3rd ed. (Calcutta: University of Calcutta, 1932), p. 47.
52. This was suggested as early as the nineteenth century by Christian Lassen, seconded by Dahlmann; see Dahlmann, *Genesis*, pp. 224ff.
53. As pointed out by Hiltebeitel, *Ritual*, pp. 175ff. Hiltebeitel does not, however, stress the fivefold composition of the groups involved, but rather, the features of sovereignty in the tales. A convenient summary of the Irish stories may be found in Alwyn Rees and Brinley Rees, *Celtic Heritage: Ancient Tradition in Ireland and Wales* (London: Thames and Hudson, 1961), pp. 73f. The Indian story is to be found in *Mahabharata* III.296f., part of which is cited above, n. 36.
54. See chap. IB, especially n. 14.
55. Rees and Rees (see above, n. 53), p. 189. On p. 118 they refer, by way of comparison, to *Taittiriya Upanishad* I.7, which states that everything that exists is fivefold; cf. *Brhadaranyaka Upanishad* I.4.17.
56. Rees and Rees, pp. 118ff. The phrase "elusive fifth" appears only later, p. 188.
57. Georges Dumézil, *The Destiny of a King*, trans. Alf Hiltebeitel (Chicago: University of Chicago Press, 1973), chap. 2.
58. Also fourfold. See Abel Bergaigne, *La Religion védique d'après les hymnes du Rig-Veda*, II (Paris: F. Vieweg, 1883), 125.
59. This is van Buitenen's translation. Literally, however, the title means "Conquest of the Directions."
60. In other similar lists, all much briefer and less prominent than the "Conquest of the World" list, the correlations between the various Pandavas and the directions are arranged differently, another suggestion of oral composition at work. III.47.11, e.g., describing the hunting of the Pandavas in the Kamyaka Forest, in the absence of Arjuna, states that Yudhishthira hunted to the east, Bhima to the south, and the twins to the west and north. III.250.7, on the contrary, in the *trishtubh* meter like III.47.11, and beginning with the identical line, has Yudhishthira hunting to the east, Bhima to the south, Arjuna to the west, and the twins to the north (van Buitenen's

translation is incorrect) at the time of the attempted abduction of Draupadi by Jayadratha (see chap. IB). Cf. too the mandala-like formation with Yudhishthira at its center, assumed during the great war for the destruction of Shalya (IX.15.19, 24f.): Bhima in front, Arjuna behind, Satyaki protecting the right wheel of the chariot, Dhrshtadyumna the left wheel (or the twins protecting the wheels). Those arrangements that place Yudhishthira in the center may perhaps be seen as truest to the Indo-European conceptualization, which allots the central portion to the king (e.g., in Irish thought the central province, Meath, was viewed as the abode of kingship; see Rees and Rees, pp. 123, 128f.). With regard to the four cardinal points and center, note also the image in III.52ff. of Nala and four "World Guardians," gods traditionally aligned with the four directions. The Pandavas are not correlated with the World Guardians, however: only one, Arjuna, is the son of the guardian of a cardinal point (Indra, associated with either north or east; see E. Washburn Hopkins, *Epic Mythology* [1915; rpt. Delhi: Motilal Banarsidass, 1974], pp. 149ff.).

61. Since numerical classification is extremely popular in Indian thought, almost all numbers, and particularly prime numbers, appear again and again. One source of the diversity may be the creation of significant numbers by the principle of "x + 1"; that is, to any given number, one more is added, to represent the totality. See Bergaigne, II, 123ff., where the classificatory numbers three, five, and seven are said often to be derived in this manner; one may surmise, however, that even such a number as six, which, as pointed out above (n. 48), is significant for the Pandava family, may be seen as being composed of x + 1. With all these points made, the fact remains that the number five is particularly popular, and of varied application: five senses (though sometimes six), five breaths, five elements (ether, air, fire, water, and earth), five fires, five sacrifices, etc. The Samkhya philosophy that runs through epic thought is a classificatory system based largely on the number five; but also three (see, especially, Appendix, n. 25). The importance of this number may also be noted in Indian thought outside the epic in such groupings as the five gods of the Smarta tradition, the five directional *dhyanibuddhas* of Tantric Buddhism, the five-member audience for the Buddha's Deer Park sermon, the five original members of the Sikh brotherhood, etc. Five is the dominant number in the Pashupata philosophy, and the traditional village council is called a *panchayat*. On fives, see further Jan Gonda, *Viṣṇuism and Śivaism: A Comparison* (Jordan Lectures, 1969) (London: Athlone Press-University of London, 1970), pp. 45ff., and David M. Knipe, "One Fire, Three Fires, Five Fires: Vedic Symbols in Transition," *History of Religions* 12 (1972–73): 28–41: "'Three' is the vertical cosmos . . . 'four' is the horizontal cosmos . . . and 'five' is quite simply both at once and therefore the most complete expression of all, one that provides transcendent closure to the world view" (p. 35).

62. Dahlmann (*Epos und Rechtsbuch*, pp. 89 ff.) views this marriage primarily as an expression of the unity of the joint family.

63. Both the structure of the Pandavas and the chaos of the Kauravas are noted by Biardeau, "Etudes" II, p. 103. In support of her interpretation of the number one hundred, one may refer to *Mahabharata* I.209.8, which van Buitenen translates as

follows: " 'Hundred' and 'thousand' and 'always' all bespeak infinity." This infinity is, however, as often positive as negative: generally, one hundred sons are considered a great boon, as in III.281.37, 44.

64. In the *Mahabharata* itself: the five sons of Vasu Uparichara (I.57.28), the five sons of Yayati (I.70.31f., etc.), the five sons of Ilina (I.89.15f.), the five sons of Kuru (I.89.44), the five sons of Jamadagni (III.116.4), the five Kekayas, the five Trigartas. Note that Yayati, dividing the world between his five sons, is Dumézil's prime example of a "first king"; for reference, see above, n. 57. Note too the emphasis in V.144.22 on the promise that Kunti will always have five sons (here the twins are evidently considered her children): Karna will kill Arjuna or die himself in the war, but none of the other Pandavas will be killed by him (see chap. IIA3). Cf. the statement of Vyasa's disciples, also five in number, that they want no sixth added to their ranks (XII.314.37f.; and see XII.327.16).
65. Officially assumed by one son. But note in the sons-of-Daire story that Daire is told that his son named Lugaid will become ruler, and so names each of his five sons Lugaid (Rees and Rees, p. 74).
66. Dumézil, *Mythe et épopée* I, pp. 53ff.
67. Dumézil, *King*, passim.
68. Implied by Dumézil in *Mythe et épopée* I, pp. 101f. Stated specifically by Gehrts, pp. 173ff.
69. See Dumézil, *Mythe et épopée* I, p. 45.
70. For bibliography on the recurrence of the number three in folklore and epic, see *The Study of Folklore*, ed. Alan Dundes (Englewood Cliffs, N.J.: Prentice-Hall, 1965), p. 133, n. 4. In the *Mahabharata*, three is a significant number, particularly apparent in the concept of the "three worlds"; also the three *gunas* ("qualities" in nature), etc.
71. On the theme of the successful youngest son, see Stith Thompson, *Motif-Index of Folk Literature: A Classification of Narrative Elements in Folktales, Ballads, Myths, Fables, Mediaeval Romances, Exempla, Fabliaux, Jest-Books and Local Legends*, rev. ed., 6 vols. (Bloomington: Indiana University Press, 1955–58), nos. H1242 ("Youngest brother alone succeeds on quest") and L10 ("Victorious youngest son"). Sometimes the successful youngest is the last of five, as in the case of Niall; cf. Puru (I.70.31ff.) and Rama Jamadagnya (III.116.4ff.; cf. I.60.46f.) in the *Mahabharata*.
72. So great is Arjuna's position that in Indian literature outside the epic he is occasionally viewed as the oldest Pandava. Such, e.g., is the case in the Buddhist *Jataka* no. 536.
73. This chapter seems to support the idea of divine kingship (see v. 1). See also III.183.22ff.; XII.73.26; XII.91.38, 41; XII.137.99.
74. See *Rg Veda* X.131.4f. Note too that *Mahabharata* I.3.60ff. preserves an Ashvin prayer in archaic style.
75. Primarily in I.189 (see further, chap. IB). Note the epic's means of reconciling the idea of the Pandavas as five Indras with their connection with the gods who are said to have fathered them: in I.189.27 the Indras say:

We shall go from the Gods to the world of men
Where release is declared to be hard to obtain.
But Gods must beget us upon our mother,
God Dharma, the Wind God, God Indra, the Aśvins.

Elsewhere the Pandavas are commonly said to be *like* five Indras. In this case it is difficult to tell whether the mythic or the formulaic usage came first.

76. For a short account of the basic theories, see Archer Taylor, "The Biographical Pattern in Traditional Narrative," *Journal of the Folklore Institute* 1 (1964): 114–29. Taylor discusses the work of J. G. von Hahn, Otto Rank, Lord Raglan, Joseph Campbell, and Vladimir Propp. He omits the work of Jan de Vries, *Heroic Song and Heroic Legend*, trans. B. J. Timmer (London: Oxford University Press, 1963), pp. 210ff., also of significance in this regard.
77. On such panegyrics in the Indian context, including *Atharva Veda* XX.127, lines 7–10, addressed to a King Parikshit, see Chadwick and Chadwick, II, 482, 617, etc.
78. Van Buitenen, *Mahābhārata*, I, 469.
79. Showing him to be a future *chakravartin* ("wheel turner"), a world ruler.
80. The child Bharata, like all heroes, has many Vayu/Bhima-like qualities.
81. Both naming and performance of the *samskaras* are referred to rather vaguely in the case of the Pandavas. No etymologies of the names are given, although this oversight is later corrected with regard to Arjuna (see Appendix). The priest who performed the *samksaras* is not named; the Pandavas acquired the services of their priest, Dhaumya, only much later (I.174). The southern recension, however, makes Kashyapa the priest who attended the Pandavas in their childhood; see Prolegomena to the Critical Edition, p. xxxv.
82. In the course of an incident during which Arjuna is trying intentionally to insult Yudhishthira with a greater purpose in mind (see chap. IIA3, n. 86).
83. Cf. the slightly different version in VIII.52.33. Are these stanzas meant to be taken literally? Are they simply symbolic indications of Arjuna's warrior prowess? Or is their credibility completely undermined by the context in which they are spoken?
84. See, especially, I.119.15ff. Unlike Arjuna's ability, which is partially learned, Bhima's prowess is primarily innate; see, e.g., I.114.13. Unthinking, he inspires the hatred of his cousins through his boyhood pranks.
85. On Arjuna as Drona's favorite: I.123.1, etc. On Drona's preference for Arjuna above Ashvatthaman: I.125.7, etc.
86. Here van Buitenen translates "Brahmā-Head"; elsewhere (III.41.8), "Brahmā's Head."
87. E.g., Arjuna figures out for himself how practice will lead to mastery of archery, and then starts to practice shooting in the dark (I.123.2ff.). I.123.68ff. relates how Arjuna among all the pupils of Drona was the most capable of saving his teacher from a Ganges crocodile. For this feat, Drona gave Arjuna the *brahmashiras* weapon.
88. On several occasions, Arjuna shoots five arrows, as if shooting for his whole family; see, e.g., I.123.71. Such is certainly the case when Arjuna shoots five arrows to win Draupadi (I.179.16). Marie Delcourt, in "The Legend of Sarpedon and the Saga of

the Archer," *History of Religions* 2 (1962–63): 40ff., suggests a directional significance for these five arrows. Cf. Pandu's shooting of five arrows at a deer in I.109.6 (an act that leads to his being cursed to impotence; thus the requirement of a magic charm to engender his sons).

89. Cf. Skanda receiving the powers and gifts of all the gods in IX.44f.; likewise, the goddess Devi in the Puranic "Devimahatmya" (see *Markandeya Purana* LXXXII).
90. He apparently learns of it only in V.138ff.
91. See above, n. 22.
92. Cf. Arjuna's jealousy and anger when his superiority is threatened by another archer, Ekalavya (I.123.10ff.). At Arjuna's prodding, Drona manages to reduce Ekalavya's ability by virtue of an extremely unkind trick: he asks Ekalavya to cut off his right thumb as the fee for his instruction in archery—instruction that Drona in truth can scarcely claim to have given.
93. Ekalavya (see preceding note), like Karna at this point, is of inferior caste; thus the particular resentment against him. The requirement that the hero be of noble birth is mentioned by Hopkins in "Position," p. 99 n.
94. Dumézil views the Arjuna-Karna opposition as a transposition of storm-sun opposition to be found in the Vedas; see *Mythe et épopée* I, pp. 130ff., following an earlier article, "Karṇa et les Pāṇḍava," *Orientalia Suecana* 3 (1954): 60–66.
95. E.g., in V.90.17.
96. Note earlier attempts to destroy Bhima alone (I.119.34ff.). Threats to his life in childhood are a typical aspect of the biography of the hero; see Taylor, p. 118 (citing Raglan), etc.

IB. MARRIAGES

One of the typical exploits of the epic and saga hero is wife winning by various means. Wife winning is an initiatory exploit insofar as it is a major step toward full manhood, and heroic stories of wife winning are based upon what may have been real social events such as bride stealing and marriage tests. Since a number of different types of marriage have traditionally been accepted as legal in India,[1] there has been much scope for variety in the marriage episodes of the *Mahabharata*. The figure who benefits most from this scope is the most frequently married of the epic's major characters, Arjuna, who has four wives.[2] As the following discussion will suggest, Arjuna's success with women is part of his connection with fertility, noted above.

The Polyandrous Marriage to Draupadi, Prosperity (Shri) Incarnate

Of Arjuna's marriages, the most important for the heroic story of the Mahabharata is the one to Draupadi (I.174ff.), taking place before any of Arjuna's three other marriages, which are grouped together. In fact, the marriage to Draupadi becomes the basis of the heroic plot of the epic, for it is an insult to her, perpetrated by the Kauravas, that leads eventually to the Kurukshetra War itself. The story, briefly told, is as follows. The Kauravas, headed by Duryodhana, are envious of the successful rule of the Pandavas at Indraprastha, and they challenge Yudhishthira to a dice game, with the hope of winning the Pandavas' kingdom. Compelled to play by the legalities of the situation,[3] and cheated by the maternal uncle of the Kauravas, Shakuni, who plays for the Kaurava side,[4] Yudhishthira loses the kingdom, then his brothers and himself, and finally Draupadi. She is brought before the assembly of men during her period, when she should be in seclusion, and insulted with obscene innuendo by Duryodhana and his brother, Duhshasana, who feel she is now theirs. Eventually, however, she is returned to the Pandavas, and the dice game is replayed. After losing again, the Pandavas go into exile for thirteen years (the first twelve to be spent in the forest, the last, incognito in a place of their choice), in accordance with the wager agreed upon before the replay.[5] When the period of exile is over, the Kauravas refuse to return to the Pandavas their rightful share of the kingdom,[6] and the Kurukshetra War ensues. The insult to Draupadi has not been forgotten by the Pandavas, and it provides an incentive to violent action for them in the war. In order to understand the meaning of this story fully, it is necessary to bear in mind that Draupadi is considered by the epic to be an incarnation of the goddess Shri, personified Prosperity (I.61.95, etc.). Thus, although she is returned to the Pandavas, and is able to go into exile with them, she is not really regained until they have won back their kingdom. One is reminded of the prophecy at Arjuna's birth, quoted in chapter IA: " . . . he shall . . . rescue the lost fortune." The word for "fortune" there is *shri*.

The theme of a war fought for the purpose of winning back an abducted wife has a number of Indo-European parallels, the most fully developed of which is, of course, to be found in the *Iliad*.[7] Such a war is likewise the central event of the *Ramayana*, and this basic parallelism with the *Ramayana* is recognized fully by the *Mahabharata* itself.[8] Within the *Mahabharata*, the near abduction of Draupadi by Jayadratha in the forest (III.248ff.) and her attempted seduction by Kichaka in the Matsya country (IV.13ff.) are abbreviated reduplications of the same theme. Note too the parallel in the war between the gods and the demons of Indian mythology—for these two groups are always fighting over such objects as the earth, or the sacrifice, or immortality—all of which hypostatize prosperity—and the story of Shri's abandonment of the demons in favor of the gods is told frequently in the epic.[9]

The central importance of Draupadi for the heroic plot of the *Mahabharata* may be adduced as evidence for the pivotal role of the Panchalas in some earlier version of the epic tales, a theory mentioned in chapter IA of this study; for Draupadi is the princess of Panchala, often referred to as the Panchali in the epic. In the extant epic, the marriage to Draupadi creates an alliance that is basic to identification of the Pandava and Panchala causes, reversing an earlier Pandava-Panchala enmity (see below).

In terms of the issue of fertility, the marriage to Draupadi is extremely significant, largely because of Draupadi's identification with Shri. The scene of Draupadi's *svayamvara* ("bridegroom choice," according to van Buitenen's translation) involves Arjuna in a test of bow bending, a typical marriage test in Indo-European literature, which includes obvious sexual symbolism.[10]

The test has been geared to Arjuna's particular ability by Drupada, Draupadi's father, who admires Arjuna and wants him as a son-in-law (I.176.8ff.). That the test is the culmination of an initiatory sequence may be seen from its relationship to the story of Drona and Drupada. The brahmin Drona had been wronged by his friend King Drupada, in one of the epic's many brahmin-*kshatriya* confrontations, after which Drona had become the weapons instructor for the Pandavas and the Kauravas (I.122; I.154.1ff.). At the beginning of their course, Drona had asked his pupils to promise that as his teacher's fee they would defeat Drupada for him. As noted in chapter IA, only Arjuna had promised this; and he had eventually fulfilled his promise, the defeat of Drupada being the Pandavas' first military victory. Humiliated, Drupada had then performed a sacrifice to beget a son who would be able to defeat Drona, and Dhrshtadyumna had been born from the sacrificial fire. Draupadi, Shri incarnate, had taken birth incidentally at the same time, from the sacrificial altar.[11] Meanwhile, Drupada had conceived such an admiration for Arjuna that he wished to secure this great warrior as the husband of his daughter, and constructed the marriage test accordingly. At this time, the Pandava brothers, having escaped from the lacquer house (see chap. IA), were living together, disguised as brahmins, in the town of Ekachakra, in a preview of their later exile, especially its thirteenth year. When Vyasa advised them to go to Draupadi's *svayamvara*, they went still disguised, and revealed their identity only after the marriage test had been completed.

Here, then, are the usual requirements of a literary pattern of initiation: a break with childhood lifestyle and connections, a period of isolation, preparation (with instruction) and victorious adventure, and a reemergence and reincorporation into society, clinched by a marriage.[12] This pattern, which is one of death to the old life and rebirth to the new one (that is, the overcoming of death), is marked here by the deaths of substitutes, which make possible the continuing life of the central figures: a low-caste family dies in the lacquer house, in place of the

Pandava family (I.136.7ff.).[13] The initiatory pattern will be repeated several times in the *Mahabharata*, with emphasis on different aspects each time, as the Pandavas—and primarily Arjuna, the great initiatory hero of the group—prepare for their adult challenge, the war at Kurukshetra. Certainly the composite nature of the poem is largely responsible for its repetitive tendencies in this regard, as in others.

The aftermath of Draupadi's *svayamvara* is the decision of the Pandavas to share Draupadi as their joint wife, a decision that is justified by the epic and accounted for by modern scholars in a variety of ways. The epic itself offers three justifications, the first being the story, told by Vyasa twice, that in a former life Draupadi was a young woman who prayed to the god Shiva for a husband five times, and was thus condemned by Shiva to have five husbands (I.157.6ff. and I.189.41ff.). This justification, then, has to do with karmic fruition of past lives. In addition, a legal justification is offered (I.182.1ff.): when the Pandavas had won Draupadi, they brought her home, calling out to Kunti, who was inside the house, "Look what we found!" Thinking her sons had brought home alms from their day of begging in brahmanic disguise, Kunti told them to share what they had brought. So as not to falsify their mother's words, the Pandavas were forced to share Draupadi. At this juncture Arjuna showed his great respect for his older brothers by refusing Yudhishthira's offer to let him have Draupadi for himself (I.182.8ff.); evidently polyandry seemed less of a sin to him than marrying before Yudhishthira and Bhima. Yudhishthira then decided upon the sharing arrangement to prevent strife between the brothers (I.182.15), and was soon heard defending its legality on the grounds of obedience to his mother (I.187.28ff.). A third justification is the story of the five Indras, which, as mentioned in chapter IA, identifies the Pandavas with five Indras of the past (the same god born in five different ages), so that Draupadi is really marrying only one individual when she marries all of them (I.189).

From a modern point of view, perhaps the most satisfying explanation of the polyandry is a variant on that suggested by the story of the five Indras: that in a sense the Pandavas are really only one composite figure. From this point of view Draupadi's role is also largely symbolic, in that she represents the prosperity and sovereignty of the composite Pandava king.[14] The symbolism may, however, reflect real tribal polyandry, such as is still practiced here and there in northern India.[15] That among the Pandavas Arjuna is the primary husband of Draupadi may be ascertained as much from the fact that it was he who won her[16] as from the accusation leveled against her much later, in XVII.2.6, that she always preferred Arjuna to her other husbands (see chap. IIC).[17] In the latter point, one may find an additional piece of evidence for regarding Arjuna as the central heroic or kingly figure of the epic. Arjuna has one son by Draupadi, whose name is reported variously as Shrutakirti or Shrutakarman.[18] His brothers have one son each by her as well, creating another fivesome known metronymically as the Draupadeyas (I.57.102f.).

With regard to Arjuna's three other marriages, as with regard to this one, various legal issues and questions are raised, indicating the epic's concern with *dharma*. In all four cases, the epic ultimately accepts the marriage as legitimate, although it seems originally to have appeared problematic to the epic poets. Much of the difficulty may be attributed to the incorporation of folkloric motifs and outmoded customs into the epic framework; these are absorbed at the heroic level as acceptable practice for a hero, whose very purpose in life is to settle questions of *dharma* neatly. The settling of *dharma*-related questions and impasses will be a continuing theme in the *Mahabharata*; in fact, it has already been of major importance in the genealogical history of the Pandavas, which dominates the earlier chapters of Book I. On the occasion of Arjuna's marriages, however, the Pandava brothers themselves face issues of *dharma* for the first time.

A Woman in Every Direction: Ulupi, Chitrangada, and Subhadra

The necessity of sharing Draupadi leads eventually to Arjuna's other marriages, as follows (I.200ff.). The Pandavas are advised by the seer Narada, who illustrates his point with the dire example of the *asura*s Sunda and Upasunda (I.201ff.), that they ought to share Draupadi equally, on the basis of set rules; otherwise, there might be strife among them (as in fact comes about later between the Pandavas and the Kauravas over Draupadi). They agree that each brother will have Draupadi as his exclusive partner for a year at a time, and that any brother interrupting any other's private meeting with her will have to go into exile as a celibate (*brahmacharin*) for a year.[19] Such a breach is committed by Arjuna, inadvertently and with excellent reason (he enters the room to get weapons in order to be able to protect the cows of a brahmin), yet requiring him to go away to fulfill the agreement. Refusing Yudhishthira's offer to free him from this responsibility, Arjuna sets off for a year of *brahmacharya*, with the impressive heroic statement: "I have also heard you say not to follow the Law with pretenses. I shall not waver from my truth, I am armed with my truth!" (I.205.29).[20]

The striking point often raised regarding this year of exile is that Arjuna is not, after all, celibate during it; rather, he marries three times. Arjuna's seeming neglect of his agreement is one of the reasons adduced by Hopkins for regarding the *Mahabharata* as a composite work.[21] How can the epic approve of such behavior? In answering this question, one must first note that even Draupadi's *svayamvara* is approached by the Pandavas in the guise of *brahmacharins*, a disguise that is guarded zealously by the brothers, although it leads to great controversy (I.180f.). Furthermore, Arjuna's generally chaste character is referred to explicitly on that occasion, by the *gandharva* ("celestial musician") Chitraratha (I.159.13). Chastity seems in this context to be the forerunner of marriage, as it is in the Hindu analysis of the ideal stages of life: studentship (*brahmacharya*), householdership, and so forth.[22] *Gandharvas*, whose friendly relations with Arjuna, after initial quarreling, are emphasized several times in the epic, are symbols of fertility;[23] Chitraratha's appearance here suggests impending sexuality. The *brahmacharin* disguise gives way at the proper moment in the story pattern: such too is its role in the story of Arjuna's exile.

Arjuna's exile, and his behavior during it, may also be regarded from a different point of view, according to which the story of the agreement between the brothers and Arjuna's breaching of it seems to be a secondary accretion.[24] Arjuna's marriages, that is, may be viewed as being of central importance to the epic structure, for they set up the alignment of forces for the Kurukshetra War. In some sense, one may view Arjuna's exilic journey as a preliminary "conquest of the world," since he travels in all directions during it, and has an adventure with some female, usually a conquest, at each cardinal point.[25] Or if one takes his earlier marriage to Draupadi into account, one may note that in the end he has four wives, obviously comprising one for each direction (Panchala being in the south).

The first of Arjuna's three post-Draupadi marriages, that to Ulupi, daughter of the *naga* ("snake") king Kauravya (I.206), is a version of the folkloric motif of marriage to an animal or, more specifically, the "animal paramour,"[26] which has accrued to Arjuna. As a snake, Ulupi is a fertility figure connected with the earth. To Arjuna she bears one son, Iravat, who is not, however, mentioned until much later in the epic.[27] Ulupi will serve later as a female helper figure[28] for Arjuna, restoring him to life (see chap. IIB). In the course of Arjuna's Book I encounter with Ulupi, his first meeting with a female during his year of exile, he attempts to be true to his *brahmacharya*, but fails because Ulupi says she will die if he refuses to make love with her (I.206.29). She offers the legal justification that his vow of chastity is binding only with regard to Draupadi (I.206.26). Here Arjuna, in his heroic role of protector of the weak (I.206.31), is evidently absolved of any negative consequences of his action. Besides, the Ulupi marriage is necessary, one may note, to secure the northern direction.[29] The marriage between Arjuna and Ulupi is what is traditionally referred to as a *gandharva* marriage, in that it is sealed by a purely private agreement between the two parties. Arjuna spends just one night with her.

Arjuna's next marriage, to Chitrangada of Manalura in the east (I.207),[30] is offered as an example of the legal fiction of *putrika* ("daughter") inheritance: Chitrangada's father, Chitravahana, has no sons, so her son becomes successor to his line. This son, Babhruvahana, unlike Arjuna's other sons, stays conveniently at home (in Manalura) during the great Kurukshetra War; however, he plays an important role in Book XIV (see chap. IIB). The marriage to Chitrangada is apparently of the *asura* type, in that Arjuna requests her and is given her by her father for a bride price (the son). They live together for three months (that is, one quarter of the year) (I.207.23),[31] and he visits her again later (I.209.23f.).

Although not as important to the central heroic tale as the marriage to Draupadi, the marriage to Subhadra at Dvaraka in the far west at the end of the year of exile (I.211ff.) is extremely significant; it may even provide some insight into the composition of the epic as a whole, since it is a connecting link between Arjuna and Janamejaya: Arjuna and Subhadra give birth to Abhimanyu, who fathers Parikshit, who fathers Janamejaya. Subhadra is the sister of Arjuna's dear companion and cousin,[32] Krishna (see chap. IC, etc.). Her name, meaning "glorious" or "auspicious," suggests that she too is a fertility figure, much like Shri (Draupadi) in character. In the typology of folklore, she represents the beautiful younger wife, a theme that becomes quite popular in later Indian drama.[33] Draupadi is duly jealous, until a reconciliation is effected (I.213.14ff.).

Arjuna's marriage to Subhadra is a marriage by capture, a *rakshasa* marriage, such as is common in Indo-European heroic literature, a typical heroic feat. Arjuna's capture of Subhadra is undertaken at Krishna's instigation, after Arjuna has expressed infatuation with her. Although the Bhojas, Vrshnis, and Andhakas (Krishna's people) at first object to Arjuna's action, Krishna manages to mollify their anger, primarily by a legal argument:

> Guḍākeśa [Arjuna; see Appendix] has showered no contumely on our line, but doubtless has shown us superior honor! The Pārtha knows that you Sātvatas [another name for Krishna's people] are not greedy for riches, and he also judged that he could not win at a bridegroom choice. Who would approve of giving the girl away, as though she were cattle? And what man on earth would barter his offspring? I believe that Arjuna saw all these difficulties, and hence abducted the girl lawfully. [I.213.2–5][34]

Krishna goes on to speak of how wonderful it will be to have Arjuna marry into their group and how, anyway, Arjuna could never have been defeated by force (I.213.6ff.). The gift-giving scene that follows (I.213.22ff.) shows that the marriage has cemented an alliance between Krishna's people and the Pandavas; thus the Pandavas acquire one of their staunchest supporters.

Another major Pandava alliance, that with the Panchalas, had likewise been acquired through one of Arjuna's marriages, the marriage to Draupadi. The final major Pandava alliance, with the Matsya people, will be clinched by a marriage arranged by Arjuna for Abhimanyu (although the girl will first be offered to Arjuna himself, much as Draupadi was [see chap. ID]). Arjuna may thus be viewed as the alliance-maker of the Pandava family, the performer of a typically royal, and heroic, ordering function. The connection between marriage, alliance, and prosperity may be observed in its fully developed form at the horse sacrifice late in the epic, where all four of Arjuna's wives appear together (XIV.90.2ff.). Ideally, four wives of the king were to participate in the horse sacrifice,[35] which was meant to establish the king's universal rule and the prosperity and fertility of the kingdom.[36] In the epic itself, the role of the wives is not described in detail, beyond the statement that they gathered at the time of the ceremony and Draupadi was made to lie beside the horse after it was sacrificed (XIV.91.2)—a gesture symbolizing fertilization. The wives present on this occasion are those of Arjuna, not those of the official king and celebrant of the sacrifice, Yudhishthira, another indication of Arjuna's own kingly character.

In the epic's description of the newborn Abhimanyu, one finds strong elements of the standard heroic childhood, that praise due to royal ancestors or patrons discussed in chapter IA:

> Subhadrā, Keśava's [Krishna's] dear sister, gave birth to Abhimanyu Saubhadra as Paulomī [a name of Indra's wife] did to the effulgent Jayanta. He was a long-armed, mettlesome, bull-eyed, enemy-taming bull of a man, the hero Abhimanyu whom Subhadrā bore. He was fearless and wrathful [*abhish cha manyumamsh chaiva*], and hence they called Arjuna's enemy-taming, bulllike son by the name Abhimanyu.[37] The superior warrior was begotten on the Sātvata woman by Dhanaṃjaya [Arjuna; see Appendix], as fire is begotten at a sacrifice upon the womb of the *śamī* [tree] block that is drilled.[38] At his birth the strong-armed Yudhiṣṭhira, son of Kuntī, gave ten thousand cows to the brahmins and as many coins. From childhood on he was Vāsudeva's [Krishna's] favorite, and like the moon[39] to his fathers[40] and all his subjects. From his birth onward Kṛṣṇa celebrated the sacred rites for him, and the child grew as the moon in the bright fortnight. The enemy-tamer learned from the *Veda*-wise Arjuna the entire four-membered, tenfold Science of Archery, both human and divine. The powerful child learned the niceties of the sciences of weaponry, of deftness in handling missiles, and of all actions. Arjuna made him his equal in learning and application, and the sight of his son by Subhadrā brought contentment to Dhanaṃjaya. Like Indra, the Terrifier [Bibhatsu, yet another name for Arjuna; see Appendix] saw a son all muscle, marked with all good lines,[41] unassailable, with the shoulders of a bull and the wide mouth of a snake, a great archer with the pride of a lion and the power of a mad elephant, the voice of a thundercloud and a kettledrum, the face of the full moon, the match of Kṛṣṇa in bravery, might, beauty, and shape. [I.213.58–70]

In this passage one sees an Arjuna who has become the proud father rather than the central heroic figure: his fatherly pride is compared to that of his own father, Indra, presumably at the time of Arjuna's birth as well as Jayanta's (for Arjuna too is Indra's son). Thus the succession of generations is being stressed, and connected with the central hero's fertility.[42] Henceforth, the epic will always compare Abhimanyu favorably with Arjuna, or stress that he has surpassed his father.[43]

In I.213.71ff., just after the birth of Abhimanyu, the birth of Draupadi's children, the five Draupadeyas, including Arjuna's son Shrutakarman, is mentioned for the first time (outside the introductory materials at the beginning of Book I). The Draupadeyas are destined not to survive to bear offspring, a fact that, with so many others, the epic audience is undoubtedly expected to realize from the start: juxtaposed with Abhimanyu, they already seem less important, almost shadowy, although most of their names are expressive of royal virtues.[44]

The main point still to be made is that with the births of these children the entire cast of the Kurukshetra War has come into being, and Book I of the *Mahabharata* is ready to end with its final initiatory adventure, the burning of the Khandava Forest (see chap. IC). The only important *Mahabharata* figure as yet unborn is Parikshit who, as Abhimanyu's son, will be a member of the next generation, born after the war is over. Arjuna has played the major role in the last generation of scene setters, as he will be the major fighter in the war.

By the end of Book I, Arjuna has organized a family and network of alliances that will endure throughout the time portrayed in the epic and determine the direction of the story. He has procreated to assure his family's continuity and has acquired for it prosperity and protectors. The feeling at the end of the book is extremely positive, and one may assert that Arjuna's heroic side remains a positive force throughout the *Mahabharata.*

In conclusion of this chapter, one more point must be mentioned: Arjuna's propensity for relationships with women is an important part of his popular image, and sometimes a source of amusement.[45] More than in India, perhaps, this emphasis has come to dominate the characterization of "Ardjuna" in Indonesia. As H. Ulbricht writes in *Wayang Purwa: Shadows of the Past*, a discussion of Javanese shadow plays:

> Ardjuna became the idol of the Javanese people. He is the hero who not only excels in physical prowess but also in intelligence, feeling and refinement. Because of his versatility Ardjuna is depicted as the favourite of the weaker sex [*sic*]. It seems that a child was later born to almost every house he entered. Conflicts between princes and princesses who were unaware of their common descent from Ardjuna are a familiar dramatic occurrence, and Ardjuna's own encounters with his unknown sons likewise give rise to much confusion and many surprises.[46]

Ulbricht goes on to recount a story of Ardjuna's transformation, on one occasion, into a well of water.[47] In no way could his propensity to fertility be more aptly expressed. In south India, meanwhile, to the present day, Arjuna and the Pandavas are worshiped in the context of a cult of Draupadi as Mother Goddess.[48]

Notes

1. Several lists of different types of marriage are to be found in the *Mahabharata*, of which the longest, I.67.8f., includes eight types, named for various classes of beings: *brahma, daiva, arsha, prajapatya, asura, gandharva, rakshasa, paishacha*. This list is the same as that found in *Laws of Manu* III.21. Not all these types are recommended for all social classes, and the fifth and eighth (marriage by purchase, and seduction of a woman while she is mentally unfit) are condemned altogether; this despite the fact that Madri's marriage to Pandu was of the *asura* type (see *Mahabharata* I.105.5) and Arjuna's marriage to Chitrangada fits loosely into this type as well. In this list, the *svayamvara* ("bridegroom choice") is not included; but see I.96.8ff. and I.211.21 (the latter is quoted below, n. 34). A list of five types of marriage is found in XIII.44.2ff.
2. The other Pandavas have two wives each (including Draupadi), except for Bhima, who has three. The additional wives and the sons they produced are mentioned in passing at I.90.83ff. (This list omits two wives of Arjuna, Ulupi and Chitrangada, and their respective sons.) None of these sons plays a role in the war except Bhima's important *rakshasa* son, Ghatotkacha, whose birth story is told in greater detail in I.139ff. (It seems that some additional wives may appear briefly in XV.32.11ff.)
3. The specific reason given by the text is Yudhishthira's vow: "Once challenged, I will not refuse,/ For so I have sworn for eternity" (II.52.16). See further, chap. IIIB1, n. 17. Recent scholarship sees the dice game as a requisite of the royal consecration ritual that Yudhishthira is engaged in throughout Book II, and necessary to establish his kingship; see van Buitenen, *Mahābhārata*, II, 27ff., following his article "On the Structure of the Sabhāparvan of the Mahābhārata," in *India*

Maior: Congratulatory Volume Presented to J. Gonda, ed. J. Ensink and P. Gaeffke (Leiden: Brill, 1972), pp. 68–84. Otherwise, the epic considers gambling a great vice for a king.

4. Maternal uncles are of extreme importance throughout the *Mahabharata*, offering the strongest support to their nephews. Some examples: Shakuni of Duryodhana, Krpa of Ashvatthaman, Krishna of Abhimanyu, Vasudeva and Shalya of the Pandavas, Dhrshtadyumna and Shikhandin of the Draupadeyas.
5. The story of the dice game is told in II.43ff., the replay, specifically, in II.66ff.
6. See, especially, V.57.18.
7. See, e.g., the chapter entitled "Elopements" in Rees and Rees, pp. 279ff. See, more broadly, Thompson, *Motif-Index*, under classification R, "Captives and fugitives," and Grintser, Part II, chap. 4.
8. The story of Rama Dasharathi is recounted to Yudhishthira in *Mahabharata* III.258ff. because he has asked to hear the adventures of someone as unfortunate as himself. Note that in the *Ramayana* not only is the main plot, the abduction of Rama's wife, Sita, of this pattern, but also the subplot of the abduction of Sugriva's wife.
9. See, e.g., XII.218 and XII.221. Cf. XII.34.14, where the gods and the demons are said to be fighting *shrinimittam* ("for the sake of prosperity" or "on account of Shri").
10. On bow bending as a marriage test, see Delcourt, discussing parallels from the *Odyssey, Ramayana, Lalitavistara*, etc.
11. I.155 tells the basic story of the births of Dhrshtadyumna and Draupadi.
12. To refer to this pattern as one of initiation is not to insist upon a ritual origin for it; nor is it the present author's intention to overemphasize the "myth-ritual" interpretation elsewhere in this study, although it is sometimes worth suggesting (as in chap. IC). The pattern referred to here as "a literary pattern of initiation" is that discovered by most of the scholars treated in the Taylor article cited above (chap. IA, n. 76), and others.
13. The classic case of substitute death in epic poetry is the death of Patroklos in place of Achilles; see, e.g., Whitman, pp. 200ff., and Nagy, *Achaeans*, pp. 33ff.
14. On the female figure of Sovereignty, see, especially, Dumézil, *King*, pp. 70ff., and Hiltebeitel, *Ritual*, pp. 143ff. Dumézil views Draupadi as the transposition of a trifunctional Indo-European goddess; see *Mythe et épopée* I, pp. 103ff. It is Hiltebeitel who discusses—most cogently—the connection between the Draupadi/Shri figure and the Sovereignty figure. On the matrilineal flavor of these figures and their relationship to the pre-Indo-European Goddess, see Ruth Katz (Arabagian), "Cattle Raiding and Bride Stealing: The Goddess in Indo-European Heroic Literature," *Religion* 14 (1984): 107–42.
15. On the current practice of polyandry in India, see, e.g., Gerald D. Berreman, "Pahari Polyandry: A Comparison," *American Anthropologist* 64 (1962): 60–75. Berreman points out that the Paharis often attribute their polyandry to the Pandava precedent (p. 67). Besides the interpretations of Draupadi's polyandry that stress prosperity and sovereignty and those that stress tribal prototypes, many other suggestions, including the following, have been offered by modern scholars: nature-

myth interpretations such as that of Ludwig (p. 14), who sees Draupadi as the earth, the Pandavas as the seasons; Dahlmann's idea that the multiple marriage of Draupadi represents property sharing by a joint family (see chap. IA, n. 62); and a political interpretation, stressing the alliance created (Sadashiv Ambadas Dange, "The Pāndava Riddle [Birth and Marriage in a New Light]," *Journal of the University of Bombay*, NS 26, no. 2 [1957]: 167ff.). One further, probably related, explanation may be suggested: a connection with Indo-European story patterns. A parallel is to be found, e.g., in the Irish story of Derdriu and the sons of Uisliu in the forest (Kinsella, pp. 8ff.), as well as in the *Ramayana* episode of Sita's forest sojourn with Rama Dasharathi *and* Lakshmana (though in each of these cases the central female figure is married to only one of her men).

16. By shooting five arrows, as pointed out in chap. IA, n. 88.
17. It must be pointed out, however, that Draupadi and Bhima also have a very special relationship: he is her primary protector on a number of occasions throughout the epic; see, e.g., IV.16ff. (and an additional example may be noted in chap. IIIC, below). On Bhima as the major killer of the Kauravas proper (as opposed to the Kaurava allies) in the Kurukshetra War, see chap. IIA2, n. 34.
18. Shrutakirti: I.57.102, etc.; Shrutakarman: I.213.72. The names of the Draupadeyas are unstable. Note the change at X.8.50ff., where Shrutakarman and Shrutakirti appear as two separate figures.
19. Taking, as van Buitenen does, the reading of the southern recension, which is in agreement with the critical text in I.55.32. Elsewhere the critical text says that Arjuna's exile was twelve years in duration. See van Buitenen, *Mahābhārata*, I, 446, 466.
20. The phrase *satyenayudham alabhe*, which van Buitenen translates as "I am armed with my truth," might better be rendered as "I touch my weapon with truth"; Arjuna is swearing an oath (see chap. IIA2).
21. Hopkins, *Great Epic*, pp. 370f.
22. See, e.g., *Laws of Manu* III.1–4; also *Mahabharata* XII.184.8ff.; XII.234.13ff.; etc.
23. On the connection between *gandharvas* and love, see Hopkins, *Epic Mythology*, p. 156. Indeed, the *gandharva* is sporting in the water with his women when Arjuna encounters him on his way to Draupadi's *svayamvara* (I.158.4). Note that Arjuna's connection with *gandharvas* runs parallel to Bhima's connection with *rakshasas* in the epic.
24. Hopkins (*Great Epic*, pp. 370f.) treats Arjuna's breaking of his *brahmacharya* as a prime example of contradiction in the epic resulting from conflation of stories.
25. In the south, Arjuna encounters five *apsarases* ("celestial dancers") who have been changed into crocodiles through a curse. He breaks the curse, but no marriage results, at least according to the extant account (I.208f.). Arjuna's journey is, in fact, a traditional pilgrimage to pilgrimage places in the various directions, but this fact is not stressed by the epic.
26. Thompson, *Motif-Index*, B600–699, "Marriage of person to animal," includes B610, "Animal paramour." More narrowly, B613.1 is the widespread motif of the "Snake paramour"; but B613.1.1, "Snake woman as paramour," includes an

Indian listing only. In the present context, the "paramour" classification is preferable, since the Ulupi encounter is not called a marriage until Book XIV.

27. Iravat is first mentioned in VI.43.66f. He is first called Arjuna's son in VI.86.6ff., and is said to have a snake mother: Ulupi is not specified, but is implied. Iravat is not mentioned on the list of the eleven sons of the Pandavas in I.90.82ff., nor is Arjuna's son by Chitrangada, Babhruvahana.
28. Cf., e.g., Nausikaa in the *Odyssey* and Siduri in the *Epic of Gilgamesh*.
29. Taking Gangadvara (I.206.6, etc.) as a northern site. Biardeau also sees this marriage as a king's necessary act to secure the (fertile) *naga* world; see "Etudes" V, p. 132.
30. Book XIV, however, knows the place as Manipura (see chap. IIB).
31. Or three years out of the twelve-year period (see above, n. 19).
32. Arjuna's mother, Kunti, is the sister of Vasudeva, Krishna's father (I.104.1). Arjuna's marriage to Subhadra is, thus, a standard cross-cousin marriage (strikingly, permissible in this epic context, but not at all favored by strict Hindu *dharmashastra* ["lawbooks"]; on which, see further Thomas R. Trautmann, *Dravidian Kinship*, Cambridge Studies in Social Anthropology, 36 [Cambridge, Eng.: Cambridge University Press, 1981], chap. 5, especially pp. 334ff.).
33. It is found, e.g., in the *Malavikagnimitra* of Kalidasa and the *Ratnavali* and *Priyadarshika* of Harsha.
34. Cf. Krishna's advice to Arjuna in I.211.21–22: "The baron's marriage is the bridegroom choice, bull of men. But that is dubious, Pārtha, since one's own sentiments have no influence on the outcome. Forcible abduction is also approved as a ground of marriage for barons who are champions, as the Law-wise know. Abduct my beautiful sister by force, for who would know her designs at a bridegroom choice?"
35. See P. E. Dumont, *L'Aśvamedha: Description du sacrifice solennel du cheval dans le culte védique d'après les textes du Yajurveda blanc* (Paris: Paul Geuthner, 1927), p.16: "Les quatre femmes du roi sont présentes et s'approchent. Ce sont: la mahiṣī (la reine consacrée, celle qui a été épousée la première . . .), la vāvātā (la favorite), la parivṛktā (la dédaignée) et la pālāgalī (femme de caste inférieure . . .)." ("The four wives of the king are present and approach. They are: the mahishi [the crowned queen, she who was married first . . .], the vavata [the favorite], the parivrkta [the disdained] and the palagali [woman of inferior caste . . .].") To line up all these ideal roles with wives of Arjuna is not possible, although Draupadi is clearly the *mahishi* and Subhadra probably the *vavata*. Yet the number four seems more significant than the individuals, being necessary, it seems, for the completeness of the ceremony. Cf. the four wives of Vasudeva (XVI.8.18ff.); although in other passages the epic limits a *kshatriya* to two or three wives (see XIII.47.47).
36. T. N. Ramachandran, "Aśvamedha Site Near Kalsi," *Journal of Oriental Research* (Madras) 21 (1951–52): 7.
37. Here what van Buitenen calls a pseudo-etymology is offered.
38. This simile draws a connection between fertility and sacrificial acts. For further discussion of the latter, see chaps. IC and IE.
39. Abhimanyu, said by I.61.86 to be an incarnation of the son of Soma (the Moon), is described several times in this passage in terms of the imagery of that heavenly

body. Though commonly applied to other figures as well, lunar imagery is particularly appropriate for Abhimanyu, since he is the descendant of the Lunar Dynasty, the dynasty that gave birth to the major participants in the Kurukshetra War (see III.147.3; V.112.6; XII.329.31); as pointed out by Hiltebeitel, *Ritual*, p. 338, and Biardeau, "Etudes" V, p. 168.

40. Note the plural, which is in line with Indian kinship terminology, but also suggestive of the unity of the Pandava group.
41. The adjective used here, *sarvalakshanalakshita*, actually means "marked with all signs," and thus refers to the special markings that are often viewed as characteristic of a hero (see chap. IA).
42. Succession of generations is an important theme in epic and saga, as well as myth. See further, chap. IIB, n. 3.
43. With regard to Abhimanyu's equality with or superiority to Arjuna, many passages might be quoted; in these passages, Arjuna (or Arjuna and Krishna) becomes the standard of comparison inserted into formulas, in place of Indra. See, e.g., VII.22.26, which speaks of Abhimanyu, "whom they say is one and a half times as excellent as Krishna and the son of Prtha in battle"; cf. XI.20.1. Meanwhile, VII.22.25 uses the phrase *parthasama* ("equal to the son of Prtha") with reference to Shrutakirti, Arjuna's other son, who also tends to be compared with him.
44. E.g., Shrutakirti = "he of famed glory"; Shrutakarman = "he of famed action."
45. A letter received by the author from an Indian friend, Mr. Mohan Francis of Madras, who wrote on 22 July 1979, having just learned of her choice of dissertation topics, stated: "Just like you to select such a romantic subject as Arjun for your thesis! I am sure you have read up all the interesting tidbits about that inveterate lady-killer of yore and are ready to face your examiners at any time."
46. H. Ulbricht, *Wayang Purwa: Shadows of the Past* (Kuala Lumpur: Oxford University Press, 1970), p. 60.
47. Ulbricht, pp. 60ff.
48. See Alf Hiltebeitel, "Śiva, the Goddess, and the Disguises of the Pāṇḍavas and Draupadī," *History of Religions* 20 (1980–81): 152f. The first volume of Hiltebeitel's *The Cult of Draupadī*, entitled *Mythologies: From Gingee to Kurukṣetra* (Chicago: University of Chicago Press, 1988), has just appeared (see above, Acknowledgments).

IC. THE BURNING OF THE KHANDAVA FOREST, I

Martial Ecstasy

Chapter IC of this study will argue that the episode of the burning of the Khandava Forest (I.214–25), the last episode of Book I of the *Mahabharata*, reflects an ancient heroic ideal, which, in determining Arjuna's actions, emphasizes a Vayu/Bhima-like side of his character hitherto unrevealed and later hidden again: here extreme violence in support of world order is accepted as the hero's warlike role. That this picture of heroic activity was common to other ancient civilizations, both Indo-European and Semitic, will be suggested through comparison of the Khandava episode with materials from two other epics, the *Iliad* and the *Epic of Gilgamesh*. After presenting a picture of Arjuna as an embodiment of this ideal of heroism, the discussion will focus on one aspect of the ideal, the hero's friendship with his companion, as portrayed in the friendship of Arjuna and Krishna.

The story of the Khandava burning is as follows. Arjuna and Krishna one day meet the god Agni (Fire), who asks them to give him help in burning the Khandava Forest, a feat that he cannot accomplish on his own because Indra, as storm god, invariably extinguishes with rain the fire that Agni sets there. Agni needs the forest as food. Since he is disguised as a brahmin, whom Arjuna and Krishna have volunteered to feed before they recognize his true identity, they are obliged to help him. Yet their help goes far beyond what one might expect of them. For besides fighting Indra and a number of other gods who come to his assistance, and stopping Indra's showers, "the two tigerlike men started a vast massacre of the creatures on every side" (I.217.1). From the description, which is obviously based on the terrors of a real forest conflagration, it becomes clear that Agni is not the only killer: the two heroes are themselves killing creatures and feeding them to Agni—even creatures who would otherwise have escaped from the forest—eventually wiping out all the inhabitants of the forest, with only a few exceptions. The scene is described as follows:

> Indeed, whenever the heroes saw live creatures escaping, such as lived in the Khāṇḍava, they chased them down. . . . As the Khāṇḍava was burning, the creatures in their thousands leaped up in all ten directions, screeching their terrifying screams. Many were burning in one spot, others were scorched—they were shattered and scattered mindlessly, their eyes abursting. Some embraced their sons, others their fathers and mothers, unable to abandon them, and thus went to their perdition. Still others jumped up by the thousands, faces distorted, and darting hither and thither fell into the Fire. All over, the souls were seen writhing on the ground, with burning wings, eyes, and paws, until they perished. As all watery places came to a boil . . . the turtles and fish were found dead by the thousands. With their burning bodies the creatures in the forest appeared like living torches until they breathed their last. When they jumped out, the Pārtha cut them into pieces with his arrows and, laughing, threw them back into the blazing Fire. Their bodies covered with arrows and screeching fiercely, they leaped upward nimbly and fell back into the Fire. The noise of the forest animals, as they were hit by the arrows and left to burn, was like the ocean's when it was being churned. The huge flames of the happy Fire jumped up to the sky and caused the greatest consternation among the Gods. [I.217.2, 4–14]

Arjuna's and Krishna's behavior, augmenting the horrors of an already ghastly situation, is presented here objectively; that is, the two are not censured, nor are their victims dwelt upon with sympathy.[1] The composers of the episode admire the behavior of the heroes in this situation, and here and ever afterward in the epic, the burning of the Khandava Forest is praised as a great feat.[2]

The episode of the Khandava Forest burning is one of the most difficult sections of the epic to understand. For not only does it offend modern sensibilities (both Hindu and Western); it also goes against the morality propounded by the extant epic. This it does not only by deliberately flouting the doctrine of nonviolence, which is important in classical Hinduism and is advocated in many of the *Mahabharata*'s didactic passages.[3] The behavior extolled as heroic in the episode also violates the rules of warfare, the *kshatriya* code, set forth throughout the *Mahabharata*, which state clearly that innocent bystanders are never to be slain in battle.[4] The Khandava episode, on the contrary, depicts a berserker ideal of martial ecstasy, as Arjuna and Krishna, laughing, slay all creatures who cross their path. It is apparent, then, that the episode represents a way of thinking anterior to the extant epic.

In other episodes of the *Mahabharata* as well, supposedly good characters behave immorally from the point of view of the extant epic, either because their actions reflect outmoded behavioral patterns or for some other reason. Generally, however, an attempt is made to show that the actions performed are actually moral (as has been seen in chap. IB with regard to Arjuna's marriages); or else they are condemned as unacceptable at the heroic level. In the latter case, the material's significance, the reason why it is not omitted altogether, or better disguised, must be sought at another level, and this is the subject of chapter IIA3, below. But of major episodes, the Khandava episode is unique in its amorality, its freedom from apologetic or moralizing commentary. The question, then, is what the imagery means here, and why it has been accepted into the epic without correction or amendment.

To attempt to answer the latter half of this question first, one may point to one important fact. The heroes of the *Mahabharata* generally perform their feats in battle against human or semidivine enemies somewhat like themselves. The Khandava Forest battle, however, is a battle with cosmic forces. It is possible that the episode has survived intact just because a battle with natural forces may have been viewed by the compilers as free from the moral dilemmas that battle with human enemies would entail. True, animals are generally accorded good treatment by Hindu doctrine; yet in this episode at least, no compassion is shown to them. The hero's joy in battle and use of brute force are glorified in a situation where there are no human victims.

With regard to the meaning of the imagery, the following may be said. Comparison shows that similar battles with nature are to be found in other heroic literatures. In fact, the cosmic battle provides symbolic language for portraying the hero's power.[5] Study of parallel scenes may cast some light on the significance of the scene in the Khandava Forest.

Permissible Violence: A Parallel from the *Iliad*

As a parallel scene found elsewhere in Indo-European literature, the episode of Achilles' battle with the river Skamandros (Xanthos) in *Iliad* XXI.211ff. is striking. During Achilles' *aristeia* ("grand heroic moment")[6] against the Trojans,[7] Skamandros, angered at the fact that Achilles is filling his waters with corpses, attacks the hero, and threatens to drown him until Achilles is strengthened somewhat by the intervention of Poseidon and Athena. Then Skamandros calls upon his tributary, Simoeis, for help, and once again threatens to overwhelm Achilles. It is only when Hera, supporter of the Greeks, prevails upon her son Hephaistos (the smith) to bring fire to combat the water of the river that Achilles finds an ally to make the river give up the battle.

Like the Khandava episode, the Skamandros episode presents a battle between the structurally opposed cosmic forces of fire and water, with an anthropomorphic hero figure as intermediary. In the Khandava episode, fire wins because of heroic intervention, while in the Skamandros episode, fire intervenes and is itself victorious, thus saving the life of the hero, who was at first losing the battle. The difference seems to have to do with the difference in emphasis between the two episodes in their present contexts: the Khandava episode is aimed at showing the greatness of the heroes, while the point of the Skamandros episode seems to be that "gods are stronger than mortals."[8] There can be no doubt, however, that both episodes are based upon a common Indo-European symbolism, which visualizes the hero's activity as resembling that of fire, against which fire's opposite, water, is a natural opponent.[9] In Indian thought, this symbolism is inherent in the notion of the energy (*tejas*) of the warrior, which will be discussed further in chapters ID and IE, below; two points regarding it must, however, be mentioned in connection with the Khandava episode.

The first point is that the association of the hero with fire may account in part for an aspect of the Khandava episode's symbolism which could be considered problematic (although the epic itself does not question it): the fact that in this episode, unlike any other episode of the epic, Arjuna fights against his own father, Indra. The second point has to do with the intimate connection, in the vocabulary of *Mahabharata* imagery, between fire and sacrificial activity, combined with the fact that the epic, in line with the mainstream of ancient Indian (Vedic) thought, sees sacrificial activity as the basis of universal order, the central task of the king or hero (see chap. IE). In the Khandava episode, Arjuna and Krishna, by supplying the needs of Fire through their own fiery activity, are supporting the sacrificial order of the universe. Thus, although their activity seems unlawful according to the epic rules of "chivalry," it is accepted by the epic as being fully supportive of the higher *dharma*: the burning of the Khandava Forest is simply a very violent sacrifice.

That Indian thought accepts the concept of permissible violence in sacrifice may be seen not only from statements in Indian legal texts,[10] but also from various images presented in the *Mahabharata* itself. The mammoth churning of the ocean by the gods and the demons, using a mountain as their implement, recounted in I.15ff., is clearly a sacrificial act, resembling as it does the priestly actions during the Vedic Soma sacrifice.[11] The churning is described in part as follows:

> Then, as Gods and Asuras churned the ocean with Mount Mandara, a mighty roar rose from it like rumbling thunder in the clouds. All kinds of creatures that inhabit the deep were crushed asunder by the big mountain and by the hundreds went to their perdition in the salty ocean; and the mountain drove sea animals of all sorts, such as dwell in submarine abysses, to their destruction. While Mount Mandara was being driven around, large trees crashed into one another and tumbled down from the peak with their nestling birds. The friction of the trees started fire after fire, covering the mountain with flames like a black monsoon cloud with lightning streaks. The fire drove out the elephants and lions and burned them, and all creatures of many kinds found their death. Then Indra the Lord of the Immortals flooded the fire that was raging everywhere with rain pouring from the clouds. [I.16.18–24]

The description in this passage is quite comparable to that in the long passage on the burning of the Khandava Forest quoted above (which in fact concludes with a reference to the ocean churning),[12] the one real difference being that Indra's actions benefit the sacrificial activity in the ocean-churning episode, while hindering it in the Khandava episode. This shift in Indra's role does not, however, affect the basic image, in which fire and water are both important participants in sacrificial activity. Here water (including the liquid of the ocean itself and the sap of Mount Mandara's plants [I.16.25f.]) quickens the sacrificial site and seems to produce the precious objects that soon rise from the ocean as a result of the sacrificial work.[13] In the Khandava episode, several creatures survive the burning of the forest, one of them the snake king Takshaka, Indra's friend, for whose sake Indra has been trying to extinguish the fire, another the *asura* architect Maya. These survivors may be compared to the objects arising from the ocean churning; for like the latter they seem to represent the principles of world order, as their names and characters suggest.[14] Note that in the Book III tale of the digging of the ocean by the sons of Sagara, a picture of violent activity is presented, which has many of the same elements as those to be found in the accounts of the Khandava Forest burning and the ocean churning, although the description of the suffering caused is briefer, as follows:

> While it was being dug into by the joint forces of the Sāgaras, Varuṇa's realm [the ocean-to-be], rent on all sides, suffered extreme pain. Asuras, Snakes, Rākṣasas ["ogres"], and all kinds of creatures cried out in pain, when they were being killed by the Sāgaras.
>
> Once-alive creatures were now seen decapitated, trunkless, with knees, bones, and skulls shattered—by the hundreds and thousands. [III.105.20–22][15]

Insofar as digging and plowing activities may be seen as sacrificial,[16] this episode may also be said to have sacrificial overtones. Like the Khandava-burning and ocean-churning stories, it is etiological: it accounts for the creation of the ocean.

Biardeau interprets the Khandava Forest burning as a picture of *pralaya*, the dissolution of the universe at the end of a cosmic age.[17] The imagery of *pralaya*, she asserts, is modeled after the imagery of the funeral sacrifice, in which the body is burned and the ashes quickened with water, so that rebirth (or in the case of *pralaya*, a new creation of the universe) may ensue.[18] She supports her interpretation of the Khandava episode in this light by referring to a tale that is attached to the episode in many manuscripts of Book I, but not included in the critical version: the tale of King Shvetaki who, with the help of the god Shiva, sacrificed so excessively that he made Agni ill (Poona Edition, I, Appendix I, no. 118).[19] The story is told to explain why Agni had to eat the Khandava Forest: he needed the good food found there in order to cure himself. Shiva is known to Indian mythology as a disrupter of sacrificial order, as is brought out in the well-known tale, found in the *Mahabharata* and elsewhere, of his destruction of Daksha's sacrifice,[20] and in connection with this characterization is often regarded as the destroyer of the universe at the time of *pralaya*[21] (the all-consuming conflagration of dissolution being envisioned, as Biardeau points out, as a Shaivic [Shiva-informed] sacrifice).[22] Biardeau sees the connection of the Shvetaki story with the Khandava episode as direct confirmation of the pralayic reference of the events described in that episode.[23] Besides emphasizing that Indra fights Agni in this *pralaya* because he cannot cooperate in world destruction even if renovation is its ultimate goal (his role properly being one of maintenance),[24] she treats the fire-and-water imagery of the episode as a reflection of the fire and storm that overcome the universe in the classic *pralaya* scenario, and the survivors of the conflagration as reflections of the remnant that survives *pralaya* to provide the basis of a new creation.

The feeling of the present author is that Biardeau's interpretation goes too far; for it seems that the participation of Agni and Indra has broader application than simply to the funeral sacrifice or *pralaya*, as may be seen in the role of fire and water, for example, in the ocean-churning story.[25] The goal of every sacrifice is creative, with sacrificial fires bringing down rain.[26] Furthermore, the order of the entrances of fire and water in the Khandava episode does not conform particularly well to the order of their entrances at *pralaya*. Nor does Indra's uncooperative role in the Khandava Forest burning have to be explained in terms of specifically pralayic, rather than more generalized sacrificial imagery, even though he is, as its beneficiary, more usually thought of as one who encourages sacrifice than one who opposes it. Indra's opposition in this episode seems to have resulted from the combination of fire-and-water battle imagery with a picture of violent sacrifice performed by Arjuna and Krishna. The story of Shvetaki may indeed be meant to suggest a connection with *pralaya*, but in the view of the present author this story must be regarded as a late addition, not only because it is excluded from the critical text,[27] but also because it creates a reduplication in the activity of Shiva; for the main body of the Khandava episode regards Shiva merely as one of the many gods who rush to Indra's assistance (I.218.31), not as the cause of the entire affair.[28]

Although the present study does not agree that the imagery of *pralaya* provides the structure of the Khandava episode, it does not doubt that *pralaya* imagery is used descriptively throughout this scene. Fire's activity is said to resemble that at the end of an age (I.216.32),[29] and omens are seen which are similar to those appearing at such a time (I.218.38). It seems that the imagery of *pralaya* has become formulaic and may be employed to describe any wild and intensely destructive scene, even where it has little connection with the real structure of the event being recounted (see chap. IE for further discussion).

A commonly offered interpretation seems to come closer to the original significance of the Khandava episode than that advanced by Biardeau: the idea that it represents a historical burning of forests for the purpose of conquest or land clearing, the animals killed representing the local tribes wiped out during the expansion.[30] In fact, it is said in the epic that the Khandava tract became the site of Khandavaprastha (Indraprastha), the Pandavas' capital (I.199.24ff.). The name of the snake king Takshaka, threatened by the Khandava Forest burning, may well stand for the city of Takshashila: the early chapters of Book I suggest an identification between the two by stating that both are enemies of Janamejaya. Takshashila is attacked and conquered by Janamejaya (I.3.18); Takshaka, Janamejaya tries, but fails, to kill along with other snakes in his great snake sacrifice (the sacrifice that provides the setting for the first public telling of the *Mahabharata*), performed in revenge for Takshaka's slaying of Parikshit, Janamejaya's father (I.36ff.). The description of the snake sacrifice, quoted at the opening of this study, is so similar to that of the Khandava Forest burning as strongly to suggest a connection between the two. Note too that here, as in the Khandava episode, Takshaka is particularly protected by Indra, and survives (I.48.14ff.).[31] This snake sacrifice must be viewed as symbolic, since it apparently corresponds to no historical practice;[32] and it seems probable that both it and the Khandava Forest burning represent the conquest of lands and peoples, viewed as a creative, sacrificial act—with the human dimension, strikingly, repressed.

That a similar concept may have existed among the Greeks may be suggested in noting the resemblance of the following image from the Skamandros episode to the sacrificial imagery cited above, bearing in mind that the Skamandros River marks the boundary between Greeks and Trojans, conquerors and conquered:

> . . . The elms burned, the willows and tamarisks,
> the clover burned and the rushes and the galingale, all those
> plants that grew in abundance by the lovely stream of the river.

The eels were suffering and the fish in the whirl of the water
who leaped out along the lovely waters in every direction
in affliction under the hot blast of resourceful Hephaistos.[33]

The image as presented here has, however, passed completely out of the realm of sacrificial activity (if such was indeed its origin), and into the realm of poetry.

Initiatory Companionship: A Parallel from the *Epic of Gilgamesh*

Having compared the Khandava episode to the Skamandros episode of the *Iliad* in an attempt to understand the significance of its fire-and-water imagery, one may now turn to another comparison, which should serve to clarify other aspects of the Khandava story: a comparison with the story of the battle of Gilgamesh and Enkidu together against Huwawa (Babylonian version) or Humbaba (Assyrian), the terrible spirit dwelling in the cedar forest, in the *Epic of Gilgamesh.*[34] In this tale, the image of two friends going together into the forest to prove their heroism for the first time directly parallels the image in the Khandava episode of Arjuna and Krishna proving their might in the forest. The enemies fought by the heroes in the two episodes also have much in common: in the Khandava episode the enemy is a forest protected by a storm god, while in the Humbaba episode it is a forest spirit appointed by a storm god, Enlil.

There are differences, however, the main one having to do with the nature of the enemy described; for Humbaba combines both fire and storm in himself:

To preserve the cedar [fore]st,
Enlil has appointed him as a terror to mortals.
Ḫumbaba—his roaring is (like that of) a flood-storm, his mouth
is fire, his breath is death![35]

Humbaba must therefore be counteracted with yet another force; and for this the *Epic of Gilgamesh* chooses the wind, sent by the sun, who is always on Gilgamesh's side, as recounted in the Hittite:

The heavenly Shamash [Sun] heard the prayer of Gilgamesh;
And mighty winds arise against Ḫuwawa:
The great wind, the north wind, [the south wind, the whirlwind],
The storm wind, the chill wind, the tempe[stuous] wind,

> The hot wind; eight winds arose against him
> And beat against the eyes of [Ḫuwawa].[36]

In the Khandava episode, on the other hand, the role of the wind god, Vayu, is minor and completely subordinated to that of Indra, whom he supports (I.218.15ff.).[37]

The differences in distribution of the various natural phenomena between the two episodes may perhaps be attributed to the fact that the Khandava episode is Indo-European (as is the Skamandros episode of the *Iliad*), while the Humbaba episode probably is not. The defeat of the natural enemy by winds may be thought of as a Semitic characteristic, especially insofar as it is also reflected in the *Enuma Elish* (Babylonian creation epic):

> Ti'âmat (and) Marduk, the wisest of the gods, advanced against one another;
> They pressed on to single combat, they approached for battle.
> The lord spread out his net and enmeshed her;
> The evil wind, following after, he let loose in her face.
> When Ti'âmat opened her mouth to devour him,
> He drove in the evil wind, in order that (she should) not (be able) to close her lips.
> The raging winds filled her belly;
> Her belly became distended, and she opened wide her mouth.
> He shot off an arrow, and it tore her interior;
> It cut through her inward parts, it split (her) heart.[38]

Against this explanation, one may point to the fact that it is specifically an Indo-European version of the Humbaba story, the Hittite version, which stresses the wind's role in support of the heroes. Furthermore, many parallels may be drawn between Marduk's killing of Ti'amat and the Indo-European story of Indra's killing of Vrtra, especially certain versions of the latter,[39] so that a common source may exist after all. In that case the difference in imagery could be attributed to a Lévi-Straussian permutation of symbols, although it must be admitted that comparison of the hero's activity with that of fire is particularly characteristic of Indo-European thought. For the purpose of the present discussion, the most important points to be made with regard to the Khandava and Humbaba episodes are that each has originated in a quest for natural imagery to depict the fiery, stormy battle of great heroes and that in each the battle, unlike that of the Skamandros episode, is fought in and against a forest.

What is the meaning of the forest setting? It may be suggested that such a setting points to the initiatory character of the events recounted. Indeed, each battle may be said to be the first major feat, the military initiation, of its respective heroes; and the forest is the appropriate site for such an adventure.[40] Into the forest the fire-and-water battle imagery enters easily, providing an occasion for the heroes to prove themselves.

As discussed earlier, the experience of initiation is an experience of death and rebirth; and it is surely for this reason that imagery of the forest often becomes part of the initiatory scenario. As explained by Mircea Eliade: "The bush symbolizes both hell and cosmic night, hence death and virtualities."[41] The initiation rites undergone by young men in tribal societies tend to include a period of isolation in the forest,[42] and this symbolism has also found its way into literature recounting the adventures of such initiatory heroes as Arjuna and Krishna in the Khandava story and Gilgamesh and Enkidu in the Humbaba story. These figures' fight with the forest may be related to the initiate's attempt to survive there.

To view the Khandava adventure as a rite of initiation helps cast light on certain of its aspects, in particular the wildness of the heroes' behavior. A sentence from the chapter on initiation rites in Arnold van Gennep's classic work, *The Rites of Passage*, seems directly applicable to the case of Arjuna and Krishna in the Khandava episode: "The novices are outside society, and society has no power over them, especially since they are actually sacred and holy, and therefore untouchable and dangerous, just as gods would be."[43] From this perspective, then, the *Mahabharata*'s acceptance of unchivalrous behavior in its heroes may be explained quite satisfactorily, as a result of the poets' recognition that the incident takes place during an amoral and chronologically premoral stage in the heroes' lives. Further light is also cast on the nature of the combat between Arjuna and his father: to regard the Khandava episode as primarily initiatory suggests that Arjuna's main purpose in fighting Indra is simply to prove himself a man in his father's eyes. Such an interpretation goes far toward explaining why the *Mahabharata* does not treat the combat between Arjuna and Indra in this scene as anything unusual, although it is in direct contradiction to their relationship elsewhere in the epic. At the end of the episode, Indra expresses delight with his son[44] and promises to give him many weapons in the future (I.225.7ff.). Arjuna has not only proved himself to his father, but has also fulfilled a formulaic requirement of heroism: to be able to face the archetypical hero, Indra, in battle.

Finally, to view the Khandava episode as initiatory casts light on the friendship of the hero and his companion depicted in it. Although Arjuna, as Indra's son, must be seen as the central hero of the story, the friendship of Arjuna and Krishna is treated as one of equals. This conception too may be viewed as related to the initiatory scenario. One may refer in this regard to a passage from Victor Turner's *The Forest of Symbols: Aspects of Ndembu Ritual*:

> If complete obedience characterizes the relationship of neophyte to elder, complete equality usually characterizes the relationship of neophyte to neophyte, where the rites are collective. This comradeship must be distinguished from brotherhood or sibling relationship,[45] since in the latter there is always the inequality of older and younger, which often achieves linguistic representation and may be maintained by legal sanctions. The liminal group is a community or comity of comrades and not a structure of hierarchically arrayed positions. This comradeship transcends distinctions of rank, age, kinship position, and, in some kinds of cultic group, even of sex. Much of the behavior recorded by ethnographers in seclusion situations falls under the principle: "Each for all, and all for each."[46]

It may be suggested that initiatory companionship provides a basis for the very common theme of heroic friendship throughout epic literature. Thus the Arjuna-Krishna friendship in the Khandava episode closely resembles the friendship of Gilgamesh and Enkidu in their initiatory adventure.[47] (The *Iliad* also portrays a close friendship on the part of the hero Achilles, his friendship with Patroklos, but that relationship is not one of equality; it is, rather, to the glory of Achilles.)[48]

In the *Mahabharata*, mutually supportive companionship of equals is frequently depicted. For example, warriors often join together to accomplish their goals, although such conspiracy is forbidden by the extant rules of battle, which prescribe single combat, more along the lines of the Greeks on the Trojan battlefield.[49] Meanwhile, too great egoism is condemned as a positive evil, as in the example of Duryodhana: in one sense, the entire tragedy grows out of his reaction to an insult.[50] Beyond other friendships portrayed in the epic, that of Arjuna and Krishna is taken to be perfect.

As portrayed in the Khandava episode, the friendship of Arjuna and Krishna is easygoing and pleasant, a camaraderie that begins with quiet withdrawal from the other picnickers by the Yamuna River and cheerful conversation reminiscing over past events, and extends into boisterous, almost childlike or ecstatic routing of the forest. Throughout the epic, the friendship of Arjuna and Krishna is so close that the two are often said to be aspects of one another, or even one and the same. Their names, meaning "white" and "black," suggest twinship;[51] and, as mentioned in chapter IB, they are cousins (and brothers-in-law). Their closeness is brought out several times in the Khandava episode by the use of a dual phrase that recurs throughout the epic, calling them both by the same name: "the two Krishnas" (I.214.27, etc.).[52] At the end of the episode, Krishna chooses eternal friendship with Arjuna as a boon from Indra (I.225.13). During the war scenes that dominate the *Mahabharata,* Krishna will become Arjuna's helper, in what seems to be a reflection of the Vedic Indra-Vishnu relationship (see chap. IE). It would appear, then, that the true spirit of equality in the friendship is reflected better in the Khandava episode than elsewhere in the epic action.

Throughout most of the Khandava episode, it is not mentioned that Krishna is "God." Rather, he is Arjuna's friend and equal, a participant in a warrior friendship of equality. When Agni supplies weapons to Arjuna just before the battle begins, he also supplies them to Krishna, who seems to need them just as badly (I.216.21ff.). (They are the famous discus and club, standard attributes of Vishnu.) Yet turning once again to the comparative materials, one can see that Krishna's divinity may be implied in the given situation, even at the heroic level. For in both the Humbaba and Skamandros episodes, divine intervention is necessary to assist the central hero, although he himself is semidivine. In the Khandava episode, one sees divine intervention incorporated into the companionship motif itself, for the hero's companion is God. This point will be pursued further at the level of devotion.

The Ideal of Chivalry

In the preceding discussion, comparison between the Khandava Forest burning and two non-Indian parallels has provided an understanding of Arjuna's violent behavior in the former—behavior appropriate chronologically in Arjuna's life, as he passes into full manhood, and acceptable to the epic poets as lawful in the given situation. In conclusion of this chapter, it is necessary to point out that even as Arjuna fights in a Vayu/Bhima-like manner in the Khandava episode, certain aspects of his behavior continue to indicate that he is in fact Arjuna and not Bhima, that as he matures he will channel his violent side into martial energy in place of martial ecstasy. First, Arjuna fights with his own special weapon, the bow Gandiva, rather than his bare hands, a club, or the trunk of a tree, more Bhima-like weapons;[53] in fact, he has been presented with this bow, which is to characterize him in the future, by Varuna at the beginning of the episode (I.216.5ff.). Second, even in this episode, Arjuna acts in his usual chivalrous manner for one brief moment at least, when he permits Maya, who has supplicated him, to escape. Unlike most of what Arjuna does in the Khandava episode, such an act is fully in line with the rules of battle set forth in the epic[54] and is particularly characteristic of Arjuna's chivalrous heroism.[55] Finally, and most important, Arjuna's overall behavior in the episode is ultimately not amoral; he fights wildly, but with a *dharma*-related goal in mind, and this contributes to the extant epic's approval of his actions. For the epic as a whole far prefers the "arjunic" ideal to the "bhimic"; in fact, if the Vayu/Bhima and Indra/Arjuna types are already clearly distinguished from one another in early Indo-European thought, as Dumézil claims, it may also be said that the epic itself, by propounding a precise warrior code, is responsible for much conceptual development with regard to the latter type. The Khandava episode, however, presents Arjuna primarily as stark "hero," in an undeveloped form. (Discussion of the Khandava episode continues in chap. IIIA.)

Notes

1. One might, however, speculate that the incident involving the Sharngaka birds at the end of the episode (I.220ff.) was appended in part to fill this gap.
2. The burning of the Khandava Forest is the only one of Arjuna's heroic feats foretold specifically in his birth prophecy (see chap. IA). It is generally listed among the great feats of Arjuna, as an example of his unmatched strength.
3. For references, see chap. IA, n. 35
4. See, e.g., the rules of VI.1.28–32, quoted in chap. IIA3, n. 1.
5. Certainly with mythic antecedents.

6. For this translation of *aristeia*, see Nagy, *Achaeans*, p. 28, n. 2.
7. *Iliad* XX ff.
8. *Iliad* XXI.264. (Quoted [as is the passage on pp. 78–79] from Richmond Lattimore, trans., *The Iliad of Homer* [Chicago: University of Chicago Press, 1951].)
9. See the statement of Whitman (p. 140): "Xanthus threatens to quench the fire of Achilles, and fire itself must answer the challenge." In fact, the Hephaistos-Achilles connection runs all through the *Iliad*: Hephaistos made Achilles' armor (XVIII.368ff.). Besides the Skamandros battle, another well-known Indo-European example of the opposition of water to warrior heat is to be found in the story of the cooling of the hero Cuchulainn in vats of water after his first great adventure; see Kinsella, p. 92. The *Mahabharata* mentions many versions of the common Indian theme of the fire in the ocean (for instance, in the story of Aurva [see I.171.17ff.]).
10. See *Laws of Manu* V.39: "Svayambhû (the Self-existent) himself created animals for the sake of sacrifices; sacrifices (have been instituted) for the good of this whole (world); hence the slaughtering (of beasts) for sacrifices is not slaughtering (in the ordinary sense of the word)." (Quoted from Georg Bühler, trans., *The Laws of Manu*, the Sacred Books of the East, vol. 25 [1886; rpt. New York: Dover, 1969].)
11. Sadashiv Ambadas Dange, *Legends in the Mahābhārata* (Delhi: Motilal Banarsidass, 1969), pp. 248ff.
12. Compare also the role of Mount Mandara in the Khandava episode (I.218.46ff.) with its role in the ocean churning.
13. In this version of the story: Sun, Moon, Shri, Liquor, the horse Uchchaihshravas, the Kaustubha jewel, and the divine physician, Dhanvantari, bearing the nectar of the gods, the object of the entire endeavor.
14. See Biardeau, "Conférence," vol. 79, p. 141; "Etudes" V, pp. 140ff. Hiltebeitel agrees with Biardeau on this issue in part, but not completely; see his article, "The Burning of the Forest Myth," in *Hinduism: New Essays in the History of Religions*, ed. Bardwell L. Smith, Studies in the History of Religions (Supplements to *Numen*), 33 (Leiden: Brill, 1976), p. 219. The case of Maya, an architect whose name implies "magic," "illusion" (see chap. IIA3, etc.), is clear. For Biardeau's interpretation of "Takshaka," see below, n. 31.
15. The fiery element is soon introduced in the form of Kapila (III.105.25), who in anger burns the sons of Sagara. Their ashes are afterward purified by Ganges water descending from the sky and filling the ocean (III.106ff.).
16. Cf. the activity of Kuru, described in IX.52.2ff.; also the plowing up of Sita by her father, Janaka, in *Ramayana* I.65.14.
17. Biardeau, "Etudes" V, pp. 139ff. The cosmic age succeeded by *pralaya* is precisely a *kalpa* ("eon"), that is, one thousand *mahayugas* ("great *yugas*"; a *mahayuga* is a four-*yuga* ["world age"] period), but the epic often, and particularly in formulas, refers to it simply as a *yuga*. The fact that the terminology on this subject is often imprecise is discussed by Biardeau in "Etudes" IV, pp. 123ff.
18. Biardeau, "Etudes" III, pp. 31, n. 1; 75ff.; etc. Indeed, the main description of *pralaya* in the *Mahabharata* (III.186.56ff.) follows this pattern.

19. Found in the northern recension of the epic.
20. See *Mahabharata* VII.173.29, 41ff.; XII.274; etc. See further, chap. IIIC, including n. 26.
21. Mentioned here and there in the *Mahabharata* (V.195.13, etc.), this role is only hinted at in the epic's main account of *pralaya*; see III.186.72. In later Hindu thought, Brahma is known as the creator, Vishnu as the preserver, and Shiva as the destroyer of the universe (see Introduction), although each of these gods may likewise encompass the other two.
22. Biardeau, "Etudes" III, pp. 79ff. Scheuer (especially pp. 350f.) clarifies: all sacrifice has its Shaivic (that is, violent) aspect, but the sacrifice that is *pralaya* particularly so: "C'est dire que non seulement Śiva catalyse le danger inhérent à tout sacrifice, la violence nécessaire à toute vie en société: il représente aussi, potentiellement, un *danger pour la sacrifice*, pour la société . . . tout entière. Lorsque ce danger potentiel devient un réalité, nous sortons du cadre normal du sacrifice, nous entrons dans un periode de crise" (p. 350). ("That is to say that Shiva not only catalyzes the danger inherent in all sacrifice; he also represents, potentially, a *danger for the sacrifice*, for society . . . as a whole. When this potential danger becomes a reality, we go outside the normal bounds of sacrifice, we enter a period of crisis.")
23. Biardeau, "Kārtavīrya," p. 297; "Etudes" V, pp. 143ff.
24. Biardeau, "Conférence," vol. 79, p. 141; "Etudes" V, p. 140.
25. As against, e.g., the sons-of-Sagara story, which does reflect funeral imagery (see above, n. 15).
26. See, e.g., *Bhagavadgita* III.10ff. = *Mahabharata* VI.25.10ff.
27. Biardeau would not be impressed by this argument (see Introduction, n. 58).
28. Hiltebeitel ("Burning," p. 220) notes this discrepancy. But note Biardeau's disagreement here ("Etudes" V, p. 146, n. 1): Shiva as one of Indra's supporters is not the best reading of the stanza (despite its acceptance by the Critical Edition), etc.
29. Cf. I.217.16.
30. Hiltebeitel ("Burning," pp. 213ff.) summarizes various versions of this view, as presented by Holtzmann (younger), C. V. Vaidya, Irawati Karve, and van Buitenen.
31. Why Indra should be depicted as protecting a *naga* against an Aryan sacrifice is a difficult question to answer; Hiltebeitel notes the problem in "Burning," p. 216. Biardeau's identification of Takshaka, on the basis of his name, as *démiurge* ("Etudes" V, p. 140), protected by Indra in his world-maintaining role, does not address his *naga* persona. The present author's inclination is to explain the image by a historical interpretation: a group that proved powerful against the conquerors was seen as being protected by Indra. Yet if one is to search for meaning within the Khandava episode itself, the obvious explanation is that structural oppositions make strange bedfellows: Arjuna opposes the forest and Indra in the course of his initiatory exploit; thus, forest and Indra find themselves on the same side.
32. Unless some sort of "magic"; see Moriz Winternitz, "The Serpent Sacrifice Mentioned in the Mahābhārata," *Journal of the Bombay Branch of the Royal Asiatic Society*, NS 2 (1926): 74–91.

33. *Iliad* XXI.350–55.
34. Alexander Heidel, *The Gilgamesh Epic and Old Testament Parallels*, 2nd ed. (1949; rpt. Chicago: Phoenix-University of Chicago Press, 1963), pp. 33ff.
35. Heidel, *Gilgamesh*, p. 35.
36. Heidel, *Gilgamesh*, pp. 48–49.
37. As an illustration of the flexibility of imagery within structural and formulaic limitations none, perhaps, is better than the juxtaposition between this passage and the statement in the very next chapter that wind is fire's charioteer (I.219.36), a common figure of speech. In terms of the realism of the imagery, wind as storm's helper or fire's helper is equally convincing.
38. Alexander Heidel, *The Babylonian Genesis: The Story of Creation*, 2nd ed. (1951; rpt. Chicago: Phoenix-University of Chicago Press, 1963), p. 40.
39. See, e.g., XII.273.6: "Then when he [Vrtra] was yawning, Shakra [Indra] cast his thunderbolt [at him]."
40. Hiltebeitel at first ("Burning," pp. 216ff.) emphasized the initiatory side of the Khandava episode, but more recently retracted his argument in favor of Biardeau's *pralaya* scenario: his reference to initiation had been, he admitted, too vague (see Hiltebeitel, "The Two Kṛṣṇas on One Chariot: Upaniṣadic Imagery and Epic Mythology," *History of Religions* 24 [1984–85]: 7, n. 22). (Biardeau had maintained ["Etudes" V, pp. 137f., n. 1] that she preferred the word "test" [*épreuve*] to the word "initiation" in this case.) It is hoped that the present discussion may succeed to some extent in fleshing out the argument for initiation.
41. Mircea Eliade, *Rites and Symbols of Initiation: The Mysteries of Birth and Rebirth*, trans. Willard R. Trask (New York: Harper Colophon Books, 1975), p. 36.
42. See, e.g., Arnold van Gennep, *The Rites of Passage*, trans. Monika B. Vizedom and Gabrielle L. Caffee (Chicago: Phoenix-University of Chicago Press, 1960), pp. 74, 81.
43. Van Gennep (see preceding note), p. 114.
44. Actually, the fact that Indra and Arjuna are father and son is not often mentioned in the Khandava episode. There is one brief reference to their relationship in I.218.46, in a phrase that van Buitenen translates as "mocking his father," when it would seem rather to mean "frightening his father," but when Indra expresses his delight with Arjuna at the end of the episode, he does not mention that Arjuna is his son. Nevertheless, one may assume that such a relationship is implied throughout the episode; otherwise Arjuna's prowess might frighten Indra all the more, rather than ultimately pleasing him.
45. A particularly interesting point in relation to the *Mahabharata*, in which brotherhood is such a central element.
46. Victor Turner, *The Forest of Symbols: Aspects of Ndembu Ritual* (Ithaca: Cornell University Press, 1967), pp. 100–101.
47. That Gilgamesh and Enkidu are equals is an important aspect of their relationship throughout the epic: Enkidu is created specifically to equal Gilgamesh. See Heidel, *Gilgamesh*, p. 18.

48. Following Maurice B. McNamee, *Honor and the Epic Hero: A Study of the Shifting Concept of Magnanimity in Philosophy and Epic Poetry* (New York: Holt, Rinehart and Winston, 1960), pp. 13ff. Note, in particular, how Achilles instructs Patroklos in *Iliad* XVI.87ff. to limit his fighting so as not to take the glory from Achilles.
49. Equals ought to be matched, and one must not attack a warrior who is already engaged against another; see, e.g., the rules of VI.1.28–32, quoted in chap. IIA3, n. 1. That the Kauravas as a group fought and killed Abhimanyu is considered reprehensible (see chap. IIA2); that Arjuna could fight the Samshaptaka group en masse is seen as an almost superhuman feat (see chap. IE).
50. See II.43.3–10: "One time the princely Dhārtarāṣṭra ['son of Dhrtarashtra'] came, in the middle of the [assembly] hall [of the Pandavas], upon a crystal slab, and thinking it was water, the flustered prince raised his robe; then, bitter and shame-faced, he roamed about the hall. Again, seeing a pond with crystalline water adorned with crystalline lotuses, he thought it was land and fell into the water with his clothes on. When they saw him fallen in the water, the servants laughed merrily and gave him clean clothes at the king's behest. Mighty Bhīmasena saw him that way, as did Arjuna and the twins, and they burst out laughing. A choleric man, he did not suffer their mockery; to save his face he did not look at them. Once more he pulled up his robe, as though crossing a pool, to ascend firm land, and again those people all laughed at him. He once tried a door, which appeared to be open, and hurt his forehead; another time, thinking the door was closed, he shrank from the doorway." Such illusion is not, to be sure, surprising, in view of the fact that "Maya" (see above, n. 14) had built the hall. The light, folkloric flavor of this incident, actually expressive of an extremely serious heroic—and religious (see chap. IIIB2)—situation, is striking: the incident becomes all the more ominous.
51. On Indo-European twinship names, see Donald Ward, *The Divine Twins: An Indo-European Myth in Germanic Tradition*, Folklore Studies, 19 (Berkeley: University of California Press, 1968), p. 6. In particular, note the following: "In some instances the twins share the same name in the singular with a differentiating adjective, for example, 'Halfdan the Black' and 'Halfdan the White.' "
52. Again, see Ward, p. 6: "It is common for a pair of twins to be called by a single name in the plural, or dual: for example, 'Dioskouroi,' 'Alcis,' and 'Aśvínā.' Sometimes the proper name of one twin is applied to both, for example, the Roman 'Castores.' "
53. Examples of Bhima using such a weapon abound. In one of the outstanding passages of the epic (IV.32.17–19), Yudhishthira advises Bhima to avoid a weapon of this type, so as to escape recognition: "Yudhiṣṭhira, the King Dharma, said to his gallant brother who like a mad elephant was eyeing the giant of the forest [that is, a tree], 'Don't commit violence, Bhīma! Let that tree stand, Bhārata ["descendant of Bharata"], lest the people, when you do your superhuman feats with a tree, recognize you for Bhīma. Get hold of some other, human weapon, a bow or spear, a sword or battle-axe.' " Of course, Bhima can also shoot, but the bow is not his preferred weapon.

54. See, e.g., VII.118.8, quoted on p. 147: one should not strike another who is beseeching him.
55. An interesting twist makes Maya the brother of Namuchi (I.219.39), the demon killed by Indra (see chap. 1A, etc.). Note that Krishna immediately follows Arjuna's lead in letting Maya go.

ID. THE ENCOUNTER WITH THE MOUNTAIN MAN, AND CONNECTED EVENTS

The episode of Arjuna's encounter with a Kirata ("mountain man," according to van Buitenen's translation), who is Shiva in disguise, and his subsequent visit to Indra's heaven and fight against Indra's enemies, the Nivatakavacha, Pauloma, and Kalakeya demons (henceforth referred to as the "mountain-man sequence," a heading that will also subsume connected later events of Books III and IV),[1] is important for what it adds to the definition of the hero in the Indian context. What it says in effect is that to be a true Indian hero a character must be capable of great ascetic feats, which, in addition to the more universal skills, will be at the root of his power.[2] In making this statement, the sequence presents a fuller initiatory scenario than does the Khandava episode, stressing a different aspect of Arjuna's character, while not at all negating that aspect emphasized in the forest burning.

During the mountain-man sequence, Arjuna is apart from the other Pandavas who, having lost the dice game, are engaged in an enforced forest seclusion, itself initiatory in nature.[3] He goes on a long journey, is nearly killed in a fight with the mountain man, wins weapons, receives instruction, wins the approval of his father, Indra, through battles resembling that in the Khandava Forest, but this time fought on Indra's behalf, and eventually returns to his brothers fully equipped for battle.

Similarities to the Khandava Episode: Further Initiation

Some of the events of the mountain-man sequence indicate that it has indeed been constructed to express many of the same ideas as those presented in the Khandava episode: for example, the weapon winning is a clear reduplication, although much expanded. The hero's receipt of his characteristic weapons is a virtually universal aspect of heroic initiation, for like the bow bent at Draupadi's *svayamvara* (see chap. IB), weapons as a class represent manhood, virility, and thus, the coming of age of the hero.[4] In Arjuna's case, weapons are won on a number of different occasions, two of the most important being the burning of the Khandava Forest and the mountain-man sequence.[5] In the Khandava episode, weapon winning is presented merely as a preliminary to the central initiatory exploit. In the mountain-man sequence, on the other hand, weapon winning is central, the goal and major accomplishment of the journey, in anticipation of the war to come.

A second similarity between the Khandava episode and the mountain-man sequence may be noted in a comparison of Arjuna's Khandava Forest battle with his battles against the various groups of demons listed above (III.166ff.).[6] Like the Khandava Forest battle, the demon battles fought toward the end of the mountain-man sequence, of the nature of *pralaya* in fierceness (III.168.21), represent a heroic initiation anticipatory of the great Kurukshetra War. The following passage of description by Arjuna of his battle with the Nivatakavachas utilizes the same sort of imagery of fire, water, and other natural phenomena as was used in the Khandava episode; this imagery, which has become basically formulaic, or at least completely detached from its naturalistic origins,[7] is again used to illustrate Arjuna's more than human prowess:

> On all sides there appeared a shower of rocks, which sorely pressed me with terrifying stones as big as mountains, but with my swift lightning-like arrows shot from Indra's weapon I shattered each into a hundred pieces. When the rocks had been pulverized, a fire broke out, and the powdered rocks fell into it like sparks. With the rock shower abated, a powerful rain of water descended upon me with jets as wide as cart axles. The jets poured from the sky by the thousands with fiery force and covered all of heaven and space entirely. The downpour of the rains, the whistling of the wind, and the roaring of the Daityas ["demons"] blocked out everything. All space between heaven and earth was one sheet of water, and the jets that incessantly poured on the earth disconcerted me; I hurled the divine desiccating missile that Indra had taught me,[8] and the fearful blazing thing dried up the water.

> With the rock shower abated and the water dried up . . . the Dānavas ["demons"] set loose their wizardry, fire, and wind. I blew out all the fire with the water missile, and halted the impact of the wind with the great rock missile. [III.168.1–10]

Here the violent fight is against demons, as the Khandava Forest battle was against natural phenomena and animals; the issue of human warfare has not yet been faced, in this episode of pure heroic activity.[9] In fighting these battles, Arjuna is performing the perfect Indra role of demon fighter.

In both the Khandava episode and the mountain-man sequence, Arjuna fights against gods along with his other enemies. As has been discussed above, the god Indra is Arjuna's enemy at the Khandava Forest burning. In the mountain-man sequence, on the other hand, Arjuna and Indra are on excellent terms, as if to emphasize their father-son relationship,[10] which becomes a focus of attention: now Indra participates in Arjuna's initiation through instruction rather than battle. The god against whom Arjuna fights in order to prove himself is now Shiva. The fight with a god is another way of showing what has already been indicated in Arjuna's birth story: that the hero is semidivine, and strong enough to encounter the gods in battle. Even if he cannot always win, as he clearly fails to do in the mountain-man sequence,[11] his performance is extremely impressive, serving to please the opposing god and win boons from him.

As in the Khandava episode, one finds an example of Arjuna's battle frenzy in the mountain-man sequence. The following is a passage from the description of Arjuna's fight against the mountain man himself, which, with the loss of Arjuna's divine bow and his sword in turn (III.40.33ff.),[12] becomes increasingly Vayu/Bhima-like:

> Phalguna [Arjuna; see Appendix] went on to fight with trees and rocks, and the giant lord in the mountain man guise withstood the rocks as well as the trees. The powerful Pārtha, belching smoke from his mouth, struck blows at the invincible mountain man with fists that impacted like thunderbolts. The blessed Lord in his aspect of a mountain man then struck Phalguna with fists that were like Śakra's [Indra's] bolts, and a ghastly crackling sound rose from the fists of the embattled Pāṇḍava and the mountain man. The hair-raising grand battle went on for a while with hard striking arms, as that battle of yore between Vṛtra and Indra. The powerful Jiṣṇu [Arjuna; see Appendix] seized the mountain man by the chest, and

> the other struck his wrestling foe with great force. From the grinding press of their arms and the rubbing of their chests a fire with embers and smoke blazed up in their limbs. [III.40.42–48]

Juxtaposed with the more controlled, though still wild, weapons display of the ensuing demon battles, themselves set against a sedate period of instruction in Indra's heaven, this scene rounds out the sequence's picture of an incipient total warrior, part Shiva (here in place of Vayu), part Indra.

Difference from the Khandava Episode: The Hero as Lone Ascetic

Up to now, emphasis has been placed in this chapter on those aspects of the mountain-man sequence that are essentially permutations of Khandava-episode imagery. There is, however, a great difference in emphasis between these two initiatory adventures, epitomized in the fact that the Khandava episode's insistence on the companionship of Arjuna and Krishna is not repeated in the mountain-man sequence. In the mountain-man sequence, Arjuna sets off on his own, on a purely individual initiatory journey. As in the Khandava episode, he goes away from established society; this time he does so doubly, since he first leaves the city for the forest with his brothers (II.71) and then leaves even his brothers for the mountains. At no time does Krishna accompany him. In fact, Arjuna's individual responsibility for this adventure and, further, for the eventual fate of all the Pandavas, is stressed in a prophecy made by Vyasa to Yudhishthira some time before Arjuna's departure (III.37.26ff.).[13]

Only at one point in the mountain-man sequence is there any hint of a real companion: for the demon battles, Arjuna has a charioteer, Matali, sent along with him by Indra. (Matali is traditionally Indra's charioteer, and comes along with Indra's chariot, which Indra lends to Arjuna, just as Agni had supplied a chariot for him before the Khandava Forest battle.) It is noteworthy that Arjuna's companion here fills precisely the role that Krishna will fill in the Kurukshetra War, the role of chariot driver. In the mountain-man sequence, Matali serves as Arjuna's helper during Arjuna's military initiation, the main focus, however, being Arjuna's individual prowess: Arjuna has to encourage Matali at least as much as Matali encourages him (III.168f.).

That Arjuna faces the first part of his journey completely alone, and strives with Shiva alone and unarmed, permits the addition of a new dimension to the picture of his heroism: this is the ascetic dimension mentioned above. Ascetic activity, so important in the Indian context, is ultimately an individual affair. To perform it, Arjuna has helpers: Vyasa, who abets Arjuna's *yoga* (approximately, "discipline") with esoteric knowledge taught to Arjuna through Yudhishthira (III.37.27ff.), and Indra who, disguised as a brahmin, advises him (III.38.30ff. and III.163.10ff.; III.164.2ff.);[14] but he has no constant companion.

To apply technical terminology: such lone activity is actually more typical of shamanic initiation than warrior initiation.[15] Certainly Arjuna's exploit appears to have a shamanic dimension, as may be seen from the emphasis in it on bodily ascent: "In just one day the spirited Pārtha reached the holy mountain, for with his Yoga he had become fast as thought, like the wind" (III.38.28). In addition, a heavenly sojourn plays a major role in the sequence. Included too is total destruction of Arjuna's body—that typically shamanic version of initiatory death and rebirth—as he is temporarily reduced by the mountain man to "a ball of flesh with his limbs mangled" (III.40.50).[16]

It is possible to hypothesize some real shamanic influence here because in this episode Arjuna travels in a northward direction, through the Himalaya (toward the heartland of shamanism, Central Asia). Arjuna has already been associated with the northern direction in the "conquest of the world" episode. In this association, he appears once again to represent the Pandava group as a whole; for all the brothers were born in the Himalaya and spent their early childhood there, until Pandu's death. At the end of the mountain-man sequence, the other Pandavas will go again to the Himalayan region, to rejoin Arjuna after his heavenly sojourn.

The symbolic role of the Himalaya (over and above its possible historical connection with the Pandava-"Janamejaya" line [see Introduction]) is striking in the *Mahābharata*, as in later Indian poetry. In fact, the entire northern region has taken on a magical flavor in traditional Indian thought, being known, for example, as the home of a fantastic race called the Northern Kurus (Uttarakurus).[17] The *Mahabharata* considers the north to be the best of all directions.[18] A major aspect of the special significance of the northern mountains is referred to in the mountain-man sequence itself, when Indra, disguised as a brahmin, accosts Arjuna upon his arrival at Indrakila Mountain, with the following words:

> Who are you, son, arriving here in armor, with bow and arrows, with sword and wrist guards tied on, who follow the Laws of the baronage? Weapons are of no use here; this is the land of the serene, of ascetic brahmins who control their anger and joy. There is no use for bows here, nor for any fighting. Lay down your bow, you have reached the end of your journey. [III.38.32–34]

The brahmin ascetic (heir to shamanism?) is thus viewed as the typical inhabitant of the north, defining the characteristic lifestyle of that region: even Indra wears brahmanic garb there. A journey to the Himalaya is an otherworldly journey for an initiate, representing initiatory death and rebirth.[19]

It is in these surroundings that Arjuna must prove himself in order to win weapons; which means, of course, that he must perform austerities (*tapas*) equivalent to those of a brahmin.[20] If this aspect of heroism was originally propounded by brahmins, it had been incorporated into the heroic code by the time of the extant epic, which closely identifies primarily brahmanic *tapas* with primarily warrior *tejas* (see chap. IC), both symbolized by heat. The extant epic regards asceticism as a means of obtaining warrior and kingly power.[21] There can be no doubt that Arjuna will be able to meet the ascetic standard: his power of yogic concentration, already demonstrated in his skill at shooting as a youth, has foretold his ascetic capabilities, as has the *gandharva* Chitraratha's comment upon his chastity (see chap. IB). Furthermore, Arjuna's connections with the northern direction and his innate brahmanic affiliation (see chap. IA) suggest in advance that his *tapas* will be successful. As if to reinforce these points, it is said, as mentioned above, that Arjuna's power has been increased through special knowledge passed to him from the brahmin Vyasa through Yudhishthira. Both *tapas* and *tejas* are combined in the scene of Arjuna's austerities:

> Delighting in a beautiful spot in the woods, the spirited man of awesome heat [*ugrateja*] devoted himself to awesome austerities [*tapasy ugre*]. Dressed in grass and bark and carrying stick and deerskin, he passed one month eating fruit every fourth night, a second month he ate every eighth night, a third month only once a fortnight, subsisting on a dead leaf that had fallen on the ground. When the fourth month came and the moon was full, the strong-armed scion of Pāṇḍu lived on wind alone, with arms raised, without support, balanced on the tips of his toes. And because of his ceaseless bathing the braided hair of the great-spirited hero of

boundless might took on the sheen of lightning and lotus. [III.39.20–24]

The reaction of the seers (that is, the greatest of the ascetics) is predictable: they feel threatened by the amount of power Arjuna is obtaining (III.39.25ff.).[22] But because of the greatness of Arjuna and the righteousness of his mission, Shiva decides to grant him the weapons he desires: Arjuna's efforts, he points out, have not been made for selfish purposes.[23] The fight between Arjuna and Shiva, shaman par excellence, disguised as a mountain man, follows (III.40 and III.163.17ff.)—another initiatory test for Arjuna, an escape from near death, culminating in the giving of the *pashupata* (*brahmashiras*) weapon by Shiva, and instruction in its use.

Sojourn in Indra's Heaven

In the following segment of the sequence, in which Arjuna ascends from the mountains to Indra's heaven, where he spends five years, the simpler warrior ideal familiar from the Khandava episode is dominant, although faint brahmanic echoes are still apparent here and there. In fact, the entire conception of the story is a warrior conception, which visualizes Indra's heaven as a suitable abode for the greatest of warriors. As in the Khandava episode, Arjuna has won the approval of his father; this he has accomplished by his success in the encounter with the mountain man, for Indra had promised formerly to give weapons to his son only after Arjuna had met with Shiva (III.38.43). As Biardeau points out, it is noteworthy that Indra approves fully of Arjuna's ascetic accomplishments, since he traditionally fears and discourages such feats, which threaten his power.[24] In the mountain-man sequence, Indra actually gives Arjuna additional instruction in the ways of *tapas* (III.164.22). Indra delays his own weapon giving until after Arjuna's arrival in his heaven, but the other World Guardians, Yama, Varuna, and Kubera, assembling from the various directions, give characteristic weapons to Arjuna immediately, along with words of encouragement.[25] In obtaining these weapons, Arjuna is implicitly obtaining the powers of the respective gods, incorporating them into himself, as befits a king.

When Arjuna then rides up to heaven on Indra's divine chariot, the connection between his austerities and his warrior power is stressed again:

> Not the most lordly sacrificing kings, generous with stipends, nor godlings nor Dānavas may ascend this superb chariot. No one who has not done austerities is able even to set eyes on this great divine chariot, or to touch it, much less to ride in it! [III.43.16–17]

At this point, however, Arjuna bids good-bye to the Himalaya in an expressive speech, which emphasizes his own relationship to the area (III.43.22ff.),[26] and assumes his full identity as Indra's son. At no time, with the possible exception of his birth story, is this identity stressed more strongly, for in Indra's heaven Arjuna sits on his father's throne "like another Indra" (III.44.22). When the sage Lomasha visits, he finds Arjuna occupying half of Indra's throne (III.45.10).

It is noteworthy that just at this juncture the scene shifts to Dhrtarashtra's court, where Dhrtarashtra is asking Samjaya what he may expect of the now fully prepared Arjuna in battle (III.46ff.). Perhaps the entire conversation was invented to provide a framework for the seemingly ancient[27] stanza in the *trishtubh* meter, which forms part of Samjaya's answer:

> Pouring out and pouring forth his shafts,
> The diademed man [Kiritin = Arjuna; see Appendix] will stand, bow drawn,
> By the creator created our all-snatching death—
> But what must be cannot be avoided. [III.46.18]

During his stay in Indra's heaven, Arjuna learns from Indra how to use the weapons he has acquired. At the end of his stay, he is asked by his father to pay his teacher's fee by defeating the Nivatakavacha demons (III.165.10–11).[28] The story of this request and the subsequent battle, quoted in part above, as well as the story of Arjuna's battle with the Paulomas and Kalakeyas, is told only later in Book III, as the mountain-man sequence events are recounted in Arjuna's own words.[29] Here the relationship between Indra and Arjuna is carried almost to the point of identification, when it is said that Brahma had once predicted to Indra, regarding the Nivatakavachas: "You yourself shall be their end, but in another body, Slayer of Vṛtra" (III.169.31). But there is also the clear implication that Arjuna has surpassed his father, as is appropriate for a great hero.[30] It is said by Matali himself that Arjuna rides Indra's chariot even better than Indra does (III.164.37ff.); and Matali finds Arjuna's battle with the Nivatakavachas more terrifying than any he has ever experienced with Indra (III.168.17ff.). In fact, in destroying the

Nivatakavachas, Paulomas, and Kalakeyas, Arjuna performs a task that was too difficult for Indra. These demons all had won a boon to the effect that the gods could not kill them, and thus a semidivine hero has to perform the task (III.45.22ff.; III.170.6ff.; V.98.1ff.).[31]

Arjuna's connection with the *gandharvas*, and thus, as it appears, with fertility (see chap. IB), is of some importance in the account of his heavenly sojourn; for here, besides weapon usage, Arjuna learns singing and dancing from the *gandharva* Chitrasena. The critical text mentions this fact only briefly (III.45.6–8 and III.164.54), but a number of manuscripts of Book III stress the contrast between asceticism and eroticism[32] in Arjuna's character by enlarging the account of his dealings with Chitrasena into a complete short story (Poona Edition, III, Appendix I, no. 6).[33] Here, just following mention of Arjuna's instruction by the *gandharva*, it is said that Arjuna admired the *apsaras* ("celestial dancer," female counterpart of a *gandharva*) Urvashi. Noticing this admiration, Indra sent Chitrasena to suggest to Urvashi that she and Arjuna should become lovers. Urvashi was most pleased, since Arjuna was superhumanly handsome, strong, and virtuous (as Chitrasena expounded at length). When she appeared to wait upon him, however, Arjuna refused her overtures, on the grounds that she was his ancestress; he had only looked at her out of curiosity and interest because she was the mother of the Paurava (thence, the Kuru) race. Urvashi then cursed Arjuna to become a eunuch dancer, a curse that he had earned, she said, by disregarding a woman pierced by Kama's (Cupid's) arrows. Arjuna ran to Chitrasena, and Chitrasena told the story to Indra, who transmuted the curse into a blessing: in the thirteenth year of exile, while the Pandavas must live incognito, Arjuna would be able to disguise himself as a eunuch, but he would regain his virility after that year.

That this episode is rejected by the Critical Edition suggests that it is a late addition to the *Mahabharata*, the purpose of which is to provide a connecting link with the fourth book of the epic, the *Virataparvan*, also possibly late,[34] which recounts the thirteenth year. The story, however, is nonetheless useful in emphasizing qualities of Arjuna's character that are only suggested in the brief stanzas of the critical text which tell of his studies with Chitrasena; for here one finds that Arjuna is a symbol of male fertility who nevertheless has astounding self-control and can do what many a famous seer failed to do, fulfilling an Indian ideal: that is, resist temptation by an *apsaras*.[35] Arjuna as eunuch is thus, in one sense,

Arjuna as the supreme practitioner of discipline and abstinence already observed in the earlier stages of the mountain-man sequence. Arjuna's connection with *gandharvas* is also pursued in the critical text of Book III, where one of the later episodes is a battle in which Arjuna succeeds in saving the Kauravas from *gandharva* captors headed by Chitrasena himself (III.229.18ff.).[36]

The forest exile culminating in the thirteenth incognito year may be viewed as a sort of consecration (*diksha*) for future action (see chap. IE).[37] Posing as a eunuch during the thirteenth year enables Arjuna to survive and meanwhile gather up his vital powers (a yogic task) for future use. Only a true hero would be able to control himself in this way. Thus, in the mountain-man sequence, Arjuna prepares himself to be a model of both asceticism and fertility, which are themselves interconnected, and are to be viewed as two aspects of heroism in its Indian version.

In Book IV, Arjuna's abilities along both these lines are employed when he refuses Virata's offer of his daughter Uttarā in marriage, and gives her to his son Abhimanyu instead (IV.66.27ff.). In this one action, he both shows that in his year as a dancing master he has not violated this girl (asceticism) and provides for the family's continuity (fertility); for the child of Abhimanyu and Uttarā will be the one surviving descendant of the Pandava (and Kaurava) line (see chap. IIIC).

The fourth book of the *Mahabharata* is at least partially humorous in nature, particularly because in it the Pandavas take on disguises that exaggerate or reverse their true characters;[38] van Buitenen, with this in mind, suggests a connection between Book IV and the Hindu spring "New Year's" festival of Holi, "the Indian form of saturnalia," or its equivalent in classical India.[39] Arjuna's disguise as a eunuch is amusing in that it completely reverses his strength and emphatic virility, making him appear and act weak, almost "feminine."[40] On the other hand, the disguise may be taken quite seriously as a symbol for what Arjuna has actually become during the exile: powerless. In fact, all the Pandavas—their "weapons" left hanging on a tree outside of town (IV.5.9ff.)—are like eunuchs during this period, with Arjuna as usual embodying the situation of all five.[41] That Arjuna is able to accept his powerlessness gracefully, and act the part of the eunuch he temporarily is, is a sign of his heroic self-control. As soon as it becomes necessary for him to do battle in defense of King Virata's cattle, raided by the Kauravas just as the thirteenth year is ending, Arjuna's heroic identity reveals itself to all observers, under the eunuch disguise, which is about to be removed (IV.36.30ff.).[42] At this point, Arjuna's own analysis of his situation is as follows:

> It is at the behest of my eldest brother that I observe for this year a vow of chastity; I swear this is the truth. I am not a eunuch . . . but under another's orders and compliant with the Law. Now, to be sure, I have fulfilled the vow and am released. [IV.40.12–13]

Notes

1. The *Mahabharata* gives two different, though similar, versions of the central mountain-man sequence events, one told by a narrator and one in Arjuna's own words: III.38ff. and III.163ff.
2. On the figure of the warrior-ascetic as it developed in post-epic Indian literature, see Indira Viswanathan Shetterly, "Recurrence and Structure in Sanskrit Literary Epic: A Study of Bhāravi's *Kirātārjunīya*," Dissertation, Harvard 1976. (The *Kiratarjuniya* is a sixth-century poem based on the mountain-man sequence of the *Mahabharata*, which became well known—and a popular artistic subject—in its own right. [On the famous relief of "Arjuna's penance"(?) at Mahabalipuram, South India, see, especially, T. N. Ramachandran, "The *Kirātārjunīyam* or 'Arjuna's Penance' in Indian Art," *Journal of the Indian Society of Oriental Art* 18 (1950–51): 58ff.])
3. Involving such initiatory activities as receiving instruction, fighting with *rakshasas* (mainly on Bhima's part), etc. However, Arjuna's feats during this period are the focal point of the Pandavas' preparation for adulthood and war.
4. Lord notes that Yugoslav epic singers often elaborate upon the arming of the hero as he sets out on his great adventure, and remarks (p. 88): "It may well be that the presence of the elaboration at this point and in connection with this particular hero is a survival from rites of initiation or dedication."
5. The following are Arjuna's major weapon acquisitions. As a child he is given the important *brahmashiras* weapon by Drona (I.123.74ff.). Drona also gives Arjuna the *agneya, varuna, vayavya, parjanya, bhauma, parvata*, etc. weapons (I.125.18ff.). Just prior to the Khandava Forest burning, Varuna, told to do so by Agni, gives Arjuna the bow Gandiva, two inexhaustible quivers, and a chariot with a monkey on its standard (see Appendix) and *gandharva* horses; to Krishna, Agni gives a discus and a club (I.216). After the forest burning, Indra promises Arjuna future acquisition of *agneyas*, *vayavyas*, and other weapons (I.225.12). During the mountain-man sequence, Arjuna is given the *pashupata* (*brahmashiras*) weapon by Shiva (III.41.7ff. and III.163.48ff.); in the same chapter, Gandiva, which had been taken from him by the mountain man, is returned to him. In III.42 the World Guardians give weapons to Arjuna, including the *danda* ("staff") from Yama, etc.

In III.45 Indra gives Arjuna various weapons, including the thunderbolt itself. Most of the weapon giving of the mountain-man sequence is repeated in III.163f. In III.165 Arjuna is said to have been given his conch, Devadatta, and various other accoutrements before his battles with the Nivatakavachas and other demons; but III.171 states that he was given these things after the battles. Devadatta, however, had supposedly been given to him much earlier by the *asura* Maya—just one example of the inconsistency among these various accounts, the purpose of which is to supply Arjuna ultimately with all the weapons and accoutrements that characterize him. Finally, another acquisition of the *pashupata* weapon by Arjuna is recounted in VII.57.79: it is won by Arjuna after a dream ascent to Shiva in preparation for his battle against Jayadratha (see chap. IE, n. 32, and chap. IIA2).

6. These battles are included only in the second telling of the mountain-man sequence.
7. Note Matali's use of it in an exclamation in III.168.21.
8. Note the strange fact that Indra has given Arjuna a drying weapon. So goes the permutation of symbols, over and above the basic mythic identities of the characters; see chap. IE for further discussion of this point.
9. The grieving Pauloma and Kalakeya city (III.170.55ff.) tends in that direction, but not enough to undermine the joy in Arjuna's victory: the city suddenly vanishes, like a mirage (III.170.59).
10. At one point Arjuna even sits on Indra's lap (III.44.21).
11. Paralleling Achilles in the Skamandros episode (see chap. IC). Failure in a battle against the gods points to the human component of the hero. (On the hero's humanity, see Part II of this study.)
12. Arjuna's inexhaustible quivers are exhausted during this battle. (Van Buitenen omits *akshayau* ["inexhaustible"] in his translation of III.40.36.) Cf. the failure of the sword Hrunting and Beowulf's resorting to the might of his arms in his fight against Grendel's mother (*Beowulf*, lines 1518ff.).
13. Beginning: "The time shall come of your fortune, best of the Bharatas ['descendants of Bharata'], when Dhanaṃjaya the Pārtha overpowers the enemies in battle." (The word for "fortune" here is *shri*.)
14. In the later chapters, however, the brahmin who appears is not identified explicitly with Indra. See chap. IA for a brief discussion of Indra's brahmanic tendencies.
15. On shamanic initiation, see Mircea Eliade, *Rites and Symbols*, pp. 87ff., and *Shamanism: Archaic Techniques of Ecstasy*, trans. Willard R. Trask, Bollingen Series, 76 (New York: Pantheon, 1964), pp. 110ff.
16. In calling these manifestations "shamanic," the present study is guided by the following statement made by Eliade at the beginning of his chapter entitled "Shamanic Ideologies and Techniques among the Indo-Europeans" (*Shamanism*, p. 376): "Our role is limited solely to discovering to what extent the various Indo-European peoples preserve vestiges of an ideology and technique that are shamanic in the strict sense of the term, that is, which exhibit one of its essential features: ascent to heaven, descent to the underworld to bring back the patient's soul or to escort the dead, evocation and incarnation of the 'spirits' in order to undertake the ecstatic journey, 'mastery over fire,' and so on." Eliade himself mentions "Arjuna's ecstatic ascent of the Mountain of Śiva" as resembling shamanic ascent, though

not actually shamanic (p. 420); surprisingly, however, he refers here only to the brief episode in *Mahabharata* VII.57 (see above, n. 5, etc.), entirely omitting mention of the much more developed episode in Book III. On destruction of the body, generally dismemberment, see *Shamanism*, pp. 34ff., etc. Biardeau ("Etudes" V, p. 150, etc.) interprets *pinda* (the word that van Buitenen translates as "ball of flesh") as an *oblation* (sacrificial), which Arjuna becomes at this moment; see further, Scheuer, pp. 232ff.

17. Cf. the Hyperboreans of Greek legend. See II.25.7ff. on Arjuna's meeting with the Northern Kurus during the "conquest of the world." These capitulate to him without battle, making the following statement (vv. 9–13): "Pārtha, you are incapable of conquering this city in any fashion. Turn back, good man, this should suffice you, invincible champion! Any human who enters the city must die. We are pleased with you, hero; your conquests should suffice. There is nothing left for you to conquer, Arjuna. This is the land of the Northern Kurus, and no war can happen here. And if you were to enter it, Kaunteya ['son of Kunti'], you would not be able to see anything, for no human eye can see what is here. Yet, if there is something else that you wish to accomplish here, tiger among men, then speak and we shall do it at your behest, Bhārata."
18. See, e.g., V.109.24 (note the punning between *uttara* meaning "north" and *uttara* meaning "best"); XIV.43.10.
19. The forest environment serves the same function for the other Pandavas, only less emphatically. Note too that when the others decide to ascend the mountains to meet Arjuna they are advised that they can do so best by way of austerities (III.141.22; to be taken either literally or figuratively). Later it is said that the Pandavas had to be carried up by *rakshasas* (III.145.7). Cf. Yudhishthira's statement (III.155.70) that the Pandavas have reached a superhuman place; also the fact that at a certain stage of their ascent, they are stopped by the sage Arshtishena, with the following words (III.156.21–23): "From here onward it is impossible to go, bulls of the Bharatas, for here is the play garden of the Gods, beyond the course of humans. All the creatures here hate a human who errs in the slightest, and the Rākṣasas kick him. . . . Beyond the peak of this mountain . . . lies the course of the fully perfected divine seers." But these words do not dissuade Bhima from proceeding after a while, and combating the *yakshas* ("sprites") and *rakshasas* who would oppose him (III.157.25ff.); and the other Pandavas later follow him (III.158.3).
20. Note Eliade's discussion of *tapas* as a probable Indian illustration of shamanic "mastery over fire" (*Shamanism*, pp. 412ff.).
21. See, e.g., II.14.11, with reference to Arjuna Kartavirya. Regarding Arjuna the Pandava, the most specific statement of this principle is in VII.52.24. The epic also provides the extreme example of Vishvamitra, a king who manages to transform himself into a powerful brahmin by his austerities; see, especially, I.165.41ff.
22. This is the usual reaction of the gods or divine beings to the ascetic power of a mortal.
23. See Shiva's statement (III.39.29): "He does not desire heaven, nor sovereignty, nor long life." Arjuna had earlier made the same point to Indra, refusing the temptation of other boons besides weapons, offered to him by that disguised god, with the following words (III.38.40–41): "I do not want wishes or worlds, or divinity, still

less happiness, nor the sovereignty over all the Gods, overlord of the Thirty [the whole pantheon]! If I leave my brothers in the wilderness without avenging the feud, I shall find infamy in all the worlds for time without end."
24. Biardeau, "Etudes" V, p. 176.
25. For references on the giving of weapons to Arjuna by the World Guardians and Indra, see above, n. 5.
26. "It is by thy grace, Mountain [specifically, Mount Mandara], that brahmins, barons, and commoners attain to heaven and devoid of pain walk with the Gods. . . . I have happily lived on thee! Many are the peaks of thine that I have seen, the valleys, rivers, and springs, and thy very holy places" (III.43.23–25).
27. On the basis of its (slight) irregularity; see M. C. Smith, "The Core of India's Great Epic," p. 74. Cf. too V.51.18.
28. A reduplication of Drona's earlier request.
29. See above, n. 1.
30. Here again, then, one finds the theme of generational succession (see chaps. IB and IIB).
31. The implication is that Indra would have been able to combat them before the boon was given (III.165.20).
32. A phrase coined by Wendy Doniger O'Flaherty to refer to the structural oppositions inherent in the character of the God Shiva (*Asceticism and Eroticism in the Mythology of Śiva* [London: Oxford University Press, 1973]), but which also applies well to Arjuna.
33. The introduction to the critical text of this book states (p. xix): "Although this piquant story has permeated all versions of the epic except the Kaśmīrī . . . there is no reason to doubt that it is a late addition."
34. See van Buitenen, *Mahābhārata*, III, 18ff. The relative lateness of Book IV was argued, in particular, by Hopkins; see, e.g., *Great Epic*, pp. 382f.
35. The *apsaras* is often, though not always, one sent by Indra specifically to tempt the seer, who seems to be gaining too much power by way of his asceticism; see, e.g., *Mahabharata* I.65.20ff.; I.120.5ff. Note the reversal of that pattern here, where the *apsaras* is sent by Indra as an affectionate gift instead of a curse.
36. Arjuna is doing well against the *gandharvas* when Chitrasena, who has remained invisible up to then by way of his magic, reveals his true identity (III.234.25ff.).
37. Or a sort of initiation, a death and rebirth in the belly of a fish (*matsya* = "fish"), that is, the womb (IV.66.10), à la Jonah.
38. Yudhishthira as a brahmin master of dicing, Bhima as a cook (with a sideline of wrestling), Arjuna as a eunuch dance teacher, Nakula as a groom, and Sahadeva as a cowherd (IV.1–3). In addition to these disguises, there is much more humor in Book IV. Perhaps the best example of this humor is to be found in the obvious parody of the *Bhagavadgita* scene of Book VI (see chaps. IIA1 and IIIB1) at IV.36; noted by Dumézil, *Mythe et épopée* I, pp. 93f.; van Buitenen, *Mahābhārata*, III, 15f.; etc. Note also Arjuna's tying on of his armor upside down (IV.35.18 [van Buitenen's interpretation]), etc.
39. Van Buitenen, *Mahābhārata*, III, 5. On the basis of *Mahabharata* IV.42.22, Hiltebeitel questions the Holi connection; see "Disguises," p. 148, n. 5. For further critique, questioning the "carnival spirit" of Book IV, but not the shared New

Year's/Book IV/initiation characteristic of reversal, see J. W. de Jong, Review of *The Mahābhārata*, vol. III, trans. J. A. B. van Buitenen, *Indo-Iranian Journal* 22 (1980): 58f.

40. As pointed out in chap. IA, a eunuch is the precise opposite of a hero in *Mahabharata* parlance. An Indo-European parallel to Arjuna's eunuch disguise may be noted, e.g., in Achilles' female disguise, taken on when he was hidden by his mother on the island of Skyros, to forestall his participation in the Trojan War; see Apollodorus III.174; Ovid, *Metamorphoses* XIII.162f. (and Eliade, *Initiation*, p. 109, on the initiatory meaning of this episode). Arjuna's disguise also seems to have a basis in the mythology of Indra; for as early as the *Rg Veda*, Indra is said to have taken on a female disguise (*Rg Veda* I.51.13), and elsewhere he is said to have once been castrated temporarily (*Mahabharata* XII.329.14.2; *Ramayana* I.47.27). Hiltebeitel ("Disguises," pp. 153ff.) argues that Arjuna's disguise turns him into a Shiva-like figure (insofar as a well-known persona of Shiva is the man-woman Ardhanarishvara ["half-woman lord"]), the disguise being an aspect of the "pervasive identification of Arjuna with Śiva" (p. 160) throughout the epic. (Shiva, Hiltebeitel points out, is also a dancer; thus, he suggests, the profession Arjuna assumes here. Cf. Biardeau, "Conférence," vol. 82, p. 91.) The present author finds Hiltebeitel's discussion of the Shiva imagery applied to Arjuna here convincing, and sometimes amusing (e.g., the discussion of Arjuna's "firm" "non-masculinity," on p. 155), but doubts the imagery's mythic significance for the epic as a whole. Cf. the points made regarding Shiva below, chap. IE, n. 17; chap. IIIB2, n. 19; etc. For Hiltebeitel's discussion of Shiva-related elements in the Book IV disguises of the other Pandavas, see "Disguises," pp. 172f.
41. Because of the ascetic overtones of the forest exile and the several cases of enforced sexual abstinence in their family, Biardeau favors an interpretation that would connect the very name "Pandava," via "Pandu," with a word for eunuch, *panda*; see "Etudes" IV, pp. 261f.; "Etudes" V, p. 191. By way of contrast, Draupadi puts forth the claim, during the entire incognito year, that her supposedly absent husbands are five *gandharvas* (IV.8.27ff., etc.). Note that Bhima's cook disguise, his emphasis upon luxurious eating, is considered by his detractors to be a eunuchlike (unheroic) tendency (V.157.16; VII.114.69ff., part of a long battlefield insult by Karna). (The word used for "eunuch" as applied to Bhima, here and elsewhere, is *tubaraka*.) Bhima also plays a female role for a few moments during the Book IV action (IV.21.38ff.), pretending to be Draupadi, to save her from Kichaka. For more on the symbolism of the weapons in the tree, see chap. IE, n. 45.
42. The cattle raid is a typical Indo-European heroic theme, known particularly from Irish examples, of which the most famous is the *Tain Bo Cuailnge*. The theme is also associated with the figure of Indra himself, who is said in the Vedas to have stolen the cows of the "Panis" (see Arthur Anthony Macdonell, *Vedic Mythology* [1898; rpt. Delhi: Motilal Banarsidass, 1974], p. 157, etc.). For a full discussion of the role of cattle in Indo-European culture, see Bruce Lincoln, *Priests, Warriors and Cattle: A Study in the Ecology of Religions* (Berkeley: University of California Press, 1981).

IE. ON THE BATTLEFIELD AT KURUKSHETRA, I

In his supreme heroic effort, his activity against the Kauravas on the battlefield at Kurukshetra ("the Field of the Kurus"), Arjuna fights as he has been trained to fight, and ultimately proves himself to be what he is purported to be and has indeed been since his training began, that is, the best of all the warriors. As Indra told him after his training in arms:

> Now even the multitudes of the Gods cannot vanquish you in battle—not to speak of humans in their world, [with their unperfected souls][1]—for you are beyond measure, unassailable, and matchless in war. [III.165.2]

Or again, after his defeat of the demons for Indra (see chap. ID):

> Not a man on earth can overcome you. Bhīṣma, Droṇa, Kṛpa, Karṇa, Śakuni, and all the kings are not worth a fraction of you when you stand on the battlefield. [III.171.2–3]

Not only can Arjuna defeat any single comer; he is also able to hold off an entire contingent that opposes him simultaneously. (This group is known as the "Samshaptakas" because they have "sworn together" [*sam-shap*] to kill Arjuna or themselves die.)[2] Specifically, Arjuna is the greatest of all archers, as suggested by his common epithet "Savyasachin" ("Left-handed Archer"), given to him, apparently, because he shoots ambidextrously (see Appendix).[3] In short, Arjuna's fighting wins the war for the Pandavas.[4]

Nominated by Arjuna (V.140.18ff.), Dhrshtadyumna has been made the general (*senapati*) for the Pandava side; but Arjuna himself is the *senapatipati*, the master of the general or, as van Buitenen translates it, "the marshall's marshall" (V.154.12f.). Krishna, who has agreed to help the Pandavas without fighting actively (V.7), serves as Arjuna's charioteer and adviser throughout the war, which lasts for eighteen days, aiding him as Vishnu, out of friendship, aided Indra, pacing out his path.[5]

Heroic Battle Imagery

It has been pointed out previously that it is necessary to distinguish in the *Mahabharata* between a character's or situation's mythic associations and purely literary associations, the latter being qualities that are attributed to the character or situation formulaically only. Regarding the battle books (VI–IX), which are particularly formulaic, this consideration must be taken especially seriously.[6] Here one finds Arjuna and other warriors described in many stock terms that define them rather as archetypical great heroes than as specific individuals. These heroes' identities remain essential to the overall structure of the war, but are often lost sight of completely in a given formulaic description. One of the results of oral formulaic composition is a tendency in epic (not just Indian) that parallels the so-called henotheistic tendency of some Indian mythic thought:[7] attention shifts from hero to hero, and often whichever hero is the center of concern at a given moment is described at that moment as the greatest imaginable. Another result is that almost any formula of praise may be applied to almost any great warrior at his moment of glory (with the possible exception, in the *Mahabharata*, of Bhima, whose style of fighting deviates from the norm, and a few others). Thus, regarding Arjuna, one finds that although his superiority is established by the epic's statement that he is Indra's son and partial incarnation, and his victory what one must expect of the son of Indra (in effect, a recapitulation of the mythic victory of the gods over the demons), the description of his behavior in battle is often indistinguishable from that of other chariot warriors. The formulaic imagery of the battle books must be studied, keeping in mind the mythic affiliations that it so often bypasses, in order to complete the discussion of Arjuna as hero.

One finds, for example, formulaic comparison of Arjuna fighting an opponent to Indra fighting Vrtra or some other enemy;[8] but this comparison is applied very frequently to other warriors as well. The most striking illustrations of the point being made here may be found whenever Karna, who is Arjuna's archenemy, is compared to Indra. For example, the brahmins and bards praising Karna at his investiture as commander (the third) of the Kaurava army compare him to Indra, the Pandavas to the demons (VIII.6.42), a comparison that reverses the mythic framework of the epic, but is quite appropriate formulaically. One may imagine that this sort of reversal is occurring only because Kaurava lackeys are the speakers, but will soon discover that even a relative neutral like Samjaya (the narrator of most of the battle-book description) mixes his metaphors: the epic compares any current victor to Indra, and praises him. Sometimes confusion seems to set in, as when both Arjuna and Karna are compared to Indra in the same stanza:

> Both had prowess equal to great Indra's. Both were great charioteers resembling great Indra. And with arrows resembling great Indra's thunderbolt, they struck at one another like great Indra and Vrtra. [VIII.65.7]

The words are Samjaya's, and the confusion may be attributed to the free use of formulas typical of oral epic poetry.

Description of warrior activity in terms of natural phenomena must also be considered. One may first note that the image adopted in the Khandava episode, which is essentially a comparison between the hero's behavior and that of fire, is picked up by the battle books. The impression produced by the image here is different from that produced in the Khandava episode, partly because the description is more standardized than it was there, partly because human beings and their just or unjust causes, rather than natural catastrophes, now lie behind the action (see further, Part II). Nevertheless, the basic picture is identical, justifying a statement made by Biardeau, that the Khandava Forest battle is a symbol (*figure*) of the great war.[9] It must be remembered that Arjuna is not the only hero of the Kurukshetra War who is compared to a fire, or even a forest fire. Rather, the image applies to all the great heroes. It is appropriate, however, to concentrate on Arjuna here.

The comparison with fire is implicit in the epithet "foe burner" (*paramtapa*, etc.), which is applied continually to Arjuna and others, throughout the epic. More specifically, comparison with a raging forest fire may be seen in the following example, in the words of Samjaya to Dhrtarashtra:[10]

> As a roaring, blazing, scorching [*pratapi*] fire let loose in the forest by woodsmen would, well nourished, burn the thicket with its abundant trees and canopy of dry creepers, so did he [Arjuna], scorching [*pratapi*] with his host of arrows, having arrows as his flame, with fiery energy [*tejas*] reaching upward and downward, unforgiving, swift, swiftly burn your son's entire army. [IX.23.61–62]

In these stanzas[11] one finds echoes of the complementary concepts of *tapas* and *tejas* referred to in chapter ID, above.

Even nearer the imagery of the Khandava episode is this passage, in which the Kauravas flee from Arjuna like animals from the burning forest:

> Your great army, tormented by arrows, shone like a bamboo forest on a great mountain, blazing in the night. . . . Like herds of deer devoured by a fire in the great forest, the Kurus ran about, burned by Savyasachin. [VIII.58.16, 18]

The following passage suggests the wind imagery mentioned in chapter IC:

> As fire, urged by the wind, would burn a forest with abundant trees, creepers, and bushes, with grass and shrubs as dry fuel, so Dhanamjaya, the fire of the Pandavas, having arrows as his flame, angered, urged by the Krishna-wind, burned the forest of your army. [VII.68.53–54]

From these quotations one may recognize some of the thought behind the imagery. Two major points become clear: as stated previously, the energy of the hero (*tejas*) burns like fire; and for a warrior of Arjuna's type on the battlefield, the particular conduit of heat is the arrows he sends forth, themselves compared to flames that scorch and burn.[12] In fact, the comparison of an arrow to a flame, and the image of the heat of arrows, is common throughout the epic.

This imagery appears quite simple and straightforward, until one notes that it is complemented by imagery that compares Arjuna equally to other natural phenomena, including the one which is directly opposed to fire, and which also corresponds to Arjuna's mythic identity, based on his paternity: the storm. Besides the very frequent references to "showers" (*varsha, vrshti*) of arrows poured by Arjuna and others, a few more specific examples may be cited. Just before the image of the bamboo fire quoted above (for images are often piled upon one another in the epic), the following image is found, specifically comparing Gandiva to Indra's storm weapon, the thunderbolt:

> He made the very great and terribly loud Gandiva resound like the awful crashing of the thunderbolt from the thundercloud in the sky. Then the army, struck by the arrows of Dhanamjaya, split apart, like a great ship in the ocean, shaken by a strong wind. The arrows released by Gandiva, multiform [and] attacking, resembling firebrand, meteor and the planet Saturn, burned up your army. [VIII.58.13–15]

In addition, however, one finds that Arjuna is compared frequently with the sun; see, for example, VI.112.122f., where this image is preceded directly by the common image of a smokeless fire. And he is also compared to the moon[13] and the wind.[14] The complexity of the natural imagery here quite outdoes that in the Khandava episode.

In an attempt to glorify Arjuna and others further, the extremes of these phenomena are also presented as images of the hero's behavior. The comparison with fire pushed to its limit results in comparison with the *samvartaka* ("destroying") fire, which destroys the world at the end of a cosmic age; one may find it applied to Arjuna, for example at VII.64.15, preceded by comparison with various gods. One also finds the image of the *yuga* ("world age") sun,[15] applied to Arjuna, for example, in VII.31.44, VII.66.20, and many other stanzas. Such imagery, along with comparison of various warriors to Shiva,[16] and the passing statement that Shiva preceded Arjuna on the battlefield (VII.173.9f.; XII.330.69f.),[17] fits well with the frequently presented picture of the battlefield as a whole paralleling the chaos of the time of universal dissolution.[18] As she does in the case of the Khandava episode, Biardeau takes the *pralaya* imagery found in the battle books to be mythically, that is, structurally determinative.[19] Dumézil's studies suggest a similar conclusion, when he stresses the parallels in theme and structure between the story of the Kurukshetra War and the eschatological battle of Scandinavian mythology.[20] The viewpoint of the present author regarding the pralayic interpretation of the Khandava Forest burning has been discussed above, and the point made there may also be reiterated regarding the battle books: it seems preferable to view eschatological imagery in the battle scenes as primarily formulaic.[21] The battles are described as resembling *pralaya* in intensity, but this says nothing about the time frame of the epic, which places the war at the onset of the Kali age, not at the time of dissolution. Nor does *pralaya* imagery seem to mold the events of the war or the characters involved.[22] Furthermore, it clearly may be said of the battle books, if not the Khandava episode, that if an eschatological battle underlies them, it has been subordinated almost completely to the idea of a heroic rather than a mythic cosmic struggle. (Further discussion of these points follows in chaps. IIA3 and IIIC.)

Arjuna also creates a river of blood (VII.15.42f.), corresponding to the river whose image is used quite frequently to suggest the horrifying aspect of the battlefield, and which is sometimes identified as Vaitarani, the Hindu river of death (VI.55.125, etc.). (The image of the armies resembling oceans is also used,[23] reminding one of the imagery of the ocean-churning story, discussed in chap. IC.) One cannot help but be reminded here of Skamandros in the *Iliad*, filled with corpses.

Although natural imagery appears to be rather randomly applied to Arjuna, some logic may be noted in its distribution. The one rule that seems to be applicable consistently is a perfect Lévi-Straussian permutation of binary oppositions. A hero is a hero, the epic seems to say, primarily in the face of an opponent. (This conception leads, for example, to the notion, which dominates the battle books, that each hero has a "share" [*bhaga*], his fated and most appropriate opponent in battle.)[24] In a given stanza or group of stanzas, any natural phenomenon may be linked with any hero, as long as the opposing natural phenomenon is linked with his opponent in the fight being described. The image chosen often seems to have little to do with the mythic affiliations of the warriors concerned.

Excellent examples of the fluidity of natural imagery may be discovered in the continuing Arjuna-Karna conflict. Beginning in childhood, the conflict has turned into a "share" relationship,[25] the outcome of which will be decisive for the ending of the war. If Karna were to be true to his mythic connections he would, as Surya's son, always be represented by the "sun" half of a battle simile; his opponent would have to be compared to an opponent of the sun, such as clouds that cover the sun. Instead, one finds the following reversal in a boast by Karna:

> Like a huge cloud, I will cover Dhanamjaya with arrows, though he burns like the sun, has ample rays, and is blazing with glory, dispelling darkness. [VIII.29.13]

In the very next stanza, a different image may be noted, which is again untrue to Karna's mythic identity:

> Having become a cloud, I will extinguish the son of Prtha with showers of arrows in battle, as [one might extinguish] fire, Agni, smoke-crowned, blazing, energetic, burning this world. [VIII.29.14]

Later, however, in the *Striparvan* (Book XI), as Gandhari, mother of the Kauravas, mourns the lost warriors, she reverses the imagery once again, stating that Karna was like a blazing fire in battle, extinguished by Arjuna's energy (XI.21.1).

In the stock descriptions of battle, then, one must not expect to find any particular emphasis on the fact that Arjuna is the son of Indra, the storm god. He will not be compared to the storm more than to other natural phenomena. With no uniformity, all images of force will be applied to him. One is reminded of the fact that the king's activity is supposed to resemble that of a number of natural phenomena together (see chap. IA). On the other hand, it is noteworthy that the image of fire is for all great warriors—including Arjuna—the predominant image, although, mythically speaking, Dhrshtadyumna is the warrior who is Agni incarnate (I.61.87). One is thus brought back again to the portrayal of the Khandava episode, in which fire or heat is the image of *tejas*, culminating in the pralayic heat of warrior frenzy. The sun may also provide a point of comparison for warrior energy, but only fire captures fully the motion of the warrior on the battlefield.[26]

Besides depiction of the warrior's behavior as paralleling a force of nature, one finds other images, of which one very frequently recurring example should be mentioned here: the image of the warrior or his arrows as snakelike. Dumézil and others have shown that animal imagery is commonly used to represent warrior frenzy in Indo-European literature: for example, the image of the wolf or bear, the latter probably the eponym of the "berserkers," in the Germanic tradition.[27] Animal imagery has been noted above (chap. IA), as part of the standard description of heroic childhood presented by the epic; the battle books, however, show that animal-like behavior is also characteristic of heroic adulthood. Snake imagery is the most often used animal imagery expressive of warrior activity in the *Mahabharata*, although suggestions of other animal images may be noted in such common phrases as "tiger among men," "bull among men," or "Wolf-Belly" (an epithet of Bhima). Many other scattered examples might be cited: for example, warriors are said to wheel around the battlefield like eagles,[28] or charge like elephants.[29] (Regarding Arjuna's characteristic "monkey banner" and white horses, see Appendix.)

Whatever their usual overtones of "fertility" (see chap. IB), snakes in the *Mahabharata* more commonly carry with them a particular connotation of wrath or even vengeance: one hisses like a snake when angered or distressed. One may observe the idea of vengeance at work especially clearly in an episode related in Book VIII: the story of the snake Ashvasena (VIII.66, especially vv. 15ff.).[30] Ashvasena, Takshaka's son and one of the few escapees (with his father, but without his mother) from the Khandava Forest fire, was a sworn enemy of Arjuna. During the Kurukshetra War, he became one of Karna's arrows in order to take revenge on Arjuna, revenge that ultimately failed to materialize.[31] This incident is interwoven with what appears to be a simpler original account of the shooting of a particularly powerful arrow by Karna (VIII.66.5ff.).

Snake imagery is sometimes applied to Arjuna, as in the following passage:

> But the son of Prtha, quickly releasing the sharp poison of his anger, well accumulated over a long period of time, at the king of Prasthala [Susharman, a major figure among the Samshaptakas], having filled him with a hundred arrows . . . then killed the horses of that bowman. [IX.26.40–41]

Here Arjuna is seen again in his frenzied state, as, for example, in the Khandava episode. It is difficult to say how much of the imagery of extreme behavior finds its way into the *Mahabharata* battle books by virtue of being formulaic, how much is chosen deliberately. Regarding Arjuna, however, the emphasis of the battle books is upon chivalrous heroism, not frenzy as in the case of Bhima. Thus, most of the snake similes applied to Arjuna refer to his snakelike sighs or the power of his arrows, rather than to his style of fighting.[32]

The stricter mythic significance of snake imagery in the Kurukshetra War, over and above its literary significance, may be summarized as follows: just as the Kauravas are correlated with the demons, the natural enemies of the gods, they are, it seems, correlated with the snakes, natural enemies of the birds.[33] (That there is some connection between demons and snakes may also be maintained, in view of the fact that Vrtra, Indra's archenemy, was a serpent [Vedic: *ahi*].)[34] The outstanding point of comparison between

Kauravas and snakes is that both are envisioned as chaotic masses.[35] The connection between the two groups is reinforced by the fact that Dhrtarashtra, the father of the Kauravas, shares his name with a snake king; and another great snake king is named "Kauravya" (which is an alternative designation for "Kaurava," used on occasion in the epic).[36] Such arguments have been elaborated by Gösta Johnsen,[37] as also by D. D. Kosambi, who equates the snake (*naga*) figures in the epic with Nagas, members of the indigenous (non-Indo-European) Indian population.[38] To Johnsen's and Kosambi's statements, the observation must be added that snake symbolism is particularly prevalent in the early chapters of Book I of the *Mahabharata*, where various stories about snakes are grouped around the central motif of Janamejaya's snake sacrifice, to explain why that sacrifice was undertaken (I.3ff.). Perhaps the snake sacrifice may be regarded as a reduplication of the Kurukshetra War, insofar as the "snakes" (see chap. IC), who because one of them killed Janamejaya's father are Janamejaya's mortal enemies, are identified implicitly with the great enemies of Janamejaya's ancestors. (Note how the Kauravas try to destroy the Pandavas in childhood by poisoning them [I.119.36ff.].) Despite these strong connections between Kauravas and snakes, however, the correlation is not carried through the epic clearly and consistently. The Pandavas also have substantial *naga* affiliations: outstandingly, Arjuna's marriage to Ulupi (daughter of Kauravya) and *naga* son, Iravat.[39] Nor are the Pandavas clearly connected with the complementary bird imagery, Yudhishthira's assumption of the alias "Kanka" ("heron") for the duration of the *Virataparvan* (IV.1.20, etc.) providing only an isolated exception;[40] Biardeau, in fact, argues that it is after all the Kauravas, not the Pandavas, who have absorbed bird imagery, albeit that of birds of bad omen.[41] Perhaps the chief effect of a Kaurava-snake correlation may be felt, overall, at the level of suggestion: the Kauravas, as a chaotic snakelike mass, are dehumanized and a fair target for the world-ordering Pandava heroes. On the other hand, formulaic application of snake imagery to Arjuna and other warriors on the battlefield at Kurukshetra breaks the boundaries even of this somewhat impressionistic mythic alignment.[42]

War as Sacrifice

Having concluded discussion of the natural imagery in the *Mahabharata* battle books with consideration of snake imagery, one may now turn to that image in which snake imagery converges with fire imagery, and the two converge with the heroic concepts of order and fertility: the image of sacrifice. The battle books refer again and again to the Kurukshetra War as a sacrifice, in passages such as the following, in which Karna predicts the impending cataclysm in a discussion with Krishna:

> Vārṣṇeya [Vrshni = Krishna], the Dhārtarāṣṭra ["son of Dhrtarashtra" = Duryodhana] will hold a grand sacrifice of war. Of this sacrifice you shall be the Witness, Janārdana [Krishna], and you shall be the Adhvaryu priest at the ritual. The Terrifier with the monkey standard [Kapidhvaja = Arjuna; see Appendix] stands girt as the Hotar; Gāṇḍīva will be the ladle; the bravery of men the sacrificial butter. The *aindra, pāśupata, brāhma*, and *sthūṇākarṇa* missiles will be the spells employed by the Left-handed Archer. Saubhadra [Abhimanyu], taking after his father, if not overtaking him, in prowess, will act perfectly as the Grāvastut priest. Mighty Bhīma will be the Udgātar and Prastotar, that tigerlike man who with his roars on the battlefield finishes off an army of elephants. The eternal king, law-spirited Yudhiṣṭhira, well-versed in recitations and oblations, will act as the Brahmán. The sounds of the conches, the drums, the kettledrums, and the piercing lion roars will be the Subrahmaṇyā invocation. Mādrī's two glorious sons Nakula and Sahadeva of great valor will fill the office of the Śamitar priest. The clean chariot spears with their spotted staffs will serve as the sacrificial poles at this sacrifice, Janārdana. The eared arrows, hollow reeds, iron shafts and calf-tooth piles, and the javelins will be the Soma jars, and the bows the strainers. Swords will be the potsherds, skulls the Puroḍāśa cakes, and blood will be the oblation at this sacrifice, Kṛṣṇa. The spears and bright clubs will be the kindling and enclosing sticks; the pupils of Droṇa and Kṛpa Śāradvata ["son of Sharadvat"] the Sadasyas. The arrows shot by the Gāṇḍīva bowman, the great warriors, and Droṇa and his son will be the pillows. Sātyaki shall act as Pratiprasthātar, the Dhārtarāṣṭra as the Sacrificer, his great army as the Wife. Mighty Ghaṭotkaca [Bhima's son, a *rakshasa*][43] will be the Śamitar when this Overnight Sacrifice is spun out, strong-armed hero. Majestic Dhṛṣṭadyumna shall be the sacrificial fee when the fire rite takes place, he who was born from the fire. [V.139.29–44]

The statement that Duryodhana will be the performer of the sacrifice corresponds to his position as king at the start of the war; as one might expect, his sacrifice includes its full quota of destruction. In the passage quoted, one should not look for absolute meaning in any of the individual comparisons, replete with technical terms, which might well have been lined up differently,[44] but rather, in the general comparison. In a broader sense, certain aspects of the *Mahabharata* narrative contribute to the picture of the war as a sacrifice, although they may not even be included in such a passage: Dhrshtadyumna, the general of the Pandava army, incarnating sacrificial fire; Drona as the necessary priest (although behaving as a warrior); a consecration prior to the war (see chap. ID) resembling one before a Vedic sacrifice;[45] even, perhaps, the sacrificial style of many of the killings.[46]

The metaphor of the Kurukshetra War as a sacrifice captures the central meaning of the epic at the heroic level, which is built upon the structural opposition of order and disorder, both represented by the imagery of fire and sacrifice. In simplest terms, order is represented by the rightly performed sacrifice; disorder is represented by the wrongly performed sacrifice, which gets out of control. In practice, however, the imagery becomes more complex, since even rightly performed sacrifice has its frightening and destructive aspect (see chap. IC). Sacrificial destruction is, however, viewed as ultimately creative, the extreme example being the destruction and recreation brought about by the fire of universal dissolution, described in terms of the funeral pyre, that sacrifice which best illustrates sacrifice's ambiguity. All of the considerations above may be applied to the fire and sacrificial imagery in the *Mahabharata* battle books. Or to put it another way: whether sacrificial fire is constructive or destructive depends upon whose point of view is taken, its beneficiary's or its victim's. By the same token, a "sacrifice of war" such as that at Kurukshetra may be viewed either as an effort to preserve order or as a scene of horrible destruction, or both. At the heroic level, however, the ultimate outcome is the preservation of order by the good, and the creative effort of the hero in the face of great odds is emphasized. Kurukshetra, "the Field of the Kurus," is seen as the *dharmakshetra* ("field of *dharma*"), the field of world order (VI.23.1 [*Bhagavadgita* I.1]; XIV.93.2).[47]

The metaphor of sacrifice is important not only in the battle books, but throughout the entire *Mahabharata*, as the following points will illustrate. Two early recitations of the epic take place at sacrifices: Janamejaya's snake sacrifice and a twelve-year *sattra* ("session") in the Naimisha Forest. That the Kauravas try to destroy the Pandavas in childhood by burning them in the lacquer house may also have sacrificial overtones.[48] Arjuna first proves his prowess by burning the Khandava Forest, a sacrificial effort on behalf of Agni. Yudhishthira's royal consecration (*rajasuya*) sacrifice is the occasion of Duryodhana's jealousy, which leads to the dice game, and eventually the war. (A dice game was, in any case, a standard event in a royal consecration rite; here it takes on narrative rather than strictly ritual significance.)[49] During the night attack just after the war, described in Book X of the epic, Ashvatthaman offers himself as a sacrifice to Shiva and thus gains power and support (X.7). At the same time, two other Kaurava partisans, Krpa and Krtavarman, set three fires in the Pandava camp and wait at its gate to kill all those who try to escape, as Ashvatthaman slaughters the others like sacrificial animals (X.8.100ff.)—this being a clear parallel to the Khandava Forest burning by Arjuna and Krishna in Book I.[50] Significantly, Krpa, Krtavarman, and Ashvatthaman are compared later to the three fires of Vedic sacrifice (X.9.7), a comparison that underscores the sacrificial reference of the episode. Here, however, sacrifice is viewed from its destructive side. (See chap. IIIC for discussion of the night attack and connected events.) The *Striparvan*, which follows, brings with it portraits of mourning women and funeral pyres, such as are commonly found in heroic literature.[51] After the war, Yudhishthira, on the advice of Vyasa, absolves himself of the guilt of having slaughtered his kinsmen by performing a horse sacrifice (see below), the greatest sacrifice a king can undertake. In Book XV, Dhrtarashtra, Gandhari, and Kunti die in a fire in the forest to which they had retired in their old age, a fire that spread from their own sacrificial fires there (XV.45.19ff.).

Regarded from the point of view of his behavior on the battlefield, Arjuna's heroic (or kingly) role may be characterized most accurately as that of the perfect sacrificer. Arjuna's very name (as well as one of his epithets, Phalguna) seems to point to this sacrificial function (see Appendix). Indeed, sacrifice was the ancient ideal task of the Indian king, whom Arjuna represents. The epic itself often speaks of the greatness of a king (more than likely a Pandava ancestor) primarily in terms of the impressive sacrifices he has performed,[52] and it is even stated that Indra (of whom a common epithet is "Shatakratu" ["he of one hundred sacrifices"]) himself won his kingdom by sacrificing (XIV.94.4) or surpassed other kings by sacrificing (XII.20.11). Like father like son: sacrifice, whether performed by him or offered to him, is Indra's ritual, the Vedic ritual; thus it is also Arjuna's. In a sense, the Kurukshetra War has possession of the sacrifice, or the power generated by the sacrifice, as its object, as did so many fights between gods and demons.[53] In all these contexts, the designation "sacrifice"—a Vedic inheritance—is a shorthand for "maintenance of world order" or "support of *dharma*,"[54] the kingly, or heroic, role most emphasized in Indian epic thought.

The culminating and also most straightforward example of Arjuna as sacrificer comes in the *Ashvamedhikaparvan* (Book XIV), and represents his final successful heroic action in the *Mahabharata*. In this book, Yudhishthira performs the horse sacrifice that will expiate his guilt, incurred in the war; here the troubles accumulated from the time of the skewed royal consecration onward are finally set right. As will easily be understood from the earlier discussion regarding the complementary roles of the Pandava brothers, it is Arjuna who is chosen to oversee the major portion of this sacrifice, that is, to follow the sacrificial horse and defend it during a prescribed period of wandering, before it is actually offered up (XIV.71.14ff.). (Here he takes the active role of warrior, not the relatively passive role of sacrificing king, although, as pointed out in chap. IB, the fact that it is his wives who gather for the ceremony suggests that the epic visualizes him in the kingly role as well.) During the horse sacrifice, Arjuna goes, as at the time of his exile, in all directions, staking out Yudhishthira's empire. More clearly than Janamejaya's snake sacrifice, this horse sacrifice is a recapitulation of the great war, for during it Arjuna encounters the relatives of many of his former opponents from Kurukshetra.[55] Thus the heroic role of Arjuna in the *Mahabharata* is reduced to its common denominator: sacrificial activity. One is reminded of the prediction made by the celestial voice at Arjuna's birth, that he would "offer up the three sacrifices."

Regarding the imagery of the battle books, it is most striking that the idea of war as sacrifice serves very successfully to unite all formulaic descriptions and all mythic affiliations. Fire imagery and the imagery of all other natural phenomena come together in the picture of a sacrifice, which, through the agency of fire, destroys the chaotic snakes, eats up the snakelike arrows, and dispenses a natural order in which all phenomena participate. The coordinator of this activity is the hero, preeminently Arjuna.

Where *Dharma* Is, There Is Victory

Personally, the hero fights to win kingdom and wealth or, failing these, heaven and glory.[56] The *Mahabharata*'s heroic ideal is not, however, primarily selfish: the selfish Kauravas are the villains of the epic.

Rather, victory or death is seen as the duty of a *kshatriya* (V.133.11, etc.). The hero fights for the good of all creatures, the support of *dharma*, so described: "*Dharma* is established among *kshatriyas* [which is] full of clear happiness, self-evident, free from deception, beneficial to the whole world" (VII.64.5).[57]

At the heroic level, the result of the Kurukshetra War is the victory of the Pandavas through the prowess of Arjuna, whose epithet is "Jaya" ("Victory") (see Appendix)—a name that is, further, applied on occasion to the epic as a whole or in part, in passages that also promise *jaya* to the hearer, for example:

> This history, which is entitled the *Triumph* [*jayah*] should be heard recited by one who desires to triumph: that king shall vanquish his enemies and conquer the earth. It is the best sacrament to secure the birth of a son, and an avenue to welfare, which both a queen and a crown prince should hear recited many times. [I.56.19–20][58]

As in the case of the Khandava Forest burning, creation of order by sacrifice seems to be the heroic meaning of the Kurukshetra War and the epic as a whole. At this level, a Pandava victory is entirely predictable, since the Pandavas perfectly combine *dharma* and force; thus their path is often marked by prophecies of success and favorable omens,[59] which indicate that the universe is on their side. In fact, the ultimate victory of the Pandavas over the Kauravas is inevitable insofar as the epic story is based upon the god-demon battle, which the gods always win: "Where *dharma* is, there is victory."

Notes

1. Note the slight alteration of van Buitenen's translation here. He translates: ". . . who have not made their souls."
2. See, especially, VII.16–31, the "Samshaptakavadhaparvan" ("Section of the Killing of the Samshaptakas").
3. That Arjuna's characteristic role in the war will be that of archer is foretold in II.71, where the gestures of each Pandava brother on the occasion of the group's going forth into exile after the dice game are recounted; see II.71.14–15: "Kuntī's son Arjuna, the left-handed archer, follows his king while scattering about sand to forecast the number of enemies that will burn with his arrows. Just as his grains of sand are separated from one another, as severally shall he loose on his enemies the

showers of his arrows." (Yudhishthira meanwhile covers his eyes so as not to burn the enemy with his glance [see chap. IA] and Bhima displays his arm muscles; the twins, less strikingly, cover themselves with dust.) For specific statements on Arjuna as the greatest of all archers, see, e.g., V.26.21. Arjuna is said to be capable of shooting five hundred arrows in a moment (V.59.16ff., etc.).

4. See, e.g., XII.151.32f. In fact, the decisive victory of the war is apparently Arjuna's victory over Karna, after which the Kauravas seem to know that the war is lost for them (see chap. IIA3).
5. Evidently a given of the story, Krishna's position as charioteer for Arjuna is established more than once in the epic: see III.48.15; V.7.34f.; V.154.14. For Vishnu pacing out Indra's path, see *Rg Veda* VIII.12.27 and VIII.52.3; see also *Rg Veda* IV.18.11 and VIII.100.12. On the Indra-Vishnu friendship/assistantship, see further Gonda, *Aspects*, p. 109; on the resemblance of the Arjuna-Krishna friendship to it, *Aspects*, pp. 157, 161ff. Dumézil prefers to correlate the steps of the Vedic Vishnu, more narrowly, with Krishna's steps as he runs forth from the chariot, threatening to fight actively (on which, see chaps. IIA1 and IIA3), a gesture that prompts Arjuna to action; see *Mythe et épopée* I, p. 212, following Dumézil's earlier article, "Les pas de Kṛṣṇa et l'exploit d'Arjuna," *Orientalia Suecana* 5 (1956): 183–88.
6. On the predominance of formulaic material in the battle books, see Grintser, p. 416. On general *Mahabharata* imagery, including much discussed in the present chapter, see Ram Karan Sharma, *Elements of Poetry in the Mahābhārata*, University of California Publications in Classical Philology, vol. 20 (Berkeley: University of California Press, 1964)
7. Namely, Vedic thought; as discussed first by Max Müller (see Macdonell, pp. 16f.).
8. E.g., in VIII.47.12, in Arjuna's own words.
9. Biardeau, "Conférence," vol. 79, p. 141.
10. Like a number of examples offered in this chapter, just one of many that might have been chosen. Comparison with forest fires is also to be found in the *Iliad*: XI.155; XV.605; XX.490ff.; XXI.12ff. There, however, the image is generally used to describe the entire scene of battle, while in the *Mahabharata* it refers, as a rule, to the activity of an individual warrior.
11. One might speculate that these stanzas, which are in the *trishtubh* meter, represent a different layer of the epic than the preceding two stanzas (IX.23.59–60), in the more usual *shloka* form, which also contain variations on the forest-fire theme. A comparison of Arjuna with the sun also appears in these *shloka*s.
12. *Archi*, the word for "flame," also means "ray" of the sun. Throughout the epic, arrows are also compared to sunrays, the word *rashmi* likewise being used.
13. E.g., in VII.60.20.
14. E.g., in VII.64.57.
15. That is, the sun that destroys the world at the end of a *kalpa* (see chap. IC, n. 17).
16. For application of this comparison to Arjuna, see, e.g., p. 150.
17. The importance of this statement has been, in the present author's opinion, overestimated, as an aspect of Arjuna's "'concealed' identification" with Shiva (Hiltebeitel, "One Chariot," p. 24). The present study would suggest that Shiva

imagery, like other divine imagery applied to the Kurukshetra War participants, is essentially formulaic—or, in the present case, descriptive, an extension of formulaic usage, touting Arjuna's prowess in battle through comparison with Shiva; either this or an interpolation (see chap. IIIC, n. 13). Regarding a point made by Hiltebeitel in "One Chariot" (p. 24): the comparison of Arjuna to Shiva as bow bearer in *Mahabharata* VIII.49.93 is not necessarily mythically significant; it is suitable poetically, in that bow bearing is an important trait shared by Shiva and Arjuna, but is just one of many comparisons applied to Arjuna, as the present study indicates.

18. See VII.100.5, and many other passages.
19. See, especially, Biardeau, "Etudes" IV, pp. 208ff.
20. Dumézil, *Mythe et épopée* I, pp. 222ff.
21. Hiltebeitel originally seemed to be of a somewhat similar opinion (preferring, however, the designation "allegoric" to "formulaic"); see *Ritual*, p. 312, and "Draupadī's Garments," *Indo-Iranian Journal* 22 (1980): 110f., n. 29. Lately, however, as in his interpretation of the Khandava episode (see chap. IC, n. 40), he has moved in the direction of Biardeau's interpretation: the Kurukshetra War as *pralaya* ("One Chariot," p. 25); connected, apparently, is his recent emphasis on Arjuna-Shiva identity (see chap. ID, n. 40; above, n. 17; etc.).
22. As Biardeau would have it; see, e.g., her discussions of Karna as the *pralaya* sun ("Etudes" IV, pp. 229f.; "Etudes" V, pp. 174f.; etc.) and Yudhishthira as Yama, the god of death (especially, "Etudes" V, pp. 95ff.).
23. E.g., in VII.95.2ff.
24. See, especially, V.56.12ff. and V.161.5ff. In addition, many battle descriptions include long lists of who fought with whom in the given battle, where the pairing may or may not be according to the foreordained "shares," or may correspond to them in part. The pairing continues even after the war is over, as each Pandava is assigned, as booty, the house of a corresponding Kaurava (XII.44.6ff.); Arjuna is given Duhshasana's.
25. V.56.15 lists Karna, Ashvatthaman, Vikarna (who, however, is killed ultimately by Bhima [VII.112.30]), and Jayadratha as the special shares of Arjuna. V.161.5 specifies Karna.
26. It may be suggested that the sun, as opposed to fire, is often an image of warrior splendor used to describe the calmer activity of older warriors; this would, however, be difficult to maintain consistently. Some randomly chosen examples: regarding Bhishma, VI.102.77; regarding Drona, at the time of his death, VII.165.40f. (but Dhrshtadyumna is also compared to the sun in this chapter [vv. 25 and 53]). Note that Skanda, the archetypical warrior god of Hinduism, is sometimes said to be Agni's son (IX.45.8ff), although later thought, including much of the epic, knows him as actually Shiva's son.
27. Dumézil, *Warrior*, pp. 139ff.
28. Cf. the eagle array assumed by the Pandava troops with Bhima as its beak, at VI.65.7ff. See VII.76.34 for an application of eagle imagery to Arjuna and Krishna.
29. For battle-book stanzas that apply an elephant comparison to Arjuna, see VII.102.36, quoted on pp. 31–32, and VII.66.41, quoted on p. 139.

30. Ashvasena is not mentioned by name in the critical version of the episode, but the story told (VIII.66.23) is his; cf. I.218.5ff. And cf. IX.60.35, quoted on p. 165.
31. See chap. IIIB2, n. 30.
32. Snakelike sighs: applied to Arjuna at VI.91.1, where he sighs like a snake at the news of his son Iravat's death; see also, e.g., VII.54.1, with regard to Arjuna and Krishna. Snakelike arrows: note how one such simile has, it seems, developed into an entire brief story (VII.57.68ff.): when Arjuna goes on his second visit to Shiva, to win the *pashupata* weapon again (see chap. IIA2), he and Krishna, who accompanies him, first encounter two huge snakes. These snakes turn into a bow and arrow, on which Arjuna is instructed by Shiva, before they are thrown back into the lake they had come from. On the snake-arrow comparison, see further Hopkins, "Position," p. 278; also F. D. K. Bosch, *The Golden Germ: An Introduction to Indian Symbolism* (The Hague: Mouton, 1960), p. 102.
33. On the snake-bird enmity, see the Kadru-Vinata story of I.14ff. Like the gods and the demons, the Pandavas and the Kauravas, these two groups are cousins.
34. An Indian version of the (primarily) Indo-European/Semitic mythic/folkloric "dragon" antagonist; on which, see, e.g., Joseph Fontenrose, *Python: A Study of Delphic Myth and Its Origins* (Berkeley: University of California Press, 1959). Pushing this point, Arjuna's war against the Kauravas could be interpreted as his own particular dragon fight, modeled after Indra's.
35. Note the parallelism in birth stories between Kauravas (I.107) and snakes (I.14); though see below, n. 41.
36. For Dhrtarashtra as a snake, see I.3.142, etc. Dhrtarashtra is also a *gandharva* name (I.114.44, etc.), and King Dhrtarashtra of the *Mahabharata* is said to be a *gandharva* incarnate (I.61.77f.). For Kauravya as a snake, see I.31.13, etc.
37. Gösta Johnsen, "Varuṇa and Dhṛtarāṣṭra," *Indo-Iranian Journal* 9 (1965–66): 255ff.
38. E.g., in D. D. Kosambi, "The Autochthonous Element in the Mahābhārata," *Journal of the American Oriental Society* 84 (1964): 31–44. Some sort of *naga*-autochthon identification (via totemism? fertility religion?) would, of course, go far toward explaining the Indo-European antipathy toward snakes (as witness Vrtra's role). As Kosambi makes clear, however, there is more to the Kauravas, even regarding historical antecedents, than a *naga* connection.
39. In this regard, recall Biardeau's statement that it is necessary for a king to secure the *naga* world as well as this world (see chap. IB, n. 29). A further suggestion may also be offered: May a general connection between heroes and snakes be posited for India, as for Greece? (On the Greek case, see W. K. C. Guthrie, *The Greeks and Their Gods* [Boston: Beacon Press, 1951], p. 246. On the Indian, see Charles Autran, *L'Epopée indoue: Etude de l'arrière-fonds ethnographique et religieux* [Paris: Les Editions Denoël, 1946], p. 68.) In support of this idea, note the famous Sanskrit name "Nagarjuna." Structurally, the Pandava-Kaurava opposition sometimes comes to grief against its *naga* connections: when Arjuna and Karna oppose one another in their final battle, as all deities and supernatural figures take sides in the conflict, the great snakes take Arjuna's side, the small ones, Karna's (VIII.63.36f.). Note too that "Janamejaya" is included among snake names in the epic (II.9.10).

40. See too above, n. 28. Conversely, note the striking passage in which Arjuna calls upon the *naga* weapon while his opponent, Susharman, invokes the *sauparna* ("bird") weapon against it (VIII.37.21ff.). (In line with the binary oppositions established in the epic, weapons associated with opposing natural forces often neutralize one another.)
41. Biardeau, "Conférence," vol. 89, pp. 222f., 236ff. She also argues (p. 238) for a birdlike Kaurava birth; cf. above, n. 35.
42. For Duryodhana's *naga* standard, see VII.80.26f. Here *naga* is generally taken as "elephant," but of course it also means "snake" ("dragon"?).
43. See chap. IB, n. 2.
44. And have been, e.g., in V.57.12–13, in the words of Duryodhana to Dhrtarashtra: "I and Karṇa, father, have laid out the sacrifice of war and here we stand consecrated with Yudhiṣṭhira as the victim, bull of the Bharatas. This chariot is the altar, this sword the spoon, this club the ladle, this armor the *sadas*. My steeds are the four sacrificial priests, my arrows the *darbha* grass, my fame the oblation!"
45. That the Pandavas, at Arjuna's suggestion, hide their weapons in a *shami* tree, a type of tree whose wood is closely associated with sacrificial fires (see, e.g., above, p. 64), during their last year of exile, contributes to the imagery of this period as a sacrificial consecration; see IV.5.12ff. Biardeau has much to say regarding this consecration, and especially the *shami* tree; see, especially, her "Mythe épique et hindouisme d'aujourd'hui," *Indologica Taurinensia* 5 (1977): 43–53 (also "Conférence," vol. 82, p. 93; "Etudes" IV, pp. 207f.; etc.).
46. An idea much favored and intricately argued by Biardeau; see, especially, her discussion of Jayadratha (see chap. IIA2) as the symbolic focal point of a failed Kaurava horse sacrifice ("Conférence," vol. 86, pp. 146ff.; vol. 87, pp. 148ff.; vol. 89, p. 245; [and with a Pandava counterpart] vol. 90, pp. 150ff.; vol. 91, pp. 161ff.), and her discussion of Drona's death ("Etudes" IV, p. 251). See also Gehrts, pp. 246ff., and chap. IIIC, below. For Scheuer's treatment of the Kurukshetra War as a sacrifice, emphasizing Shiva's role as *shamitr* ("slaughterer"), see Scheuer, pp. 285ff.
47. Some epic accounts of Kurukshetra as pilgrimage place stress the fact that it was once the site of great sacrificial activity performed by Kuru himself; see, e.g., IX.37.24.
48. Biardeau also compares this episode to *pralaya*, and sees the imagery of the funeral sacrifice in it ("Conférence," vol. 78, p. 158). She regards it, thus, as a foretelling of the Kurukshetra War ("Conférence," vol. 79, p. 141).
49. See chap. IB, n. 3.
50. See further, chap. IIIC, n. 9.
51. The most well-known parallels are, of course, to be found in the *Iliad*. (Nagy [*Achaeans*, pp. 113ff.] argues that funeral imagery has entered the *Iliad* from popular hero cult.) Cf. also *Beowulf*, lines 1107ff.
52. See, especially, the stories of the sixteen kings in XII.29 (with great emphasis on the gifts given to the brahmins at the sacrifices).
53. See Devasthali, p. 19, and Sylvain Lévi, *La Doctrine du sacrifice dans les Brâhmaṇas*, 2nd ed., Bibliothèque de l'Ecole des Hautes Etudes, Section des Sci-

ences Religieuses, vol. 73 (Paris: Presses Universitaires de France, 1966), chap. 2; see also chap. IB, above.

54. See *Mahabharata* XII.260.33: "The whole world follows sacrifice and sacrifice always follows the world."
55. At least one definite comparison between an act performed during the war and the horse sacrifice is to be found in the battle books: see VIII.62.24.
56. See, e.g., VI.24.37 (*Bhagavadgita* II.37): "Either killed you will obtain heaven or having conquered you will enjoy the earth. Arise, therefore, son of Kunti, resolved upon battle!" On heaven and glory, see *Mahabharata* VI.3.45f.; VI.89.40; VII.100.17f.; etc. The quest for glory is apparently an ancient Indo-European theme; see Rüdiger Schmitt's discussion in *Dichtung und Dichtersprache in indogermanischer Zeit* (Wiesbaden: Otto Harrassowitz, 1967), pp. 61ff. Cf. Heidel, *Gilgamesh*, p. 36 (Semitic): "If I fall, I will establish a name for myself!"
57. Cf. V.37.36: "A prince should do what benefits all beings and brings himself happiness, for that is the root on which Law and Profit prosper."
58. Cf. the very similar wording of XVIII.5.39–40 (p. 268). That the promises made in these passages are aimed in particular at the *kshatriya* class becomes all the more apparent through comparison with the closely related statement of V.134.17–18, appended to the explicitly *kshatriya* Vidurā speech, itself called *Jaya* (the wording is actually closer to that of I.56.19–20 than van Buitenen's translation would suggest): "This history called *Victory* [*jayah*] should be heard by him who wishes to triumph; and having heard it he will soon conquer the earth and shatter his enemies. It causes the birth of a son, it causes the birth of a hero: a pregnant woman who hears it again and again is sure to bear a hero." Here an explicit connection is made between *Jaya* and heroism. Cf. V.18.16, 19f., on the merits of *Indra-* or *Shakravijaya*. A story called *Narayanajaya* is told in XII.330.42ff., in which Narayana defeats Shiva (see XII.330.67). *Jaya* is sometimes seen as one-third of the epic story, consisting of *bhedo rajyavinashash cha jayash cha* ("the Breach, the Kingdom's Loss, and the Triumph") (I.55.43) or *bheda* ("breach"), *yuddha* ("war"), and *jaya* (van Buitenen, *Mahābhārata*, I, 446).
59. One of the best examples of favorable prophecies and omens is to be found before the war, in V.47.92ff; see further, p. 141.

PART II: HUMAN

IIA. ON THE BATTLEFIELD AT KURUKSHETRA, II

IIA1. THE EPISODE OF THE *BHAGAVADGITA*, I

Arjuna's Dejection

In a move unprecedented by any other Indo-European epic hero, and absolutely unexpected in view of his earlier successes, Arjuna sits down and refuses to fight at the start of the Kurukshetra War, not out of pride (as in the cases of Karna, and Achilles in the *Iliad*),[1] but out of disgust with war: he acts out what Yudhishthira always threatens, but never actually does, and is only brought back into activity by the words of his charioteer, Krishna, the *Bhagavadgita*. This episode is reminiscent of an episode in the *Tain Bo Cuailnge*, in which Cuchulainn, about to fight his foster brother Ferdia, tells his charioteer, Laeg, to "abuse and insult and mock" him if he seems near defeat, or praise him if he seems near victory.[2] Likewise, in a subordinate episode of the *Mahabharata*, Krishna's charioteer, Daruka, incites Krishna himself during a difficult moment in his battle with Shalva, king of the Saubha (III.23.20ff); and the charioteer Matali encourages and advises Arjuna, whom he is driving during the Nivatakavacha battle (see chap. ID) (III.169.12). This, then, was an important role of the Indo-European charioteer: to urge on the warrior he drove during battle—and Krishna does so frequently throughout the Kurukshetra War. It may have been out of such an event that the episode of "Arjuna's dejection" (*arjunavishada*)[3] developed, but it has grown into far more: a protest against the endeavor of war itself. From where does this sudden horror emerge, in a warrior who has until now awed his audience with his fabulous feats of prowess and who, overcoming his dejection, will eventually succeed in performing such feats again? That is, why does this war appear more unpleasant to Arjuna than those that he has fought already? The answer is that the Kurukshetra War raises issues which touch the human half of Arjuna's semidivine heroism; specifically, as Arjuna himself emphasizes in the *Bhagavadgita* (henceforth to be referred to as the *Gita*) episode, because the enemies here are the Pandavas' own kinsmen. Arjuna faces a personal crisis from the moment he has to meet such an enemy in serious battle,[4] and begins to question the *kshatriya* role, which was glorified at the heroic level, and which he himself plays better than any other warrior.

Just as the hero of epic and saga is generally partially divine, he is also partially human by definition. Sometimes his human side is emphasized, as in the case of Achilles in the *Iliad*, for whom the conflict between divinity and humanity may be viewed as a central issue.[5] Most often, however, a hero's humanity only makes more impressive the standard heroic feats based upon power and skill which he performs. For example, the death of Patroklos brings out Achilles' humanity but at the same time leads to his superhuman show of strength, his avenging *aristeia*.[6] During the *aristeia*, Achilles loses briefly to the Skamandros River, but rallies with divine aid, and wins a decisive victory over the Trojans. Nor does death, the great humanizer of heroes at the end of many epics, come to Achilles at the end of the *Iliad*, although it has been clearly foreshadowed, and predicted for the future.[7] Similarly, although the heroic Arjuna of Book III loses his fight with the mountain man, the consequences of the battle show it to be a positive accomplishment of the hero: a victory over death.

By comparison, the Kurukshetra War is ambiguous in outcome: although the Pandavas win, theirs is a Pyrrhic victory, a victory at great human cost, for two major reasons. First, many kinsmen and elders of the Pandavas, fighting on the Kaurava side, are killed; second, many of those fighting on the Pandava side are also killed, including, at the very end of the war, all the Pandava survivors except the brothers themselves, Krishna, and Krishna's compatriot, Satyaki. Equally striking: the warfare itself is ambiguous in that, besides being forced to fight against people who are legally and morally entitled to respect, the Pandavas are able to win only by means of trickery and deceit. It is prophetic of this ambiguity that Arjuna at first refuses to fight at all.

Arjuna has long been a voice of reason among the *Mahabharata* characters, particularly during the dice game, when he mediated between Yudhishthira and Bhima.[8] Seemingly, it is this capacity for reason that prepares him for a humanizing shift from a purely martial hero to a man sensitive to the human condition. Thus, although the ambiguity of the Kurukshetra War brings out the human complexity of all of its participants, Arjuna is probably the most involved of all in his human situation. Bhima is perhaps the least so, although even he expresses human doubts at times.[9] The shift that Arjuna undergoes in the *Gita* episode is especially striking because he has been such an active hero up to this point; contrast, in particular, Yudhishthira.

Moral Ambiguity

As characterized in Part I of this study, the hero forges ahead in pursuit of right, without pausing to ponder the moral ramifications of each of his actions; real moral consideration is only possible for a hero when he is forced to the realization that some of his best deeds may have evil consequences. In general such realization comes about only when a hero's humanity makes him vulnerable, after the fact, to negative results of his behavior. Good examples from outside the Indian context might be the humanization of Achilles after the death of Patroklos, or of Gilgamesh after Enkidu's death: the latter in particular undergoes a great change, from brute warrior to seeker after truth. Both these deaths were caused by lack of self-control and careful consideration on the part of the central hero, who was otherwise acting rightly. The human weakness that brings about regret in both these cases is friendship. Arjuna has a similar human weakness in the *Gita* episode: love of his kinsmen. But Arjuna first succumbs to his human feeling in anticipation of the evil that may occur, rather than, like Achilles and Gilgamesh, only after the fact. (For an after-the-fact emotional response by Arjuna, see chap. IIA2.) Arjuna's ability to recognize the ambiguous nature of the war in advance has to do with his innate sensitivity to *dharma*-related issues, his basically moral and chivalrous nature; this, more than pure emotion, lies at the root of Arjuna's humanization in the *Gita* episode. Yet even Arjuna does not hesitate to fight until his understanding of *dharma* is challenged by the sight of his kinsmen arrayed before him on the battlefield, itself an emotional experience.[10]

What Arjuna recognizes then is that his own *dharma* (*svadharma*), the *kshatriyadharma*, which should work in support of eternal *dharma* (*sanatanadharma*), is not so neatly correlated with eternal *dharma* as he might have assumed. It is indeed his duty as a warrior hero to fight to defend *dharma*, but in so doing, he will actually disrupt it as much as, or perhaps more than, he will preserve it; for the enemy force is made up of his kinsmen, and to kill them will represent destruction of world order:

> When the family is destroyed, the eternal family laws [*kuladharmah sanatanah*] perish. And when the law is destroyed, lawlessness [*adharma(h)*, the opposite of *dharma*] overcomes the whole family. Due to the prevalence of lawlessness, O Krishna, the women of the family are defiled. When the women are defiled, O Vrshni, mixture of classes arises. Mixture [of classes] results in hell for the family destroyers and the family; for the ancestors of those people fall, since their rites of food and water are neglected. By these sins of family destroyers, causing class mixture, caste laws and eternal family laws are ruined. [*Gita* I.40–43 = *Mahabharata* VI.23.40–43]

The breakdown of family law, as outlined here by Arjuna, is one of the characteristics of the Kaliyuga, the fourth, degenerate age of world history; this will be discussed further in chapter IIA3, below. What is most important for the present discussion is that Arjuna clearly sees the wider threat to *dharma* behind the immediate issue of war against one's own kin. So much, in human terms, for the Field of the Kurus as the field of *dharma* (*Gita* I.1 = *Mahabharata* VI.23.1) (see chap. IE).

Pacifism

Beyond the issue of kinship loyalty, Arjuna's reaction in the *Gita* episode suggests another major issue sometimes raised by the epic: the evil of war in general. In fact, throughout the *Mahabharata* a continuing antiwar statement is to be found, which is more explicit than that found elsewhere in epic literature; it is interspersed with the heroic episodes of the epic in such a way as to cast doubt on their very validity, the pendulum swinging back and forth again and again, but appears in its most concentrated form in Book V, during which various conciliatory missions to avoid the impending war are sent out by the two sides. Often this statement is placed in the mouth of Yudhishthira, as in V.70.55–58:

> War is evil in any form. What killer is not killed in return? To the killed victory and defeat are the same. . . . I don't think that defeat is different from death; the victor too is surely diminished: in the end some others will kill a loved one of his; and behold, when he has lost his strength and no longer sees his sons or brothers a loathing for life will engulf him completely. . . . It is the modest warriors, noble and with a sense of compassion, who are killed in war, and the lesser men escape. There is always remorse after the killing of others. . . . The aftermath is evil, for survivors do survive. The survivors regain their strength and themselves leave no survivors but aim at total annihilation to put an end to the feud.[11]

In the *Gita* episode, this antiwar statement is made by Arjuna, who turns it from a theoretical position to the clear action of refusing to fight—Arjuna's action being more striking than Yudhishthira's continual lamentation. Thus Arjuna's objection at the start of the *Gita* episode represents a recurrent strain of thought in the *Mahabharata*, in its most impressive form.

The general nature of the epic's antiwar statement suggests a broader explanation than that offered above for the fact that Arjuna reserves his protest for the beginning of the Kurukshetra War, rather than refusing some of his earlier battles: simply, the Kurukshetra War, unlike the battles against the Khandava Forest or the various groups of demons and *gandharva*s faced earlier, is a battle against human opponents. Approximations of human feeling may perhaps be noted in the reaction of some of the animals being slaughtered at the Khandava Forest burning and the Pauloma and Kalakeya women mourning their demon husbands,[12] but in neither of these cases is the epic audience—or Arjuna—very much moved by the suffering: those killed are not human enemies. How different does one find the lengthy scene of mourning in the *Striparvan*. As suggested in chapter IE, the destructive side of the "sacrifice of war" is especially apparent when viewed from the perspective of the victim; this is the *Striparvan*'s perspective. It is the human opponent, so clearly depicted in that book and elsewhere in the description of the Kurukshetra War, who brings out a human reaction in Arjuna. Note that when multitudes of ordinary soldiers are killed in the battle books,[13] the epic composers pass over this fact quickly; it is only when sharply defined and humanized characters are killed that a strong response is evoked. In the broadest sense, the significance of the blood relationship between Arjuna and his enemies in this war lies in the fact that it forces him to recognize their common humanity.

The Hero-Human Dialectic

In one sense, the *Gita* episode marks another initiation in the hero's life: here Arjuna confronts his humanity, specifically, his moral compunction, and overcomes it, enabling him to embark upon his mature warrior tasks. The episode marks Arjuna's initiation into wisdom, with Krishna acting as, in the words of Gerrit Jan Held, Arjuna's "genius of initiation."[14] Noting again that Krishna was alongside Arjuna during Arjuna's great initiatory exploit in the Khandava Forest, one may conjecture that perhaps there too Krishna was serving subtly as a guide for Arjuna.[15] Here such a relationship is more explicit, with Krishna serving specifically as Arjuna's instructor, his guru. Both as Arjuna's charioteer and as his teacher, Krishna is acting as a helper for the humanized Arjuna, who cannot succeed alone. That Krishna has made an agreement not to fight, but only to advise, thrusts him into the helper role, in contrast with his apparent role of friend and equal in the Khandava episode.

At its most obvious, the teaching of the *Gita* is that Arjuna should arise from his human nature to his heroic nature and fight. This teaching reaffirms the absolute necessity of heroic action for the preservation of the world (*lokasamgraha*) (*Gita* III.25 = *Mahabharata* VI.25.25): the most important thing for Arjuna is not to abandon his *kshatriyadharma*. The *Gita* also advocates adherence to class duties by people at all other levels of society (*Gita* III.35; XVIII.47 = *Mahabharata* VI.25.35; VI.40.47); yet the message is delivered specifically to a warrior hero and is, at one point, called *rajavidya rajaguhyam* ("the knowledge of kings, the secret of kings") (*Gita* IX.2 = *Mahabharata* VI.31.2).

In order to support the *kshatriyadharma*, which has just been cast into doubt, the *Gita* must resolve the moral dilemma raised by Arjuna's questions; this it does by implying that general world order may have to be preserved at the expense of lesser moral considerations: Arjuna is told to go ahead and fight against his own family (including teachers and elders) for the larger purpose of adhering to his class duty, the duty of a *kshatriya*. One might say, thus, that the amorality of heroic action—

amorality such as has been noted in the Khandava Forest burning (killing defenseless victims for the sacrificial order)—is approved of tacitly by the *Gita*. As will be seen, this condoning of amorality will open the door to immorality, the deliberate flouting of rules. Immorality will arise when illegal action is called for to preserve world order, or when (amounting to the same thing) *dharma* reaches an impasse, evoking two alternative actions, both wrong, of which one must be chosen for the higher good. It will be argued, as Part II of this study continues, that such impasses or moral ambiguities are, in the *Mahabharata*, a humanizing component of the heroic condition;[16] that they are a basic issue of the Kurukshetra War is seen in the *Gita* episode, set at the war's opening. In order to assuage Arjuna's conscience regarding amorality, the *Gita* advocates desireless action: the expectation of reward (in *Gita* parlance, "fruit" [*phala*]), either personal or general, which surely exists at the heroic level, is to be discarded stoically (*Gita* II.47 = *Mahabharata* VI.24.47, etc.). Thus, although a return to heroism is advocated, the change in attitude is significant, producing lowered expectations characteristic of the human condition.[17] (Discussion of the *Gita*'s teaching continues in chap. IIIB1.)

Arjuna is sufficiently influenced by the *Gita* lecture to fight with all his might afterward. It is important, however, to note that he lapses into his human condition again and again throughout the subsequent chapters of the epic, as will be the subject of the remainder of Part II. That is, Arjuna wavers between heroism and humanity—or one might conjecture that the impression of wavering is a product of the repetition inherent in epic, and especially the heavily interpolated *Mahabharata*. Certainly Arjuna is never fully comfortable with the necessity of killing his relatives or, similarly, his teachers and elders. Krishna himself, presumably doubting Arjuna's firmness on this issue, twice jumps out of the chariot he is driving for Arjuna in order to take over the fighting, although to do so would mean violating his agreement not to participate actively (VI.55.86ff. and VI.102.53ff.). (Arjuna stops him both times.)[18] Even more striking, perhaps, is a statement that Arjuna himself makes to Krishna at VI.102.36–37, just prior to killing his "Grandfather,"[19] Bhishma:

> Sovereignty, with hell later, having killed those who ought not to be killed, or the tribulations of forest dwelling—which should I

> choose? Drive the horses to where Bhishma is! I will do your bidding. I will fell that invincible elder, the Grandfather of the Kurus.

In this reiteration of his *Gita*-episode objection, Arjuna again expresses his fear that a supposedly heroic action will in fact lead to the precise opposite of a heroic reward—to hell instead of heaven—and considers retiring to the forest as an alternative. Such self-doubt is always a clear indication of descent from the heroic level to the human; here, as elsewhere, it is overcome in short order, only to reemerge later. It may be suggested, then, that the *Gita* episode agrees with and encapsulates much of the attitude of the epic as a whole on this point.[20] Other heroes of epic and saga are also forced to face their humanity, but none, perhaps, so often and severely as Arjuna. In the end, that side of the *Gita*'s argument which favors pure heroic activity for the preservation of the world cannot possibly be convincing to such a figure.

Humanity is not the opposite of heroism but, rather, part of heroism. Nonetheless, the combined force of human weaknesses in the hero can result in an outlook that is actually antiheroic. The hero is self-assured: he almost feels invincible and is certain that his actions are right. Insofar as he acknowledges his humanity, however, his conceit diminishes and the tone of his activity changes. The heroic outlook and the human outlook are as sharply opposed to one another, therefore, as are divinity and humanity, the true opposites; this will be the underlying assumption of Part II of this study. In effect, then, it is useless for a hero to try to maintain his normal heroic behavior once he has faced his humanity.

The human reactions of heroic Arjuna reduce him to human proportions and make it possible for the audience truly to identify with his feelings for the first time. In terms of the Pandava hierarchy, "central" Arjuna becomes "average" Arjuna, no longer towering above the audience as semidivine but, rather, coming to represent "everyman."[21] Here too is an Arjuna who is suddenly dwarfed by the monstrous dimensions of the crisis he confronts in this greatest of his battles: the unprecedented hugeness of the Kurukshetra battlefield, and the problem of universal proportions, reaching almost to the level of *pralaya* in its severity, and threatening the entire earth.

Notes

1. In the *Mahabharata*, Karna refuses to fight until Bhishma is dead, after Bhishma slights Karna's skill in battle (V.61.7ff.; V.153.25; V.165.3ff.). The entire plot of the *Iliad* revolves around Achilles' refusal to fight after an insult by Agamemnon.
2. Kinsella, p. 193. For reference to a discussion of this episode by Hiltebeitel, see chap. IIA3, n. 20.
3. The name given traditionally to the first chapter of the *Gita*, evidently based on the words of *Gita* I.28 = *Mahabharata* VI.23.28: "krpaya parayavishto vishidann idam abravit . . . " ("Filled with compassion, despairing, he said this . . . ").
4. Evidently the preliminary encounter in Book IV is not meant to be taken quite seriously.
5. See the chapter entitled "Achilles: Evolution of a Hero" in Whitman, pp. 181–200; more recently, Seth L. Schein, *The Mortal Hero: An Introduction to Homer's Iliad* (Berkeley: University of California Press, 1984), chaps. 4–5.
6. For reference, see chap. IC, n. 7.
7. See, e.g., *Iliad* I, passim; IX.410ff.; XIX.408ff. See further Schein, especially pp. 129ff. Likewise, Odysseus' death is foretold, but never shown, in the *Odyssey*.
8. When Bhima, in anger at Yudhishthira for gambling away Draupadi, threatened to burn Yudhishthira's arms, Arjuna reminded him of the need for respect for an older brother (II.61.1ff.). See III.255.59ff. for an occasion on which Yudhishthira, backed by Arjuna, restrains Bhima's violent action. Cf. also Arjuna's attempt to calm Bhima in XV.17f.
9. Note his uncharacteristic desire for conciliation with the Kauravas, at V.72.1ff.
10. Throughout Book V, Arjuna has been willing to fight if necessary (V.76), and has even become quite bellicose on occasion (V.47). When Yudhishthira expressed horror at having to kill teachers and elders, Arjuna reminded him of the necessity of fighting (V.155.19ff.).
11. This statement is a prediction of things to come: Drona's inability to fight when he thinks his son has been killed, and Ashvatthaman's revenge (see chaps. IIA3 and IIIC). Other antiwar statements in Book V include V.26.3. More generally, the *Mahabharata* contains many complaints about the tragedy of *kshatriyadharma*. Klaes, following Zaehner (see Introduction), explains Yudhishthira's compunction as an expression of conflict between *svadharma* and personal conscience (leaning toward nonviolence and compassion); but the paradigm suggested for Arjuna above, *svadharma* versus *sanatanadharma*, might also be applied: *kshatriya-dharma*, that is, conflicts with both personal feelings and universal norms. Chap. IIA3 of the present study suggests that Yudhishthira may be viewed as *sanatanadharma* incarnate: thus his extreme discomfort with *kshatriya* duty.
12. See chap. ID, n. 9.
13. In XI.26.9 Yudhishthira gives the number killed in the war as "a myriad of ten myriads and twenty thousand and six and sixty crores." (See the following stanza for the [much smaller] number of survivors.)
14. Held, p. 182 (or "initiatory genius," p. 183).

15. Cf. the emphasis in the Humbaba episode (see chap. IC) on Enkidu guiding and counseling Gilgamesh; see Heidel, *Gilgamesh*, pp. 39ff.
16. Note the parallel case of the *gessa* ("taboos") of Celtic tradition; see Rees and Rees, especially p. 327.
17. This shift may be observed most clearly in the *Gita* itself by comparison of *Gita* II.37 = *Mahabharata* VI.24.37 (quoted in chap. IE, n. 56), a fully heroic stanza promising victory or heaven, with *Gita* II.47 = *Mahabharata* VI.24.47, just cited, advocating abandonment of all heroic expectations. Two such contradictory sentiments appear only ten stanzas apart.
18. On the reduplication here, see S. K. Belvalkar, "Some Interesting Problems in Mahābhārata Text Transmission: Problem #3," *Annals of the Bhandarkar Oriental Research Institute* 26 (1945): 106–19. For a suggested Puranic parallel, the *arjuna* trees, see Biardeau, "Conférence," vol. 84, p. 185.
19. A generalized title given to Bhishma as elder, though not precisely ancestor, of the Pandavas and the Kauravas; not to be confused with the real Pandava grandfather, Vyasa (see chap. IA). The same title is often applied to the god Brahma; for an example, see p. 256.
20. In this and other senses, the *Gita* seems to serve as a summary of issues intrinsic to the epic as a whole, such as has prompted van Buitenen to write (*Bhagavadgītā*, p. 5): "The *Bhagavadgītā* was conceived and created in the context of the *Mahābhārata*. It was not an independent text that somehow wandered into the epic." There has nevertheless been great controversy over the question of whether the *Gita* is an integral part of the *Mahabharata*, or a late interpolation. Favoring the former view are Lévi ("*Tato jayam,*" p. 16); Vittore Pisani ("The Rise of the Mahābhārata," in *Volume of Eastern and Indian Studies Presented to Professor F. W. Thomas C.I.E. on his 72nd birthday 21st March 1939*, ed. S. M. Katre and P. K. Gode, *New Indian Antiquary*, Extra Series, 1 [Bombay: Karnatak Publishing House, 1939], p. 171); Sukthankar (*Critical Studies*, p. 307); Suvira Jaiswal (*The Origin and Development of Vaiṣṇavism [Vaiṣṇavism from 200* B.C. *to* A.D. *500]* [Delhi: Munshiram Manoharlal, 1967], pp. 13f.); Biardeau ("Etudes" IV, p. 173, etc.); etc. Favoring the latter are Hopkins ("Position," p. 204 n., and *Great Epic*, pp. 384, 402); Winternitz (*History*, I, 437); etc.; see also Georg von Simson, "Die Einschaltung der *Bhagavadgītā* im *Bhīṣmaparvan* des *Mahābhārata*," *Indo-Iranian Journal* 11 (1968–69): 159–74. These views depend, of course, on the respective scholar's conception of the nature of the *Mahabharata* in its earliest identifiable form, and even within the two groups the conceptions vary.
21. In this regard, note the statement of XII.26.28: "Those who are the most foolish in the world and those who are the wisest flourish happily. The middle one suffers."

IIA2. THE DEATH OF ARJUNA'S SON, ABHIMANYU, AND CONNECTED EVENTS

Grief: Parallels from the *Iliad* and the *Shahnamah*

The sequence of events surrounding Arjuna's loss of his son Abhimanyu in battle and his killing of the man he considers responsible for Abhimanyu's death, the Kauravas' brother-in-law and ally, the king of Sind, Jayadratha[1] (VII.32–121, to be referred to henceforth as the "Abhimanyu sequence"),[2] is reminiscent of the events of Achilles' loss of his friend Patroklos and subsequent *aristeia* in the *Iliad*.[3] This sequence also has something in common with Rustam's loss of his son Suhrab in the *Shahnamah*,[4] although other elements of that tale may be found in the *Mahabharata* in the story of Arjuna's fight with another of his sons, Babhruvahana (for which see chap. IIB). In all three cases from different epics, the human element of the hero is brought out through his loss in battle and mourning of a loved one: in Achilles' case a friend, and in Rustam's and Arjuna's cases, sons.[5]

Overwhelming grief after a loss is a human trait felt by those who have mortal connections with other mortals; thus Arjuna's grief is far more pronounced at the death of his human son Abhimanyu than it was at that of his half-*naga* son Iravat, killed earlier in the war (VI.86ff.). Furthermore, one might say that Abhimanyu's death was caused indirectly by Arjuna's own human imperfection, since Arjuna had taught his son how to penetrate a certain military formation, but not how to exit from it (VII.34.19, etc.). Arjuna also laments the fact that, not knowing what was happening, he was unable to come to his son's rescue in mortal danger (VII.50.46f.). As Arjuna resorts to pathetic contrast in his elegy for his son,[6] one is reminded of the brevity of heroic careers; this point is emphasized by the fact that Abhimanyu's youth is mentioned constantly,[7] but it incidentally applies to Arjuna's career as well.[8] In sum, the opening event of the Abhimanyu sequence serves to remind the audience in various ways of Arjuna's humanity.

Undoubtedly, Abhimanyu is stressed above Arjuna's other sons, human or otherwise, particularly because he provides the direct ancestral link to Janamejaya. May one see in the lamentation over his death a genre of royal mourning that, stressing the humanity (mortality) of an ancestor, balances the genre of royal praise, which emphasizes his pure heroism (see chap. IA)?[9] In Abhimanyu's death there is the implication that Arjuna has lost his progeny; one does not learn until later that Uttarā is pregnant with Abhimanyu's child (see chap. IIIC).[10]

The portrayal of Arjuna as mourner for his son adds a depth to his character that was lacking at the heroic level: the depth of fully rounded humanity. Here Arjuna is seen in the role of victim, like the women of the *Strīparvan*. His humanity having been established, however, Arjuna returns to his heroic role during his search for revenge. The subsequent events of the Abhimanyu sequence are most helpful for determining the balance between the heroic and the human Arjunas; before analyzing them, however, it is necessary to discuss briefly the comparative materials mentioned above.

It has already been noted that the friendship of Achilles and Patroklos was not one of equality but, rather, one in which Achilles was the dominant party. It is not surprising, therefore, that Achilles is able to rise above his grief to attain revenge and, at the same time, preserve his own pride by killing the killer of Patroklos—the result being his *aristeia*. Thus, although the common humanity of Achilles is one of the major points developed in the *Iliad*, an equally important point made is that Achilles is "the best of the Achaeans," that is, the greatest hero;[11] and this latter is the conclusion of the *aristeia* proper, in which only Achilles' encounter with Skamandros is explicitly short of divine.

Rustam does not participate in a grand heroic moment after Suhrab's death; his reaction is, rather, to renounce heroic action entirely. Here, however, the situation is complex, since Rustam has killed his own son, which is itself a heroic fault, far beyond human proportions.[12] Although Rustam's mourning reveals his human emotions, the point of the story appears to be that he is the last and most outstanding of a heroic line, whose son could not hope to supersede him.[13] In the case of Arjuna, on the contrary, stress is placed upon the fact that he generated a kingly line.

To understand where in this hero-human dialectic the Abhimanyu sequence of the *Mahabharata* stands will be the aim of this chapter. As in the *Iliad*, the hero's bereavement is followed by a vengeful, furious, and glorious advance. This *aristeia* (to use the Greek term) is Arjuna's most important in the *Mahabharata*; that it is, however, a humanized *aristeia* (particularly in some versions) will be argued here.[14]

Mortality and Morality: A Humanized *Aristeia*

To speak first of the heroic activity: it is in the Abhimanyu sequence at least as much as at any other time during the Kurukshetra War that Arjuna is depicted as a Vayu/Bhima-type hero. Here images of Bhima-like rage abound, as in the following passage, which the concluding comparison makes one of the stronger statements of this sort with regard to Arjuna:

> They[15] resisted Arjuna, tortured with grief for his son, angry, like Death the destroyer, abandoning his life in the tumult, equipped, fighting wonderfully, plunging into the troops like the leader of an elephant herd, a great archer,[16] boldly advancing, a tiger among men. . . . United, they warded off that one who was aiming to kill Jayadratha, approaching, that bull among men, as a cure [wards off] a disease that has arisen. [VII.66.39–41, 43]

However, the Abhimanyu sequence also provides a picture of Bhima in action, as if to suggest that Arjuna's behavior is controlled by comparison:

> But the son of Kunti, with weapons exhausted, rushed at by Karna, entered weaponless among the elephants slain by Arjuna, which he saw fallen, resembling mountains, for the sake of blocking the path of his [Karna's] chariot. . . . Then, having lifted up an elephant killed by the arrows of Dhanamjaya, desiring to interpose it,[17] the son of Prtha stood there, that conqueror of the enemy's cities. Karna then blew away that elephant with his arrows. Then the

> Pandava, roaring, hurled the elephant's limbs at Karna [and], angered, threw wheels and horses and vehicles, whatever he saw on the ground, at Karna. [VII.114.62, 64–66]

(Note also VII.103.15, in which Bhima actually lifts up Drona's chariot and throws it.) Such contrast is too obvious to ignore, and one must conclude that the key to Arjuna's particular character in this episode lies elsewhere than in his strength, or Vayu/Bhima qualities.

What of Arjuna's chivalrous or "Indra" side, that moral or *dharma*-conscious quality which controls his premoral or amoral side? It is here that one must look for a change in Arjuna in the Abhimanyu sequence, a change that throws off the entire balance of Arjuna's heroic nature by emphasizing his humanity.

In the Abhimanyu sequence, Arjuna's Indra-like heroism is represented by his taking and fulfilling an oath to kill Jayadratha, whom he blames for Abhimanyu's death, before the sun sets on the fourteenth day of battle (VII.51.20ff.). In traditional Indian thought oaths are connected directly with the proper functioning of world order, insofar as their fulfillment depends upon and helps to preserve that order; likewise, to frame it as an oath seems to raise any act to the level of action in support of *dharma* and truth. (Indeed, one may swear by truth itself [several examples follow].)[18] To fulfill an oath is a proud and heroic accomplishment, attempted by many *Mahabharata* heroes,[19] but preeminently Arjuna, since he is preeminently aware of world order and, at the same time, preeminently active. Regarding his oath taking, Arjuna says: "I do not recall untrue speech [of mine]. I do not recall defeat. I do not recall, having promised, leaving any at all [of the promise] undone" (VII.12.13). Arjuna's oath to kill Jayadratha is just one of many oaths he takes in the *Mahabharata*,[20] but it is the one most carefully followed to its conclusion by the epic composers. They show it to be fraught with problems.

Just after Arjuna takes the oath, Krishna tells him he was rash to do so without Krishna's approval, and informs Arjuna that after hearing Arjuna's vow, the Kauravas have appointed six warriors specifically to protect Jayadratha: Drona will be organizing a special military formation, under his own command, for this purpose (VII.53.1ff.).[21] Arjuna's reaction to this news is merely to repeat his oath in a different version, now swearing by truth and touching his weapons, in a gesture that typifies his

Indra nature (VII.53.31ff.). He adds that his first step will be to get past Drona. Shortly thereafter, however, one finds that Krishna is plotting a way to help Arjuna, and that the Pandavas are all extremely worried about Arjuna because his vow seems so impossible to fulfill (VII.56.6ff.). Krishna is next seen instructing Daruka, his charioteer, to equip his chariot so he may fight the next day on Arjuna's behalf (VII.56.18ff.).[22] Daruka replies: "His victory is certain. From where could defeat come, O tiger among men, for him whose charioteer you are?" (VII.56.40).

The next chapter, VII.57, in the face of a sudden lack of confidence on Arjuna's own part (VII.57.10ff.), recounts a dream sequence in which Arjuna, accompanied by Krishna, journeys again to Shiva, and again wins the *pashupata* weapon from that deity (compare chap. ID), with a promise that his vow will be accomplished (VII.57.79). But when that apparently interpolated[23] episode is over, one finds further reference to Arjuna's predicament, as Yudhishthira begs Krishna for help, and Krishna promises to give it (VII.59).[24]

Beyond the obvious point that all the expressions of concern cited here seem to cast doubt upon Arjuna's heroic status, his formerly unquestioned ability to fulfill his oath, another issue is also raised: Arjuna, in taking his oath, has opened himself up to the possibility of death, and with it the failure of his entire enterprise. His oath (compare first version and the Pandava lament) states that he will enter fire if he fails to kill Jayadratha before sunset (VII.51.37 and VII.56.13). At most points in the Kurukshetra War, Arjuna as hero does not really seem vulnerable to death: the heroic fantasy of the epic permits a great warrior to rally even when wounded by many hundreds of arrows.[25] For Arjuna at Kurukshetra, the hero's obligatory choice of victory or death is brought into sharp focus only by means of his oath regarding Jayadratha. It has been noted earlier that the characteristic act of an initiatory hero is to overcome death. But what if a hero fails to do so? Mortality may perhaps be seen as the primary mark of humanity in a hero.[26] Certainly Arjuna's humanity is emphasized by the expressed fears that he will have difficulty performing the action he has sworn to accomplish, and will thus be liable to death.

As Arjuna sets out against Jayadratha the next morning, the omens are good (VII.60.22ff.), indicating that nature is on his side. When he approaches the Kaurava formation, the omens for the Kauravas are bad

(VII.64.4ff.). At the start of his advance, Arjuna evidences both Vayu/Bhima- and Indra-like behavior. Altogether, he is very much the hero.

Nonetheless, Arjuna's first major encounter in this *aristeia* is somewhat ambiguous. He greets his teacher, Drona, and asks for a blessing and permission to pass (VII.66.3). Drona, however, refuses to grant these, saying that Arjuna will have to vanquish him before he vanquishes Jayadratha (VII.66.7). A fight ensues, but finally Krishna, as charioteer and adviser, reminds Arjuna that such a fight is a waste of time, since it is delaying their reaching the real enemy. At this point, Arjuna informs Drona that Drona is his "teacher. . . . not my enemy. I am your pupil, the same thing as your son. And there is not a man in the world who could defeat you in battle" (VII.66.33). Then Arjuna and Krishna proceed right past Drona, into the Kaurava army (VII.66.35); Drona and his soldiers fall back and now only pursue Arjuna from behind (VII.67.1). Can this inexplicable advance reflect a desire on the part of the epic composers to skirt temporarily the issue of Arjuna's humanizing relationship in battle with his teacher?

Arjuna's wildly heroic advance continues in the terms quoted on p. 139, above. A number of single combats follow, along with some display of virtuosity on Arjuna's part, as one against many. Eventually, Dhrshtadyumna intervenes, dividing the Kaurava ranks (VII.70.15ff.).

After the slaying by Arjuna of Vinda and Anuvinda, princes of Avanti (VII.74.17ff.), a fabulous episode takes place in which Arjuna, dismounting from his chariot, holds off the entire Kaurava army so that Krishna may unyoke the tired horses for a brief respite (VII.74.36ff.). Arjuna also shoots water from the ground for the horses to drink, creating a lake and a house (stable) of arrows (VII.74.56f.).[27] This episode serves to heighten the suspense by delaying Arjuna's advance; but even more important is its illustration, once again, of Arjuna's unbelievable skills, particularly his archery:

> Like Tvashtar,[28] the son of Prtha, performer of marvelous actions, made a marvelous house of arrows, with crossbeams of arrows, pillars of arrows, and a covering of arrows. [VII.74.57][29]

Afterward, the mad rush toward Jayadratha continues, and Arjuna seems even more formidable than before. Earlier it was said that "there was not one at all . . . who abandoned the battle out of fear" (VII.70.34). Now, however, the Kaurava army is described as "falling apart, as if drowning . . . out of fear" (VII.76.1)—although it rallies in the next stanza. Arjuna's onrush is portrayed as a race against time, as the audience is reminded that the sun is moving westward (VII.75.28).

Arjuna's next major encounter is with Duryodhana. Krishna must now urge Arjuna on with a reminder of Duryodhana's deceit in taking the kingdom; in his response, Arjuna recalls the insult to Draupadi at the dice game (VII.77.1ff.). Perhaps these reminders are intended to draw attention to the fact that in this encounter too Duryodhana is resorting to a trick, which, while not illegal, is certainly out of the ordinary: Drona has tied on Duryodhana's armor in a special way, so that it is all but impenetrable (VII.78.11ff.).[30] That Arjuna triumphs only by fabulous skill (combined with rage) is greatly stressed with regard to this encounter (VII.78.26ff.).

After more combat and a certain number of delaying tactics (including description of the various battle standards [VII.80]), the scene shifts to an unsuccessful attempt by Yudhishthira to counter Drona (VII.81). Again, more combats follow, including that in which the *rakshasa* Alambusa is killed by Bhima's *rakshasa* son, Ghatotkacha (VII.84), and another of Drona against the Vrshni Satyaki and others (VII.85.1ff.). Just at this moment, Krishna's conch, Panchajanya, is heard by Yudhishthira who, assuming that it is a call for help, and declaring that he cannot live without Arjuna, dispatches Satyaki to defend him (VII.85.35ff.). Yudhishthira's fearful words to Satyaki cast new light on the situation developed up to this point:

> I do not grieve for Dasharha [Krishna], protector of the world, the Lord. He is indeed able to conquer in battle even the three worlds together, my dear—I tell you this truly, O tiger among men—how much more so these very weak forces of Dhrtarashtra's son. But Arjuna, O Vrshni, oppressed by many in battle, might lose his life. Therefore, I feel faint. [VII.85.86–88]

Yudhishthira's explanation of his distress is the first reminder during the *aristeia* of the fact that Arjuna is actually quite human, and could be killed. In the sentences that follow, Yudhishthira emphasizes Arjuna's bravery rather than his strength.

Not wishing to abandon Yudhishthira, whom he has promised Arjuna to guard (since Drona has vowed to capture Yudhishthira),[31] Satyaki counters Yudhishthira's fears with praise of Arjuna's pure heroism:

"Consider the destiny, perfection in weapons, *yoga*, and also impatience in battle, perfected knowledge, and likewise compassion of your brother" (VII.86.33).[32] Thus a dialectic is set up.

Satyaki had been Arjuna's archery pupil (II.4.29, etc.), and his behavior is Arjuna-like: when he decides to set out, he avoids Drona just as Arjuna had (VII.88.27). In fact, Satyaki's accomplishments in the ensuing battle are shown to be recapitulations of Arjuna's feats, as Satyaki says to his charioteer:

> We are mere instruments here, O charioteer. Our enemies have [already] been burned by Keshava and Phalguna. Let us now slay those killed by that bull among men, born of the self of the lord of gods. [VII.94.2]

Satyaki, comparing his opponents to grass consumed by a fire (VII.95.7), follows the path of dead bodies left by Arjuna (VII.95.8). He thinks that Arjuna is near, because he hears Gandiva's noise (VII.95.9). Meanwhile, the scene shifts again to Yudhishthira, who once more expresses fear that Arjuna is in mortal danger or dead (VII.102), because he *cannot* hear Gandiva (VII.102.6). Another heroic description of Arjuna (VII.102.35–36, quoted on pp. 31–32, above) is interwoven with Yudhishthira's lament. As will be apparent, the contrasts displayed in the Abhimanyu sequence are impressive, drawing the audience back again and again to the dialectic of Arjuna's humanity as opposed to his heroism. Yudhishthira also expresses fear that Satyaki has been killed (VII.102.39).

The fighting style of Bhima, now dispatched into the Kaurava formation by Yudhishthira, is in marked contrast to Arjuna's and Satyaki's. A brief excerpt describing Bhima's actions has been quoted above; another follows, which shows how differently Bhima deals with Drona than Arjuna did:

> But the teacher, thinking, "Bhima will reverence me as Phalguna did," said to Wolf-Belly: "O Bhimasena, one of great strength, you cannot enter the enemy's division without having defeated me in battle in the midst of the enemy. Even though that younger brother of yours, Krishna [Arjuna; see Appendix], entered with my consent, you will not, sir, be able to enter the army." But then fearless Bhima, having heard that speech of the teacher, angered, hissing,

> with copper-red eyes, declared to Drona: "O relative of brahmins, Arjuna, hard to assail, entered the battlefield *without* your consent, even as he would enter the forces of Shakra. I am not, O Drona, compassionate Arjuna, by whom you are honored with the highest reverence. I am Bhimasena, your adversary! 'You are our father, our teacher, likewise our relative, and we are your sons': thus we all think, continually bowing to your honor. Speaking to us today, you will see that to be reversed. If you think of yourself as our enemy, let it be so now! I, this Bhima, will act towards you as befits an enemy!" Then, having brandished his club, like the destroying staff of Time, he cast it at Drona. . . . He [Drona] jumped down from his chariot. He then crushed Drona's vehicle, with horses, charioteer, and standard, and destroyed his many soldiers powerfully, as wind [destroys] trees. [VII.102.79–88]

After achieving some success, Bhima sights Arjuna, also fighting, and roars with joy; Arjuna and Krishna answer him with Bhima-like roars (VII.103.25ff.). Yudhishthira, hearing the noise, rejoices, and lists again the heroic feats of Arjuna. One is, however, reminded of the difference between Bhima and Arjuna a few lines later, when it is stated that after a fight in which Bhima unseated Karna, as warriors shouted and conches were blown:

> The son of Prtha [here, Arjuna] discharged Gandiva and Krishna sounded his conch. Drowning out that noise, the sound of Bhima roaring was heard all through the armies. [VII.104.31–32]

Still more combats follow, of which the most interesting is the continuation of that between Bhima and Karna. The issue of oaths is raised again here. At one decisive moment, it is stated, Karna did not kill the unarmed Bhima because of a promise he had made to Kunti (VII.114.67).[33] Certain manuscripts (not the critical text) juxtapose with Karna's action in sparing Bhima the statement that Bhima was also considerate of oaths: he spared Karna's life so as to leave Karna for Arjuna, who had sworn to kill him (Poona Edition, VII, 910*, lines 2ff.). But Bhima is generally not so sensitive to matters of order and chivalry; compared to Arjuna's, his vows are much more violent in character.[34]

Now the situation is restated in the form of a lament by Arjuna, which emphasizes the burden of heroism (through the example of Satyaki), even as it creates cliff-hanging suspense:

> . . . . And the sun is sinking. . . . I trust that Satyaki, of true valor [*satyavikramah*][35] and great power, bull among the Shini people, having crossed the ocean, would not [now] come upon a puddle and despair. . . . I consider it negligence on the part of King Dharma that having cast off fear of the preceptor, he sends Satyaki forth. Drona constantly strives to capture King Dharma, as a flying eagle [strives to capture] prey. I hope the king will be safe! [VII.116.31, 33, 35–36]

An impossible single combat is described in the words of Arjuna, Krishna, and Samjaya: Satyaki is tired; Bhurishravas, his current opponent, is not. The two fight with various weapons, and finally wrestle (VII.117.19ff.).[36] Bhurishravas wins. He drags Satyaki by the hair, strikes Satyaki's chest with his foot, and is about to cut off his head (VII.117.53).

Krishna, in his traditional charioteer's role, incites Arjuna with descriptions of this conflict as it progresses, finally stating:

> See the tiger among Vrshnis and Andhakas, your pupil, O great-armed one, not inferior to you in archery, fallen under the power of the son of Somadatta [Bhurishravas]. Valor is no real thing [*asatyah*], O son of Prtha, if Bhurishravas outdoes the truly valiant [*satyavikramam*] Vrshni, Satyaki, in battle. [VII.117.55–56]

There is some suggestion in these lines that *dharma*, or truth (*satya*), its counterpart, is being threatened here in the person of Satyaki:[37] the truth of his valor, which should be the key to its effectiveness,[38] threatens to malfunction. Thus are some of the issues represented by Arjuna's vulnerable oath reduplicated in Satyaki's plight. As a hero, Arjuna must protect Satyaki; yet an impasse of *dharma* has been created. If Arjuna acts to save Satyaki, as Krishna is encouraging implicitly, he will be going against the accepted rules of single combat, which state that one should not attack a warrior who is already engaged against another.[39] But if Arjuna does not act, *dharma* will be threatened even more severely. It has been stated above (chap. IIA1) that impasses of *dharma* are typical of the human condition. Here Arjuna responds as "heroically" as possible, as he was told to do in the *Gita*; but his action, if necessary, is also illegal. As if to emphasize the illegality, the epic composers give a gruesome twist to the act: Arjuna shoots off Bhurishravas's arm (VII.117.62). In case there is any doubt as to whether or not Arjuna is aware of the illegality of his deed (in other words, whether the deed is really immoral or simply amoral), the epic recounts Bhurishravas's rebuke against Arjuna, and a certain amount of self-defense on Arjuna's part: Arjuna recognizes the moral conflict, at least after the fact. Bhurishravas says in part:

> Was this weapon taught to you by noble Indra, embodied, or by Rudra [Shiva], O son of Prtha, or by Drona or Krpa? Surely you, who are superior to others in the world, know your own *dharma*. How were you able to strike one not fighting [with you] in battle? Those who are wise [who know the rules] do not strike one who is heedless or frightened or deprived of his chariot or beseeching or in trouble. [VII.118.6–8]

Bhurishravas concludes that Arjuna must have learned his behavior from the Vrshnis, that is, from Krishna (VII.118.13ff.). At first Arjuna does not respond,[40] but when the Kauravas continue to censure him, he defends his own heroism by suddenly citing a great vow (*mahavrata*) of his not mentioned previously, and apparently invented by the epic composers for the occasion: "No one of my men shall be killed within the range of my arrows" (VII.118.23). Arjuna goes on to say:

> Not discerning *dharma*, it is inappropriate to censure another. That I in battle cut off the arm of one wielding a weapon, intending to slay the Vrshni hero, was an uncensurable duty. [VII.118.24–25]

Yet Arjuna never answers Bhurishravas's objections with real success; rather, his words make apparent the impasse of *dharma* created by the incompatibility between rules of battle such as those Bhurishravas has cited and the rule that lies implicitly behind Arjuna's own self-defense: "The gods with Agni at their head would bring bad fortune to him who, having abandoned his comrades, should come home safe" (VI.73.28).

Finally, an additional justification offered by Arjuna emphasizes, at this crucial moment, a point that has already been raised by the epic, but which now assumes major importance:

> What virtuous person [*dharmikah*] indeed . . . would honor[41] the killing of Abhimanyu, with weapon cast down, a child, deprived of his chariot, deprived of his armor? [VII.118.26]

Here Arjuna implies that his illegal attack against Bhurishravas was in response to the earlier illegal slaying of Abhimanyu: two wrongs make a right.[42] Such justification will be appealed to again in many forms throughout the epic, whenever either side commits an illegal action (see chap. IIA3). With regard to Abhimanyu's slaying, the additional argument that he was killed by many warriors who had banded together against him while he fought alone will generally be included.

As if to undermine Arjuna's self-defense, however, Satyaki now commits an act that cannot be defended either in terms of the rules of battle (no matter how greatly stretched) or by the impasse of the moment: he kills Bhurishravas who, having decided that now his only recourse is to fast to death,[43] is sitting still in yogic meditation (VII.118.36). Satyaki justifies his act by referring to Abhimanyu's murder (VII.118.43). He then cites a vow of his own, not mentioned previously:

> I promised in some moment of agitation that any enemy alive who, having crushed me in battle, should strike me in anger with his foot would be killed by me, even if he had taken a vow of asceticism. [VII.118.44]

No one approves Satyaki's defense (the celestials are busy applauding Bhurishravas [VII.118.38f.]), but no one objects very vigorously. Samjaya relates to Dhrtarashtra the complete story of Satyaki's vow, and praises the Vrshni heroes in the highest terms, with reference to their honesty as well as their prowess (VII.119). And so the dialectic continues with regard to Satyaki, here Arjuna's double.

The concluding treatment of the hero-human dialectic in the Abhimanyu sequence again revolves around Arjuna, as he prepares to close in for the killing of Jayadratha. The central issue is Arjuna's oath. In VII.120 Duryodhana is seen inciting Karna with the statement that the sun is about to set:

> If the King of Sind is protected until sunset, the son of Kunti, his vow falsified, will enter fire. And if the earth were without Arjuna for even a moment, O respectful one, his brothers, with their followers, could not endure living. When the Pandavas are destroyed, we will enjoy this earth, O Karna, with its hills, woods, and forests, with that thorn removed. [VII.120.13–15]

In other words, Arjuna will have failed to perform his heroic duty: to protect the world. A major battle follows, in which Arjuna is compared to all conceivable natural phenomena; included is outstanding sun imagery (the sun now being a focal point): "All creatures were unable to look at the Pandava, [who was] like the midday sun burning in the sky" (VII.121.2). Finally, Arjuna kills Jayadratha's charioteer, and shoots down his standard. Yet suddenly it is stated again that the sun will go down imminently: "At the very moment when the sun was setting . . . " (VII.121.15). And so one is reminded of Arjuna's mortality in the midst of his heroic exploit, and up to the moment before he finally succeeds.

A few manuscripts include a version of the killing of Jayadratha that makes the hero-human dialectic tremendously more impressive than it is in the critical text (Poona Edition, VII, Appendix I, no. 16).[44] Krishna speaks up, telling Arjuna that in order to kill Jayadratha, he will have to kill the six warriors who are protecting that hero. The implication is that such a feat would be impossible in the remaining time. Krishna, however, offers help:

> I will now employ *yoga* for covering the sun. That King of Sind alone will see it clearly and think: "It has set." Joyful on account of your destruction, that ill-behaved one, desirous of life, will not protect himself in any way, O lord. You must strike at his weak point, O best of Kurus. Thinking, "The sun has set," he will not be paying attention. [VII, Appendix I, no. 16, lines 5–10][45]

Krishna performs this trick and, having covered the sun, incites Arjuna. A few stanzas later, Arjuna kills Jayadratha with an especially fierce arrow (VII.121.30ff.). Even the critical text here includes Krishna's advice to Arjuna on how to avoid certain death as the result of a curse that has been placed by Jayadratha's father, Vrddhakshatra, upon the future slayer of his son—advice that Arjuna is able to follow due to his superior shooting ability. The curse states that the head of anyone who causes Jayadratha's head to fall in battle will burst into a hundred pieces. Arjuna is able to shoot the head onto the lap of Vrddhakshatra himself as he sits far away performing religious devotions. Not noticing, Vrddhakshatra stands up; so it is he who drops his own son's head (VII.121.17ff.).

After the killing of Jayadratha, the critical text brings the hero-human dialectic to a close for the Abhimanyu sequence with repeated emphasis on Arjuna's heroic qualities. Krishna praises him for keeping his vow, with the statement:

> Heroism and strength similar to Rudra's, Shakra's, and Death's are yours. No one at all would be able to display in battle such prowess as you, alone, the enemy burner, have displayed today. Even so will I glorify you, with conquered and killed enemies, still more when evil Karna is killed, together with his posterity. [VII.123.25–26]

Duryodhana too feels at this point that "No fighter equal to Arjuna is found on earth. Neither Drona nor Radheya [Karna][46] nor Ashvatthaman nor Krpa is strong enough to stand in the face of that one when he is angered" (VII.125.1–2).

It is clear, nonetheless, that the Abhimanyu sequence has portrayed Arjuna's human side along with his heroism. Arjuna has responded to the human emotion of grief with a superhuman *aristeia*, but has encountered human weaknesses along the way. In particular, two humanizing aspects of Arjuna's heroic activity have emerged. First, Arjuna has had to face the fact that his heroic attempt could fail and he might be killed; according to certain versions, he has been forced to resort to Krishna's superhuman abilities to make up for his own human weakness. (Note the contrast between the pure heroic friendship of the Khandava episode and the relationship of human and helper depicted here.) Second, Arjuna has had to face an impasse of *dharma* and make and justify a choice that is not necessarily the right one; his heroism has in no way helped him circumvent this very human situation. It is this latter issue that will become central in the next chapter of this study.

Notes

1. In fact, Jayadratha caused Abhimanyu's death only indirectly by preventing other pro-Pandava warriors from following him into the Kaurava formation, which he had penetrated (VII.41.6ff.). An unnamed son of Duhshasana actually killed Abhimanyu with a club (VII.48.12), and generally six warriors, Drona, Krpa, Karna, Ashvatthaman, Brhadbala, and Krtavarman (VII.45.19, etc.), are blamed for conspiring together to kill the youth. Jayadratha had attempted earlier to seize Draupadi in the forest (see chap. IB). That he was a "share" of Arjuna is reported at V.56.15.
2. Included are the following subsections: "Abhimanyuvadha" ("Killing of Abhimanyu"), "Pratijna" ("Oath"), and "Jayadrathavadha" ("Killing of Jayadratha").

3. *Iliad* XVI ff.
4. See *The Sháhnáma of Firdausí*, trans. Arthur George Warner and Edmond Warner, II (London: Kegan Paul, Trench, Trübner and Co., 1906), 119ff.
5. Gilgamesh's humanization through the loss of Enkidu (see chap. IIA1) provides another parallel, yet the setting is rather different, and Gilgamesh a rather different type of hero from Achilles, Rustam, or Arjuna, a wisdom hero.
6. See VII.50.37–40: "A tender youth, always a hero, accustomed to a very fine bed, now the best of protectors lies on the ground like one without a protector. He whom, in repose, the best of women attended formerly, today, with scattered limbs, is attended by inauspicious jackals. He who, sleeping, was awakened formerly by *sutas*, *magadhas*, and *bandins* [types of bards], now today wild beasts awaken with unnatural noises. That beautiful face of his was used to the shade of umbrellas. Now today dust will cover it in battle." Cf. Subhadra's words of VII.55.6ff.
7. The death of "children" in battle is part of the *Mahabharata*'s antiwar statement; see, e.g., XI.20.32, where, besides Abhimanyu, Uttara (Virata's son, the brother of Uttarā), Sudakshina, and Duryodhana's son, Lakshmana, are mourned as children killed in battle. None of these figures, however, gets attention nearly so great as that paid to Abhimanyu; nor is the grief of their fathers dwelt upon at all. Note that Lakshmana is killed by Abhimanyu himself (VII.45.17; see v. 18 for Duryodhana's reaction of anger, mentioned briefly). Another youth killed in the war is Vrshasena, Karna's son, who dies, shot by Arjuna, at VIII.62.60f. Karna's reaction is passed over quickly in VIII.62.62 and VIII.63.1
8. Arjuna is not, of course, young in the same sense as Abhimanyu: the epic's single clue as to his age at the time of the war states, during the thirteenth year of exile, that he has owned Gandiva for sixty-five years (presumably since the time of the Khandava Forest burning) (IV.38.41). Still, he is called "youthful" formulaically throughout the epic; see, e.g., all three passages describing his appearance quoted on pp. 31–32. Indeed, the Pandavas, once grown up, do not really age further; the *Mahabharata* tends to ignore chronological detail unless essential to the story line, and the Pandavas retain that youth characteristic of heroes.
9. Some manuscripts insert a long passage in just such a genre into Book VII, soon after Abhimanyu's death; see Poona Edition, VII, Appendix I, no. 8, lines 329ff. The passage, which recounts the lives of sixteen great kings—who nevertheless had to die ultimately—is spoken by Vyasa, quoting the seer Narada, in an attempt to comfort Yudhishthira.
10. Note that even in VII.54f., where Krishna consoles Subhadra, Draupadi, and Uttarā, Uttarā's pregnancy is not mentioned.
11. Nagy, *Achaeans*, pp. 26ff.
12. Cf. Herakles' killing of his children by Megara, in a fit of madness set upon him by Hera; see, especially, Apollodorus II.4.12: he received the name "Herakles" only after this act.
13. Cf. the death of Connla at the hand of his father, Cuchulainn; see Kinsella, pp. 39ff.
14. On humanizing details in and around Achilles' *aristeia*, over and above the Skamandros episode, see Schein, chap. 5. That the Indian case is far more explicit, far less subtle, will become apparent as the present chapter continues.

15. Refers to a number of contingents (many of which are Samshaptakas [see chap. IE]) rushing en masse against Arjuna, as listed in the preceding stanzas: the Abhishahas, Shurasenas, Shibis, Vasatis, Machellakas, Lalitthas, Kekayas, Madrakas, Narayana Gopalas (= Narayanas [see chap. IIIB2]) and Kambojas (VII.66.37f.).
16. As always, even in the midst of his wildest behavior in battle, Arjuna is preeminently the archer.
17. Reading *vyavadhanam* ("intervention") in place of *vyavasthanam*.
18. See E. Washburn Hopkins, "The Oath in Hindu Epic Literature," *Journal of the American Oriental Society* 52 (1932): 316–37. Specifically regarding the so-called act of truth (based on an ancient Indian "belief that Truth has a power which a person with the right qualifications can invoke to accomplish wonders or miracles" [p. 252]), see W. Norman Brown, "Duty as Truth in Ancient India," *Proceedings of the American Philosophical Society* 116 (1972): 252–68. In the *Mahabharata*, oaths take many forms, formal and informal, and are referred to by a number of terms, which may be translated variously, e.g., *pratijna, satyavachana, vrata, samkalpa*; the verb *shap* is also used.
19. Outstandingly, the Samshaptakas. On Bhima's oaths, see below, n. 34. For some oaths of Yudhishthira (who in a sense has no need to take an oath, since he himself is "oath" personified), see chap. IB, n. 3, and chap. IIC.
20. Outside the Abhimanyu sequence, Arjuna takes oaths at II.68.32ff. (to kill Karna and others); VI.55.100 (to destroy the Kurus [that is, the Kauravas]); VI.102.67f. (to destroy the enemy); VII.12.7ff. (not to let Yudhishthira fall into the hands of Drona); VII.123.16f. (to kill Karna, Karna's son, and others); VIII.50.18ff. (to kill Karna or die himself). Elsewhere he reports permanent vows: VII.16.39 (not to turn back when summoned; this is reminiscent of Yudhishthira's vow reported in II.52.16 [see chap. IB, n. 3]) and VIII.49.9 and 61 (to kill anyone who would tell him to give up Gandiva). At IV.63.53 Yudhishthira, in connection with the episode mentioned in chap. IA in which his blood must be caught in a golden bowl, reports a vow made by Arjuna to the effect that he will kill anyone who wounds Yudhishthira outside of battle. Sometimes the fine line between taking oaths and boasting is bridged, so that, e.g., Arjuna's prewar statement that he will kill Bhishma (V.160.8ff.) is later called a "promise" or "oath" (*pratijnatam . . . parthena*) by Krishna who, however, seems mistaken about the place where the oath was taken (VI.103.35). Cf. also chap. IIC, especially n. 13. To take an oath is, perhaps, more typically Indra/Arjuna-like, to boast more typically Vayu/Bhima-like, but Arjuna and Bhima each do both.
21. The six are Karna, Bhurishravas, Ashvatthaman, Vrshasena, Krpa, and Shalya.
22. Somewhat cryptic, as Krishna has agreed not to fight, nor does he.
23. Because the end of VII.56 connects perfectly with the beginning of VII.58.
24. Here Yudhishthira uses the common epic simile of a boat with reference to Krishna: Krishna must act as a boat to allow the Pandavas to cross over their ocean of grief; this role he can fulfill specifically as a charioteer (VII.59.12f.).
25. In the course of the war, Arjuna himself has one outstanding near-death (meaning that the enemy soldiers think him dead), followed soon by a revival: VII.68.11ff.; see also VIII.38.30f.

26. Note Shiva's statement to Arjuna in III.163.45, where he offers Arjuna anything except immortality. The immortality of the gods is, on the other hand, much stressed (thence the entire notion of the nectar [*amrta*; literally, "immortality"] of the gods [see chap. IC, n. 13]); although, as Macdonell points out (p. 17): "According to the post-Vedic view their immortality was only relative, being limited to a cosmic age" (this except, of course, for the great divinities of *bhakti* [see Introduction]).
27. This ability to shoot water from the ground recalls Arjuna's heroic connection with fertility, discussed in chap. IB. Arjuna had performed a similar feat earlier, at VI.116.1 (see chap. IIA3).
28. The divine artificer.
29. See Poona Edition, VII, 538*, for an even more fabulous description of Arjuna's creation.
30. That, however, Abhimanyu was wearing similarly tied armor was stated at VII.47.27.
31. Satyaki's promise to guard Yudhishthira: VII.60.26ff. Drona's vow to capture Yudhishthira: VII.11.20ff. Note the interlocking vows. The teacher-pupil relationship between Arjuna and Satyaki further complicates matters here.
32. Note, however, the quality of compassion mentioned here, moving beyond heroism in the direction of human feeling.
33. On this promise made by Karna, see chap. IA, n. 64, and chap. IIA3.
34. Bhima's two major vows are both made during the dice game: to drink Duhshasana's blood (II.61.45f. and II.68.21) and to break Duryodhana's thigh with a club (II.63.14). Both vows are kept (VIII.61.6ff. [but denied in XI.14.14f.] and IX.57.43f. [for which, see chap. IIA3]). Note, however, that both are made in anger and neither is sworn to formally, with the invocation of truth or world order, as are some of Arjuna's oaths; rather, the stake is, in all cases, Bhima's attainment of heaven. Yet the repetition of the first vow is combined with a truth vow to kill the sons of Dhrtarashtra (II.68.22). In fact, Bhima is responsible for the deaths of almost all of these.
35. The formula *satyavikrama* could also mean "whose valor is truth" (see chap. IA, especially n. 31).
36. Cf. Arjuna's fight with the mountain man (see chap. ID).
37. The element *satya* in Satyaki's name lends itself to punning, but also seems to have real significance for the epic composers. Satyaki's combination of goodness and evil (see also chap. IIC) is striking. Note that he is the only Vrshni who fights actively on the Pandava side.
38. W. Norman Brown, pp. 259ff.
39. See VI.1.31 (quoted in chap. IIA3, n. 1), etc.
40. Some manuscripts do include a defense here, which seems to correlate directly with the *Gita* teaching, and which is also found elsewhere in the epic (see, especially, chap. IIA3): *kshatriya* duty; for this passage, see Poona Edition, VII, Appendix I, no. 13, lines 7ff.
41. Reading *nu* instead of *na*.

42. In fact, the killing of Abhimanyu when he was deprived of his chariot was in opposition to one of the very rules invoked by Bhurishravas on the list quoted on p. 147.
43. A not uncommon epic expedient, the *praya* ("going forth") vow (see further, chaps. IIA3, IIB, IIIC).
44. Found mainly in Bengali and Devanagari manuscripts.
45. Cf. God's act of making the sun and moon stand still in Joshua 10:12f.; borrowed by the *Song of Roland, laisses* 179f. Many more parallels may be discovered in Thompson's *Motif-Index*, under such headings as D2146.1, "Day controlled by magic"; D2147.1, "Cloud magically made to cover sun"; etc.
46. Metronymic with reference to the charioteer's wife who raised him after Kunti abandoned him (see chap. IA, etc.).

IIA3. VICTORY BY TRICKERY, I

One of the most crucial controversies of *Mahabharata* scholarship centers upon the observation that the Pandavas win the Kurukshetra War by trickery and deceit. In fact, all their ultimately effective actions in the war are opposed to the Indian rules of warrior chivalry reiterated in the epic, which both sides have accepted before the war begins (VI.1.28–32),[1] if not to more universal moral imperatives. That most of these acts are construed as immoral by the epic poets may be inferred from the fact that they are censured strictly by various characters, including the narrator, Samjaya (compare the words of the victim, Bhurishravas, quoted on p. 147, above). The Pandavas themselves seem to be aware that their behavior is questionable in certain cases, although they justify it in various ways, often displaying a certain moral innocence or inconsistency. The most striking examples of their trickery entail deliberate infringement of the previously accepted rules, not just mistaken behavior due to the mass confusion on the battlefield. With regard to the subject of this study, one must note that Arjuna himself is the central agent in many of these actions,[2] and that his decisive victories in battle may be reduced uniformly to the perpetration of improper acts. It is also noteworthy that in almost all cases, deceit on the part of the Pandavas is instigated by Arjuna's friend and helper, Krishna.

One example of this type of behavior, the illegal shooting of Bhurishravas, has been discussed in the preceding chapter of this study, where it was shown that the Abhimanyu sequence draws attention to grief, mortality, and moral ambiguity as aspects of Arjuna's human condition. That sequence, however, concludes on a note of praise for Arjuna's heroism (at least in the critical version): Arjuna has been no more decisively humanized than many another epic hero who has had his heroism brought into question at some point in his career.[3] The episodes to be discussed in the following pages emphasize many times one part of the message of the Abhimanyu sequence: Arjuna's involvement in the ambiguity of human morality. It is by such an accumulation of examples that the idea of Arjuna's humanity is conveyed, even as his heroism continues to be praised.

Permutations: The Cases of Bhishma, (Bhurishravas), Drona, Karna, and Duryodhana

It will first be necessary to review briefly the major cases of trickery or deceit perpetrated by the Pandavas during the Kurukshetra War, simply noting the one that has already been discussed in relation to the Abhimanyu sequence, and treating the others in more detail. Apart from the Abhimanyu sequence, the deceitful killings of the war are primarily those of extremely important Kaurava leaders: the first three Kaurava generals, Bhishma, Drona, and Karna. In addition, the killing of Duryodhana by Bhima must be considered.

The first major Pandava victory by deceit is the victory over Bhishma, whom Arjuna kills by the expedient of shooting from behind Shikhandin, breaking the rule against assailing one who is already engaged in battle with someone else (VI.1.31, quoted in n. 1 of this chapter). Arjuna has sworn earlier that he will kill Bhishma (V.160.8ff.), but then seems unable to do so without deceit. Bhishma's vulnerability is, meanwhile, entirely the product of his own absolute adherence to an oath: specifically, an oath never to do battle against a woman (or "a former woman, one with the name of a woman, [or] an apparent woman") (V.193.63–64). The issue of deceitfulness is brought out especially clearly here, as Bhishma himself associates this personal taboo with the standard rules of battle (with which it coalesces neatly), which he recites, in his own version, in a fairly exhaustive form:

> Battle with one who has thrown down his weapon, one who has fallen down, one with loosened armor or [fallen] standard, or one running, or frightened, or one saying "I am yours," a woman or one

> who bears a woman's name, or one who is maimed, one who has only one son, or one with no children, or one who is unpleasant to look at does not please me. (VI.103.72–73)

Bhishma makes this statement in the course of a conversation with Yudhishthira, who has gone specifically to sound out this seemingly invincible elder on how he might be defeated. He goes on to remind Yudhishthira:

> O King, your honor knows all, exactly as it happened, regarding this son of Drupada who is a great charioteer in your army, Shikhandin, desirous of battle, and a hero victorious in battle, and who was a woman formerly and afterward became a male. Let the hero Arjuna, having placed Shikhandin before him in battle, run toward me swiftly, armored, with arrows. Since that one has an inauspicious standard, and especially because [he was] formerly a woman, I in no way wish to strike that one, who is grasping his arrows. Obtaining that opening, let the Pandava, Dhanamjaya, kill me quickly, with arrows from all sides, O bull among the descendants of Bharata. [VI.103.75–79]

That is, in the baroque cast of characters of the Kurukshetra War there is one who was formerly a woman but is now a man, the Panchala Shikhandin.[4] Bhishma will not fight him/her, so the most effective strategy for defeating Bhishma must be based on sending Shikhandin against him, as a decoy. Naturally, the fact that Bhishma has given permission for the use of this tactic against him justifies it somewhat; yet the epic still holds it against Arjuna (see below).

An even more basic moral issue raised in the course of the episode is the question of fighting against an elder at all, an issue that was touched upon in the discussion of the *Gita* episode in chapter IIA1, above. Arjuna's words to Krishna summarize this issue as follows:

> How, O Madhava [Krishna], will I fight in battle with the Grandfather, venerable, senior in the family, wise, intelligent? O Vāsudeva, that high-minded, noble one was soiled by me, playing in my childhood, with dirt-smeared limbs. That father of my noble father, Pandu, whose lap indeed I climbed into as a child and called [him] "Daddy," O Gadagraja [Krishna], who spoke to me thus in my childhood: "I am not your daddy. I am your father's daddy, O descendant of Bharata"—how shall he be slain by me? Let my army

> be slain! I will not fight that noble one. Let victory or death be mine! But what is your opinion, O Krishna? [VI.103.85–89]

Certainly the very human hesitation evidenced here by Arjuna is the same as that which has already led Krishna twice to jump out of the chariot and, in defiance of his promise not to fight, rush toward Bhishma with the intention of killing him if Arjuna will not (see chap. IIA1). Both times, Arjuna managed to stop Krishna, to prevent him from breaking his promise, and then swore to proceed more firmly against Bhishma himself. (To stir up Arjuna and exact such an oath from him was undoubtedly Krishna's intent.) But it is only late in VI.103 that Krishna manages to provide a threefold justification for a fight against Bhishma which, in conjunction with Bhishma's instructions, seems to inspire Arjuna sufficiently.

Krishna first reminds Arjuna that it is his duty as a *kshatriya* to fight. Second, he reminds Arjuna that the overthrow of Bhishma has been ordained by fate. Third, Krishna concludes with a legal statement, which is actually a sharpening of his first argument, *kshatriyadharma*, at the end of which he summarizes:

> . . . Hear these words of mine, as were spoken formerly by wise Brhaspati[5] to Shakra: "O Shakra, one should kill even an elder, even one endowed with virtues, who has summoned one with bowstring drawn, prepared to kill." This stands as the perpetual *dharma* of *kshatriyas*, O Dhanamjaya. It is necessary that men without ill will fight and protect and sacrifice. [VI.103.94–96]

Although Arjuna gives in to Krishna's advice here, he later bypasses a fight with Drona on the grounds of not wishing to fight an elder (see chap. IIA2). That is, Arjuna never quite gets used to fighting such opponents, and continues to avoid elders and teachers in battle. It seems that this sort of hesitation contributes to Arjuna's unforeseen inability to win in fair combat.

In fact, Arjuna's response to the arguments offered by Krishna, at the end of VI.103, implies that he will let Shikhandin accomplish the killing of Bhishma, while he himself merely holds off other warriors: "I will restrain the other great archers with arrows. Let Shikhandin, the best of fighters, assail Bhishma" (VI.103.99). Such an arrangement would correspond to what one scholar has suggested may have been part of an early Bhishma story cycle, in which Shikhandin alone fought Bhishma.[6] Bhishma is considered to be Shikhandin's "share" in battle (V.56.12);[7] though compare V.186.19–20, where it is said that Arjuna is destined to kill him. In a version where Shikhandin killed Bhishma, almost all the moral conflicts would be avoided: Shikhandin has every right to attack Bhishma, since he has been Bhishma's sworn enemy from birth.[8] Instead, the dominant version of the killing of Bhishma in the extant text of the epic stresses both the fact that it is Arjuna who is shooting his elder and that he is doing so illegally, as Bhishma complains that the arrows hitting him are surely too strong to be Shikhandin's (VI.114.55ff.).

That this action was censured immediately is implied by the generalized statement, "and others derided kshatriyahood" (VI.114.110). Later passages leave no doubt that it was considered highly unfair; it is brought up often by characters who wish to defame the Pandavas.[9] As for Krishna's role, one must concede that he does not suggest this particular deceit; but he encourages both Yudhishthira and Arjuna to do what they have to, to fight this enemy, insisting that they not give up the battle.[10]

Having already discussed the main occasion of illegal fighting in the Abhimanyu sequence, it is necessary only to note again that Arjuna (with his double, Satyaki) is the major figure here. Krishna's role, meanwhile, is quite complex. At first he simply urges Arjuna to act, when Satyaki is in trouble; he does not tell Arjuna exactly what to do. But later the dying Bhurishravas says that Arjuna's action must have been based on Krishna's counsel (since Arjuna would never have done such a thing on his own) and blames the Vrshnis for the treacherous behavior that has entered the warriors' repertoire.[11] After the Bhurishravas shooting, Arjuna's attitude may be discerned as he justifies the act and refuses to admit his guilt. Nonetheless, others have censured the act already,[12] and soon include it on lists of Arjuna's immoral deeds. The censure, however, is mainly from the Kaurava side.

The Pandava brothers do not themselves admit any guilt until the Drona killing, which takes place as follows. Just before the war, Yudhishthira had honored his elders and asked their advice (VI.41).[13] Among other things, he had asked Drona how he might kill him in battle. (Bhishma had been asked the same question at this time, but did not give his answer until later.) Drona's answer was:

> I see no enemy, my dear, who could kill me, standing firm in battle, fighting, greatly agitated, showering a stream of arrow showers, except, O king, that one could kill me in battle with warriors [when I had] resorted to the *praya* vow [to fast to death], with weapon cast down, unconscious; I tell you this truly. And I would abandon my weapon in battle, having heard a very unpleasant thing from a credible man; truly I say this to you. [VI.41.59–61]

When, thus, Krishna suggests the contrivance of telling Drona that his son Ashvatthaman has been slain in battle, in order to make Drona give up the fight, it is obvious that this suggestion is modeled directly on Drona's earlier advice. Arjuna, however, disapproves immediately; the others approve, but Yudhishthira does so only with great reluctance (VII.164.70). The next scene, VII.164.71ff., is famous: Bhima kills an elephant named Ashvatthaman, and proclaims that Ashvatthaman has been killed. Drona is horrified at first, but then remembers that his son is invincible. As Drona continues to fight, however, certain celestial seers come and inform him that his time of death has arrived. They tell him he is fighting unfairly, since his deeds are too cruel for a brahmin. Drona, having received this warning on top of Bhima's words, is miserable. He now decides that he must ask Yudhishthira whether Ashvatthaman is really dead. Drona is certain that Yudhishthira would never tell a lie, "even for the sake of lordship of the three worlds" (VII.164.95). Urged on by Krishna and Bhima, Yudhishthira now repeats that Ashvatthaman has been killed, indistinctly muttering "the elephant" at the end of his statement (VII.164.106).[14]

That Yudhishthira's lie is considered censurable (and humanizing) by the epic poets is indicated by the fact that they have Samjaya relate here that Yudhishthira's chariot, which formerly drove above the ground, sank to the earth from this moment onward (VII.164.107). Just then, however, Dhrshtadyumna rides against Drona, and a violent battle takes the interest of the audience away from moral issues (VII.164.111ff.). Yet reminders appear from time to time in such statements as "He [Drona] set out to cast off his life by fair fighting" (VII.165.13)—which, of course, Bhima does not permit when he repeats the lie about Ashvatthaman (VII.165.32). It is also stated directly, several times, that the act was wrong.[15]

The role of Dhrshtadyumna in the slaying of Drona is much like that of Satyaki in Bhurishravas's slaying: that is, he kills one who has already given up his life through *yoga* (VII.165.33ff.). Fighting in the coarsest Vayu/Bhima style, Dhrshtadyumna is evidently oblivious of any moral dilemma: he grabs Drona's head, cuts it off, and, "when the son of Bharadvaja [Drona] had been struck down, he [Dhrshtadyumna], with great joy, gave a roar like a lion's roar, waving his sword in challenge" (VII.165.48). He then throws the head in front of the opposing army, which is forced by this gesture to flee in fright (VII.165.54f.). As the Kauravas search for Drona's headless body, the Pandava army roars with joy and makes other victory noises (VII.165.61f.). As usual, the most noise is made by Bhima who, slapping his arms, makes the earth tremble and the enemy flee (VII.165.65f.).

In contrast, the humanizing ambiguity of Arjuna's reaction is portrayed clearly; in fact, this episode provides one of the best examples of contrast between Bhima and Arjuna. With others, Arjuna asks Dhrshtadyumna to take Drona alive, rather than slaying him (VII.165.51). Not only is his disapproval of the lie reiterated in Krpa's account of the incident to Ashvatthaman (VII.165.112), but later Arjuna is quoted as censuring it at some length (VII.167.25ff.). In particular, his speech proclaims the infamy of unrighteously slaying a teacher. (The word "teacher" [*guru*] is repeated many times in the speech.) Drona, Arjuna says, had trusted that Yudhishthira would not lie because "this Pandava is endowed with all *dharma*, and is my pupil" (VII.167.34). Arjuna also blames himself for having failed to intervene. Compare Yudhishthira who, having lied, does not look back before the job is done; and Bhima, who is adamantly in favor of the trick, even accusing Arjuna, after he expresses regret, of not fighting to the utmost of his ability (VII.168.13f.).

Although the episode of the killing of Drona has to do with the issue of fighting elders and, secondarily, fighting brahmins,[16] the lie is the dominant aspect of the story. As an example of Pandava deceit, the killing of Drona is a high point in the epic, in that Pandava admission of guilt (primarily Arjuna's) is found here for the first time; for this reason, it seems as though the earlier deceits have culminated here, or as though this incident may be considered the epic's typical case of trickery. In addition, this episode is the first in which Krishna's role as inciter is absolutely clear. Most important for the purpose of the present study, however, is the fact that this episode has much to say regarding Arjuna's humanity.

The next deceitful killing in the *Mahabharata* is that of Karna. Here again, Arjuna is found committing an unfair act without real self-examination, this time simply because Krishna has recommended it. In fact, this unfair act is more explicitly opposed to the rules of battle than any of the preceding unfair acts perpetrated by the Pandavas. One may conclude, therefore, that there is no linear moral development on Arjuna's part; for his moral sensitivity appears to have regressed since the Drona-slaying episode. As usual, the *Mahabharata* offers various versions, permutations: in this case, variations on Arjuna's involvement in deceitful action in battle, each making the same basic point.

The way has been prepared deceitfully for the deceitful killing of Karna at several points earlier in the epic. Karna, it is said, was born with earrings and armor, but he has been deprived of these by Indra's trickery, mentioned previously (chap. IA);[17] he has also been tricked into using the spear given to him by Indra in exchange for the earrings and armor (I.104.20; III.294.20ff.),[18] which he had been planning to save for use against Arjuna. This latter trick was perpetrated by Krishna, who sent the *rakshasa* Ghatotkacha against Karna, specifically with this end in mind (VII.157.11ff.);[19] Krishna also kept Arjuna out of Karna's way until the spear had been used (VII.122.31ff.; VII.148.31ff.). There is yet another stratagem aimed against Karna: Shalya, the maternal uncle of the Pandava twins, has been set up to treat Karna unfairly. At the time he went over to the Kaurava side, he promised Yudhishthira that, acting as Karna's charioteer, he would revile and discourage Karna in battle (V.8.25ff.); this he does at length in VIII.26ff. Note the reversal of the charioteer's usual role of encouragement.[20] In sum, the deceitful nature of Karna's slaying is greatly emphasized. Another story is also told (VIII.29.44ff.). Karna had pretended to be a brahmin so as to be able to study with Rama Jamadagnya, the noted hater of *kshatriya*s. One day, however, when Jamadagnya was asleep, Indra, disguised as a worm, had bored into Karna's thigh. This Karna had suffered stoically, so as not to awaken his teacher, but when, upon waking, Jamadagnya had seen the wound, he had realized that Karna must be a *kshatriya*, not a brahmin: only a *kshatriya* could have stood such pain without saying a word. He had then cursed Karna to forget the divine weapon that Jamadagnya had taught him, at his hour of greatest need.[21] To complete the picture of the web of circumstances ensnaring Karna: Karna has also been cursed by a brahmin to have the wheel of his chariot fall into a hole in battle (VIII.29.31; XII.2.23ff.), and has made a promise to his mother, Kunti, to avoid killing any of her other sons except, if possible, Arjuna (V.144.20ff.).

As might be expected, Arjuna makes a vow before proceeding against Karna. Here is an especially clear statement of the issue at hand, for the oath states that Arjuna will kill Karna or himself die. As when he repeated his oath to kill Jayadratha before sunset, Arjuna swears by truth, touching his weapons (he also swears by his brothers here) (VIII.50.18ff.). As in the Abhimanyu sequence, Arjuna's vow indicates that he will be in an ambiguous situation, for his life will depend upon his slaying Karna by any means: he will either have to win by heroic skill and/or power, or succumb to human status, either in death or in trickery. Arjuna, incited by Krishna, chooses the last alternative, killing Karna by shooting him while he is trying to lift the sunken wheel of his chariot, having asked for a brief respite (VIII.66.42ff., especially 59ff.).[22] In asking for the time out, Karna, lest there be any doubt, lists the rules upon which he is basing his request:

> O Arjuna, heroes do not strike in battle one whose hair is disheveled, one whose face is averted, a brahmin or one who is supplicating, one who has sought refuge, one with weapon cast down, nor one who has gotten into difficulty, one without arrows, with armor fallen off, nor with fallen or broken weapon. . . . And you are a hero, O son of Kunti. Therefore have patience for a moment. [VIII.66.62–63]

It is clear from the number of repetitions of these rules in the epic that Karna's request is justified, and Arjuna's denial of it illegal.[23]

The final unfair slaying perpetrated by the Pandavas in the Kurukshetra War is also performed in fulfillment of a vow; in this case, the vow governs the precise form of the action. Bhima swore during the dice game to break Duryodhana's thigh in battle;[24] this justifies his killing of Duryodhana by striking, unexpectedly, below the belt. Besides, Duryodhana had been cursed to die in this way by the seer Maitreya, for refusing to seek peace with the Pandavas (III.11.33f.).

The slaying of Duryodhana is the third major killing in Book IX (*Shalyaparvan*), the first being that of Shalya himself, the second that of Shakuni. The killing of Shalya, who has become the fourth Kaurava general, by Yudhishthira, explicitly without assistance, is entirely fair (IX.15f.).[25] Shalya is, thus, the first of the Kaurava generals to die by fair means. In fact, one may say, trickery is unnecessary because the war is really over after Karna's death; note Krpa's advocacy of peace in IX.3.9ff. Sahadeva kills Shakuni in another fair fight by shooting off his head (IX.27.57).[26]

The circumstances surrounding the death of Duryodhana are extremely strange. After seeing his generals defeated one by one, Duryodhana flees and hides in a lake, solidifying the water over himself by means of his (demonic) magic (*maya*) (IX.28.52).[27] Yudhishthira goes to the lake and, after mocking Duryodhana, convinces him to come out and fight (IX.30.15ff.). Ever the gambler (for which Krishna rebukes him in IX.32.1ff.), Yudhishthira promises at this late date that Duryodhana will be given back his kingdom if he wins in single combat with any weapon of his choice against any Pandava of his choice (IX.31.24f.). The peculiarity of Yudhishthira's offer is matched only by the peculiarity of Duryodhana's acceptance of it, in view of all the Pandava tricks he has seen; nevertheless, he agrees upon a club fight against Bhima.[28] For the epic story line, the main effect of this pact between Yudhishthira and Duryodhana is that it heightens the importance of the impending fight by making the outcome of the war once again uncertain. The pause that follows the making of the pact, for a long account of a pilgrimage undertaken by Krishna's older brother, Rama (Baladeva, not to be confused with Rama Dasharathi or Rama Jamadagnya), contributes to the suspense of this denouement of the war (IX.34ff.),[29] as does the fact that Duryodhana takes the lead in the early stages of his fight with Bhima.

Krishna first suggests the deceit that Bhima eventually uses to kill Duryodhana in a conversation with Arjuna; Arjuna signals the message to Bhima by slapping his own left thigh (IX.57). After Bhima has committed his unrighteous deed, he boasts and dances wildly, and touches Duryodhana's head with his foot (IX.58). Despite the fact that such behavior may not seem surprising in a warrior of Bhima's type, Yudhishthira feels it necessary to justify Bhima's action and his own implicit compliance, which he does in the following words:

> Considering that Bhimasena is extremely pained at heart . . . I disregarded this. Therefore, let the Pandava obtain his desire, right [*dharme*] or wrong [*adharme*], having killed that foolish, greedy one who had succumbed to desire. [IX.59.33–34]

How much more does the active participation of Arjuna, who must have known better, require justification.

Baladeva, arriving on the scene just in time to watch the unfairly won battle, is disgusted (IX.59.3ff.).[30] Trying to rush against Bhima and hold him back, he is prevented by Krishna, who justifies Bhima's action; but Baladeva clearly and volubly condemns it. So does Duryodhana, showing once again that there can be no more effective condemnation of Pandava misconduct than that uttered by its Kaurava victims. Duryodhana's speech here is particularly important in that it summarizes all the major deceits perpetrated by the Pandavas in the war; it is aimed specifically at Krishna, whom Duryodhana regards as the instigator in every case:

> O heir of Kamsa's slave,[31] are you not ashamed that I was struck down wrongly [*adharmena*] in the club fight, when you reminded Bhima falsely: "Break his thighs." Do I not know what you said to Arjuna? Having killed kings, who were fighting fairly, by the thousands in battle, by many crooked means, are you not ashamed? Are you not disgusted? Day by day you perpetrated a great slaughter of heroes. Having put Shikhandin in front [of Arjuna], you killed the Grandfather. O great evildoer, having killed an elephant with the same name as Ashvatthaman, you caused the preceptor to cast down his weapon; was that not known by me? And that hero was killed by that malicious Dhrshtadyumna, watched by you, and you did not prevent him. And that spear requested for the purpose of killing the son of Pandu you foiled on Ghatotkacha—who is more evil than you? Likewise, powerful Bhurishravas, with his arm cut off, resorting to the *praya* vow, was killed by that evil grandson of Shini [Satyaki], authorized by you. And Karna did his best, desiring to defeat the son of Prtha, through the deception of Ashvasena, son of the snake king.[32] But when his wheel had sunk, Karna, foremost of men, fallen into difficulty, defeated, was struck down in battle, intent upon the wheel. If you had fought both me and Karna, and Bhishma and Drona, fairly in battle, you surely would not have won. But the princes who were following their own *dharma*, both

> ourselves and others, were killed by you ignobly, crookedly. [IX.60.27–38]

These accusations will be echoed in various forms, particularly by Ashvatthaman in justification of the revenge he decides to take for his father's death, a night raid at the very end of the war, during which almost all the remaining Pandava partisans will be killed (see chap. IIIC).

The Pandava deceits of the Kurukshetra War having been reviewed, a brief summary is in order. First, the *Mahabharata* conveys the message repeatedly that the Pandavas have won the war largely by virtue of deceitful tactics. Second, as pointed out above, Arjuna is often the central figure in a deceitful action, although Yudhishthira, Bhima, and others also play their roles, and Krishna is as a rule behind the deceits, in his capacity as helper and adviser to the Pandavas. The two questions that must now be considered are the following: why do the Pandavas have to resort to deceit to win the war, and what is the *Mahabharata*'s attitude toward this deceit? (Krishna's role in the war will be treated particularly in chap. IIIB2.)

The first question is answered clearly by the epic itself, which states that the Pandavas have been forced to use deceit to fight deceit. Most blatantly, the Kauravas engaged in trickery against the Pandavas during the dice game. In addition, they attempted to destroy the Pandavas on many occasions by unrighteous means (the lacquer house, etc.). The list of evil acts committed by Duryodhana and his brothers is invoked again and again by various characters as a litany each time Pandava trickery must be justified. One example may be quoted here, in juxtaposition with the list of Pandava evils quoted above, which it follows immediately in the text (being the gist of Krishna's response to Duryodhana):

> Having followed an evil path, O son of Gandhari, you are killed today, along with your brothers, sons, relations, followers, and friends. Due to your evil deeds alone, the heroes Bhishma and Drona have been struck down, and Karna, following your [evil] custom, has been killed in battle. Although asked by me, O foolish one, you were not willing to give the Pandavas their paternal portion, half your own kingdom, out of greed, by the design of Shakuni. Poison was given by you to Bhimasena, and all the Pandavas were burned in the lacquer house together with their mother, O great fool. And Yajnaseni [Draupadi] was dragged into the court

> during her period, at the dice game; therefore, indeed, you, shameless, are to be killed, O evil-souled one. Since you wished to conquer by deceit that one who did not know dice but knew *dharma*, by means of the son of Subala [Shakuni], who knew dice, therefore you are killed in battle. Since Krishnā [Draupadi] was troubled in the forest at the hermitage of Trnabindu by the evil Jayadratha, when they [the Pandavas] had gone hunting,[33] and since Abhimanyu, a child, one against many in battle, was killed due to your crimes, O evil one, therefore you are killed in battle. [IX.60.39–46]

The Kauravas committed evil acts long before the Pandavas ever did, and in particular are guilty of having provoked the war by refusing to give the Pandavas a share of the kingdom, breaking the agreement made before the dice-game replay. It is the initial innocence of the Pandavas that puts them clearly in the right and the Kauravas clearly in the wrong.

Having emphasized that the Kauravas are evil and in the wrong, the epic states again and again that it would be impossible to defeat this enemy without deceit. Although Arjuna is generally the greatest warrior, the "henotheistic" view of the epic composers (see chap. IE) tends to emphasize that this or that hero on either side could never be defeated even by the gods, let alone by men. For the Kaurava side, this point is made in particular regarding the first three great generals.[34] Such statements relegate the Pandavas to a strictly human defensive position, if only temporarily. Note too that the Kaurava army consists of more divisions than does that of the Pandavas (V.19.13, 27, etc.). A variation on the same theme is the epic's frequent statement that matched opponents are equal, so that neither will win if the battle is fair (this applies to occasional opponents as well as official "shares"). This point is stressed in particular with regard to Arjuna and Karna, making it clear that Arjuna will have to resort to trickery if he is to defeat Karna. More broadly, the Pandavas and the Kauravas are cousins, which implies equality.[35] During the account of the club fight between Duryodhana and Bhima, Krishna states that Bhima has greater strength, but Duryodhana has worked harder. Bhima, Krishna says, will never win if the fight is conducted fairly (IX.57.3–4); here, then, the threat of a Kaurava victory predominates. In all these cases, an impasse or danger is shown, which can be dealt with only by recourse to trickery; otherwise the war could go on forever, or the evil side could win. Vows often serve as a plot device to bring out the latent impasse and emphasize that it is a matter of life or death.

The fact that the Pandavas are fighting a great evil and must resort to expedients to conquer it is emphasized in an argument between Arjuna and Bhima, in which Bhima advocates the use of stratagems, as against Arjuna's moral scruples (VII.167.25ff.). Appropriately, this discussion takes place just after the Pandavas commit their most conscious moral transgression of the war, the slaying of Drona. When Arjuna bemoans this action, Bhima states angrily:

> O son of Prtha, you speak in strict accordance with *dharma*, like a sage who has retired to the forest [or] a meek brahmin, of rigid vows. A warrior [*kshatriyah*], protecting from harm [*kshatat*], living from harm [*kshata(j)*], and patient [*kshantah*] to the three good things,[36] quickly [*kshipram*] obtains the earth [*kshitim*], *dharma*, glory, prosperity. Your honor, descendant of our family, endowed with all warrior virtues, does not appear to advantage now, uttering a speech like a fool's. [VII.168.3–5][37]

Although its tone is quite different, the appeal made here resembles that of the *Gita*: *kshatriyadharma*, Bhima implies, is its own justification. Within these parameters, Bhima's speech suggests, the lesser *dharma* must be sacrificed for the greater, for as he says: "The kingdom of one devoted to *dharma* was wrongly [*adharmatah*] carried off" (VII.168.9). Bhima goes on to accuse Arjuna of falsehood in having proclaimed formerly that the Pandavas would strive to their utmost in the war (VII.168.13f.). Bhima's words may be seen as extreme (in fact, he has favored trickery ever since the days of the forest exile),[38] but the behavior they advocate corresponds to what the Pandavas have actually done throughout the war.

The necessity of turning to trickery to win a victory is not uncommon in heroic literature. Accounts of warfare in epic and saga tend to emphasize the relatively even matching of the opposing forces, creating, in this manner, excitement and uncertainty regarding the outcome; trickery, therefore, is sometimes the deciding factor in a dispute. Nowhere, however, is trickery stressed as much as it is in the *Mahabharata*. Take the Greek case, for example. The Greeks were great admirers of cleverness, as many of their tales show,[39] and even glorified an epic hero who was preeminently a trickster and master of disguise, Odysseus. The *Iliad* too contains a large number of deceitful actions by both sides, yet it does not dwell on them:[40] in fact, Homer omits the pivotal deception of the war, the Trojan horse, from his account entirely. Of the two major deceptions that work in favor of the Greeks, one, Hera's seduction of Zeus (XIV.159ff.), serves primarily as comic relief. The other, Athena's deception of Hektor by posing as his brother Deiphobos to put him off guard in his final battle (XXII.227ff.), is much more like a *Mahabharata* trick than any other deception in the *Iliad*; but the striking thing about the *Mahabharata* is that it concentrates more on such tricks, multiplies them, explores them from all angles, and disapproves of them at length, in a way the *Iliad* never does. Hopkins suggests that in the early heroic poems which, he feels, were incorporated into the *Mahabharata* (see Introduction), such trickery was taken for granted, much as it is through most of the *Iliad*; only later did it become an object of great concern.[41] For the purpose of the present study, however, the most important issue is the treatment of Pandava trickery in the extant epic—and there the trickery is seen as being of central importance. Furthermore, in the *Mahabharata*, as in no other epic, trickery becomes the basis of victory, completely subordinating the more usual epic expedient of heroic valor and skill.

Trickery as a Human Strategy

The *Mahabharata*'s great interest in victory by trickery is a reflection of its obsession with *dharma*: note how the epic reiterates the predetermined rules of battle, which the Pandavas go on to break. And yet some cases of victory by deceit are discussed in the *Mahabharata*, regarding which the disapproval expressed is not as great as it is regarding the Pandava deceits against the Kauravas: these are the cases of deceit employed by the gods against their demon opponents.

In fact, the theme of divine deceit against demonic enemies may be traced back to Vedic times, during which Indra's trickery, his ability to change form or combat the *maya* ("magic") of his enemies with his own *maya*, was an object of praise.[42] As the issue of trickery develops through the history of Indian mythology, many stories appear with this theme: the victory of the good by deceit.[43] When the gods fight the demons and win by deceit, their trickery is usually viewed approvingly, as cleverness: see, for example, in the *Mahabharata* itself, the story of

Vishnu's assumption of a female disguise for seduction of the demons at the time of the churning of the ocean (I.16.39ff.); the happy ending on this occasion contrasts with the ambiguous ending of the Kurukshetra War.

To be sure, some condemnation of divine deceit is found, particularly in those instances singled out by Dumézil as "sins of the warrior."[44] The most striking instance has to do with Indra's making and then breaking of a pact with the demon Namuchi—alternatively Vrtra—in order to be able to kill him; the consequences of this act are a falsehood and a brahmanicide that, hypostatized, come back to haunt Indra. It is noteworthy that some earlier versions of this tale, outstandingly those in the *Shatapatha Brahmana*, omit the evil consequences entirely: Indra's act is seen there as something to be emulated.[45] Other Brahmanas do, however, consider Indra's murder of Namuchi/Vrtra (along with other acts of his) to have been sinful,[46] and certainly by the time of the epic, the consequences, along with the disapproval of Indra's behavior that they imply, exert some fascination. Even in the epic versions, however, the moral issue is not treated with the same depth as is that surrounding the deceit perpetrated by the Pandavas in their great war. For example, in V.9ff. Shalya tells Yudhishthira a version of this tale in which Indra suffers greatly when he is forced by his dual guilt, incurred in the killing of Vrtra, to hide in the water over a long period of time, while his rival Nahusha takes over Indra's kingdom and nearly steals his wife. Indra is, however, called forth eventually with praise that absolves him completely. The brief version of the tale in IX.42.28ff. finds Indra guilty of brahmanicide and friend-slaying in the murder of Namuchi, but frees him from his guilt after he performs a sacrifice.[47] In XII.272ff. Indra combats Vrtra's power of illusion by entering Vrtra as a fever (by his yogic power), and killing him with a thunderbolt. Here brahmanicide comes to threaten Indra, who hides in a lotus stalk. (Falsehood is not mentioned here, because no pact has been made in this version of the tale, and the combat appears to be primarily a contest of illusions; similarly, XIV.11.6ff.) Brahma eventually frees Indra, by distributing the brahmanicide among certain other creatures of the world, and Indra then purifies himself through a horse sacrifice. None of these versions impresses the audience with the full and inescapable consequences of the trickery.[48] And when these mythological tales are reduced eventually to formulas, the audience is placed automatically on the side of the god.

As was discussed in chapter IA, the story of the Kurukshetra War is to some extent a transposed version of the Indian myth of the god-demon battle. It would seem too that the trickery used by the Pandavas in the war is a transposition of the trickery used by the gods against the demons. The *Mahabharata* text itself supports this conclusion, particularly in terms of the arguments chosen by Krishna in support of the use of deceit against Duryodhana.[49] In particular, IX.30.6 and IX.57.7 clearly echo the Vedic conception of the use of *maya* against one possessing *maya*, the word *maya*, while still suggesting "magic," meaning essentially "artifice" in the human context. The question that must now be asked is why the epic worries so much more about Pandava deceit than divine deceit. The answer must have to do with the *Mahabharata*'s keen awareness of the humanity of both perpetrator and victim in the former case as opposed to the latter.[50] The Kauravas, although demonic, suddenly emerge as human victims. As for the Pandavas: the issue they are fighting for no longer appears one-sidedly righteous, when their enemies no longer represent absolute chaos or evil.

As was discussed in chapters IC and ID, the *Mahabharata* finds it quite acceptable to be a hero at the expense of nonhuman victims: the demonic victims of Arjuna in Book III receive little sympathy, and although the Khandava-burning victims are murdered in defiance of every formal rule of battle, the epic raises no protest. To these examples another may now be added: the *Mahabharata*'s treatment of the shooting of the monkey Valin by Rama Dasharathi, otherwise known as the hero of the *Ramayana*, whose story is recounted to the Pandavas by the sage Markandeya during their forest exile (III.258ff.).[51] In this tale, the great hero Rama, honoring a pact with the monkey Sugriva, suddenly kills Sugriva's rival, Valin, while Valin thinks he is fighting against Sugriva alone (III.264.35ff.); yet the *Mahabharata* raises almost no protest regarding this deceitful action, nor does it consider Rama any less a hero. (In the *Ramayana*'s own version of the same story, the deceitful nature of the act is acknowledged, and an attempt is made to justify it; but even here it does not interfere with Rama's heroic stature.)[52] It must be noted too that the *Mahabharata* raises no protest over the illusions created by the various *rakshasas* who participate in the Kurukshetra War on either side, as they fight one another:[53] *rakshasas* will be *rakshasas*. Criticism of such trickery intensifies immediately, however, when the combatants are human beings. Here, then, is the logical extension of

Hiltebeitel's idea regarding changes made in moving a story from the mythic to the epic plane (see Introduction).

In the story of the Kurukshetra War, the human depth of the victims is greatly emphasized. Even the worst men on the Kaurava side, the sons of Dhrtarashtra themselves, have good points as well as bad ones: they are, for example, brave fighters, handsome, heroic;[54] Duryodhana is said to have been a good king (XV.15.19ff.). Such expression of admiration for the opponent is common in heroic literature, serving to enhance admiration for the hero himself, who can defeat such an enemy. For example, it is stated of one of the pagan enemies in the *Song of Roland* (who is entirely in the wrong morally, according to that poem's assessment): "Were he but Christian, right knightly he'd appear."[55] But better words yet are spoken of the sons of Dhrtarashtra: for unlike the pagans in *Roland*, they come from good stock (they are, after all, Kurus)[56] and have good parents, Dhrtarashtra and Gandhari. Even more striking is the fact that many Kaurava partisans are not at fault morally; they are fine men, righteously motivated, whom fate has placed on the evil side. An example of such a figure is one exceptional son of Dhrtarashtra, Vikarna, who defended the rights of Draupadi during the dice game (II.61.11ff.).[57] Yet the most important *Mahabharata* figure in this regard is Karna who, but for fate, would have been recognized as the oldest Pandava brother, and not been on the Kaurava side at all. (Born before Kunti's marriage, he had been abandoned as an infant by her and raised by a *suta*, losing his *kshatriya* status until Duryodhana elevated him to the kingship of Anga [see chap. IA].)[58] Karna is the key to Kaurava humanity. Although he is violent, and is often called sinful, since he is one of the four who "did not shed a tear" when Draupadi was mistreated during the dice game (III.28.7ff.),[59] it is generally clear that he is on the Kaurava side out of genuine friendship and loyalty toward Duryodhana,[60] and because of his undeserved rejection by the Pandavas, who do not realize who he is until after the war is over (XI.27.6ff.). It is also stressed continually in the battle books that Karna is a fair fighter: in particular, he stands by his vow to Kunti, mentioned above, that he will slay none of the Pandava brothers except Arjuna.[61] Karna is, further, a paragon of generosity: the first step of his undoing, the loss of his earrings and armor, is the result of his inability to refuse anything to a brahmin; he must give up even his innate accoutrements when Indra, in brahmanic disguise, requests them (I.104.17;

III.284.12f.). The climax of the audience's sympathy for Karna comes when he is heard, just prior to his death, lamenting the fact that although righteous, he did not attain victory:

> Unable to bear these disasters, wringing his hands, railing, he [said]: "Knowers of *dharma* have always said: '*Dharma* protects those devoted to *dharma*.' Since my [wheel] sank today, it does not protect its devotees. I think *dharma* does not always protect." Speaking thus, with horses and charioteer reeling, buffeted by blows from Arjuna's weapon and agitated in his actions due to a mortal wound, he again and again censured *dharma* in battle. [VIII.66.43–44][62]

These words are genuinely pathetic,[63] as is the Pandavas' utter dejection when they are informed, too late, of Karna's true identity.

It is also striking that the elders, who are most explicitly good, are on the Kaurava side in the war. This situation is explained by the figures involved (Bhishma, Drona, Krpa, and, incidentally, Shalya) in VI.41, where each states in turn (in almost identical words) that he is "bound" by Kaurava wealth and like a eunuch in the situation. (Shalya's explanation is a bit different in wording from the others, and his participation on the Kaurava side has been explained in greater detail earlier in the epic [V.8].)[64] The implication of these statements is clearly that fate has tied the elders to the Kaurava side; but it is extremely difficult to understand why this should be so. The overriding significance, however, is moral complexity, the fighting of the elders on the Kaurava side serving as a plot device to emphasize this complexity, particularly when it is stated that they continue to pray for a Pandava victory, even as they fight against it (VI.17.5f.; VI.41, passim).

Another attempt to explain the elders' position is to be found in VI.105.27, where Bhishma tells Duryodhana: "Today, O king, tiger among men, killed in the face of the enemy, I will pay off my great debt to you, based on food from my lord."[65] The meaning of Bhishma's statement seems to be that he is fighting for the Kauravas because he has, while living in their court, depended upon them for sustenance; the word *pinda* ("food") also encompasses anticipated funeral and ancestral offerings. Such justifications for the elders' siding with the Kauravas have to do with their powerlessness and dependence, that is, their human vulnerability. Insofar as Bhishma, Drona, and Krpa are all viewed as incarnations of gods, not demons (I.61.63, 69, 89),[66] their participation on the demonic side in the war makes better sense in human than heroic terms.[67]

On the Pandava side, humanity brings with it moral ambiguity: one observes that the right for which the Pandavas are fighting, their right to possession of the kingdom, is, in the last analysis, not so certain after all; it is not as clear-cut as the right of the gods over the demons. This dubiousness is emphasized by the confusion at every stage in the genealogical progression that leads up to the births of the Pandavas and their cousins.[68] In fact, the figure who really seems to be entitled to the throne is Karna, but due to circumstances he is never even considered for this honor, and in the end fights on the Kaurava side. Of all epics other than the *Mahabharata*, it is perhaps the *Iliad* that presents the most ambiguous division between right and wrong; but there the legal issues are not stressed as much as they are in the *Mahabharata*. For the *Mahabharata*, uncertainty regarding *dharma* becomes a defining factor of the human condition. Considering the ambiguity of the Pandava claim and the humanity of their victims, it is bad enough that they have to fight and kill at all. But far worse is the fact that the Pandavas turn to conscious deceit in order to win, deceit that sometimes makes them appear evil in comparison with the Kauravas, who (except in the killing of Abhimanyu) are generally righteous warriors—Duryodhana, for example, being praised enthusiastically by the gods after his Book IX club fight against Bhima (IX.60.51ff.).[69] As mentioned in the introduction to this study, the *Mahabharata* is sufficiently critical of Pandava trickery to have suggested a complex inversion theory to the Adolf Holtzmanns.

Having recognized moral ambiguity in the Kurukshetra War, the epic tries, on the one hand, to ignore it and return to the simpler condition of *dharma* outlined at the heroic level: insisting that the Pandavas are absolutely righteous,[70] it emphasizes that the deceits perpetrated against Bhishma and Drona were undertaken only with the implicit permission of these elders; but such statements are probably late additions.[71] The epic also insists that various curses predetermined the outcome of encounters between some of the heroes, making the Pandava trickery only incidental in that regard; "shares" were foreordained and, further, networks of oaths forced certain actions and counteractions. In short, the epic, whether earlier or later, has piled up multiple motivations to rationalize the actions of the Pandavas in the war. The issues of Pandava righteousness and the influence of fate on the Kurukshetra War will be reconsidered in Part III of this study; here one can only say that Pandava righteousness is not fully convincing at the human level, even though at the heroic level it meant that the Pandavas were demigods fighting for the kingship of Yudhishthira, Dharma incarnate, with every prospect of victory, because right was on their side.

Fate versus Effort: *Dharma* on the Eve of the Kaliyuga, the Present, Degenerate Age

Where they become fully caught up in human issues, the epic poets accept the moral ambiguity of the Kurukshetra War and understand it, even as they mourn it, by way of a pessimistic view of *dharma* which is precisely opposite that emphasized at the heroic level. What the poets present each time they focus on these issues is a picture of *dharma* on the eve of the Kaliyuga, the world age (*yuga*) of greatest dharmic decline, according to traditional Hindu reckoning. (The *yuga*s are Krta, Treta, Dvapara, and Kali. From *yuga* to *yuga*, in that order, morality is said to decline by one-fourth [*Mahabharata* III.148, and elsewhere].)[72]

The beginning of the Kaliyuga of the present cycle has been dated variously in Hindu works,[73] but the *Mahabharata* itself invariably states that the events connected with the Kurukshetra War marked the juncture between this fourth age and the preceding Dvapara age (I.2.9; III.148.37; IX.59.21; compare V.72.18; V.140.7ff.; VI.62.39; XII.326.82ff.). The chronologies set forth in the Puranas basically agree.[74] The age which began at that time is marked by a degenerated and further degenerating *dharma*, variously described in the *Mahabharata*[75] and elsewhere: a *dharma* of one-quarter strengtn, as opposed to the complete, whole *dharma* that represents the Krtayuga (golden age) ideal. It will be argued here that the preoccupation of the composers of the main body of the extant epic is the issue of *dharma*'s decline, as represented by the events of the Kurukshetra War. Considering the fact that Indian thought regards the Kaliyuga as identical to the present age of world history, the epic may be seen to provide a commentary on the present human condition, even as it recounts the adventures of past heroes.

As mentioned above, the *Mahabharata* begins with an extremely complicated genealogy, with so many breaks and confusions in it that it is impossible to tell to whom the disputed succession to the throne really belongs; it continues in the same vein, depicting impasses in which both sides are wrong, or an individual would be wrong no matter how he or she behaved. As van Buitenen has written:

> . . . The epic is a series of precisely stated problems imprecisely and therefore inconclusively resolved, with every resolution raising a new problem, until the very end, when the question remains: whose is heaven and whose is hell?[76]

Among the impasses leading up to the war, the most striking is that confronted by Yudhishthira on the occasion of the dice game, an episode of central importance for the epic narrative in that it represents the major provocation to war, and is essentially the first battle of the war or a microcosm of the entire struggle.[77] It is upon this game that one may focus first, in order to argue that the primary significance of the impasses depicted in the *Mahabharata* is the decline of *dharma*. At the dice game, Yudhishthira, Dharma incarnate, should have been the winner and thereby have established his kingship,[78] but he was not. On the contrary, the portrayal of *dharma* in the dice-game episode consistently emphasizes its confusion and improper functioning. There does not seem to be even a small detail of this game in which *dharma* functions as it should; not to mention the larger outlines of the game, which Yudhishthira is forced to play but doomed from the start to lose.[79] To take just one example: in both embattled camps, Pandava and Kaurava, during the brief period of the dice game, younger brothers challenge older ones, something which would never happen were *dharma* functioning properly.[80] Another example: Draupadi, the Pandavas' common wife (a legally questionable marriage, as is pointed out frequently [see chap. IB]), although married to five husbands, is treated "as though unprotected amidst her protectors" (II.60.24), and the formula that so designates her, *nathavatim anathavat*, is a clear sign of *dharma* gone awry.[81]

In fact, an extension of the issue of Draupadi's position, the question of whether or not Yudhishthira was Draupadi's master at the time he gambled her away, becomes the subject of a debate that dominates the dice-game scene. Yudhishthira himself cannot answer this question at all; he does not even try to respond (II.60.9, etc.). Eventually Bhishma, the eldest present, responds to the question Draupadi herself has raised:

"As the Law is subtle, my dear, I fail/ To resolve your riddle the proper way" (II.60.40). That is to say, even the elders cannot answer the riddles of *dharma* at this point: the legal impasse cannot be resolved. Draupadi indicates the reason for this breakdown a few stanzas later: "Methinks that Time is out of joint.... This ancient, eternal Law [*dharmah sanatanah*] is lost among the Kauravas" (II.62.7, 9).

The names of the *yugas* are the names of the throws of dice, *kali* being the worst throw; thus a dice game is a particularly appropriate symbol with reference to the onset of the Kali age. A mark of the Kaliyuga is discord, particularly within families, and this is precisely what the dice game and pursuant war represent, the game being called explicitly a "dice game of friends" (*suhrddyuta*) (II.53.21);[82] see the words of the elder, Vidura, when he opposes plans to hold the game: "When brothers are split, a quarrel [*kalahah*] is sure" (II.51.24). Kali personified is the evil spirit of gambling[83] who, one may assert, overcomes Yudhishthira in this game. Duryodhana, the villain of the *Mahabharata*, is said to be a partial incarnation of Kali (I.61.80; XI.8.27; XV.39.10), while Shakuni, who gambles for Duryodhana (against the rules of the game, according to II.53.16), incarnates Kali's companion Dvapara, another dice demon,[84] whose name refers to the next to worst dice throw and the second most degenerate age (I.61.72; XV.39.10; XVIII.5.18).

Beyond such explicit symbolism, one must consider the overall nature of the dice game: the fact that it is played and won with deceit, which nobody seems willing or able to prevent. This deceit is carried through the Kurukshetra War. The war, like the dice game, is a reflection of the Kaliyuga breakdown of family law, as Arjuna points out at the beginning of the *Gita* (see chap. IIA1).[85] During the war, wild confusion on the battlefield, particularly that leading to combat with relatives, even those nominally on the same side (fathers killing sons, and sons, fathers, etc.), is another mark of the Kaliyuga, in which no rules are followed.[86] It is in such an atmosphere that the intentional deceits are perpetrated.

It will be evident from the preceding discussion that the reason deceit is absolutely necessary for the Pandavas in the war is that in the Kali age good cannot be expected to win by the natural, positive functioning of *dharma*: *kshatriyadharma* has broken down; the age of heroes has ended. The connection between Pandava trickery in battle and the exigencies of the Kali age is made explicit by Krishna's statement in defense of the last great Pandava deceit in the war, Bhima's below-the-belt striking of Duryodhana:

> Know that the Kaliyuga has arrived and the promise of the Pandava [has been fulfilled]. Let the Pandava be considered to have made good his hostility and his promise. [IX.59.21]

Or to put it slightly differently: just as Yudhishthira fails in his sort of test, the dice game, the *Mahabharata* warrior heroes fail in their test of pure warrior heroism on the test site of *dharma* (see chap. IE, etc.), Kurukshetra; they are unable to win by skill, power, and righteousness in battle. In particular, such failure is obvious in the case of Arjuna, the greatest hero. The Kaliyuga has been ushered in, and one must admit that the victory of the good is incomplete; this is the meaning behind such factors as the greater size of the Kaurava force, the battle against elders and relatives, and the Pyrrhic victory, with almost all the warriors killed, as well as the deceit.[87]

Recognition of the Kaliyuga, arriving at its foreordained moment, is recognition that human effort and fate are not always in harmony with one another as they seemed to be at the strictly positive level of pure heroism. It is at the human level that the *Mahabharata*'s concern with the question of the relative effectiveness of fate (*daiva*, etc.) and human effort (*purushakara*, etc.), a concern that is reflected in a number of epic passages, may best be understood. Perhaps the most important passage on this subject is the conversation of III.28–36, where Yudhishthira predictably defends the idea that fate must be accepted gracefully, while Draupadi and Bhima argue against him, all with reference to the forest exile. Pandurang Vaman Kane summarizes the epic's treatment of the question of fate and effort as follows:

> In the Mahābhārata the topic of human effort and *daiva* (fate or destiny) comes up for treatment in numerous places and is put in the mouth of several characters with different emphasis according to circumstances. In Ādi 1.246–247, 89.7–10, Sabhā 46.16, 47.36, 58.14, Vanaparva 179.27–28, Udyoga 8.52, 40.32, 159.4, 186.18, Āśramavāsika 10.29 the emphasis is on *daiva* as all powerful, it being said that human effort is useless as against *daiva*. A golden mean is advocated in Ādi 123.21, Sabhā 16.12, Udyoga 79.5–6, Śānti 56.14–15, Sauptika 2.3, in all of which it is said that worldly affairs require both *puruṣakāra* (effort) and *daiva*. In certain other

> passages it is recommended that effort is superior to daiva and that one's business is to make efforts and not to care for fate; e.g. in Droṇa 152.27, Śānti 27.32, 58.13–16, 153.50, Anuśāsana 6.1ff, Sauptika 2.12–13 and 23–24.[88]

At the heroic level, there is no doubt that effort will succeed: fate and effort will not be in opposition to one another. At the human level, the Kaliyuga represents the interference of fate. What has been fated is the destruction of the *kshatriyas* (the heroes), as stated in a prophecy spoken at the time of Draupadi's birth: "Superb among women, the Dark Woman [Krishnā] shall lead the baronage to its doom" (I.155.44)[89]—for such is the role of Shri in the Kaliyuga. One might say that the allowance of trickery by the good side in the battle books marks an attempt to outwit opposing fate by human effort; but fate cannot really be outwitted.[90]

Kingly Policy

The full significance of the concept of "Kaliyuga" in the *Mahabharata* becomes evident when one focuses on the fact that the Kaliyuga is the present age. Emphasis upon the chronological connection between the Kurukshetra War and the Kaliyuga thus implies a connection with present conditions; and so one finds, as one might expect, that the *Mahabharata* heroes take on realistic human traits. The pull of the old heroic ideals may hold back this development to a certain extent, yet the *Mahabharata* composers acknowledge its necessity. The process of humanization has come furthest with regard to Arjuna. Why Arjuna?

Some aspects of Arjuna's personality that seem to have conduced to his humanization have already been discussed in chapter IIA1. Here one aspect of Arjuna, referred to throughout this study, which may have contributed in particular to the emphasis on his participation in stratagems, must be reemphasized: this is the fact that Arjuna is the Pandava who is seen as the direct ancestor of the king, Janamejaya, to whom the epic is supposed to have been recited. According to epic chronology, Janamejaya was an early king of the Kaliyuga, ruling just two generations after Kurukshetra—thus very much a human king who faced human difficulties.[91] In his heroic aspect, Arjuna, as Janamejaya's great-grandfather, is praised unstintingly; in his human aspect, Arjuna becomes the role model for a human ruler. The deep concern for *dharma* evidenced by the *Mahabharata* composers is an outgrowth of the observation that *dharma* does not function well in our age. Because a realistic role model for kingship is essential under such conditions, the ideal king is brought down to earth—which is possible because the traditional Indian king was not divinized completely.[92] Not only is the *Mahabharata* story a practical lesson for the human king; attached to the story is didactic material, *dharmashastra* ("lawbooks," in the broadest sense), which serves as a practical guide for kingship.[93] In the extant epic, there is a tremendous amount of such material, of which the largest portion is that included in the didactic books, expounded to Yudhishthira as the receptacle of kingly *dharma* (but with the other Pandavas always behind him) by Bhishma, on his deathbed. Bhishma is attempting, through his teaching, to settle Yudhishthira's doubts, raised in the course of the war that has just ended, as expressed in such statements as the following: "Righteous behavior [*dharmacharya*] and kingdom are continually at odds, by which [issue] my mind is confused, as I ponder constantly" (XII.38.4). The didactic books include two long subsections specifically regarding the art of ruling: *Shantiparvan* (Book XII) 1–128 is known as the "Rajadharma" ("*Dharma* for Kings"); and XII.129–67 is the "Apaddharma" ("*Dharma* for Emergency"). Also included here, and elsewhere in the epic, is a large amount of instruction for ordinary people, whose concerns Arjuna, among the Pandavas, reflects secondarily.[94]

The problem faced by the king (and, secondarily, by others) in the Kaliyuga is the subtlety of *dharma*, that very basic issue referred to by Bhishma in the dice-game episode, as quoted above;[95] this is because in the Kali age the distinction between right and wrong is at its weakest.[96] The prevailing situation is described as follows, with wordplay such as throughout the *Mahabharata* underscores the ambiguity of events: "*Dharma* becomes *adharma* and *adharma*, *dharma*" (XII.259.4).[97] A Lévi-Straussian structuralist might argue that the emphasis upon pragmatic solutions in the *Mahabharata* represents an attempt to mediate between these ideal extremes by advocating the use of evil means, where appropriate, to achieve a higher good. This balance represents the ethic of the Kali age, in which the king's primary responsibility is to preserve his basically righteous dominion, for the protection of his subjects and the world, with lesser regulations adjusted accordingly. The name for such an approach is "policy" (*niti*), the extreme of *niti* being *apad-*

dharma, such as is taught in the "Apaddharma" chapters. The Kaliyuga is a prolonged period of emergency (*apad*).[98] Kingly policy is the subject of a large body of ancient Indian literature outside the *Mahabharata*, that is, *arthashastra* ("political treatises"—with which much *Mahabharata* instruction has a great deal in common); but the epic uniquely studies policy from every moral angle.[99]

References to policy, explicit and implicit, abound in the *Mahabharata*. Policy is the use of means (*upaya*) by which a king governs his realm; it is in particular that cleverness by which he overcomes difficult situations. On the one hand, policy in a king is seen as being of paramount importance; thus Pandu foretells at the time of Arjuna's birth that his son will be "wise in policy" (I.114.25), and it is said of Parikshit that "his understanding was wide; he knew the six vices[100] and was the foremost scholar of the science of polity" (I.45.15). On the other hand, policy is often tricky; thus, Indra's use of deceit to defeat Namuchi/Vrtra is seen as an archetypical example of the use of means. Pretending friendship, Indra lulled his enemy into a sense of well-being, and only later attacked him; this is a stratagem that is often recommended for use by kings who fear a formidable foe (XII.69.23, etc.).

The Kauravas view the dice game as their means against the Pandavas, who are otherwise invincible because they are so strong and well liked. They feel that in using this stratagem they will be emulating Indra's actions (II.50.20). Yet on their tongues, policy sounds ugly, as, for example, in the following statement made by Duryodhana on the eve of the dice-game replay:

> Have you not heard . . . what the learned priest of the Gods, Bṛhaspati,[101] said when he propounded policy to Śakra? "Enemy-killer, enemies must be cut down by any means before they, with war or force, can do you evil!" [II.66.7–8]

Indeed, the instigator of the dice game and chief gambler, Shakuni, as occasionally Duryodhana (above, p. 164), has overtones of the evil magician along with the crafty politician.[102] The dicing and other early Kaurava tricks aimed at destroying the Pandavas are within the realm of permitted policy, such as is, for example, described by Bhishma in a rather pragmatic passage of his "Rajadharma" teaching (in general, the didactic books may be taken as an objective standard, although not always in line with the actual practice of the epic characters):

> And a king should not be in the power of another, even if [that other is] heroic, but the weak one, harassing that one with strength and heroism, should remain independent. And he should oppress the kingdom of that one with deadly weapons, fire, and poison. [XII.69.21–22]

Yet when the Kauravas cite policy in justification of their actions, the epic sees it as rationalization: the Pandavas have done them no harm, nor threatened them.

By way of contrast, the concept of policy really does justify the actions of the Pandavas in battle, for they are only fighting evil with evil, and their goal is just. Statements of policy that could be applied directly to the Pandavas' actions in the war are abundant; for example, XII.55.15–16:

> It is *dharma* that one should kill in battle fathers, grandfathers, sons, teachers, kinsman, and relations acting wrongly. . . . A *kshatriya* who kills in battle an evil, greedy person who has broken a pact, even if a teacher, is a knower of *dharma*.[103]

Or XII.110.26:

> In whatever way a person acts, so should he be treated; that is *dharma*. One practicing artifice [*mayacharah*] should be treated with artifice. One practicing goodness should be met with goodness.[104]

Such statements, phrased in terms of (*kshatriya*)*dharma*, serve to reconcile Yudhishthira and Arjuna to their inevitable duty, after the war is over; the statement just quoted addresses itself to an issue to which both of them had devoted much concern. Even so, the epic continues to display a certain self-doubt regarding compromise in matters of *dharma*; note, for example, the strange juxtaposition of counsels in XII.96:

> If one fights with trickery, one should oppose him with trickery.[105] But if one fights lawfully [*dharmatah*], one should check him with *dharma*. . . . One should conquer evil with good. Death by *dharma* is better than victory by evil deeds. [XII.96.9, 16][106]

At the human level, *kshatriyadharma* is quite different from what it seemed to be at the heroic level: a precarious effort to maintain order against many forces that cannot really be overcome completely, there being no longer any hope of easy or absolute success. *Kshatriyadharma* here is only the best policy, which the Pandavas learn from their clever adviser, Krishna.

As a more specific example of the legal status of trickery in the *Mahabharata*, one may turn to the issue of lying. "Truth" stands for *dharma*, and at the heroic level it is often stated that a given hero's strength is his truth; this idea, which has become formulaic, is applied to the various Pandavas, and other heroes as well (see chaps. IA and IIA2). In the didactic books of the epic, lying is often strictly forbidden (XIII.110.46; XIII.132.19; etc.).[107] On the other hand, these books more often make the point (particularly in the "Rajadharma" section) that lying is justified when it becomes a matter of policy. In fact, truth may be more wicked at certain times than falsehood is, that is, when it leads to harmful results (for example, bandits learning where their victims have hidden); a number of stories in XII.110 (compare VII.49) and elsewhere illuminate this point. Obviously, the ambiguous position of truth is a Kaliyuga phenomenon, as the following passage implies:

> *Dharma* was four-footed [whole, like a bull standing on four legs] and complete, as was truth also, in the Krtayuga. Then no other teaching at all wrongly [*adharmena*] arose. But in the others [other ages], *dharma* declined from that teaching by one foot [in each], and *adharma* increased, with theft, untruth, and illusion. [XII.224.22–23]

In the Krtayuga, thus, truth was perfect, such being too the ideal of truth at the level of pure heroism. The *Mahabharata*, on the other hand, speaks of the existence of permissible lies and, implicitly, of the subtlety of truth, in phrases similar to the one quoted above (p. 180) regarding *dharma* in general, for example: "One may voice a lie when about to expire, or when about to marry: then the lie becomes truth and the truth a lie" (III.200.3).[108] Various passages inserted into and connected closely with the epic narrative reiterate the decline of truth. Before the war it is stated by Vidura that "a lie in a high place" is "equal to brahmin murder" (V.40.3). Yet by the time of the final battle against Drona, Krishna advocates lying in words much like those of the didactic books, managing to convince even Yudhishthira (VII.164.99)[109]—and all so that a brahmin may be killed.[110]

In summary, one may note that the ideal virtues connected with heroism or kingship as seen in Part I of the present study are all relegated to an inferior position in the Kaliyuga, as stated in XII.224.26–27:

> The *dharma*s of the Krta age are different from those of the Treta, Dvapara, and Kali, constructed according to its [*dharma*'s] power [in each age]. In the Krtayuga, *tapas* is highest. In the Treta, knowledge is highest. In the Dvapara it is sacrifice, they say. In the Kaliyuga, giving.

Giving (which seems primarily to mean gifts to brahmins)[111] is assigned to the Kaliyuga as an easy means for a difficult age. The new view of kingship for this age might be summarized in the words of XII.120.4–5: "As a peacock bears tail feathers of many colors so a *dharma*-knowing king should make his form manifold: sharpness, crookedness, indomitability, and also truth and honesty." Notably, the word used for peacock here, *bhujagashana* (literally, "eater of snakes"), provides an apt parallel to the role of the Pandavas in the Kurukshetra War (see chap. IE).

Finally, it is necessary to comment upon the relationship between Yudhishthira's and Arjuna's respective roles in the epic, from the point of view of Kaliyuga kingship. As might be expected, Arjuna, as the active party, is the one who changes with the *yuga*s; he adapts, while Yudhishthira remains the still point at the center. To put it another way: Yudhishthira may be said to incarnate *sanatanadharma*, that portion of *dharma* which never changes and continues to operate—at one-quarter strength—even in the Kaliyuga. Arjuna, then, represents *varnashramadharma* ("*dharma* of classes and stages of life"); note the great emphasis on his performing the role of his class, the *kshatriya* class, in the *Gita*. It is, in fact, by virtue of being a *kshatriya* par excellence that Arjuna is forced to modify his actions to conform to the Kaliyuga. To draw the distinction more sharply, one might refer to the well-known Hindu concept of the four aims of life, *dharma, artha* ("profit," but also "practical life," "politics" [note *arthashastra*, above]), *kama* ("pleasure"), and *moksha* ("salvation"),[112] and go so far as to suggest that within this schema, Yudhishthira represents the first aim,[113] while Arjuna represents the second (not really *dharma* at all). (Bhima would then represent *kama*; on *moksha*, see further chap. IIIB1, etc.)

At the human level, adaptation of eternal standards to the requirements of the current human condition is the key to Arjuna's character.

The contrast between his heroic role and his human role is outstanding. Thus Arjuna is said to be a master of chivalry; for example, during his great move against the Samshaptakas, early in Book VII: "When they were fleeing, Arjuna, remembering the vow of a warrior, did not kill any fallen warriors or warriors with faces averted" (VII.31.48). Nevertheless, he commits acts that are equally unethical both before and after the moment referred to by this statement. Certain isolated incidents of the battle books that strongly reiterate Arjuna's heroism may best be understood as counterpoises to the signs of human weakness he so often displays. After his deceitful shooting of Bhishma, for example, only Arjuna of all the warriors present can ascertain and provide the heroic sort of pillow required by the dying elder, a pillow of arrows shot into the ground (VI.115.32ff.); Arjuna also shoots water out of the ground to quench Bhishma's thirst (VI.116.1ff.). Here are an act of judgment and one of world ordering[114] worthy of a kingly or heroic figure; yet who can forget the act of moral adaptation that preceded them?

At the human level, such adaptation—policy—is admired reluctantly, as essential to the age. At the same time there is nostalgia for eternal *dharma*, and this is where Yudhishthira's importance comes in. In fact, a certain portion of eternal *dharma* is still alive, as the respect shown in the didactic books and elsewhere for such absolute values as truth and nonviolence[115] testifies. The *Mahabharata* can still insist in places that "where *dharma* is, there is victory" (see chap. IA, etc.), and provide a victory of sorts for the good. One might say that it is *varnashrama-dharma*, how people should actually behave, that has been modified, while *sanatanadharma* lurks in the background, whole but weak. The main problem of the *Mahabharata* heroes led by Yudhishthira was, it is suggested, that they tried to behave at first as though they lived in an earlier age, where the old rules based on eternal *dharma* still applied. Their failure led them ultimately to greater transgressions, to retrieve what had been lost; with these, the Kali age opened, in time's inevitable course—for the Kaliyuga is fated, and against such fate, effort, so highly prized by heroes, is of little avail. Idealistically, the *Mahabharata* may suggest from time to time that the king creates the age: an excellent king provides a Krtayuga for his realm, a less excellent king a Tretayuga, and so on (V.130.16; XII.70.6ff.; XII.92.6; XII.139.10). This view is the heroic one; yet in its moments of realism and practicality, the epic admits implicitly time after time that the king must adapt to the age he lives in. In contrast to the variety of Kaliyuga options, the perfect *dharma* of the Krtayuga remains rather vague, since it has nothing at all to do with real experience.[116] Likewise, Yudhishthira's reaction to adversity is often vague in comparison with Arjuna's: he is bewildered, and most often suggests withdrawal. Note his failure, mentional above, to respond at all, either negatively or positively, regarding the question of *dharma* raised at the dice game.

The lie told at the time of Drona's slaying deserves special consideration, because in that episode Yudhishthira participates in the deceit. In explanation of this fact, one may point to the occasional statement in the epic that *dharma* is completely dead in the Kaliyuga, rather than one-quarter alive (XII.71.11);[117] in a like manner, Yudhishthira is shown to have lost all his integrity, the lie to Drona being a perfect reversal of eternal law. There is another way to look at this incident as well: just as all the epic characters who interact with Arjuna in his heroic aspect have heroic personalities to complement his, so they all have human personalities to interact with his humanity; Yudhishthira is no exception, as his lie to Drona, the extreme of his human adaptation, proves. Note, however, that in the Drona-slaying episode, as generally throughout the battle books, Arjuna is the figure who truly struggles with the morality of the situation. In this episode he displays his most human reaction of all regarding Pandava trickery, and it is here, in the wake of this most outstanding of Pandava deceits, that one may truly identify with Arjuna's human emotions.

Notes

1. "When our battle is in progress one fighting with speech should be opposed with speech. One who has left the midst of battle is by no means to be killed. And a chariot warrior is to be fought by a chariot warrior, a chief elephant by an elephant, a cavalryman with a horse, and an infantryman by an infantryman. . . . According to usage, with regard for heroism, according to one's power, according to age, having called out, one should strike, [but] not at one who is unsuspecting or in distress. One engaged with another, heedless or, likewise, with face averted, with weapons exhausted or without armor is by no means to be killed. One should by no means strike charioteers, bearers, weapon bringers, or sounders of kettledrums and conches." These regulations are repeated, as a whole or in part, and with variations, throughout the battle books; they also appear in

the didactic books (XII.96.7ff.; XII.97.3) and elsewhere. One version of the list has been quoted in chap. IIA2, in the rebuke of Bhurishravas against Arjuna, and others are cited in the present chapter.
2. The present author differs here from Hiltebeitel, who emphasizes Yudhishthira's, rather than Arjuna's, role in the various deceits (*Ritual*, pp. 237ff.).
3. E.g., Achilles in the Skamandros encounter (see chap. IC).
4. Shikhandin's story is told in V.170ff.
5. The priest of the gods and master of policy (see below, n. 101).
6. M. C. Smith, "The Core of India's Great Epic," p. 53. Cf. VII.126.7.
7. See also V.161.7.
8. See, especially, V.188f.
9. See, e.g., the quotation from IX.60.27–38 on pp. 165–66.
10. Like Arjuna, Yudhishthira wishes not to fight at this point; his idea is, as usual, to escape by withdrawing to the forest. Krishna says that he himself will undertake to slay Bhishma, so as to keep the oath taken by Arjuna "at Upaplavya [the Matsya capital]" (cf. chap. IIA2, n. 20). Yudhishthira tells Krishna not to falsify his (Krishna's) promise not to fight, and says that he himself will ask Bhishma how he may be slain. Krishna agrees, and all the Pandavas, with Krishna, then accompany Yudhishthira to Bhishma's abode. For these events, see VI.103.12ff.
11. For reference, see p. 147.
12. Besides Bhurishravas himself, all the soldiers (VII.118.19). Here as well, Krishna is included in the blame.
13. This act was Yudhishthira's preparation for war, as the hearing of the *Gita* was Arjuna's, and it takes place in the epic just after the *Gita* episode.
14. The Greeks, like the Indians, distinguished between real truth and literal truth. A master of the latter was Autolykos, the maternal grandfather of Odysseus; see Norman O. Brown, *Hermes the Thief: The Evolution of a Myth* (1947; rpt. New York: Vintage-Random House, 1969), pp. 8f.
15. See, again, the passage from IX.60.27–38 (pp. 165–66).
16. To kill a brahmin is one of the worst of crimes according to epic thought (see p. 183). One may nevertheless, the epic says, battle against a brahmin who fights like a warrior; see VII.135.33; XII.35.17ff.; etc. On the other hand, Drona, as a brahmin, should not be fighting at all; see Bhima's angry words of VII.165.28f. and Dhrshtadyumna's words of VII.168.22ff. See further, below, n. 67 and n. 110.
17. For references, see chap. IA, n. 44. See also XII.5.8ff.
18. In the latter account, Indra specifies that the spear may be used by Karna only once.
19. Here, then, is another substitute death (see chap. IB, especially n. 13). I.143.38 states in the course of Ghatotkacha's birth story that Indra created him *shakti-hetoh* ("on account of the spear"; van Buitenen translates, "for power's sake").
20. Hiltebeitel provides an extensive and cleverly delineated comparison between the Arjuna-Karna battle under discussion and the Cuchulainn-Ferdia battle of the *Tain Bo Cuailnge* (see chap. IIA1), emphasizing the function of the charioteer for encouragement and discouragement; see his "Brothers, Friends, and Charioteers: Parallel Episodes in the Irish and Indian Epics," in *Homage to Georges Dumézil*,

ed. Edgar C. Polomé, *Journal of Indo-European Studies*, Monograph no. 3 (Washington D.C.: *Journal of Indo-European Studies*, Institute for the Study of Man, 1982), pp. 85–111.

21. Cf. the version of the story told in XII.3. Here the worm is not identified with Indra, but is, rather, a *rakshasa*, and the theme of deceit is absent.
22. The particular trick used against Karna has been seen as the transposition of an act perpetrated against the sun god by the Vedic Indra; see Dumézil, "Karṇa et les Pāṇḍava"; *Mythe et épopée* I, pp. 131ff. That Indra perpetrated this act for a figure named Kutsa, whose patronymic is "Arjuneya" ("son of Arjuna") adds an interesting dimension to this argument; see *Mythe et épopée* I, p. 137, etc. In line with her particular interpretation of the Kurukshetra War, Biardeau sees Karna as a representation of the *pralaya* sun, that is, the sun gone out of control; for references, see chap. IE, n. 22. Surely the significance of Karna's chariot (and its aberrant behavior) in this episode has some connection with the chariot as characteristic accoutrement of the sun god in Vedic mythology (although other Vedic gods are also charioteers). An additional symbolic value also resides in Karna's predicament: he is not destined to be *chakravartin* ("wheel turner" = world ruler); his charioteer hinders him and his wheel sinks into the ground.
23. Cf. the epic's emphasis on the fact that Abhimanyu was killed when deprived of his chariot (see chap. IIA2, especially n. 42).
24. For reference, see chap. IIA2, n. 34.
25. On the lack of assistance, see IX.15.50. On the righteousness of the battle, see IX.16.55, where Shalya is referred to as "killed in lawful [*dharmye*] battle by the son of Dharma whose soul was *dharma*." Shalya is Yudhishthira's "share," "though some said they thought the two were mismatched" (V.56.13).
26. Shakuni is Sahadeva's "share" (V.56.22). Note the successive deaths of two great maternal-uncle figures.
27. Cf. Indra's hiding in the water after his killing of Vrtra (see p. 170). Duryodhana seems to have a special attraction to solidified waters (a product of magical illusion par excellence); cf. his adventures in the assembly hall (see chap. IC, n. 50).
28. Duryodhana chooses the weapon himself (IX.31.26), after which Bhima is set against him as the Pandavas' only hope. The choice is appropriate: Duryodhana is Bhima's "share" (V.56.14); the two have been enemies since childhood (I.119.24ff.); and both have always been expert at club fighting (I.123.40, quoted on p. 43).
29. Baladeva had departed on the eve of the war, to avoid taking sides (V.154.32ff.). Although he says he is neutral, his peculiar recounting of the dice game (V.2.9) suggests that he is actually pro-Kaurava.
30. Both Bhima and Duryodhana were disciples of Baladeva (V.154.32, etc.).
31. Kamsa was Krishna's demonic uncle/cousin, who threatened Krishna's life, and whom Krishna ultimately killed. Krishna is called "heir of Kamsa's slave" here because Kamsa had imprisoned Krishna's parents. The story of Krishna and Kamsa is far more pivotal to the Puranas than to the *Mahabharata*; see, e.g., *Harivamsha* (appendix to the *Mahabharata*) XLIV ff. and *Bhagavata Purana* X.1ff.

32. See chap. IE. On Krishna's foiling of Karna in this case, see chap. IIIB2, n. 30.
33. See chap. IB.
34. The final word on this issue is spoken by Krishna in IX.60.57–60: "This one of very fast weapons and these bold, great charioteers could not have been killed by us in battle by fair fighting. Therefore . . . these means were ordained by me; otherwise the Pandavas would never have won. For all these four noble men [Bhishma, Drona, Karna, and Bhurishravas], the most excellent chariot warriors on earth, could not have been killed lawfully [*dharmatah*] even by the World Guardians themselves. Likewise this son of Dhrtarashtra, with club in hand, rested, could not have been killed lawfully, even by Time himself with his staff."
35. Held (pp. 296ff.) suggests that the Pandavas and the Kauravas, like the gods and the demons with whom they are connected, are the two balanced phratries of a tribe.
36. The Ganguli-Roy translation of the epic interprets "the three that are good" here as "the gods, the Brahmanas, and [the] preceptor."
37. Note the plays on, or attempted etymology of, the word *kshatriya*, in v. 4.
38. See III.34.56ff. and III.36.31ff. The former passage is a general defense of trickery, the latter a specific recommendation: to take as thirteen years the thirteen months already spent in exile.
39. See G. S. Kirk, *Myth: Its Meaning and Functions in Ancient and Other Cultures* (London: Cambridge University Press; Berkeley: University of California Press, 1970), p. 187.
40. For various deceptions against the Greeks perpetrated by Apollo in favor of the Trojans, see *Iliad* V.443ff.; XVI.786; XXI.596ff. At XII.251ff. Zeus confuses the Greeks with a dust storm. On a number of occasions gods disguise themselves as compatriots of various warriors in order to incite them: Apollo does this for the Trojans (XVI.715ff.; XVII.70ff., 319ff.) and Poseidon does it for the Greeks (XIII.43ff., 215ff.). On the Greek side: Odysseus lies to Dolon (X.382ff.); Odysseus and Diomedes steal horses from the Thracians during a night raid (X.469ff.); Hera seduces Zeus to take his attention away from the war (XIV.159ff.); Patroklos dresses up in Achilles' armor (XVI.40ff.); Athena clouds the minds of the Trojans (XVIII.311); Athena deceives Deiphobos (XXII.227ff.) and returns Achilles' spear to him after he has once missed hitting Hektor with it (XXII.273ff.). Shooting from behind does not appear to be forbidden by the Greek rules of warfare, as it is implicitly by the Indian rules.
41. Hopkins, "Position," pp. 62ff., 227ff.; *Great Epic*, p. 376. Hopkins also suggests that it is the Pandavas' identity as unsophisticated newcomers that accounts for their particularly unchivalrous style of fighting; see "Position," pp. 64f.
42. For some Rg Vedic references to Indra's transformations, see under entry "Indra: Verwandlungen und Wunder" in *Namen- und Sachregister zur Übersetzung . . .*, by Johannes Nobel, vol. IV of Karl Friedrich Geldner, *Der Rig-Veda: Aus dem Sanskrit ins Deutsche übersetzt und mit einem laufenden Kommentar versehen*, Harvard Oriental Series, vol. 36 (Cambridge, Mass.: Harvard University Press, 1957), pp. 64f. On his combating *maya* with *maya*, see *Rg Veda* I.11.7; II.11.10; V.30.6; X.147.2; see also I.32.4; III.34.3. Jan Gonda argues that *maya* does not

necessarily imply trickery here; see his *Change and Continuity in Indian Religion*, Disputationes Rheno-Trajectinae, 9 (The Hague: Mouton, 1965), pp. 167f. Certainly, however, such was the interpretation of later Indians to whom the word *maya* meant, besides "magic," "trick" or "illusion," as it does throughout the *Mahabharata*. On trickery as a typical aspect of the Indo-European/Semitic "combat myth," including the Indra-Vrtra combat (cf. chap. IE, n. 34), see Fontenrose, pp. 11, 197, 200, 261f., etc.

43. See the discussion of three stories containing this element (the story of Garuda, the story of Kacha, and the story of the churning of the ocean) in Dange, *Legends in the Mahābhārata*.
44. Dumézil, *Warrior*, Part II. Regarding Indra, the sins are specifically brahmanicide, the breaking of a pact, and adultery.
45. *Shatapatha Brahmana* XII.7.1.10ff.; XII.7.3.1.
46. *Jaiminiya Brahmana* II.134; *Aitareya Brahmana* VII.28; *Panchavimsha Brahmana* XII.6; *Taittiriya Brahmana* I.7.1.7.
47. Cf. Yudhishthira's use of a horse sacrifice to expiate his guilt after the Kurukshetra War.
48. One version of the story in the epic does not mention the breaking of a pact, and has Indra hide in a lake only because he does not really believe that Vrtra is dead (III.98f.). The prose version of XII.329.17ff. has Indra guilty of brahmanicide only, in the slaying of Vrtra and Vishvarupa.
49. See IX.30.6ff.; IX.57.5ff.; IX.60.62.
50. Note the statement of XII.280.17: "Those acts which are done by deities and also by sages, a virtuous man [*dharmatma*] should not perform, nor should, having heard, condemn."
51. See chap. IB, n. 8.
52. See *Ramayana* IV.16.25ff. One of Rama's self-justifications (IV.18.34ff.) is that animals are generally hunted, and often by tricky means. Indeed, Rama's earlier inability to distinguish between Valin and Sugriva (IV.12.29ff.) emphasizes their lack of human individuality.
53. See, e.g., VII.84, where Alambusa is killed by Ghatotkacha.
54. Regarding Duryodhana, see VI.78.45ff.; VI.93.20ff. Yudhishthira reminds Duryodhana in IX.30.11 that he has always been called a hero. The plays attributed to Bhasa portray a more sympathetic Duryodhana than the one in the epic; see Juthika Ghosh, *Epic Sources of Sanskrit Literature*, Calcutta Sanskrit College Research Series, no. 23 (Calcutta: Sanskrit College, 1963), p. 48.
55. *The Song of Roland*, trans. Dorothy L. Sayers (Harmondsworth: Penguin, 1937), *laisse* 72. As Sayers herself states in the introduction to her translation (p. 21): "You cannot make an epic out of a conflict where all the heroic qualities are on one side."
56. And note the words of the brahmin Samba who, speaking for the other citizens (admittedly, in a flattering statement spoken after the fact), states that there has never been an unpopular king in this line. He goes on to say that fate, not Duryodhana or others, caused the war (XV.16.2).

57. The lower-caste half-brother of the sons of Dhrtarashtra, Yuyutsu, actually takes the Pandava side in the Kurukshetra War (VI.41.90ff.).
58. Cf. Esau losing his birthright to Jacob in Genesis 25:29f. The abandonment of Karna at birth and his adoption by lowly parents has parallels in many heroic life stories; thus Karna becomes one of the heroes cited in Otto Rank's "The Myth of the Birth of the Hero"; see *The Myth of the Birth of the Hero and Other Writings by Otto Rank*, ed. Philip Freund (New York: Vintage-Random House, 1959), pp. 18ff.
59. The other three were Duryodhana, Shakuni, and Duhshasana. Note the interaction among these four, who are frequently grouped together, in III.8. This chapter represents the worst of Karna's behavior, for here he advises killing the Pandavas in their forest exile (III.8.17ff.).
60. VIII.29.23 has Karna state in anger to Shalya, who has been undermining him: "[The word] 'friend' [*mitra*], O respectful one, is, they say, from [the verb] *mid*, [meaning] to delight, please, protect, or gladden, or [variants of those meanings formed] by adding the prefixes *a*, *vi*, or *pra*. And I do all those things for Duryodhana."
61. Karna has a chance to break this promise, but does not, at VII.114.67; VII.142.17; and VIII.17.95; if Poona Edition, VII, 449*, is included, that makes once with each of Kunti's sons, except Arjuna. Note also his refusal on principle to shoot the same arrow twice (VIII.66.8): "Men like me are not deceitful," he says at that time.
62. Karna had stated (admitted) earlier (V.141.33) that "yato dharmas tato jayah" (van Buitenen translates: "Where there is Law there is triumph").
63. In her interpretation of the Kurukshetra War, Biardeau generally stresses Karna's evil side: he is the epitome of bad kingship, the opposite of righteous Arjuna, consumed by passion (see "Conférence," vol. 82, p. 100; vol. 87, p. 161; vol. 88, p. 178; etc.), mythically, the sun of *pralaya*, run amuck (for references, see chap. IE, n. 22); his loss of *kshatriya* status represents class mixture ("Conférence," vol. 84, p. 178f.; vol. 85, p. 144; vol. 87, p. 147; vol. 88, pp. 174f.; etc.)—for Biardeau's view of the significance of which, see below, n. 67. But what of the pathetic *human* Karna, so well known to modern Indian thought? (See, e.g., Ram Dhari Singh "Dinkar" 's Hindi poem *Rashmirathi* ["The Sun Charioteer"] [1952], in which Karna emerges as underdog, victim of racial [caste] prejudice.) That Karna is much closer to the Karna of the present discussion.
64. Duryodhana's use of trickery to force Shalya to fight on his side seems to justify Yudhishthira's unfair use of Shalya against Karna.
65. Cf. III.37.14, etc.
66. See further, below, n. 101 and n. 114, and chap. IIIC, n. 18. Shalya, on the other hand, incarnates a demon (I.61.6); see further, chap. IIIB1, n. 31.
67. Biardeau ("Conférence," vol. 85, pp. 143ff., 163; vol. 87, p. 155; etc.—elaborated in "The Salvation of the King in the *Mahābhārata*," *Contributions to Indian Sociology*, NS 15 [1981], 81ff.) stresses the anomalous combination of brahmanic and warrior attributes in the personages of both Bhishma and Drona (Bhishma as a

renouncing *kshatriya*, Drona as a fighting brahmin) in her explanation of their participation on the evil side, that is, the side where class order is not preserved according to the stipulations of *dharma* ("Conférence," vol. 87, pp. 145ff., 153ff., 160ff., etc.). In fact, the mixture of brahmanic and warrior qualities is far from always condemned in the *Mahabharata*: it is, e.g., a very positive feature of Yudhishthira's and Arjuna's constitutions (see chaps. IA and ID, above, and Biardeau herself, "Brahmanes et poitiers," *Annuaire de l'Ecole Pratique des Hautes Etudes, v^e Section [Sciences Religieuses]* 79 [1971–72]: 40; 43f., n. 2 [contrasting the cases of Drona and the Pandavas]; etc.). Furthermore, the epic certainly does not concentrate on class mixture as a negative point (or any point) in Bhishma's case (his initial renunciation is much lauded [I.94.90ff.]), nor as much as it might in Drona's clearer case: Bhishma and Drona are presented as admirable characters, and if in Drona's case class mixture is indeed a sign of the times (see below, n. 110), it does not mar his character, nor does it interfere with Arjuna's respect for him.

68. This genealogy is the primary concern of I.57–114.
69. As noted in chap. IIA2, the celestials also praised Bhurishravas, not Satyaki.
70. A frequent statement, one of the more impressive versions of which is found, in the words of Samjaya, at VI.61.14ff.
71. See Hopkins, "Position," p. 200 n., and Simson, pp. 171ff. Cf. Drona's giving Arjuna permission to fight against him in the future, in a passage that has not, however, been included in the critical text (Poona Edition, I, Appendix I, no. 80, line 28).
72. The similarity to the generations of man in the Greek tradition (see Hesiod's *Works and Days*, lines 109ff.) has often been noted.
73. See Pandurang Vaman Kane, *History of Dharmaśāstra (Ancient and Mediaeval Religious and Civil Law)*, 2nd ed., Government Oriental Series, Class B, no. 6, 5 vols. in 8 (Poona: Bhandarkar Oriental Research Institute, 1968–77), III, 896ff.
74. However, they postdate the *Mahabharata* chronology slightly, by stating that the Kaliyuga began with the death of Krishna. One may conjecture that the *Mahabharata* is placing greater emphasis than the Puranas on the explicit connection between the events of the war and the decline in *dharma* that marks the Kaliyuga. Evidently, too, the Puranas do not like to admit that the Kaliyuga could have started while Krishna was still on earth; the *Mahabharata* admits this freely, however (IX.59.21). For the argument of this study, the general atmosphere of decline is more significant than the precise moment of its onset.
75. Particularly III.188.
76. Van Buitenen, *Mahābhārata*, II, 29.
77. The war is often compared to a dice game; see chap. IIIB2.
78. See chap. IB, n. 3.
79. Forced to play: Yudhishthira is bound by a vow (see chap. IB, n. 3). Doomed from the start to lose: this being the import of "The Kaunteya loves to gamble but does not know how to play" (II.44.18; II.45.38).
80. This is done by both Bhima and Vikarna in II.61.
81. Cf. VII.50.37, quoted in chap. IIA2, n. 6.
82. Van Buitenen translates, "family game."

83. As in the story of Nala and Damayanti, particularly *Mahabharata* III.55f.
84. For Dvapara, see "Nala and Damayanti," III.55.1ff.
85. Note the similarity between Draupadi's statement of II.62.7, 9, just quoted, and Arjuna's expression of his fears in *Gita* I.40–43, quoted on p. 130. In fact, three of the Kaurava generals represent major familial relationships, violated by the Pandavas in the war: grandfather, brother, and maternal uncle. (Gehrts [p. 239] suggests that Bhishma, Drona, Karna, and Shalya represent the four declining ages.)
86. See VI.44.45f., and many other passages. As a rule, a battle starts in an organized manner, with foes appropriately matched (chariots against chariots, foot soldiers against foot soldiers, etc.), but quickly disintegrates into chaos. For the Kaliyuga parallel, see III.188.28: "Son may kill father, father may kill son. . . ." Besides being forced to fight cousins, teachers, and elders, Arjuna himself is pushed at one point in the battle books to the height of fraternal disloyalty. Angry at him for his slowness in defeating Karna, Yudhishthira has said that Arjuna ought to give up his bow to Krishna. Arjuna has, however, sworn that he will kill anyone who tells him to give up Gandiva (see chap. IIA2, n. 20). He is thus prepared to kill Yudhishthira, when Krishna, scolding him for not knowing *dharma* well enough to be able to figure out such a strategy himself, advises him that to address his older brother in the familiar is equivalent to killing him; so he solves the impasse of oath versus fraternal duty by that lesser evil. Arjuna then wants to kill himself, but Krishna advises him to boast, to build up his morale (in many versions: to kill himself symbolically). This peculiar story, apparently designed as a study of Arjuna's sense of duty (the particular oath is not mentioned elsewhere), is told at VIII.49ff., shortly followed by the real killing of Karna, himself an older brother, unrecognized.
87. Biardeau would agree that the dice game, Pandava exile, and pursuant war represent Kaliyuga decline of *dharma* (see "Conférence," vol. 80–81, pp. 131ff.; vol. 82, p. 90; vol. 87, p. 153; "Etudes" IV, p. 207), but she differs from the present author in her assertion that this Kaliyuga yields (as at the end of a *kalpa* [see chap. IC, n. 17]) to a *pralaya* (the war [see chap. IE]), which clears the air for a new Krtayuga (Yudhishthira's ideal rule) ("Conférence," vol. 80–81, p. 131; vol. 82, p. 90; "Etudes" IV, pp. 153f. [and see p. 172]; etc.). (On trickery in the war as effective for preservation of the greater *dharma*, see "Conférence," vol. 83, p. 105; vol. 86, p. 146; vol. 87, p. 155; vol. 88, p. 178; "Etudes" II, p. 104; "Etudes" IV, pp. 148f., n. 2; 150.) Hiltebeitel cannot quite bring himself to adopt the same position; see "Toward a Coherent Study of Hinduism," *Religious Studies Review* 9 (1983): 210. The present study suggests that with the proviso that the king in some sense makes the age (see p. 185 and chap. IIIC), Yudhishthira and his successors for some generations (that is, to the eternal present) are destined to be good kings in a bad world; if nothing else, the downswing of the epic's mood for book after book once the Kurukshetra War is over—excepting Book XIV, the whole last half—supports such an interpretation: rosy premonitions (IV.27.12ff.) notwithstanding, the joyfulness of Yudhishthira's reign is definitely not emphasized. For Scheuer's opposition to the definitiveness of the Kaliyuga conception in the epic, see Scheuer, pp. 332f.: the Kaliyuga must die with the death of Duryodh-

ana, Kali. (But how would this fit in with Puranic chronology [though cf. Biardeau, "Etudes" IV, p. 154]?) Perhaps the disagreement between the Biardeau-Scheuer conception and that of the present author may best be understood as disagreement between a heroic and a human perspective on the situation depicted; and as might be expected, the conflict is resolved at the level of devotion.

88. Kane, III, 168. Kane's references are not to the Critical Edition, but the Critical Edition equivalents are as follows: I.1.186–87; I.84.6–9; II, Appendix I, no. 30, line 33; II.43.32; II.52.14; III.176.27–28; V.8.35; V.40.30; V.156.4; V.187.17; XV.16.2; I.114.15; II.15.11; V.77.4–5; XII.56.14–15; X.2.3; VII.127.17; XII.27.30; XII.58.13–16; XII.149.46; XIII.6.1ff.; X.2.12–13, 22–23. The issue is, to be sure, complicated further by the doctrine of *karma*, to which many references may be noted in the epic, sometimes in conjunction with the passages cited by Kane in the paragraph quoted; see, e.g., II.15.11. See further, III.181; III.200; etc.
89. The large-scale destruction of *kshatriya*s is an obsession of the epic. Besides its prominence in the repeated story of Rama Jamadagnya (I.2.3ff., etc.), it has become formulaic with regard to the Kurukshetra War.
90. Dhrtarashtra has been interpreted as the personification of blind fate in the epic; see Dumézil, *Mythe et épopée* I, pp. 162ff., and Gehrts, p. 169. As the war proceeds, Dhrtarashtra censures destiny again and again, but Samjaya censures Dhrtarashtra.
91. The sort of moral dilemma that Janamejaya might have faced is indicated in the story told at XII.146ff. of a King Janamejaya (whether the same one or a different one is unclear) killing a brahmin and having to expiate that sin with a horse sacrifice.
92. See chap. IA, n. 10.
93. The fact that the *Mahabharata* is a work of kingly instruction has been pointed out by Biardeau; see "Etudes" IV, p. 173, where she asserts that to recognize this fact means to acknowledge that the didactic and story portions of the epic are closely connected with one another. In making this statement, Biardeau is in part agreeing with the much earlier work of Dahlmann (see Introduction), who also saw a strong connection between the didactic portions of the epic and the epic narrative: the single editor he envisioned had seen his task as the illustration of *dharmashastra* with incidents in the epic story and had connected each epic event with the specific legal points it was supposed to portray or clarify. Dahlmann, with Biardeau, who echoes him without going as far as he does in defense of absolute epic unity, errs on the side of optimism: because he sees the epic story as one of good's victory over evil, his view of epic *dharma* is too idealized, and so he is unable to explain the contradictions between the actions of characters in the story and the laws set forth in the didactic sections, not to mention contradictions *within* the story and *within* the didactic sections. Similarly, Biardeau comes to the conclusion that Yudhishthira really brought in the Krtayuga by his rule, not the Kaliyuga: she too is more optimistic than the epic warrants.

94. Even the kingly instruction should be of concern to ordinary people, for, as the epic states at XII.308.147: "Everyone is king in his own home." That ordinary citizens loved and admired the Pandavas is stressed throughout the epic.
95. See also II.60.31.
96. See in particular XII.230.14ff. and XII.252, where lack of clear moral imperatives is tied explicitly to moral change during the four ages. In countless other places in the *Mahabharata*, the subtlety of *dharma* is mentioned as characteristic of present times. In citing examples, it is necessary to bear in mind that the *yugas* are, in a sense, calculated backward from the present Kali age; see J. F. Fleet, "The Kaliyuga Era of B.C. 3102," *Journal of the Royal Asiatic Society of Great Britain and Ireland* (1911): 480, 495. Thus any conditions of current morality portrayed in the epic may be assumed automatically to be Kaliyuga conditions. Dahlmann also notes subtlety of *dharma* (*Epos und Rechtsbuch*, pp. 62ff.), but does not pursue this point fully because of his optimistic view of the ultimate victory of good in the epic.
97. Cf., e.g., III.149.27, and see further, especially, p. 250.
98. The concept of *apaddharma* pervades the *Mahabharata* story, although it is not often mentioned explicitly outside the didactic books. It is, however, named at I.104.6, where it is stated that the magic charm by which the Pandavas were begotten was given to Kunti by the seer Durvasas, "with a foresight of the Law of Distress [*apaddharma*] that would apply"; cf. I.111.22, etc. See also V.28.3f., where Yudhishthira cites *apaddharma* to explain his current stance, a veiled threat of war.
99. That the epic views itself as connected with the *arthashastra* tradition is suggested by its use of the word *vijigishu* ("one desirous of victory") to characterize its intended beneficiary (as in I.56.19, quoted above, p. 118 [van Buitenen translates, "one who desires to triumph]). *Vijigishu* is the term used by *arthashastra* for an ambitious king: see Gonda, *Kingship*, p. 127.
100. Desire, anger, greed, lust, pride, intoxication (or a similar list).
101. Brhaspati, the priest of the gods, and Ushanas, the priest of the demons, are often-quoted authorities on policy, and connection with their names immediately identifies a statement as a statement of policy. In the *Mahabharata*, Drona is said to incarnate Brhaspati (I.61.63), but, strikingly, aligns himself with the demonic side in the Kurukshetra War.
102. See the discussion of his ability to take various forms, and of his *maya* (XI.24.23f.).
103. See also XII.32.6ff.
104. A recurrent theme. Cf. Yudhishthira's statement in praise of Arjuna at III.142.13–14: "He gave shelter and safety to him who walked the straight path; but to one who was crooked, who sought to kill by trickery, were he the Thunderbolt-wielder [Indra] himself, he was a deadly poison."
105. The word for "trickery," *nikrti*, is precisely that used repeatedly in the dice-game episode to describe Shakuni's means to victory (II.54.7ff.).
106. Probably a conglomeration of sources: the words in v. 16 seem to be those of Manu Svayambhuva.

107. See also XII.192.53ff. for a long speech in praise of truth.
108. The existence of certain permissible lies is reiterated throughout the *Mahabharata*, with their number generally taken to be five, as in I.77.16.
109. Poona Edition, VII, 1310*, expands this statement to approbation of the five kinds of permissible lie (see preceding note).
110. Though to be sure, a fighting brahmin—itself a standard example of *apaddharma* in action; see, e.g., XII.79.1 (and cf. v. 33).
111. An act encouraged throughout Book XIII (*Anushasanaparvan*), which Hopkins ("Bhārata," p. 4) and others call a *danadharma* ("[treatise on] the duty of liberality").
112. For a reference, see chap. IIID, n. 6.
113. Though cf. chap. IIID, n. 6.
114. The pillow-making too is seen by Biardeau ("Etudes" V, pp. 201f., etc.) as an act of world ordering, a propping apart of heaven, incarnate in Bhishma (I.93), and earth.
115. For some references regarding nonviolence, see chap. IA, n. 35.
116. Such discussions as those in XII.230.14ff. and XII.252, cited above, n. 96, take the Vedas, ideally conceived, as the standard of eternal *dharma*.
117. See Biardeau, "Etudes" IV, p. 160, n. 1. Of course *dharma* would approach total disappearance as the Kaliyuga proceeded.

IIB. THE HORSE SACRIFICE

During what is perhaps Arjuna's greatest heroic moment, his defense of the horse during Yudhishthira's horse sacrifice, a few incidents serve to underline his humanity. The first takes place during the fight between Arjuna and the Saindhavas, subjects of Jayadratha, whom Arjuna had killed in the Kurukshetra War (see chap. II-A2). During this battle, the omens become terrible and Arjuna begins to fail; overcome with arrows, he drops Gandiva, and returns to his senses only after the gods and various seers recite blessings on his behalf (XIV.76.12ff.). Later in the same encounter, as Arjuna begins to win, he is approached by Duhshala, the only daughter of Dhrtarashtra and widow of Jayadratha. She carries with her her grandson, the son of her son, Suratha, who had died of sorrow when informed that Arjuna, who had slain his father, had suddenly arrived in his country. Duhshala now asks for mercy for the child, reminding Arjuna that "O great armed one, just as Parikshit, killer of enemy heroes, was born to Abhimanyu, so this grandson of mine was born to Suratha" (XIV.77.33). In other words, she is appealing to Arjuna's paternal emotion, as portrayed in the Abhimanyu sequence; it is striking that she feels she can approach him in this way on behalf of a relative of Jayadratha. To this human appeal from his "sister" (for such Duhshala is, according to Indian kinship rules)[1] Arjuna responds favorably, "censuring *kshatriyadharma*" (XIV.77.39).

Arjuna Dies at the Hand of His Son, Babhruvahana—But Is Revived

The most striking incident of the horse sacrifice is also one of the most humanizing events of Arjuna's career: this is his fight with his own son,

Babhruvahana, in Manipura (XIV.78ff.). Arjuna, "remembering *kshatriyadharma*" (XIV.78.2), challenges his son vigorously (XIV.78.3ff.), but Babhruvahana does not wish to fight against his father. He is, however, encouraged to do so, to prove his heroism, by Ulupi, who suddenly appears on the scene (XIV.78.8ff.); thereupon this heroic youth defeats and kills his father. It was the feeling of Holtzmann (younger) that this event marked Arjuna's death in the original form of the epic;[2] but this is certainly not the case in the extant epic. Here Chitrangada first mourns her slain husband as the various warriors were mourned in the *Striparvan*, underlining his humanity by acknowledging his mortality; Babhruvahana also mourns, and prescribes terrible penances for himself (XIV.79.9ff.). Chitrangada and Babhruvahana then start together to fast to death (XIV.81.1). In the end, however, Ulupi tells Babhruvahana how to revive Arjuna through the use of a special gem, and Babhruvahana does so (XIV.81.2ff.). Note that it is only with the aid of a nonhuman helper that Arjuna can continue to live on this occasion.

The fight between Arjuna and his own father, Indra, at the time of the Khandava Forest burning was discussed in chapter IC, above. In fact, the fight between father and son is common in myth, epic, and saga, establishing a theme of succession of generations.[3] In most cases, however, the central hero is the last figure of his line, or at least is not challenged successfully by a son. Thus, in the fight between Rustam and Suhrab in the *Shahnamah*, which occurs because Suhrab does not recognize his father, the battle results in Suhrab's death: Rustam is shown to be the greater of the two;[4] similarly, the fight between Cuchulainn and his son Connla in the introductory tales of the *Tain Bo Cuailnge*.[5] In having a son who is capable of killing him in battle, Arjuna is unusual among great warrior heroes.[6] Fortunately, the Indian imagination is able to provide a deus ex machina to revive the hero and permit the story to continue.[7] Yet clearly the fact that Arjuna is killed by his son emphasizes his mortal weakness.

As is generally the case, acknowledgment of the hero's mortality is accompanied by recognition of the fact that his morals are less than perfect. The Babhruvahana episode brings out the underlying meaning of this connection: immorality, the failure to support the perfect world order, is a human weakness that results from, accompanies, or leads to mortality. Ulupi explains, thus, that Arjuna's death at the hand of his son was expiation for Arjuna's unrighteous killing of Bhishma

(XIV.82.8ff.).[8] When she adds that Babhruvahana was able to kill Arjuna because "the son is known as the self" (XIV.82.21), she is defending Arjuna's heroism implicitly, despite his apparent failure. Thus the hero-human dialectic, observed in the preceding chapters, continues.

The Mark of Humanity on Arjuna's Body

A most interesting exchange toward the end of the *Ashvamedhikaparvan* likewise suggests the contrast—and connection—between Arjuna's heroism and humanity (XIV.89.1ff.). Anticipating Arjuna's homecoming after following the horse, Yudhishthira asks Krishna why Arjuna has had to suffer so greatly in his lifetime (that is, in context, why he has had to fight so hard) in spite of the fact that he is wise and has a body marked with auspicious marks (that is, is a hero). Yudhishthira asks: "O Krishna, what indeed is the unlucky mark on his body, endowed with all [auspicious] marks, due to which he suffers pains?" (XIV.89.4). Krishna replies that Arjuna's single physical fault is *pindike . . . atikayatah*, which seems to mean "two disproportionately large swellings" (XIV.89.7). Whether this phrase refers to Arjuna's large cheekbones,[9] calves,[10] or testicles,[11] it still entails the ascription of physical imperfection to the otherwise physically perfect Arjuna; or if the last translation is correct, the interpretation of a heroic fertility trait as unlucky. Here, then, is a mark of humanity on Arjuna's body.

Much of Book XIV stresses the fact that Yudhishthira's horse sacrifice was performed perfectly.[12] That, however, the entire affair is denigrated in the end (in the words of a half-golden mongoose) serves to reduce it to human proportions, especially when the very small offering of a poor brahmin is contrasted favorably with Yudhishthira's far greater offering (XIV.92f.): "O kings, this sacrifice is not equal to the *prastha* of ground barley of a generous gleaner who dwelled at Kurukshetra" (XIV.92.7 and 19). Thus is the stature of sacrifice—and with it the heroic role of sacrificer (see, especially, chap. IE)—cast into doubt.

Notes

1. Duhshala is referred to as Arjuna's *bhagini* or *svasr* ("sister"), in XIV.77.24ff.
2. Holtzmann, *Arjuna*, p. 57.

3. For discussion of several examples of tales of generational conflict, see C. Scott Littleton, "The 'Kingship in Heaven' Theme," in Puhvel, *Myth and Law*, pp. 83–121. Littleton's starting point is the Greek example, as found in Hesiod's *Theogony* and Apollodorus's *Bibliotheca*. The father-son combat is Thompson motif N731.2, listed for Persia, Ireland, England, Iceland, Greece, Arabia, China, Philippines, Hawaii. The transference of power from father to son is replete with psychological meaning (for a Freudian view of the Indian case, see Robert P. Goldman, "Fathers, Sons and Gurus: Oedipal Conflict in the Sanskrit Epics," *Journal of Indian Philosophy* 6 [September–December 1978]: 325–92, specifically pp. 329ff. on the Babhruvahana episode); it also has political implications, and may be used to explain and justify current states of affairs.
4. For reference, see chap. IIA2, n. 4.
5. For reference, see chap. IIA2, n. 13.
6. Note, however, a parallel in the strikingly similar story of King Arthur's death at the hand of Mordred, in which Mordred is also killed; see Thomas Malory, *Le Morte d'Arthur* (Caxton), XXI.4. According to the *Telegony*, Odysseus was also killed by a son, Telegonus, who, like Babhruvahana, was borne to his father by a secondary "wife."
7. Or borrow one. It should be noted that the role of Ulupi in this episode resonates with that of the Goddess as a reviver of the dying-and-rising god in the mythology of the early fertility religions—which mythology passed into Indo-European/Semitic thought, as later into the Western mystery cults. A classic example of such a story is that of the rescue of the god Baal from the land of Death by his sister Anath, in the Canaanite materials (see Fontenrose, pp. 130f., etc.); cf. the Egyptian story of the search by Isis for the body of Osiris. Interestingly, a similar story is attached to Indra and recounted in the *Mahabharata*, that is, his rescue by his wife (with male help, to be sure, as would be typical of an Indo-European retelling) from a lake where he had hidden (see chap. IIA3) (V.9ff.; XII.329.17ff.). Thus is evidenced an apparently universal flip side of the active hero or warrior god: a more passive dying-and-rising figure. Might it be suggested that the Babhruvahana episode of the *Mahabharata* uncovers such a flip side of Arjuna, which could thus be appended to the consideration of Arjuna as fertility figure in chaps. IA and IB, above?
8. Also a case of "father" versus "son," as Goldman ("Oedipal Conflict," pp. 333ff.) points out.
9. See the Ganguli-Roy and Dutt translations, and Dumézil, *Warrior*, p. 164.
10. This is Nilakantha's interpretation; see his commentary on XIV.87.8 = Critical Edition XIV.89.7: "The fleshy back portion below the knees is the *pindika*." Also Otto Böhtlingk and Rudolph Roth, *Sanskrit-Wörterbuch*, 7 vols. (St. Petersburg: Buchdruckerei der Kaiserlichen Akademie der Wissenschaften, 1855–75).
11. The last interpretation is suggested by Professor Daniel H. H. Ingalls. In support of this view one may cite Draupadi's reaction, at XIV.89.10, to Krishna's words: "Krishnā Draupadi looked at Krishna askance, with annoyance."
12. See, e.g., XIV.90.18ff.

IIC. THE ASCENT TO HEAVEN, AND CONNECTED EVENTS, I

The Twilight of the Heroes

The *Mausala-*, *Mahaprasthanika-*, and *Svargarohanaparvans* (Books XVI–XVIII) of the *Mahabharata* form a unit that might aptly be named, after the Scandinavian parallel, "The Twilight of the Heroes."[1] This unit, to be referred to henceforth as the "ascent-to-heaven sequence," is filled with the sadness and mystery that characterize ultimate recognition of the hero's mortality and are so often to be noted at the end of an epic or a saga.[2] In the *Mahabharata*, the ascent-to-heaven sequence forms one more link in the chain of humanizing events in Arjuna's life.

In the *Mausalaparvan*, set thirty-six years after the Kurukshetra War (XVI.1.1, etc.; and see XI.25.41),[3] 500,000 (XVI.9.11) Vrshni warriors, impelled by fate and curses,[4] kill one another in a drunken brawl. The immediate cause of the brawl is an argument regarding deceit in the war between Satyaki, who had fought for the Pandavas, and Krtavarman, who had fought for the Kauravas (on Satyaki's role in the deceit, see chap. IIA2; on Krtavarman's, chap. IIIC); the first insult is flung and the first blow struck by Satyaki, Arjuna's disciple.[5] Baladeva and Krishna also die at this time, and Krishna's city of Dvaraka is engulfed by the ocean.

The Puranas locate the start of the Kaliyuga at the time of Krishna's death;[6] in the context of the *Mahabharata*, however, the events of the *Mausalaparvan* simply ratify the earlier onset of that age. Noteworthy is the fact that during the brawl described here, "son killed father and father killed son" (XVI.4.40), precisely as had happened in the Kurukshetra War, and indicating the same disintegration of family loyalties. The entire *Mausalaparvan* seems to mourn the death of the age of heroes, for it uses the word "hero" many times, with reference to the Vrshnis.

The Waning of Arjuna's Heroic Power

The meaning of the *Mausalaparvan* for Arjuna's life is that it marks the waning of his heroic power. Summoned by Daruka, Krishna's charioteer, sent by Krishna shortly before his death (XVI.5.2f.), Arjuna sets out to remove the Vrshni women from Dvaraka. But his weapons (that is, his heroic skills) fail him just at the moment when Abhira bandits, ignoring his battle boast (XVI.8.51), attack the caravan (the proliferation of such "barbarians" being a distinguishing mark of the Kali age):[7]

> Then Arjuna began to raise the great, unaging divine bow, Gandiva, as if with some effort. He strung the bow with difficulty, when the confusion was tumultuous, and thought of his weapons, but could not remember them.[8] And having thus seen that great deterioration in his strength of arms in battle, he became ashamed due to the loss of the divine weapons. And all those Vrshni warriors, riding on elephants, horses, and chariots, were unable to bring back those people who were being carried off. But as they were descending upon them from here and there, due to the abundance of women, the son of Prtha tried to protect the people. Then before the eyes of all the warriors, those extremely wild men drew them away on all sides; and others left of [their own] free will. Then the mighty son of Prtha, Dhanamjaya, agitated, together with the servants of the Vrshnis, struck the barbarians with arrows released from Gandiva. In a moment . . . those arrows of his were exhausted; although inexhaustible formerly, those blood-eaters were exhausted. Then, when his arrows were exhausted, struck with pain and grief, Pakashasani [Arjuna; see Appendix] killed the barbarians with the tip of his bow. Having taken the best women of the Vrshnis and Andhakas while the son of Prtha was looking on, those barbarians departed in all directions. . . . But mighty Dhanamjaya reflected on that fate in his mind. Pervaded with pain and grief, he gave himself over to sighing. Due to the loss of his weapons and the exhaustion of his strength of arms and the intractability of his bow and the exhaustion of his arrows, the son of Prtha was depressed, thinking "This is fate." He desisted then . . . and said, "All is lost." [XVI.8.52–64]

Note the parallel between the weapon failure here and that described in the mountain-man fight; but there the ending was a happy one. Not so in the *Mausalaparvan*—and here the failure is doubly emphasized, in that it manifests itself as an inability to protect women, that is, the loss of one of Arjuna's greatest heroic traits, his sexual prowess.

The dejection felt by Arjuna at this time is also described in his discussion with Vyasa in the following chapter. Vyasa sees that Arjuna is "sad minded, sighing again and again, world-weary" (XVI.9.4), and asks him why. At this point, Arjuna mourns the loss of Krishna and the Vrshni heroes, clearly expressing the irony of the situation: "Able to withstand clubs, iron maces, and spears, with arms like iron maces, they have been killed with *eraka* grass" (XVI.9.10). (The grass had turned into the clubs lethally employed in the final Vrshni brawl [XVI.4.34ff.].) And: "I consider the destruction of Sharngadhanvan [Krishna] as incredible as the drying of the ocean, the moving of a mountain, the falling of the sky, or the coolness of fire" (XVI.9.13–14).

In other words, world order, to be protected by the hero, has collapsed. Next Arjuna recounts the failure of his weapons, that is, the loss of his own heroic skill. And then again he mourns the loss of Krishna, with the clear statement that his heroic success had depended on this helper:

> Not seeing him who first, with his energy, burned the armies of the enemy, [which] I afterward destroyed with arrows released from Gandiva, I despair. . . . I cannot bear to live without heroic Janardana. [XVI.9.21–23]

Arjuna has been reduced to human status, and mortality is the consequence. Vyasa answers his lamentation with a statement that all the events are due to fate and a brahmin's curse (XVI.9.25f.).

The issue of fate versus effort, referred to frequently throughout the *Mahabharata*, is central to the ascent-to-heaven sequence. To be caught up by fate and struggle against it, succumbing ultimately, is human nature, emphasized in the *Mausalaparvan*.

Retirement from the World

Book XVII (*Mahaprasthanikaparvan*) begins with Yudhishthira attributing the end of the Vrshnis to fate. Arjuna, followed by the other

Pandavas, agrees, and all decide that the time has come for them to retire from the world. Then follow the anointing of Parikshit as king (on Parikshit, see further chap. IIIC), the performance of funeral rites for the Vrshnis, and the appointment of Krpa (in his capacity as "compassion" [the implication of his name]?)[9] as Parikshit's teacher (XVII.1.2ff.). The point being made here is similar to that made through the death of Arjuna at the hand of his son Babhruvahana: the heroic generation is being superseded. In this case, the succession of generations is carried through to its logical conclusion: a human generation takes over, and the audience is brought into the present state of the world; Parikshit was Janamejaya's father.

The scene of the Pandavas and Draupadi setting out (XVII.1.18ff.) is compared to the scene of their setting out on the eve of their forest exile, although there are now seven members in the party instead of six, since a dog (later seen to be Dharma in disguise) has joined them. But the party members are cheerful on this occasion, and there is a sense of acceptance of fate on the part of all concerned. Even the citizens they are leaving behind do not entreat the Pandavas to stay as frantically as they did years earlier. In fact, retirement from active life in old age is desirable for a householder, according to Hindu rules of *varnashrama-dharma*.[10]

Soon, however, one learns that there has been some defiance of fate, after all, on Arjuna's part, for he has kept Gandiva and his quivers with him out of greed. He agrees to give up these weapons only when forced to do so by Agni; this Arjuna does by throwing them back to the god Varuna, in the waters, who had supplied them originally (XVII.1.32ff.).[11] Divestiture of weapons marks a return backward through initiation to what could be called a "preheroic" state. The fact that Arjuna is the only one of the brothers visibly to undergo this struggle with fate accentuates his human character.

Having traveled in all directions, "desiring to circumambulate the earth, with *yoga* as their *dharma*" (XVII.1.44), the Pandavas finally turn northward and ascend into the Himalaya (XVII.2.1). Now the northward ascent takes on human meaning, as a return to origins, or a death.

At this point in the text, there follows the famous story that describes the expiring of the various human members of the party (excepting Yudhishthira) in turn, as they approach Mount Meru, practicing *yoga* (XVII.2.3ff.). In case after case, Bhima, the last to expire, asks why the person has fallen, and Yudhishthira answers him. Draupadi, Yudhishthira says, has fallen because of her partiality to Arjuna, among all her husbands (XVII.2.6). Sahadeva falls next, because of the pride he took in his wisdom, Yudhishthira says (XVII.2.10). Nakula falls because of his pride in his beauty (XVII.2.16f.).

The fall of Arjuna causes Yudhishthira to utter a statement on heroism, which, more clearly perhaps than any other in the epic, gives expression to the human weaknesses of the hero. Bhima asks:

> I do not recall any falsehood on the part of this noble one, even in insignificant matters. As the evil consequence of what, therefore, has he fallen to the earth? [XVII.2.20]

And Yudhishthira replies:

> Arjuna spoke thus: "I will indeed burn the enemy in one day." But he did not do it. Considering himself a hero, he has therefore fallen. And this Phalguna looked down upon all bowmen. One desiring well-being must do as he says he will. [XVII.2.21–22]

Yudhishthira's words stress again the importance of fulfilling vows as a heroic accomplishment. Exaggerating some boast uttered by Arjuna to rouse himself in battle, such as that reported briefly at VI.77.35 ("I will fell them today . . ."), Yudhishthira's statement has been molded specifically to encapsulate Arjuna's flaws, at the end of Arjuna's life. In every case, Yudhishthira's explanation of a character's fall summarizes important negative aspects of the character. Perhaps this point is most obvious in the case of Bhima's fall, regarding which Yudhishthira states: "Your honor has eaten too much, and you boast of your power. Not having considered the other [world?], you have therefore fallen to the earth, O son of Prtha" (XVII.2.25).[12]

In Arjuna's case, the fault is typically that of a humanized hero: in the pride of his idealized heroism, Arjuna made a statement or promise or vow[13] that he was incapable of fulfilling just because he was really human and limited. Particularly in view of Arjuna's periodic hesitation to fight to his utmost at Kurukshetra (see, especially, chaps. IIA1 and IIA3), his words are seen to have been a gross overestimation. Thus the difficulty of fulfilling a vow emphasizes Arjuna's humanity in the ascent-to-heaven sequence, as it did in the Abhimanyu sequence, but more conclusively.

The Disappointment of Heroic Expectations: Hell Instead of Heaven

Yudhishthira's bodily ascent to heaven in the third chapter of the *Mahaprasthanikaparvan* is reminiscent of Arjuna's ascent to Indra's heaven in Book III (see chap. ID). In fact, certain elements of Yudhishthira's ascent imply that Arjuna should really be the central figure here, or originally was. To begin with, Yudhishthira ascends, as Arjuna did, in a celestial chariot that Indra brings for him. At first Yudhishthira refuses to go because Indra demands that he abandon the faithful dog, the only one of his party left. Among other arguments, some versions (though not the critical text) make him refuse to do this because of a vow:

> I would indeed strive to fulfill this eternal vow of mine: never to send away, even if it means abandoning my life, one who is frightened, devoted, or afflicted, saying "There is no other [recourse]," one who has arrived, exhausted, for protection, desiring life. [Poona Edition, XVII, 13*]

This statement sounds suspiciously like a cross between Arjuna's battle vows, such as caused him to protect Satyaki (see chap. IIA2), and the more general rules of warrior chivalry (see, especially, chap. IIA3), reworked. When, after the dog reveals himself as the god Dharma, Yudhishthira does ascend, the seer Narada is quoted as saying of him:

> Having obscured the glory of those in attendance here, even of all the royal seers, the king of the Kurus indeed surpasses [them]. We have heard of no other than the Pandava who, having filled the worlds with fame, energy, [and] excellence of behavior, arrived [in heaven] with his own body. [XVII.3.26–27]

Arjuna, however, had performed this very feat in Book III.[14]

Even if Arjuna, or his prototype, was once the central figure of an episode of final bodily ascent to heaven at the end of a heroic life, Yudhishthira has taken his place here. Why should Yudhishthira be the central figure of a heroic adventure, an ascent to Indra's heaven? The answer appears to be that Yudhishthira, although he is in many ways the least traditionally heroic of the Pandavas, is also the one who manages to remain the most aloof and idealized, who succumbs the least to his human failings; this is because he embodies *sanatanadharma* (see chap.

IIA3). The other Pandavas and, in fact, all the other *Mahabharata* heroes, typified by Arjuna, have fallen from their heroic status in the Kaliyuga, when traditional heroism is dead. Yudhishthira has, from time to time, wavered on the brink of despair, but the epic's glorification of *dharma* causes him to be elevated once again, at the last moment. In light of *dharma*'s failure throughout the *Mahabharata*, however, the final glorification of Yudhishthira may seem less convincing than does Arjuna's humanized role. Certainly the humanizing pull is admitted even in the case of Yudhishthira, when his affection for his lost wife and brothers is stressed. Indra, indeed, recognizes this fact, and says to Yudhishthira, almost in surprise: "Even today the human state touches you, O king; [but] this is heaven" (XVII.3.33). In addition, Yudhishthira, who started out this sequence almost totally knowledgeable (as witness his explanations to Bhima), becomes more and more confused as the sequence continues. His continual bewilderment and need for instruction are quite human, as were Arjuna's at the start of the Kurukshetra War. Yudhishthira's confusion combined with his affection, both human qualities, cause him to insist again and again that he be brought to where his brothers are, even if it means giving up heavenly bliss. This wavering between great knowledge and almost total confusion is no more than is typical of Yudhishthira throughout the epic, marking his particular reaction to the Kaliyuga. Yet his humanization does not proceed nearly so far as that of the other Pandavas in the ascent-to-heaven section of the epic.

For while Yudhishthira has been wafted to heaven, the other Pandavas have been transported to hell; this is where Yudhishthira eventually finds them (XVIII.2.32ff.). The point of much of the *Svargarohanaparvan* seems to be the disappointment of heroic expectations of heaven, in connection with the ambiguity of human morality: it is Duryodhana who, as a great hero killed in battle, has made his way to heaven (XVIII.1.4ff.)! (Even Yudhishthira, when he sees this reversal, briefly censures *dharma*.) The epic's explanation: all people, both good and evil, go to both hell and heaven. Those who are evil go to heaven first, then hell. Good people, it is implied (if not stated directly), first expiate their sins in hell, then go to heaven (XVIII.3.12ff.). (Here again is, in structuralist terms, that attempted mediation typical of the *Mahabharata*'s treatment of the human condition [see chap. IIA3]. Note too how Karna is classed with the Pandavas, not the Kauravas, throughout the *Svargarohanaparvan.*) Yudhishthira is being shown hell, Indra says, because of his deception of Drona; the other Pandavas have been sent there for the same or similar reasons (XVIII.3.14f.). As if to underline Yudhishthira's humanity at this point, Dharma praises him for his loyalty to his brothers and wife, that is, his refusal to leave hell and go back to heaven without them (XVIII.3.33). And as if to underline the connection of these words with realistic kingly instruction, both Indra and Dharma make the identical statement: "My dear, hell must be seen [even] unwillingly by all kings" (XVIII.3.11 and 35).

There is another level of the ascent-to-heaven sequence, which, in the end, resolves all moral ambiguity by bringing both Pandavas and Kauravas to heaven, and stating that ultimately all the figures of the Kurukshetra War were reabsorbed into the supernatural beings from whom they had originated. This ending is discussed further in Part III of this study, which deals with that level of the *Mahabharata* in which the human condition is transcended. (On the ascent-to-heaven sequence, see, specifically, chap. IIID.) Before proceeding to that discussion, however, it is necessary to review the findings of the present chapter regarding Arjuna.

With regard to Arjuna, the point of the main body of the ascent-to-heaven sequence is that in the end his heroic powers desert him, and he dies a human death—mysterious and sad, in that it is a reversal of his heroic nature, but quite human. Formerly he went to the other world (Indra's heaven) as part of an initiatory sequence; that is, in a sense, he died and rose again. In fact, the hero's visit to the other world, exposing him as it does to his mortality, can have two possible results: the hero may overcome death or succumb to it. In the ascent-to-heaven sequence, the latter result occurs: Arjuna goes to the other world never to return.[15] Even if this sequence should be taken as a late addition to the *Mahabharata* (although the critical text includes it),[16] one cannot deny that it reflects an extremely significant aspect of Arjuna's personality—his humanity—and in fact caps it.

Notes

1. Note Dvaraka's far western location.
2. Thus, Sayers writes regarding *Roland* (p. 26): "It ends, like the *Iliad* and *Aeneid*, in a minor key, and on a falling cadence." Cf. the statement of Irawati Karve in *Yugānta: The End of an Epoch* (Poona: Deshmukh Prakashan, 1969), p. 16, that her family always viewed the *Mahabharata* as a tragedy, an expression of the futility of human life.
3. Fleet (p. 687) takes the thirty-six years as thirty-six years after Yudhishthira was first crowned king.
4. The first curse is that spoken by Gandhari, at XI.25.36ff. Blaming Krishna for his indifference to the killing during the Kurukshetra War, she curses him to die "by contemptible means" (v. 41) in thirty-six years, with all his relatives already dead. The second curse is that discussed in the *Mausalaparvan* itself (XVI.2.4ff.); it was pronounced upon the Vrshnis by three sages, Vishvamitra, Kanva, and Narada, after the Vrshnis tried to play a trick on these sages.
5. See XVI.7.5f.
6. See chap. IIA3, n. 74.
7. III.186.30 specifically mentions Abhiras among these.
8. Refers to the mental calling of weapons.
9. *Krpā* = "compassion" (see chap. IIA1, n. 3; see further, I.120.18).
10. See, e.g., *Laws of Manu* VI. Cf. *Mahabharata* XII.236f., etc.
11. See chap. ID, n. 5. Cf. King Arthur's means of giving up Excalibur, as in Malory, XXI.5.
12. Dumézil (*Mythe et épopée* I, p. 82) suggests that Yudhishthira's explanations in this episode have no connection with specific acts committed by the respective characters earlier in the epic; he tries (with some effort) to connect them with the trifunctional hierarchy he finds represented by the Pandavas (see chap. IA). Clearly, the faults listed represent explication by some epic composer who considered the basic story but not necessarily all the extant details. Regarding the older brothers, the basis of the accusation is clear; regarding the twins, as usual, less so. The division of beauty and wisdom between Nakula and Sahadeva may be based on an ideology that lies behind the Pandava hierarchy, as Dumézil suggests, or may be quite random.
13. See Nilakantha's commentary: "Arjuna said 'in one day' due to pride of heroism, and from falsely promising he fell—this is the meaning." Note that Nilakantha specifies false "promising" (*[mithya]pratijnatva*) here, elevating the battle boast to a full-fledged oath (see chap. IIA2, n. 18 and n. 20); XVII.2.21–22 does not, in fact, go quite so far.
14. See, specifically, III.225.29.
15. There is a suggestion that he may return in another cycle (see chap. IIIC).
16. The brevity and regularity of these books suggest that they are late in their present form, but of course their material may be early. In fact, M. J. Darmesteter, "Points de contact entre le Mahâbhârata et le Shâh-Nâmah," *Journal Asiatique*, 8th series, 10 (1887): 38ff., suggests a Persian (Indo-European) parallel to the events of the *Mahaprasthanikaparvan*. The present study will hypothesize, in chap. IIID, that the ascent-to-heaven sequence embodies, in part, a philosophy which is later than that of much of the rest of the epic.

PART III: DEVOTEE

IIIA. THE BURNING OF THE KHANDAVA FOREST, II

In Part I of this study, Arjuna's character as epic hero was explored, and in Part II it was shown how Arjuna as epic hero is reduced to human proportions. The aim of Part III will be to explore that aspect of Arjuna's total character which elevates him again to heroic status of a different sort: that is, his religious devotion. The discussion undertaken here will consist of reevaluation of all that has been said regarding Arjuna in Parts I and II in light of an additional factor: Arjuna's religious faith. Part III will consider statements about Arjuna that appear throughout the epic, many of which are attached to episodes that have been discussed already; an entirely new sequence will be added to the consideration only in chapter IIIC. The statements to be dealt with here are such as serve to raise all of Arjuna's exploits to a transcendent plane, giving them rich religious significance. It is this religious dimension of Arjuna which most strongly suggests that he be taken as a role model; it becomes apparent, from his example, that a heroism of religion is able to restore a hero to heroic status even in an age that is not conducive to heroism.

Arjuna and Krishna as Two Ancient Sages, Nara and Narayana

As a preliminary example of the manner in which the traditionally heroic, not to mention the human, dimension of a particular episode is transcended in favor of the religious dimension, one may turn again to the burning of the Khandava Forest. There Arjuna appears as epic hero, with Krishna as his heroic friend and accomplice. Another dimension is added to the episode, however, in I.219.12–18, which was not considered previously, but which may be quoted now:

> When the Gods retreated, a disembodied voice spoke to Indra with a mighty and deep rumble: "Your friend, the great Snake Takṣaka, is not here, for at the time of the burning of the Khāṇḍava he went to the Field of the Kurus.[1] You cannot defeat Vāsudeva and Arjuna when they stand fast in war, Śakra, listen to my word! They are the two divinities Nara and Nārāyaṇa, who are renowned in heaven. You yourself know well of their power and bravery. Unassailable, invincible in battle, these two ancient great seers cannot be vanquished in any world. They are most worshipful to all the Gods, and to Asuras, Yakṣas, Rākṣasas and Gandharvas, men, Kiṃnaras, and Snakes [various classes of beings]. Therefore, pray depart from here with the Gods, O Vāsava [Indra], and watch this destruction of the Khāṇḍava Forest, which has been ordained."

Here is a new standard of heroism (the word that van Buitenen translates as "power" here being *virya*, that is, "heroism," "virility" [I.219.15]). Actually, however, Arjuna and Krishna are said to be more than heroes: they are said to possess the omnipotence of divinity, and the success of their venture is regarded as a foregone conclusion; hearing who they really are, Indra simply gives up the fight (I.219.19). This impression is reinforced by the I, Appendix I, no. 118, version of the story. Here (lines 130ff.) Agni is promised by Brahma, even before he undertakes it, that his burning of the Khandava Forest will succeed, on the grounds that Nara and Narayana, incarnate in Arjuna and Krishna, will aid him. The critical version, on the other hand, saves the identification of Arjuna and Krishna with Nara and Narayana until the end, then uses it to provide a full explanation for Indra's capitulation.

The identification must not have come as a complete surprise to the traditional audience: it is in the nature of oral literature that stories are told and retold, so that suspense is not the most important element of a good tale; and the *Mahabharata* in its extant form mentions that Arjuna and Krishna are Nara and Narayana twice in earlier passages (I.1.117 and I.210.5). Nonetheless, superimposition of the Nara-Narayana identification upon the Khandava Forest burning seems totally to transform the meaning of the heroic exploit. Not to mention the divine nature of Arjuna and Krishna naturally results in a certain emphasis being placed on the human side of their heroism, their risk. As soon as the identification with divinities is mentioned, however, the human side of the heroes is obscured. This pattern, set up by the Khandava episode, is repeated again and again throughout the epic, for example, in the mountain-man sequence (here Arjuna is informed of his own identity as Nara [III.41.1, quoted below, p. 218; etc.]),[2] and at crucial moments of the battle books.[3]

It is now necessary to look more closely at the Nara-Narayana pair, with whom Arjuna and Krishna are identified. One notes first that the pair appears to have an independent mythology, which may be construed as prior to its identification with Arjuna and Krishna in the *Mahabharata.*[4] From the epic, one learns that Nara and Narayana were two seers, whose godlike power derived from a tremendously long course of austerities that they practiced at the Badari hermitage in the Himalaya (III.41.1, etc.). Any mention of the two in the epic carries with it implicitly the eternality and perfection of their friendship: it is said that as a pair, Nara and Narayana are born *yuga* after *yuga*, "for the sake of maintenance of the world" (*lokayatravidhanartham*) (VII.172.81),[5] Arjuna and Krishna incarnating the pair in the present age. Completely apart from any identification with Arjuna and Krishna, Nara and Narayana play the decisive role in the epic's account of the god-demon battle at the churning of the ocean (I.17.2ff., especially 18ff.).[6]

God as Friend

From one point of view, it may be concluded that Nara and Narayana are equals in a very successful heroic (including ascetic) companionship. This view finds support in the initiation scenario of the Khandava episode, where the identification with Arjuna and Krishna is made, as in the ocean-churning story, where it is not. The related names "Nara" and "Narayana" may even be thought of as twinship names, as suggested with regard to "Arjuna" and "Krishna" in chapter IC, above. From another point of view, however, it is clear that the source of the Nara-Narayana pair's omnipotence is actually Narayana, for it is he who is identical with Vishnu, that is, the supreme Godhead;[7] this identity is reiterated throughout the extant *Mahabharata*, which regards "Narayana" as a name of Vishnu, and Krishna as an incarnation of Vishnu/Narayana.

The name "Nara" means "man."[8] As discussed in Part II of this study, Arjuna, although heroic and semidivine, suffers from human weaknesses when left to his own devices; thus his identification with Nara in the

Nara-Narayana pair. The name "Narayana," whatever its origin,[9] was thought to carry with it the connotation of "man's [Nara's] goal [or support, or refuge]."[10] "Narayana" does seem, thus, to suggest a certain leadership or preeminence. It even appears possible, although this is by no means essential to the argument being presented here, that the name "Nara" could have been derived backward from "Narayana" taken as a patronymic. Yet even if Narayana's superiority is not inherent in his name or its history, it is certainly indicated by the epic's statement that Narayana created Nara by his austerities (VII.172.80). Similarly, a brief retelling of the Khandava Forest burning, in the context of a long chapter in praise of Krishna late in the *Mahabharata*, apparently views Krishna (Vishnu) as the unique source of power for this feat: "Once that noble lord went, satisfied, to the Khandava Forest, as fire. And having conquered the *rakshasa*s and snakes, omnipotent, he offered it all in the fire" (XIII.143.23).[11]

When Narayana/Vishnu/Krishna is taken as its supreme member, the Nara-Narayana friendship, and thus the Arjuna-Krishna friendship, takes on a new appearance. Here is a heroic friendship in which the companion or helper is God himself. As suggested earlier (chap. IC), divine help is not an uncommon theme in heroic literature. Perhaps the most outstanding characteristic of this help in the *Mahabharata*, however, is that it derives not from one god among many, but from the infallible One, Vishnu, incarnate in Krishna. The case might be compared to that of the biblical God aiding the patriarchs or the Christian God aiding Beowulf or Roland: the relationship of Arjuna to Krishna, Nara to Narayana, is a relationship of devotion (*bhakti*) to the Supreme.

In the context of the Khandava episode, this point is particularly telling, for here the enemy conquered by the heroes is Indra himself—the most important of the lesser gods (see Introduction), but not great enough to win this battle. In fact, it is possible to see in this episode a reflection of the historical process whereby the worship of the Vedic god Indra (with its characteristic ritual, the Vedic sacrifice) was superseded by worship of the fully Hindu god Vishnu, such as evidently lies, for example, behind the famous Puranic story of Krishna holding up Govardhana Mountain to protect his companions from Indra's storm.[12] Part I of the present study noted the connection between Indra and the Indian epic heroes, particularly Arjuna. Yet at another level of Arjuna's character, the level of devotion to supreme divinity, which forms the subject of Part III, Arjuna's close relationship with Indra has been surpassed by his relationship with Vishnu/Krishna, even to the extent of fighting against Indra with Krishna's help. Thus, although at the heroic level Arjuna's power is based on his being Indra's son, the power of his fully developed character is predicated upon his relationship with Krishna—and it is Krishna who is the source of this power. Correspondingly, the epic stresses the relationship between the king and Vishnu.[13]

Vaishnava theology (the theology of Vishnu worship) has viewed friendship as one of the desirable relationships between a devotee and God;[14] certainly it is the outstanding relationship with Krishna enjoyed by any character in the *Mahabharata*. At the level of devotion resides the true meaning of statements of the eternality and perfection of Arjuna's and Krishna's friendship, for *bandhava* ("friend," "kinsman") has become a devotional name of God (XII.325.4.167). Descriptions of Arjuna that merely serve to emphasize his beauty at the heroic level seem to suggest his connection with Krishna at the devotional level: such characteristics as lotus eyes[15] and dark skin[16] are seen as being typical of Vishnu incarnate in Krishna.[17] Similarly, certain of Arjuna's exploits that are merely typical at the heroic level are seen at the devotional level greatly to resemble exploits of Krishna: such, for example, is Arjuna's stealing of Subhadra, comparable to Krishna's stealing of Rukmini;[18] or Arjuna's battle with the Pauloma and Kalakeya demons in their airborne (III.170.8ff.) city, comparable to Krishna's battle with Shalva, king of the airborne Saubha (III.15ff.).[19]

Some of the heroic parallels between Arjuna and Indra may be reevaluated at the devotional level as parallels between Arjuna and Vishnu. Here Gandiva is seen to resemble Vishnu's discus as much as Indra's thunderbolt.[20] Draupadi is an incarnation of Shri, who according to the mythology is Vishnu's wife, not Indra's—the story of the five Indras (see chap. IB) notwithstanding.[21] Arjuna as demon fighter plays a role modeled after that of Vishnu's incarnations (see chap. IIIB2) as much as that of Indra. (In Indian mythology, demon fighting seems originally to have been an Indra role, which later passed over to Vishnu;[22] Arjuna borrowed it, it seems, from both these models.) Could the once-mentioned idea that Karna embodies the demon Naraka (see chap. IA) be aimed specifically at setting up an opponent for Nara and Narayana, as the similarity of names suggests?[23] One notes, finally, that Arjuna is compared to Vishnu more than Indra in his Book I birth prophecy, quoted on pp. 29–30.

Arjuna Divinized

Here too one may best understand statements of Arjuna's divinity found here and there in the epic, including that in I.219.15, quoted above. If Arjuna is semidivine as Indra's son and partial incarnation (see chap. IA), he is fully divine as Vishnu/Krishna's friend and devotee. After their battle in the mountain-man sequence, Shiva tells Arjuna:

> Nara you were in a previous body, with Nārāyaṇa your friend, and at Badarī you did awesome austerities for many myriads of years. In you there is great splendor as there is in Viṣṇu, the supreme person. The world is held up by the splendor of the two of you, who are the foremost of men. At the consecration of Indra you took the great bow that thundered like a monsoon cloud and with Kṛṣṇa chastised the Dānavas, lord. [III.41.1–3]

Here Arjuna is viewed as partaking of divinity insofar as his splendor (*tejas*) is equal to Vishnu's. Arjuna is also said to have participated with Krishna in divine exploits in defense of the gods against the demons. In the following chapter, Kubera calls Arjuna "ancient god everlasting" (*purvadeva sanatana*) (III.42.32). Even more explicit are the passages in which Arjuna and Krishna are identified with one another, as, for example, when they are referred to as the "two Krishnas" in the Khandava episode and elsewhere (see chap. IC). The full meaning of such passages is to be found only at the level of devotion: Arjuna as devotee participates in Krishna's divine nature. This idea is greatly developed in the epic. For example, Krishna states in VII.56.29–30, with obvious religious meaning:

> Tomorrow all the worlds, with gods, *gandharva*s, goblins, snakes, and *rakshasa*s, will know me [to be] a friend of Savyasachin. Whoever hates him hates me. Whoever follows him follows me. Let it be understood that Arjuna is one-half of my body.

Thus the equality of Arjuna's and Krishna's heroic friendship is restored at a higher level, where both parties are taken to be gods.[24]

Sometimes the identity of Arjuna and Krishna is stated as the poetic expression of a monistic philosophy: the two are really one self. VII.10.38 states, for example, that Arjuna is Krishna's self and Krishna is Arjuna's self, while v. 41 of the same chapter speaks of Nara and Narayana as one self that has been made twofold. At XVI.7.15 Krishna is quoted as saying: "Know that I am Arjuna and Arjuna is me." The Khandava episode itself, however, does not contain such material, preferring, as it does, the image of two Krishnas side by side.[25]

In chapter IA it was mentioned that the Pandavas are sometimes worshiped in cults in various areas of India; these seemed to be based upon the semidivinity of the hero. At the devotional level, the worship of Arjuna in particular is seen to have another meaning and dimension: Arjuna may have become an object of worship largely by virtue of inclusion in the sphere of Krishna *bhakti*, as a result of his close relationship with Krishna. In this regard, a famous passage may be cited, which seems to refer to the worship of Arjuna (unique among the Pandavas) and connect it with that of Krishna, as early as the fourth century B.C.; this is Panini (the great Sanskrit grammarian) IV.3.98, which states: "vāsudevarjunabhyam vun." The precise meaning of this phrase, which summarizes a grammatical rule, is that the suffix *aka* may be added to a name *X*, to create a word meaning "one who is a worshiper of *X*"; the two examples offered by Panini are *vāsudevaka* (Vāsudeva being a name of Krishna) and *arjunaka*.[26]

At the same time, it becomes apparent that heroic traits of semidivinity and divine traits, that is, heroic and devotional traits, closely related to one another, may easily flow into one another; and in particular, an incarnation, like a hero, is a cross between divinity and humanity. Compare with the case of Arjuna the case of Rama Dasharathi, who undergoes heroic experiences similar to Arjuna's, but with Krishna's fully divine powers: according to the extant *Ramayana*, Rama is, like Krishna, an incarnation of Vishnu. Rama is what Arjuna would be were he absorbed completely into his divine friend. In fact, a similar model may be applied to Krishna himself, who is both hero and God.

The case of Arjuna is particularly interesting for the very reason that his heroism and devotee/divinity have not coalesced completely. In parallel lines throughout the epic, Arjuna's heroism, humanity, and devotion are all emphasized; within a chapter, Arjuna's significance may fluctuate from level to level. Nonetheless, the levels are all connected, as will continue to be noted throughout Part III. To summarize the findings in this regard so far: Arjuna restores his threatened heroic potential, and transcends it, by his devotion to God. Or, to be truer to the epic narrative, one may restate the preceding as follows: Arjuna's heroism carries in itself *at all times* the seeds of its transformation.

To conclude this chapter, a final issue must be raised. That the Vishnu/Krishna devotional movement in general has had tremendous influence upon the extant epic may be seen in numerous passages, including the entire *Gita*. The name "Narayana," however, often refers specifically to the God of a particular branch of the movement, the Pancharatra.[27] Although the Pancharatra school is mentioned by name only a few times in the *Mahabharata* (XII.322.24; XII.326.100; XII.337.59, 63, 67), there is evidence that it was quite influential at some stage of the epic's redaction: passages couched in Pancharatra language are to be found, particularly, in the didactic books of the epic. The longest and best-known passage of this kind is the "Narayaniya" section of Book XII (XII.321–39), which features a yogic journey of the seer Narada northward to Badari and thence to the "White Island" (Shvetadvipa), where live the completely fulfilled worshipers of Nara and Narayana. It is specifically this section that mentions the Pancharatra school by name, and is generally accepted as an early product of this school.[28] At the devotional level, the White Islanders correspond to that ideal which at the heroic level was represented by the Northern Kurus.

But a far greater influence of the Pancharatra school than appears from the explicitly Pancharatra passages may be posited here: the identification of Arjuna and Krishna with Nara and Narayana appears to be connected with the worship of Narayana by the Pancharatrins (or some closely related group). Furthermore, many manuscripts of the *Mahabharata*, northern recension, preface the various books with a repeated invocation (*mantra*) dedicated to Nara and Narayana, which has been included in the Critical Edition before I.1.1 and in the apparatus for every other book of the epic:

> narayanam namaskrtya naram chaiva narottamam/
> devim sarasvatim chaiva tato jayam udirayet//

> Having honored Narayana and also Nara, the best of men, and also the goddess Sarasvati,[29] one should set *jaya* in motion.[30]

Here an intimate connection is drawn between Nara-Narayana and *jaya*, that is, either the *Mahabharata* as a work (see chap. IE) or victory in general (including spiritual victory), depending upon one's interpretation of the stanza.[31] Narada and Vyasa, closely associated with Pancharatra doctrine in the "Narayaniya" section (Narada as its student,[32] Vyasa as an incarnation of Narayana [XII.334.9; XII.337.4ff.])[33] and elsewhere,[34] are both important figures throughout the epic (and see, especially, chap. IIIC). Finally, a connection between the doctrines of this school and the extant epic's portrayal of certain events in Book X may be suggested (see chap. IIIC).[35]

Since the explicitly Pancharatra passages of the epic are apparently late (the name "Narayana" not being found in the *Gita* at all),[36] the specifically Pancharatra elements of the Arjuna-Krishna relationship may be thought of as late additions; this refers primarily to the Nara-Narayana identification, while other devotional aspects of the relationship must be older. It is striking, then, to see how this identification has dispersed throughout the epic, transforming the adventures of Arjuna one after another.

Notes

1. Thus Takshaka survived. A connection is drawn here between snakes and Kurukshetra.
2. Note too that V.48.13ff. refers to Narayana's participation in the antidemon battles of the mountain-man sequence (or their reduplication), along with Arjuna/Nara.
3. See, e.g., Vyasa's words to Ashvatthaman at VII.172.50ff.
4. Sushil Kumar De, "Sects and Sectarian Worship in the Mahabharata," *Our Heritage* 1 (1953): 14, n. 2, suggests, however, that the figure of Nara is derived from Arjuna, rather than merely being identified with him.
5. *Lokayatravidhana* is equivalent to *lokasamgraha*, mentioned in chap. IIA1.
6. It is, however, difficult to tell how independent of the central plot of the epic this story is.
7. Some didactic passages of the *Mahabharata* view Shiva as the supreme God, but the central narrative—and much of the didactic material—favors Vishnu/Krishna, relegating Shiva, with all other Hindu deities, to a secondary (though still important) position. For further discussion of Shiva's role, see chap. IIIC, especially n. 13.
8. This is not to imply that Nara is entirely human in origin. As Biardeau has argued ("Etudes" V, p. 91), the figure of Nara may be derived from the figure of Purusha, well known as early as *Rg Veda* X.90, who is superhuman, although his name too means "man" (he is the primal man). (The word *purusha* appears twice in III.41.1–3, quoted on p. 218, in the phrases translated by van Buitenen as "the supreme person" and "'the foremost of men.") A reflection of Nara's supernatural origin may perhaps be noted in *Mahabharata* V.186.19, where Arjuna/Nara is apparently identified with Prajapati ("lord of creatures"), who is himself sometimes identified with Purusha (see *Shatapatha Brahmana* XI.1.6.2).

9. For a good discussion, see Jaiswal, pp. 33ff. Narayana may in truth be the patronymic of some historical individual.
10. This is one etymology offered by the epic (V.68.10; van Buitenen translates, "the course of men"). XII.328.35 mentions this derivation, but seems to prefer one based on Narayana's connection with the waters (*naras*).
11. Cf. the story told in XIII.126, where Krishna burns a mountain in a display for the seers. The harm to the animals living there is stressed, but in the end the act turns out to be little more than a trick, for Krishna is able to restore the mountain. A competing version of the story, with Shiva in the central role, is told in XIII.127.
12. The Govardhana story is mentioned briefly in *Mahabharata* II.38.9, etc.; see further, *Harivamsha* LIX ff. and *Bhagavata Purana* X.24ff. With regard to the relative youth of the Vishnu/Krishna cult in comparison with the Indra cult, it is noteworthy that Vishnu/Krishna bears, throughout the epic, epithets that mean "younger brother of Indra" (Upendra, etc.). On the other hand, Krishna is said to have given Indra his sovereignty (III.13.18). See Gonda, *Aspects*, pp. 155ff., on the transposition of elements from the Indra cult to the Krishna cult and the antagonism between the two cults (Gonda discusses the Govardhana story on p. 156). And see further, O. C. Gangoly, "Indra-Cult versus Kṛṣṇa-Cult," *Journal of the Ganganatha Jha Research Institute* 7 (1949–50): 7ff.
13. See Gonda, *Aspects*, pp. 164ff., on "Viṣṇu and Kingship." As Gonda mentions, the archetypical king primarily associated with Vishnu in the *Mahabharata* is Prthu Vainya, regarding which, see XII.59.129f. (although in the same chapter Prthu is also said to be Indra-like in form [v. 104], and both Vishnu and Indra are said to have contributed to his consecration [v. 120]).
14. Edward C. Dimock, Jr., "Doctrine and Practice among the Vaiṣṇavas of Bengal," in *Krishna: Myths, Rites, and Attitudes*, ed. Milton Singer (Chicago: Phoenix-University of Chicago Press, 1968), p. 49. The reference here is to Krishna's childhood friends, the *gopa*s, but would apply equally well to Arjuna; see *Gita* XI.41, 44 = *Mahabharata* VI.33.41, 44.
15. See, e.g., XV.32.7, quoted on p. 32.
16. See all descriptions of Arjuna on pp. 31–32.
17. On the symbolism of Krishna's lotus eyes, see, especially, V.68.6: "The lotus is the highest abode, everlasting, undecaying, never-ending—so he is the *Lotus-eyed One*, because he is of such nature." Krishna's dark skin is his most characteristic physical attribute; with regard to it, see Appendix, under Krishna. At a more esoteric level, a series of peculiar physical markings, including sixty teeth each, eight tusks, four testicles, and the matted hair of an ascetic, as well as characteristic signs of Vishnu such as the discus and the *shrivatsa* (a tuft of hair on his breast), are attributed to Nara and Narayana, at XII.331.24ff. Most of these marks are not, however, shared by Arjuna; the only exceptions being, perhaps, those reflecting his eroticism and asceticism, which parallel Nara's and Narayana's (see chap. IIB, and Appendix, under Gudakesha).
18. Mentioned briefly in the *Mahabharata*, at V.47.68.
19. Though note too the explicit parallel with Shiva's classic battle against Tripura, underscored by Arjuna's decisive use of the Raudra ("Rudra-informed" [Rudra =

Shiva]) weapon (III.170.38ff.), quite appropriate against the background of the mountain-man sequence.

20. The epic states that Arjuna's bow and Krishna's discus were won at the same time (see chap. ID, n. 5). Note how they are juxtaposed in V.53.12. Arjuna and Vishnu/ Krishna both have conches as well.
21. On this issue, see Hiltebeitel, *Ritual*, pp. 144ff. Note how Poona Edition, I, 566*, cleverly equates Draupadi with Shachi, Indra's wife, rather than Shri, undoubtedly to account for her relationship with Indra incarnate; but this is not part of the critical text.
22. See Gonda, *Aspects*, pp. 122, 156. (On Indra's and Vishnu's shared trait of serpent fighting, see *Aspects*, p. 157.) Strikingly, the stories of Indra's demon slaying throughout the epic (such as those discussed in chap. IIA3, above) are sometimes Vaishnavized: e.g., in V.10.38 Vishnu enters Indra's weapon, making it possible for Indra to kill Vrtra.
23. Throughout the *Mahabharata*, Naraka is seen almost exclusively as an enemy of Vishnu/Krishna. Note, however, a hint of Indra-Naraka enmity at III.165.18.
24. Later Nara and Narayana are both seen as incarnations of Vishnu; see *Bhagavata Purana* I.3.9; II.7.6.
25. Jean Herbert's very interesting, but often bypassed, commentary on the episode (*La Mythologie hindoue: Son message*, 2nd ed., Spiritualités Vivants, Série Hindouisme [Paris: Albin Michel, 1980], pp. 137–426) tends toward a monistic interpretation somewhat reminiscent of the "metaphysical plane" of the epic as a whole, identified by Sukthankar (see Introduction, n. 10): the Khandava Forest is the world of multiplicity, destroyed by the yogic effort of guru and disciple. Herbert works out the allegory in detail, but finally opts, quite appropriately in the present author's opinion, for ultimate dualism (p. 410) or, as he earlier calls it, *l'unité duelle* (p. 204). It is also noteworthy that Herbert, like Biardeau, sees the story as one of *pralaya* and recreation, this being its cosmic meaning, running parallel to its psychological meaning (pp. 143ff.).
26. Gonda (*Aspects*, pp. 160f.) feels, however, that this phrase has been overinterpreted: it does not necessarily imply Krishna-Arjuna companionship or a devotional cult; nor does *vāsudeva* certainly refer to Krishna here. For the worship of Arjuna as Shiva in the context of the cult of Draupadi as Goddess (see chap. IB), see Hiltebeitel, "Disguises," p. 153; but in the opinion of the present author, such an identification is merely an extension of (heroic) fertility traits: it does not determine Arjuna's devotional identity.
27. On the Pancharatra school, see e.g., F. Otto Schrader, *Introduction to the Pāñcarātra and the Ahirbudhnya Saṃhitā* (Madras: Adyar Library, 1916); De, "Sects," pp. 13ff.; Jaiswal, pp. 40ff.; Gonda, *Viṣṇuism and Śivaism*, pp. 49ff.; Mitsunori Matsubara, "The Early Pāñcarātra with Special Reference to the Ahirbudhnya Saṃhitā," Dissertation, Harvard 1972.
28. That the Pancharatra school has influenced any given philosophical passage is most readily evident from the presence there of the *vyuha* (translated by Gonda [*Viṣṇuism and Śivaism*, p. 50] as approximately "arrangement") doctrine, whereby Vishnu is said to emanate through four or five successive *vyuha*s named after various Vrshnis.

29. Sarasvati is the Hindu goddess of speech and the arts.
30. An original translation, which is neutral regarding the phrase *tato jayam udirayet*, is offered here, since that phrase has been translated so variously (see next note).
31. That *jaya* in this invocation is the name of the epic is Nilakantha's view; see his gloss on this stanza. See also van Buitenen's translation: *"The Bard shall intone the song of the Triumph after having bowed to Nara and Nārāyaṇa, supreme among men, and to the Goddess Sarasvatī."* Lévi (*"Tato jayam,"* pp. 16–17), on the other hand, translates: "While adoring Narayana, and Nara the best of males, and also the goddess Sarasvati, may one make victory issue therefrom!" On *jaya* here as a spiritual victory, see Upendraray J. Sandesara, "Interpretation of the Word *Jaya* in the First Verse of the Mahābhārata," *Journal of the Oriental Institute* (Baroda) 7 (1957–58): 264: "In the verse quoted in the beginning of the Mahābhārata, *Jaya* clearly refers to a spiritual victory in the frame-story of a physical victory." On *jaya* more generally, see chap. IE and Appendix.
32. The very name "Narada" suggests a connection with Nara-Narayana.
33. Vyasa also shares Krishna's name: he is Krishnadvaipayana ("Island-born Krishna" [see I.57.71]) (for examples, see pp. 244 and 255; and see further, Appendix).
34. The two together are associated with the teaching of the identity of Arjuna and Krishna with Nara and Narayana; see, e.g., III.84.4f.; VIII.69.22f.; XIII.153.43. There are also many references to this teaching being propounded by one or the other of these two seers separately.
35. One might suggest very tentatively that the fivefold composition of the Pandava group has some connection with the Pancharatra school, since the Pancharatrins seem to have had a cult of five Vrshni heroes (*panchaviras*), who were interpreted later as the *vyuhas* of God; see Jaiswal, pp. 68f., and Gonda, *Viṣṇuism and Śivaism*, pp. 51ff. (Note the brief mention of a *vishvadeva* [type of deity] named Panchavirya in XIII.91.31.) The element *pancha-* in the term "Pancharatra" means "five" (see chap. IIIC). With regard to the connection between the *Mahabharata* and Pancharatra doctrine, one may refer, further, to the play attributed to Bhasa entitled *Pancharatram*. The subject of this play is the imposition of a five-day deadline by the Kauravas late in the Pandavas' exile: if the Pandavas can be located during this time, they will be given back their kingdom. (The ending is a happy one.) As far as the present author has been able to ascertain, this plot has no basis in the epic itself (certainly not in the critical text); nor can a good explanation of the title be found. Might a connection with Pancharatra philosophy be suggested here?
36. On the relative lateness of the "Narayaniya," see, e.g., Jaiswal, pp. 15f., suggesting a date of third or early fourth century A.D.

IIIB. ON THE BATTLEFIELD AT KURUKSHETRA, III

IIIB1. THE EPISODE OF THE *BHAGAVADGITA*, II

The highest statement of Arjuna's devotion to Vishnu/Krishna in the *Mahabharata* is the *Bhagavadgita*. Here Krishna gives private instruction to Arjuna and shows him a mystical vision of himself in his divine form—all this because Arjuna is his devoted friend and disciple. It has already been noted in chapter IIA1 that the *Gita* is Arjuna's initiation into wisdom, as opposed to his various military initiations. At the devotional level, one recognizes that God himself is Arjuna's teacher here: the wisdom Arjuna sought because of his human uncertainties has been attained through devotion.

Chapter IIIA of this study stated that Arjuna's transformation into "devotee" does not occur at a single point or period in his career but, rather, occurs again and again throughout. Nonetheless, the episode of the *Gita* and particularly the vision of *Gita* XI = *Mahabharata* VI.33 is the most striking occasion of such transformation. Although he has learned previously of his identity with Nara, has already been called an eternal god, and knows that his companion is Narayana/Vishnu (see chap. IIIA),[1] Arjuna is prepared for the *Gita* experience by virtue of having lapsed into his most vulnerable and human condition at the start of the episode: it is clear at this point that Arjuna does not know, or has forgotten, who he really is (*Gita* IV.5 = *Mahabharata* VI.26.5).[2] By the time Krishna's exposition of the *Gita* to him is concluded, Arjuna has been transformed into devotee par excellence, and has learned of his identity with Krishna himself (see below). (Nara-Narayana terminology is not used here; and the *Gita* is, it appears, a product of the Bhagavata school, not the Pancharatra school.)[3] Note, however, that Arjuna seems to forget the *Gita* teaching in the course of the war, and has to hear it again (albeit in a modified form)[4] as the "Anugita" ("Aftersong") (XIV.16–50), when the fighting is over.

In chapter IIA1 that portion of the *Gita*'s message which advocates ongoing heroic action was discussed. It was noted, however, that the fully heroic quality of such action is undermined by the moral ambiguity of the situation presented. Pursuing the issue of moral ambiguity in chapter IIA3, this ambiguity was found to be inherent in the human condition that Arjuna was fated to suffer in the setting of the Kaliyuga. It is now possible, from the vantage point of devotion, to reconsider the *Gita*'s message, and discover that in truth the *Gita* advocates a response which transcends human ambiguity. It will further be seen that in fact the *Gita*, rather than advocating the employment of heroic effort against fate (a strategy that cannot succeed for humans), favors submission to fate and its transformation at the level of devotion; this is its most impressive teaching to Arjuna.

The Path of Knowledge, the Path of Devotion, and the Path of Action

The inconsistencies to be found in the *Mahabharata* regarding the relative effectiveness of "fate" and "effort" have already been summarized (chap. IIA3). At the heroic level, it was concluded, fate and effort harmonize; at the human level, however, fate is often victorious, winning out over those efforts that oppose it. In the Kaliyuga in particular, fate's effect is very negative, undermining human actions and desires. Other levels exist, however, from the perspective of which the relationship between fate and effort appears entirely different than it does from the perspective of the first two levels. One of these levels has not been discussed so far in the present study and, except for passing reference in chapter IIIA to "a monistic philosophy" (p. 218), is being introduced here for the first time; it may be called the level of knowledge. The other level is that of devotion, so crucial to the character of Arjuna. Both these points of view are important in the *Gita*, in combination and separately.

To view the world from the standpoint of knowledge is to follow what the Hindu religious tradition calls the *jnanamarga* ("path of knowledge") or *jnanayoga* ("discipline of knowledge"). Here the word "knowledge" (*jnana*) is a technical designation for mystical knowledge, and refers specifically to the passage, via meditation, beyond opposites to *brahman*, the world soul—which is said to be identical with the individual soul (*atman*).[5] Here war is no longer opposed to peace, as at the heroic and human levels; success and failure, and even life and death (*Gita* II.11ff. = *Mahabharata* VI.24.11ff.), are one and the same, and there is no more issue of morality as opposed to immorality (*Gita* IV.36 = *Mahabharata* VI.26.36), so that the negative meaning of Kaliyuga disappears. Followed to its full conclusion, the concept of *brahman/atman*, in fact, invites the monistic (*advaita*) interpretation that all the multiplicity of the phenomenal world is illusion (*maya*).[6] There is no need to mediate oppositions here: they simply disappear.

The path of devotion (*bhaktimarga*) or discipline of devotion (*bhaktiyoga*), as defined by the *Gita*, goes one step further, broadly identifying *brahman* with God (here, specifically Vishnu/Krishna).[7] Here too opposites and multiplicities are transcended, but now transcendence takes on divine coloration: everything in the world is equivalent to Vishnu/Krishna; the *maya* ("magic") that projects the phenomenal world is Vishnu/Krishna's own (*Gita* VII.14f. = *Mahabharata* VI.29.14f., etc.). The greatest expression of this view in the *Gita* is the chapter on *vibhuti*s ("manifestations") (*Gita* X = *Mahabharata* VI.32), in which the best of every category in the world is identified explicitly with Vishnu/Krishna: these *vibhuti*s include Indra (note how this changes the meaning of the Khandava Forest battle), Shiva, and various other gods, Narada, Arjuna himself, and Vyasa. In the same chapter, Vishnu/Krishna is called the self of things, and their beginning, middle, and end. Other parts of the *Gita* and the epic as a whole echo these equations, identifying, for example, all the various other deities, Vedic and otherwise, with Vishnu/Krishna.

What do the two points of view just discussed make of the human issue of conflict between fate and effort? Clearly, in underrating the role of the individual ego, both underrate the role of individual accomplishments. Reflecting this tendency, the *Gita*, whether arguing from the position of "knowledge" or "devotion," reveals itself as powerfully fatalistic, the high point of this expression being stanza XI.32 = *Mahabharata* VI.33.32:

> I am Time, destroyer of the world, full-grown, set here upon destruction of the universe. Even without you all these warriors, assembled in opposing ranks, will cease to be.

Here is a vision of Vishnu/Krishna himself as destroying, devouring Time (or Death, or fate) (*kala*), specifically Time at the moment of *pralaya*.[8] (*Pralaya* imagery, heretofore discounted by this study [see chap. IC, etc.], does take center stage at the levels of knowledge and devotion; see chap. IIIC for further discussion, in a devotional context.) What Krishna appears to be showing Arjuna here is that as grim as the future may seem to be from Arjuna's limited, human perspective, the reality of events is even more startling. The vision functions like a suddenly widening camera angle, a back-stepping from the human to the superhuman viewpoint. It is indeed a vision awesome enough to balance out that very premonition of the Kaliyuga which had initially caused Arjuna to sit down and refuse to fight. The Kaliyuga is now seen to be only a small part of a much longer and greater cosmic cycle, which climaxes in far more gigantic destruction than could ever be conceived of in human terms.[9] Nor do individual human deeds appear to matter at all from this perspective, for they and their fruit are destined to be reabsorbed periodically. The fate-effort opposition of the human level is thus transcended in favor of a fuller recognition of fate.

Yet even as it devalues individual deeds, the *Gita* insists that they must still be performed, as pointed out in chapter IIA1. Here is the *Gita*'s insistence upon the importance of desireless action, explained earlier as a clinging to heroic values in the face of human tragedy; now justified at a higher level, from the perspectives of knowledge and devotion (those two great reconcilers), as effort in harmony with fate:

> Therefore arise! Attain glory! Having defeated your enemies, enjoy abundant sovereignty. Indeed, they have already been killed by me; be the mere instrument, O Savyasachin. Kill Drona and Bhishma and Jayadratha and Karna, likewise the other heroes among warriors, [already] killed by me. Do not tremble! Fight! You will conquer your foes in battle. [*Gita* XI.33–34 = *Mahabharata* VI.33.33–34]

That such an approach restores the weakened value of heroic action at a new level is expressed well in the following passage from the chapter entitled "The Core of the Teaching" in Sri Aurobindo Ghose's *Essays on the Gita*:

> There are in the world, in fact, two different laws of conduct each valid on its own plane, the rule principally dependent on external status and the rule independent of status and entirely dependent on the thought and conscience. [In the terminology of the present study, these would be the heroic and human levels.] The Gita does not teach us to subordinate the higher plane to the lower, it does not ask the awakened moral consciousness to slay itself on the altar of duty as a sacrifice and victim to the law of the social status. It calls us higher and not lower; from the conflict of the two planes it bids us ascend to a supreme poise above the mainly practical, above the purely ethical, to the Brahmic consciousness. It replaces the conception of social duty by a divine obligation. The subjection to external law gives place to a certain principle of inner self-determination of action proceeding by the soul's freedom from the tangled law of works. And this, as we shall see,—the Brahmic consciousness, the soul's freedom from works and the determination of works in the nature by the Lord within and above us,—is the kernel of the Gita's teaching with regard to action.[10]

(Note how Aurobindo interprets Arjuna's movement through the three levels of his personality as a movement upward.)

The reward of such desireless action, according to the *Gita*, is salvation (*moksha*); thus is Arjuna's fear of "hell for the family destroyers" (*Gita* I.42 = *Mahabharata* VI.23.42; see above, p. 130) answered. So far, this study has emphasized the evil situation of the Kaliyuga, entrapping Arjuna. The *Gita* reminds us that Kaliyuga and *samsara*, the human condition, are synonymous: liberation from both is to be sought, as the extreme example of Kurukshetra powerfully illustrates. Desireless action—apparently recommended to all people, not just *kshatriya*s (compare chap. IIA1)[11]—is really a form of walking meditation: better than nonaction, the quietistic shirking of one's duty, it removes one not only from the danger of hell, but, moreover, from *samsara* itself.[12] Behind desireless action, knowledge and/or devotion may stand. Sometimes, too, desireless action may be practiced independently. Thus it is often said that the *Gita* presents three different paths to salvation:

knowledge, devotion, and action. *Pralaya* reveals itself as an image of this salvation, the dissolution of worldly concerns, even as it redefines *samsara*.

In line with the distinction between knowledge and devotion outlined above, the concept of fate, and action in harmony with fate, just discussed may (like the *Gita* XI vision itself, and many other sections of the *Gita*)[13] be taken either personally or impersonally. Knowledge, that is, sees fate as impersonal, the spinning out of the world by *brahman*, while devotion substitutes for the concept of impersonal fate the personal concept of the will of God.

The *Gita*, as indeed the epic as a whole, does not always distinguish clearly between fate and God's will, any more than between *brahman* and God: although its language fluctuates between these two poles, possibly reflecting historical development and change, the two have become inextricably connected.[14] Or to rephrase this point: God himself cannot change the inevitable cyclical course of fate that dominates the epic world view; God *is* the *yugas* (XII.325.105–7).[15] But to say this is to say no more than that God and *brahman* are equal; it does not mean that the emotional content of the concept of God is weakened in the least. The great difference between fate and God's will is this: their relationship to God gives a favorable meaning to events that would lack such meaning or, at the human level, be construed as unfavorable, when viewed as mere products of fate; nothing is negative or meaningless when viewed through the eyes of devotion.

In connection with this point, one may consider the idea of the *avataras* ("descents," "incarnations") of Vishnu, an idea which is essential to the extant epic in that Krishna himself is such an *avatara*. The classic statement of the *avatara* doctrine appears in *Gita* IV.7–8 = *Mahabharata* VI.26.7–8:

> Whenever there is a lessening of *dharma*, a rise in *adharma* . . . then I send myself forth. For the protection of the good and the destruction of evildoers, for the sake of establishing *dharma*, I am born in *yuga* after *yuga*.

This quotation makes clear the fact that as the *avatara* establishes *dharma*, he does not interfere with fate, that is, the progression of the *yugas*. (Compare the statement on the births of Nara and Narayana in *yuga* after *yuga* from VII.172.81, mentioned in chap. IIIA, above.) Elsewhere in the epic, even more support for this idea is found, as in the following statement, which asserts that God fits into fate's pattern neatly, as he incarnates himself:

> In the Krtayuga he was full *dharma*. In the Treta time he resorted to knowledge.[16] But Krishna [that is, Vishnu] was power in the Dvapara. . . . In the Kali he came to earth as *adharma*. [XIII.143.9]

The passage goes on to state that Krishna is the creator of all beings and the cause of both good and evil actions (XIII.143.10, 12). And yet the *avatara*'s appearance, paradoxically, carries with it a very positive feeling in every case, even in the midst of the ambiguous passage just cited. Note the following stanza: "When the *dharma* of the gods diminishes, then Krishna is born among men. Established in *dharma*, with purified soul, he indeed goes to higher and lower worlds" (XIII.143.11). God, then, is seen as the protector of *dharma* even as he acts within the *yuga* structure, changing with the shifting environment.

Likewise, when the vision of *Gita* XI focuses on the end of the *yuga*s, the time of *pralaya*, the devotional perspective offers a certain comfort. It is striking that despite his human terror of the vision, Arjuna's reaction is to praise Krishna and confirm his devotion (*Gita* XI.36ff. = *Mahabharata* VI.33.36ff.).

The *Gita* itself also has another way of making the same point: knowledge, it states, is a more difficult path than devotion (*Gita* XII.5 = *Mahabharata* VI.34.5). Certainly part of the reasoning behind this assertion would be that devotion is more emotionally satisfying than knowledge, being a personal relationship and concrete, not abstract (as fraught with bliss [*Gita* V.21; VI.21, 27, 28 = *Mahabharata* VI.27.21; VI.28.21, 27, 28; etc.] as the peak of that abstract experience may be). From inception to consummation, devotion is more in touch than knowledge with the "real" world, everyday life.

Indeed, desireless action, the ideal of the *Gita*, is preeminently the province of the devotee. Although one with knowledge may decide to continue acting for the good of the world, becoming a *jivanmukta* ("one released while still alive," that is, one who still acts even though released from the bonds of *samsara*), such a person is equally likely to withdraw. The *Gita*, in fact, finds it necessary to spend many stanzas counteracting such a tendency (see, especially, *Gita* III = *Mahabharata* VI.25). Only the devotee, who is able to view preservation of the world as an imitation of God's own desireless activity (*Gita* III.22ff. = *Mahabharata* VI.25.22ff.), can readily justify his or her continued action; he or she has a positive view of the world, as God's creation. Such a view is certainly the *Gita*'s, for here the dominant picture of desireless action involves a dedication of one's actions to God (*Gita* XII.10ff. = *Mahabharata* VI.34.10ff., etc.). Thus, the *Gita*, even while including the path of knowledge and the path of action, comes out most strongly in favor of devotion. Chapters XI and XVIII = *Mahabharata* VI.33 and 40 in particular are devotional tours de force, and the *Gita* exposition as a whole is, as already established, presented as the words of Krishna, God incarnate.

It may further be suggested that the three oldest Pandavas are, ideally, embodiments of the three paths: Yudhishthira of knowledge, Bhima of action, Arjuna of devotion. To each his own role comes naturally. Although often confused at his human level, Yudhishthira is otherwise known for his wisdom (see chap. IA); and his tendency toward withdrawal is transformed easily into a leaning toward meditative activity. Likewise, his adherence to and dependence upon *dharma* are sometimes construed as fatalism.[17] The combination in Yudhishthira is a peculiar one: absolute support of *dharma* mixed with recognition of the supreme *brahman*;[18] yet these are precisely the ideas that coexist, according to Hindu teaching, in the mind of that very wisest of men, the *jivanmukta*. (At the same time, *jnana* is a suitable response to weakened *dharma*.) Seemingly, monistic tendencies were imposed increasingly by the epic poets upon the person of Yudhishthira as time passed (see chap. IIID for discussion of one episode in which this occurred). Bhima, on the other hand, as the least pensive brother, never gives up his active stance.[19] Arjuna, the most troubled by contradictions, must turn to *bhakti*, the most accessible path.

Throughout the *Mahabharata*, a special devotional relationship to Krishna is Arjuna's defining characteristic. For him, participation in universal monistic identity with *brahman* is of secondary importance: his position vis-à-vis God, as taught in the *Gita*, seems, rather, to be one of qualified union, permitting the devotional relationship to exist.[20] Krishna's role as Arjuna's charioteer, expounding the *Gita* to him and later driving and advising him in battle, is well suited to the portrayal of this connection; for it is a commonplace of Indian thought, also found in the philosophical portions of the epic, that the soul is the body's charioteer[21]—and here the charioteer is God.[22]

There are many places in the *Mahabharata*, including certain stanzas of the *Gita* itself, where devotion is not central, but the emphasis is, rather, on knowledge alone, along with the reactions it promotes: withdrawal from the world, equanimity, nonviolence. The preceding are, however, the practices at which Yudhishthira excels; they are not associated particularly with Arjuna.[23] For Arjuna, as for the *Gita* as a whole, knowledge is intertwined completely with devotion. In fact, as the preceding discussion should suggest, in the context of the *Gita*, the path of devotion may be viewed as subsuming the other two paths.[24] Both knowledge and the capacity for desireless action are brought to the hearer of the *Gita*, Arjuna, by virtue of his devotion; Krishna expounds the *Gita* purely out of love for his devotee.

Arjuna's Heroism of Devotion

From the standpoint of the *Gita*, Arjuna must be viewed as the greatest of the Pandavas, for he brings the devotional component to the whole family by way of his special relationship with Krishna.[25] It is such devotion, from the *Gita*'s point of view, that justifies the notion that the Pandavas are good, the good side, a notion which was seen to founder at the human level. In a world governed by fate, the only absolute good comes from devotion to God; devotion defines the good:

> If even a great evildoer is devoted to me and no other, he is to be thought of as good, for he is rightly resolved. He quickly becomes virtuous [*dharmatma*]; he obtains eternal peace. O son of Kunti, rest assured that no devotee of mine is lost. [*Gita* IX.30–31 = *Mahabharata* VI.31.30–31][26]

Ultimately, then: "Having abandoned all *dharmas*, go to me alone for refuge" (*Gita* XVIII.66 = *Mahabharata* VI.40.66).

The goodness of the Pandavas is symbolized by their kinship relationship with Krishna (the Kauravas, certain claims [V.7.10ff.] notwithstanding, have no such relationship with him), but the epic suggests that the real closeness of the connection is a product of Arjuna's friendship with Krishna, more than a natural outgrowth of the kinship.[27] Arjuna's restored superheroism resides in the fact that he is the chief proponent and practitioner of devotion in the epic, supplying it to the rest of his family. Kurukshetra is restored by Arjuna's relationship with Krishna to its heroic status as the true field of *dharma* (see chaps. IE and IIA1). Devotion thus overcomes the Kaliyuga by redefining morality.

In fact, the relative goodness of many *Mahabharata* characters can be measured on a devotional scale. Duryodhana rejects Krishna violently, wishing to imprison him during his peace mission (V.86.13f. and, with Karna, Shakuni, and Duhshasana, V.128.4ff.), and not relenting even after he is granted a divine vision much like that of *Gita* XI (V.129.4ff.).[28] Bhishma is a committed devotee;[29] thus, although he fights on the wrong side for various reasons (see chaps. IA and IIA3), he is a highly respected elder and teacher. Dhrtarashtra, predictably, wavers (V.67ff.),[30] and Karna seems to recognize Krishna, but rejects his overtures with regret (V.139ff.). In *Gita* XVI = *Mahabharata* VI.38, Krishna speaks to Arjuna about the "divine condition" (*daivi sampad*) as opposed to the "demonic condition" (*asuri sampad*): Arjuna, Krishna assures him, has been born to the former (*Gita* XVI.5 = *Mahabharata* VI.38.5). The demonic condition, as described by Krishna, has been redefined as one in which devotion to God is lacking, so that attachment prevails (*Gita* XVI.8ff. = *Mahabharata* VI.38.8ff.). By implication, the "divine" are devotees, who do the work of the *avatara*.[31] Compare *Mahabharata* I.1.65–66:

> The wrathful Duryodhana is the great tree, Karṇa its [trunk],[32] Śakuni the branches, Duḥśāsana the plentiful blossoms and fruits, and the witless King Dhṛtarāṣṭra the root.
>
> The law-minded Yudhiṣṭhira is the great tree, Arjuna its [trunk], Bhīmasena the branches, Mādrī's two sons the plentiful blossoms and fruits, and Kṛṣṇa, Brahman, and the brahmins the root.

From the preceding analysis, it is easy to see the similarities between the heroic and devotional levels, in terms of positive outlook and certainty of success. Yet the approach to the positive goal is different in each case: at the devotional level, heroic action is subsumed by knowledge and transformed by devotion. At this level, the significance of all actions taken throughout the *Mahabharata* is altered radically: action is no longer seen as something apart from fate or opposed to fate; fate is supreme, but action harmonizes with it to fulfill the *Mahabharata*'s paradoxical conception of united fate and effort as the components of success. The sacrificial act, in support of world order, is redefined by the *Gita* as the devotional act, in acceptance of that order (*Gita* IX.16ff. =

Mahabharata VI.31.16ff.; see further, chap. IIIB2). In connection with the figure of Arjuna, there is a great emphasis in the epic on the positive outlook and effective power of devotion. The culmination of the shamanic quest (see chap. ID) is the "secret" (*Gita* IX.1f. = *Mahabharata* VI.31.1f.) instruction of the *Gita*. To state it differently: at the devotional level, Arjuna's heroism is restored as a heroism of religious devotion. There can be no doubt that the *Gita* itself is employing the justification of devotion to vitalize the *kshatriyadharma*.[33] The ultimate beneficiaries of this "knowledge of kings" (see above, p. 132) are, of course, the "descendants" of Arjuna, to whom the epic is addressed, and, after them, all hearers, to whom the path of devotion is accessible.

Notes

1. Arjuna praises Krishna at length, recounting his adventures, as early as III.13.10ff. Krishna responds to this praise by informing Arjuna that Arjuna and he are Nara and Narayana. Arjuna also praises Krishna at V.47.64ff.
2. Hopkins's comment (*Great Epic*, p. 184): "Arjuna is a form of Vishnu. He is taught this with wonder and great amaze in the sixth book. But our amazement at his amazement is still greater, for this doctrine, apparently so new to him, was revealed to him long before, in the third book, and on that earlier occasion he appeared fully to appreciate the fact that he was divine and identical with Krishna, facts which in the sixth book he has totally forgotten."
3. On the *Gita* as a Bhagavata work, see, e.g., Jaiswal, pp. 112, 224, and Gonda, *Viṣṇuism and Śivaism*, p. 49. The historical relationship between the Bhagavatas and the Pancharatrins is unclear to modern scholarship; though see Jaiswal, pp. 44ff., for one interesting suggestion. One may, however, question her contention (p. 37) regarding the *Gita* that: "The non-mention of Nārāyaṇa in the poem does not mean anything. For the poet of the *Gītā*, *bhagavat* ["God"] meant Nārāyaṇa, and any clarification was unnecessary." Some scholars have considered the Bhagavatas and the Pancharatrins to have been one and the same school, but have maintained that the *Gita* was composed prior to the full development of Pancharatra doctrine, which absorbed it; see, e.g., R. G. Bhandarkar, *Vaiṣṇavism, Śaivism and Minor Religious Systems* (1913; rpt. Varanasi: Indological Book House, 1965), pp. 12f., 38f.
4. See below, n. 23.
5. Beyond opposites: *Gita* II.38, 45; IV.22; V.3; VI.7ff. = *Mahabharata* VI.24.38, 45; VI.26.22; VI.27.3; VI.28.7ff.; etc. Beyond opposites to *brahman: Gita* V.18ff.; VI.29, 32 = *Mahabharata* VI.27.18ff.; VI.28.29, 32; etc. *Brahman* and the identity of *brahman* and *atman* are Upanishadic notions accepted by the *Gita*; see, espe-

cially, *Gita* V.19ff. = *Mahabharata* VI.27.19ff. (Sometimes, however, the *Gita* prefers terminology borrowed from the Samkhya school of philosophy [see chap. IA, n. 61]: *purusha* ["man," "soul"] instead of *brahman/atman*.)

6. Such was, of course, the interpretation of the great philosopher Shamkaracharya (c. A.D. 788–820).
7. For more on the nature of this identification, see *The Bhagavad Gītā*, trans. and interp. Franklin Edgerton (1944; rpt. Cambridge, Mass.: Harvard University Press, 1972), pp. 150f. Later Hindu terminology expresses the identification simply: God is *brahman "saguna"* ("with qualities") as opposed to the absolute *brahman*, which is *"nirguna"* ("without qualities").
8. On *Gita* XI's connection with *pralaya*, see Biardeau, "Etudes" III, pp. 53f.; "Etudes" IV, p. 116; "Etudes" V, p. 139; Hiltebeitel, *Ritual*, pp. 114ff.; etc.
9. This is the distinction between "sociocosmic" and "cosmic" time made by Biardeau ("Etudes" I, p. 22); see further, chap. IIIC, n. 11.
10. Ghose, *Essays* (see Introduction, n. 31), pp. 31–32.
11. The *Gita*'s position in this regard is backed up by, e.g., the concrete case study of *Mahabharata* III.198ff.; discussed by Biardeau in Madeleine Biardeau and Charles Malamoud, *Le Sacrifice dans l'Inde ancienne*, Bibliothèque de l'Ecole des Hautes Etudes, Section des Sciences Religieuses, vol. 79 (Paris: Presses Universitaires de France, 1976), pp. 135ff.
12. Edgerton explains how; see p. 159: "It is desire, rather than action, which is man's enemy. . . . If a man acts unselfishly, without interest in the result, the action has no effect on his fate; it leaves him free. . . . Therefore one should act without interest in the result of the action, without 'desire or hate.' *Indifference* is the great desideratum. It is the same as inaction in effect. It guarantees freedom from the binding effect of 'karma.' "
13. E.g., the strikingly comparable *Gita* XIII.12ff. = *Mahabharata* VI.35.12ff.
14. See Otto Strauss, *Ethische Probleme aus dem "Mahābhārata"* (Florence: Tipografia Galileiana, 1912), pp. 35ff. For one passage clearly illustrating this point, see *Mahabharata* XIII.143.41f. In the *Gita* itself, XI.32 = *Mahabharata* VI.33.32 (quoted above, p. 228) and X.30, 33 = *Mahabharata* VI.32.30, 33, explicitly identify God and fate.
15. XIII.143.30 calls Vishnu the year, season, fortnight, day and night, etc.
16. Cf. XII.224.27, quoted on p. 184.
17. See, especially, the conversation of III.28–36, mentioned in chap. IIA3; also II.67.3 ("It is at the disposing of the Placer that creatures find good or ill. There is no averting of either, if we must play again."), in conjunction with Yudhishthira's other argument for participation in the dice game (see chap. IB, n. 3). See further, chap. IIID.
18. Note the prominent reference to *brahman* in two of the episodes in the epic most revelatory of Yudhishthira's wisdom, at III.177.17 and III.297.27.
19. Although he is not necessarily a representative of desireless action, but often evidences desire (see chap. IIC for Bhima as glutton). Biardeau strongly emphasizes this aspect of the religious outlook represented by Bhima, that is, in her view, the

Vedic religion (see "Conférence," vol. 77, p.171; vol. 78, p. 160; vol. 84, pp. 167f.; etc.).

20. The terminology employed here follows the traditional *bhedabheda* ("difference and sameness") or *vishishtadvaita* ("nondualism of the qualified") interpretation of the *Gita* as a whole, according to which identity and difference are both accepted.
21. *Mahabharata* V.34.57ff. (XI.228.8ff., a more complicated passage on the chariot, lines up the equivalences differently: knowledge is the charioteer here [v. 10].) In the Upanishads, see, especially, *Katha* III.3ff. and *Maitri* II.3ff. See also the Buddhist *Questions of King Milinda* II.1.1. (The Greeks also knew this comparison; see Plato's *Phaedrus*, 246ff.) The soul is commonly called *kshetrajna* ("the field knower"; the body being the "field"). The *Gita* calls Krishna himself *kshetrajna* (*Gita* XIII.1ff. = *Mahabharata* VI.35.1ff.). Such a title would, of course, apply very well to Krishna as the excellent charioteer he is (a point often stressed) on Kurukshetra. On the image of Krishna and Arjuna on one chariot, see further Hiltebeitel, "One Chariot," pp. 8ff.; here due attention is paid to the monistic undercurrent of the imagery.
22. Perhaps a *suta* poet was responsible for such glorification of the charioteer's role in the epic. Cf., though on a smaller scale, Athena's driving of Diomedes' chariot in *Iliad* V.835ff.
23. The largely knowledge-oriented "Anugita" provides an isolated exception to this rule.
24. Regarding the subsumption, in the *Gita*, of the path of knowledge by that of devotion, a confirmed monist, such as Shamkaracharya, would disagree. The interpretation presented here is based on the author's personal impression, along with the discussion by Surendranath Dasgupta in his *A History of Indian Philosophy*, II (Cambridge, Eng.: Cambridge University Press, 1932), 529ff. Interestingly, a combination of knowledge and devotion is illustrated in tangible form elsewhere in the epic, in the disembodied Narayana devotees of the "Narayaniya" section; see, especially, XII.323.23ff.
25. In connection with his identification as Nara Prajapati (see chap. IIIA, n. 8), Arjuna is called *pandavashreshtha* ("the best of the Pandavas"; van Buitenen: "first of the Pāṇḍavas"), at V.186.19.
26. Cf., especially, *Gita* IV.36 = *Mahabharata* VI.26.36, expressing the level-of-knowledge version of the same idea: the possessor of knowledge passes beyond evil (good is not mentioned); similarly, *Gita* V.10 = *Mahabharata* VI.27.10.
27. Note, e.g., the following words of Krishna to Yudhishthira, at VI.103.32–33: "Whoever is an enemy of the sons of Pandu is also my enemy, without a doubt. Whatever is your honor's profit is my profit, whatever is mine is yours. Your brother is my friend, relation, and also pupil. I would cut off my flesh and give it away for Arjuna's sake, O king." All this is not to suggest that the closeness of the Pandava-Krishna relationship is never mentioned apart from Arjuna's mediation; it is, particularly regarding Yudhishthira. See, e.g., XII.29.5: "Keshava could not be ignored by King Dharma. From childhood on, Govinda [Krishna] was dearer [to him] than Arjuna."

28. Duryodhana's basic misconception is embodied in his words to Bhishma at V.62.1–2: "The Pārthas ['sons of Prtha' = Pandavas] are the same as other men, born just as they are, so why do you think that victory is theirs solely? We are all born the same from human wombs, grandfather, so how do you know that victory will go to the Pārthas?" If Duryodhana sometimes appears to be starting to understand who Krishna really is (VI.64.11), he studiously ignores such an insight for the duration of the war. He does, however, acknowledge Krishna shortly before his death (IX.64.28f.).
29. See, e.g., II.33.27ff.
30. Note the emphasis here on Dhrtarashtra's blindness (V.69.1).
31. Thus, a demon can attain the divine condition; and indeed Hindu mythology knows of such cases, the most famous being that of Prahlada (Prahrada) (see, e.g., *Bhagavata Purana* VII.4.30ff., and in the *Mahabharata* itself especially *Gita* X.30 = *Mahabharata* VI.32.30—elsewhere in the epic [XII.215, etc.], Prahlada is sometimes seen as a paragon of knowledge). Biardeau ("Conférence," vol. 89, p. 229) points out that the *Mahabharata* knows Shalya as an incarnation of Prahlada's brother (I.61.6), and suggests that the figure of Shalya (a demon fighting on the demonic side, even while actually committed to the side of the gods [see chap. IIA3]) is an early version of the demon devotee. Note that even as the god-demon opposition of the heroic level is transcended at the level of devotion, so too is the bird-snake opposition (see chap. IE): both a snake, Shesha, and a bird, Garuda (Suparna [cf. chap. IE, n. 40]), are known to Hindu thought as counterparts and representatives of Vishnu, although the epic itself does not stress this fact.
32. Van Buitenen's translation has been altered slightly here: he translates "crotch" (likewise, in Arjuna's case).
33. The scholar who most strongly stresses this point, Lévi, discussing the *kshatriya-dharma* and its relationship to Krishna, writes ("*Tato jayam,*" p. 16): "The Mahabharata in its entirety is the illustration and the amplification of these principles, which come to a focus and stand out very clearly in the Bhagavadgita." And (p. 17): "The Mahabharata . . . glorifies the caste of the kshatriyas and the ideal rôle which is assigned to it in the totality of the Hindu society. It also points out to the kshatriyas the glory of the god who guarantees them success and safety."

IIIB2. THE KURUKSHETRA WAR RECONSIDERED

It has been noted in the preceding chapter that the goodness, the right to victory, of the Pandava brothers is determined by their relationship with Krishna. In the chapter before that it was stated that the relationship with Krishna is also a source of infallible power for the devotee, as personified by Arjuna. The goal of the present chapter will be to reinterpret the Kurukshetra War's meaning in light of the goodness and power that have been shown to reside on the Pandava side.

The Earth's Burden and the Incarnation (*Avatara*)

From the point of view of devotion, the epic's most important account of the cause of the Kurukshetra War is that found in I.58–61. I.58.4–59.6 tells the story of the earth's burden. It was the Krtayuga, and the world was prospering accordingly. Then, however, a huge group of demons was born and, becoming tremendously powerful, began to oppress the earth (creating, presumably, a Kaliyuga of sorts). Earth, personified, eventually appealed to the gods for help; whereupon Brahma gave the order for them to incarnate themselves to save her. Brahma's order was carried out through the agency of Indra, with the final approval of Vishnu/Narayana. After an intermediary passage on the genealogy of the gods, the demons, and others, I.61 provides the list of "Partial Incarnations," which identifies the major participants on both sides in the Kurukshetra War with their divine and demonic prototypes. Among these incarnations are those of Narayana as Krishna and Indra as

Arjuna (with the other Pandavas incarnating Dharma, Vayu, and the Ashvins). The story of the earth's burden recounted here is typical of stories told in various Hindu texts to account for the world-ordering appearance on earth of Vishnu's *avataras*,[1] and serves to Vaishnavize the epic's account of the cause of the war (of which it is, of course, a reduplication, substituting "Earth" for Draupadi/Shri);[2] juxtaposed with the list of partial incarnations, it Vaishnavizes that as well. In other words, Indra incarnate in Arjuna is now Vishnu's assistant (compare the process of Vaishnavization described in chap. IIIA). Those passages of the epic that view Arjuna as an incarnation of Nara, not Indra, have simply carried the Vaishnavization even further.[3] In one sense, the stated task of the divine incarnations, that is, battle against demonic forces, is a latter-day version of traditional heroism. It is only logical, however, that linked to an *avatara* story, the task itself—and the manner of its performance—should be redefined accordingly.

In her work, Biardeau has analyzed the role of Arjuna against this backdrop: Arjuna, she says, is the king whose role is by definition that of assisting the Vishnu *avatara*.[4] The morality for kings expounded in the epic is a Vaishnavized morality: while superficially equivalent to that of pragmatic *arthashastra*, it is altered radically by its connection with *bhakti*.[5] In fact, Biardeau asserts, the entire aim of the *Mahabharata* is to advocate *bhakti* (which she sees as related intimately to desireless action) as essential to the king/warrior role:[6] through *bhakti* this violent career will become salvific in and of itself; for *bhakti*, that is, action in the name of God, free from selfish desires, can turn even the generally evil *asura* into a paragon of morality.[7] As will be apparent, Biardeau's findings agree with that of the preceding chapter of this study: that the Pandavas are good by definition because they are (primarily through Arjuna) devotees of Krishna. Biardeau has not, however, pushed this line of thought to its extreme conclusion, with reference to the tricks perpetrated by the Pandavas in the name of policy during the Kurukshetra War.

Victory by Trickery, II: The War as God's Game

It is now appropriate to focus with more precision on the meaning of this trickery, interpreted from the point of view of devotion. What exactly is the relationship between Krishna, as supreme God, and policy? And why is policy necessary if victory is assured anyway, particularly when the *avatara*'s purpose is to restore *dharma*, not undermine it?

It was Hopkins's belief that Krishna's role in instigating the various Pandava deceits of the Kurukshetra War was a late addition to the epic, aimed at justifying actions which, originally quite acceptable, were now seen as evil: if a ploy was suggested by God, it had to be approved of by the epic audience.[8] Although not provable, Hopkins's view may be correct. Barring its chronological emphasis, this view is not too different from Biardeau's idea (and that of chap. IIIB1, above) that *bhakti* informs the *Mahabharata*'s conception of *kshatriyadharma*. There is an additional point, however, which Hopkins and Biardeau have not stressed: this is the fact that trickery is a basic element of Krishna's character, practiced by him even long before the war.[9] Krishna is the *avatara* suitable to the juncture of the Kaliyuga,[10] who is seen as the embodiment of policy.[11] In short, Krishna is a playful trickster. At least for the extant *Mahabharata*, Krishna's trickery implies an open defiance of traditional morality, which is of major significance for the total meaning of the work: even as it recapitulates the human condition (see chap. IIA3), it is also the sign of Krishna's transcendence.[12]

In fact, at the devotional level the Kurukshetra War becomes little else than God's game, into which the human participants have been drawn despite themselves.[13] The epic supports this idea by the use of game imagery with reference to the war. This imagery derives in part from the connection drawn between the war and the dice game that led to it. Shakuni calls the dicing a substitute for fighting to win the desired kingdom (II.51.1ff.), and Sahadeva, swearing to kill Shakuni, warns him, shortly after the dicing is over, that the dice used by him "are not dice but honed arrows that you have chosen for war!" (II.68.39). Later, in the battle books, this imagery is repeated to show that cause and effect did, in fact, proceed as predicted:

> Which bulls among men played the dangerous dice game with life as its stake, where the foolish gamblers entered a hall strewn with the bodies of men, elephants, and steeds, with dice of arrows, spears, clubs, swords, and javelins, frightful, hard to approach in battle? [VI.15.66–67][14]

As Hopkins points out, *dyuta* ("gambling") becomes, throughout the epic, a word used to refer to the war, as are words for "play" and "dance."[15]

In and of itself, comparison of the war with a game of dice would imply only that the war is fateful—as it is, being a repetition of the cyclic god-demon battle, which always has the same outcome (see chap. IA, etc.). Behind the imagery of fate, however, the imagery of divine action is apparent at the level of devotion: the supreme God himself is the dice player. Note that Shiva is found playing precisely this role in I.189.14ff. (Outside the epic, he is as often portrayed as a dancer, with a similar, if even more ominous, connotation.)[16] Play imagery is traditionally linked to the figure of Vishnu/Krishna in terms of his *maya* (see chap. IIIB1) and his *lila* ("game" or "dance");[17] thus Arjuna's words to Krishna: "Enjoyment, consisting of play, is yours. Your *maya* is heaven and earth, O Lord" (XIV.51.9). Indeed, at the level of devotion, Krishna's *maya* is seen to have set the Kurukshetra War in motion. So, at least, may one interpret the epic's statement that the immediate cause of the dice game, culminating in the war, was the triggering of Duryodhana's jealousy by an illusion-filled assembly hall built for the Pandavas by the *asura* named Maya (one of the escapees from the Khandava Forest burning [see chap. IC]) at Krishna's instigation.[18] And so it goes throughout the epic, for Krishna's game is the conception that underlies the portrayal of Krishna as trickster at Kurukshetra.[19]

Where Krishna Is, There Is *Dharma*; Where *Dharma* Is, There Is Victory

At the human level, the game of God (fate) has some negative connotations: during a sarcastic speech in III.31, Draupadi complains that God toys with his creatures like a puppeteer playing with puppets (III.31.22)[20] or a child playing with his playthings (III.31.36). Of course the continuing game of God is responsible for a period such as the Kaliyuga. Bhurishravas, condemning the deceit used against him in the war from the point of view of a human victim, blames it angrily upon the Vrshnis, that is, upon Krishna (see chaps. IIA2 and IIA3). Yet God's games and tricks create no moral dilemma when viewed at a level above the human, for the supreme God is beyond such considerations;[21] and this, apparently, is the point being made in the epic's portrayal of Krishna as trickster.

At the devotional level, moral oppositions are transcended, as discussed in chapter IIIB1: God defines goodness in his own terms. Most significant in this regard is the following stanza from the *Gita*, already quoted in part on p. 233, above: "Having abandoned all *dharma*s, go to me alone for refuge. I will release you from all evils. Do not grieve" (*Gita* XVIII.66 = *Mahabharata* VI.40.66). Here one returns to the freedom from moral trepidation of the heroic level; yet the quality of this freedom is different, for the devotee sees all divinely inspired actions as good by definition. At the devotional level, Krishna (or Nara and Narayana) is seen as the offspring of Dharma (VII.172.51; XII.321.8f.; XII.330.40f., 58; etc.), even as Yudhishthira is at the heroic level, or Dharma is seen as Krishna's son (XIV.53.11). Or, alternatively, Krishna and *dharma* are identified with one another (III.86.22).

It was noted in chapters IA and IE that at the heroic level the victory of *dharma* is seen as automatic: "Where *dharma* is, there is victory." At the human level, however, right was seen not to be automatically victorious, due to the ambiguities and conflicts of interest that are inherent in the human condition. The level of devotion restores the maxim of *dharma*'s victory, with a different emphasis: now Krishna is mediator. That is, Krishna, as omnipotent God, defines *dharma* even as he guarantees its victory; thus the devotional version of the saying: "yato dharmas tatah krishno yatah krishnas tato jayah" ("Where *dharma* is, there is Krishna; where Krishna is, there is victory") (VI.41.55; IX.61.30);[22] or, as stated in VI.62.34 and XIII.153.39: "yatah krishnas tato dharmo yato dharmas tato jayah" ("Where Krishna is, there is *dharma*; where *dharma* is, there is victory").[23] It is easy to see how such a view might have appealed to a king who was a Krishna devotee.

At the conclusion of an episode (V.7) that involved the resolution of a complex moral dilemma (Which side was he obligated to support?), Krishna had agreed to give his troops, the Narayanas, to the Kauravas for the duration of the war, while himself aiding the Pandavas. He would not fight, he said, but would only serve as Arjuna's charioteer.[24] Both sides are pleased with the arrangement—have, in fact, chosen it. The satisfaction of the Pandavas (particularly Arjuna, who made the choice for his side) shows them to be ardent devotees of Krishna, and what appears on the surface to be the usual ambiguous solution to an ambiguous situation turns out to be weighted absolutely in their favor. Note that Arjuna later describes this choice as one of Krishna over Indra (V.47.61–63).[25]

Because of their devotion, Krishna has offered himself as helper to the Pandavas. Considering, however, that both the right and the power of the

Pandavas come from Krishna, it might be more accurate to say that the Pandavas are Krishna's helpers, the helpers of God, rather than the other way around. That is, at the heroic level, Krishna is the helper of the Pandavas, but at the devotional level the situation is reversed. Krishna's need for Arjuna is expressed, for example, in the following lines, spoken to his own charioteer:

> Neither my wives nor friends nor kinsmen nor relatives nor any other is dearer to me than Arjuna, the son of Kunti. I am unable to look at this world without Arjuna [in it] for even a moment, O Daruka; and it will not be that way. [VII.56.23–24]

In reflection of Krishna's love for him, Arjuna tends to be called Krishna's "self," rather than the other way around (III.13.37, etc.)[26] All in all, however, each half of the pair needs the other half, a symbiosis that is characteristic of the Vaishnava conception of God and devotee.[27]

At the devotional level, it is obvious that Krishna's grace (*prasada*) to his devotees is the reason for the Pandava victory in the war. The epic makes this point directly a number of times, the best statement, perhaps, being in the words of Yudhishthira, at IX.61.27–30:

> O crusher of enemies, who other than you could withstand the *brahma* weapon released by Drona and Karna: [not] even the possessor of the thunderbolt, Puramdara [Indra], in person. Many were conquered in battle by the grace of your honor; and the son of Prtha was not made to flee in the great battle. And thus too, O great-armed one, continuity of actions and a high level of energy [were enjoyed] by me, through many vicissitudes. At Upaplavya [the Matsya capital] the great seer Krishnadvaipayana [Vyasa] said to me: "Where *dharma* is, there is Krishna; where Krishna is, there is victory."

As may be noted from the quotation of *Gita* XI.33 = *Mahabharata* VI.33.33 on p. 228, above, Krishna himself states in the *Gita* that he has already killed the enemy; Arjuna need fight only as his "mere instrument."[28] In line with his pledge, however, Krishna does not tend to intervene actively, despite occasional threats to do so, the exception, of course, being the VII, Appendix I, no. 16, version of the Jayadratha killing (see chap. IIA2) (although even here Krishna does not actually fight).[29] He does make his power felt, however, through advice, excellent driving,[30] and his very presence on the battlefield; and even in that version of the slaying of Jayadratha where Arjuna apparently accomplishes the act entirely through his own power, Arjuna himself attributes the victory to Krishna's grace (VII.123.27ff.). From the devotional perspective, when the epic states that Arjuna's is the decisive heroism of the war, its meaning may be specifically that it was he who mediated Krishna's power, bringing it over to the Pandava side in battle. Note the last stanza of the *Gita*, in the words of Samjaya: "Where Krishna, the lord of *yoga*, is, where the son of Prtha, the bowman, is, there, I believe, are prosperity, victory, well-being, and sure policy" (*Gita* XVIII.78 = *Mahabharata* VI.40.78). Together, then, *avatara* and devotee bring about a certain victory of *dharma* in the world; the outcome is never really in doubt.

As at the heroic level, the war may be viewed at the devotional level as a sacrifice, epitomizing the functioning of *dharma*. Like all other aspects of the battle description, the sacrificial imagery takes on new meaning in light of devotion. This change is particularly important in that it reflects a historical change in ritual: Vedic sacrifice is giving way to devotional ritual (*puja*). As noted in chapter IIIB1, the transformation may be observed in the *Gita*; there the ideal of desireless action, performed out of devotion to God, replaces that of huge sácrifices, performed with their fruit in mind.

Yet the change is not quite as great as one might imagine, for the sacrifice has long been identified with Vishnu, and Vishnu with the sacrifice,[31] and the Pancharatrins in particular (as witness the "Narayaniya" section [XII.325.4, etc.]) continue to stress this identity in the interest of legitimating their religion by linking it with the old Vedic religion. As the sacrifice is absorbed into Vishnu, so too is the entire Kurukshetra War. The fire imagery of the sacrifice/war is also absorbed by Vishnu, for he is Agni as well as all the other deities: the flaming *tejas* of the warrior has become his, as *tapas* is his.[32] Because of the intimate connection between Vishnu and the sacrifice, devotion can redefine sacrifice, and ensure victory in the war which is a sacrifice.[33]

Notes

1. See S. L. Kātre, "Avatāras of God," *Allahabad University Studies*, Arts and Sciences 10 (1934): 49. The stories referred to are to be found in great numbers in the Puranas. Cf. Indra's statement of III.45.18ff.: Nara and Narayana incarnate will relieve the earth's burden by killing the Nivatakavacha demons.
2. Which is not really much of a change; for Draupadi/Shri is an earth goddess, as her epithet Krishnā, meaning "black" (see Appendix), would suggest. On Draupadi as earth goddess, see further Hiltebeitel, "Draupadī's Garments," pp. 102ff. For Arjuna as earth protector in a heroic/human context, see VII.120.14–15, quoted on p. 148.
3. Cf., in particular, XV.39.11, which, in a chapter that basically duplicates part of the list of I.61, simply substitutes the Arjuna-Narayana connection for the Arjuna-Indra one.
4. This point is made, e.g., repeatedly throughout Biardeau, "Etudes" V; see also Biardeau, "Salvation," p. 88.
5. Biardeau, "Etudes" IV, p. 258. The present study regards the epic's kingly instruction as a combination of secular *arthashastra* and religious *dharmashastra*, with a strong Vaishnava bias.
6. Biardeau, "Etudes" IV, p. 173; "Etudes" V, p. 195; etc. Cf. Lévi's view: see chap. IIIB1, n. 33.
7. Biardeau, "Salvation," pp. 93ff.; "Etudes" IV, pp. 181ff.; etc.
8. Hopkins, "Position," pp. 63ff.
9. In the *Mahabharata* itself, the best example of Krishna's prewar trickery is the slaying of Jarasamdha (II.18ff.); on which, too, see the words of Shishupala (see below, n. 33), at II.39.1ff. At VII.155.29ff. Krishna, proposing a stratagem to be used against Karna, tells Arjuna that he killed Jarasamdha, Shishupala, and Ekalavya "by various means," for Arjuna's sake, before the war, so that they would not go over to the enemy; if they had, with Karna, they would have burned the earth. Note that Shishupala finds illegality even in Krishna's killing of Kamsa (see chap. IIA3, n. 31) (II.38.11ff.).
10. See chap. IIA3 and Appendix, under Krishna.
11. Bhima's statement at II.14.9, at the time of the Jarasamdha slaying, "In Kṛṣṇa is policy, in me strength, in Dhanaṃjaya victory . . . ," is echoed at II.18.3 and II.18.20. Note too Krishna's statement of *Gita* X.38 = *Mahabharata* VI.32.38: "I am policy for those wishing to conquer." Besides Krishna, several other *avatara*s of Vishnu are known for their use of trickery, but not against humans: most did not even fight against humans.
12. For an excellent discussion of Krishna's activity beyond the bounds of conventional morality in a context outside the *Mahabharata*, see John Stratton Hawley, *Krishna, the Butter Thief* (Princeton: Princeton University Press, 1983), pp. 261ff.
13. On war as a game, see Johan Huizinga, *Homo Ludens: A Study of the Play-Element in Culture* (1950; rpt. Boston: Beacon Press, 1955), pp. 89ff.
14. See too VII.105.14ff., etc.
15. Hopkins, "Position," p. 199 n. (see too "Position," p. 122).

16. This is the common image of Shiva as Nataraja ("lord of the dance"), reflected in the *Mahabharata* at VI.58.53; XIII.17.49; XIII.19.17f.
17. *Harivamsha* LXIII; *Bhagavata Purana* X.29ff.; etc.; but not described in the *Mahabharata* proper.
18. The building of the assembly hall: II.1ff.; Duryodhana's misadventures in the assembly hall: II.43.3ff. (see chap. IC, n. 50).
19. Hiltebeitel (*Ritual*, pp. 86ff.) suggests that Krishna's absence from the dice game makes of that game a Shaivic affair, which Krishna later rights. (Cf. Biardeau, "Conférence," vol. 80–81, p. 122: the dice game has been placed under the sign of Shiva; but the passage she cites, Poona Edition, II, Appendix I, no. 30, lines 26ff., is not part of the critical text.) Indeed, in view of the epic image of Shiva as dice player, there can be no doubt that a certain Shaivic flavor adheres to the game. The extant epic in its critical version nonetheless avoids explicit reference to this fact, and appears to regard Krishna, as omnipotent God, as having overseen the game even in his physical absence. Some manuscripts, as is well known, have Krishna appear at the game to restore Draupadi's garments, removed by Duhshasana (Poona Edition, II, 544*); but even in the critical version, where Krishna does not actually appear, his presence is felt. Note the following lines, spoken by Duhshasana to Draupadi, at II.60.26: "To Kṛṣṇa and Jiṣṇu, to Hari [Krishna] and Nara,/ Cry out for help! I shall take you yet!" (but he does not). In support of the present argument, cf. *Gita* X.36 = *Mahabharata* VI.32.36, where Krishna says: "Of deceivers, I am gambling"—that is, Krishna alone, without any need for Shiva in this particular version of the image. In terms of the present study, then, the bad luck of the dice game may be attributed to a human surrender to fate (see chap. IIA3 and chap. IIIB1, n. 17), permitted by Krishna; it is not necessarily Shaivic.

   As to imagery of Shiva's game/dance in the Kurukshetra War itself, the most striking comparison has been made by Hiltebeitel ("One Chariot," p. 24): Arjuna's "dance" on the battlefield at Kurukshetra, like his dancing in Virata's court (see chap. ID, especially n. 40), is the dance of Shiva. The present study, however, holds to its contention of chap. IE, n. 17: the imagery of Shiva in the Kurukshetra War is not essential mythically. (Hiltebeitel himself ["Disguises," p. 155] provides reference to *Bhima's* battlefield "dance" also resembling that of Shiva [VI.58.56]; to be sure, he goes on in this article [pp. 168ff.] to argue that *all* the Pandavas together are evocative of Shiva.) One should not be surprised, therefore, to discover imagery of Krishna's dance in the war as well: compare the illusory multiplication of Arjuna and Krishna at one point in battle (VII.18.11ff.) to Krishna's self-multiplication during the *ras lila* (*ras krida*, etc.) ("*ras* dance") (*Bhagavata Purana* X.33.20, etc.).
20. "Like wooden puppets" is van Buitenen's translation. The literal translation would be: "like a wooden maiden," "a wooden doll."
21. Cf., e.g., biblical Job, especially 38ff. That Indra is cited for misbehavior in the *Mahabharata* (see chap. IIA3) is in part an indication of his fallen status; see O'Flaherty, *Origins of Evil*, p. 146.
22. Cf. the more elaborate version of the same, in V.66.9.
23. Cf. VI.21.11 (". . . where *dharma* is, there is victory") in juxtaposition with VI.21.12 and 14 (". . . where Krishna is, there is victory"). For the view that

Krishna is a late addition to the phrase "where *dharma* is, there is victory," see Simson, pp. 166, 174. Lévi, however, seems to hold the opposite view (*"Tato jayam,"* p. 15): "where Krishna is, there is victory" and "where *dharma* is, there is Krishna" (and combinations of these) are the primary phrases; "where *dharma* is, there is victory" is derivative.

24. This complex condition seems to be aimed specifically at stressing the ambiguity of the situation, that is (Held, pp. 299f.), the balance between the two sides.
25. One morning when I had done with my prayers
And done with the water, a brahmin said kindly,
"There awaits you a difficult task, son of Pṛthā.
You must fight with your enemies, left-handed archer.

"Let either the bay-horsed, bolt-hurling Indra,
Destroying the enemies, go in your front,
Or let Vāsudeva protect your rear
On his chariot yoked with his steed Sugrīva."

I chose, over Indra the Thunderbolt-Wielder,
In this battle for Vāsudeva as helper. . . .

The seriousness of the decision is emphasized here by the added condition.
26. Cf. *Gita* VII.18 = *Mahabharata* VI.29.18, where the highest type of devotee (in that context), the *jnanin* ("knower"), is called Krishna's self.
27 See John Braisted Carman, *The Theology of Rāmānuja: An Essay in Interreligious Understanding* (New Haven: Yale University Press, 1974), pp. 190ff.
28. Cf. the words of VII.94.2, quoted on p. 144.
29. In one other passage (VII.28.16ff.) Krishna is said to have intervened. Here he stops a special weapon (inconsistently, the *vaishnava*) before it can hit Arjuna: hitting Krishna, the weapon becomes a garland. Arjuna rebukes Krishna here for taking such an active role in defiance of his promise, but of course this action hardly qualifies as active fighting on Krishna's part.
30. Even to the extent of pushing down the chariot (VII.66.10f.) so that an arrow (the snake Ashvasena in disguise [see chap. IE]) will miss Arjuna.
31. See Gonda, *Aspects*, pp. 77ff.
32. Agni is mentioned as a manifestation of Vishnu/Krishna at *Gita* X.23 = *Mahabharata* VI.32.23. Elsewhere, the epic speaks of "Hrshikesha [Krishna], with the immeasurable, shining energy of fire" (XIII.143.25).
33. Note how Krishna is consulted about, and gives permission for, both the royal consecration and the horse sacrifice (II.12.25ff., etc. [note too the participation of Narada, in II.5ff.]; XIV.70.18ff.), as well as the war itself (V.70ff.). To the present author, it seems that the terrible insult delivered to Krishna by the demonic Shishupala at the start of the royal consecration ritual (II.34ff.) must be a major factor in the disastrous problems of this sacrifice and the pursuant war. The situation is not really righted until the time of the horse sacrifice.

IIIC. THE NIGHT ATTACK, AND CONNECTED EVENTS

Of all the sequences in the *Mahabharata* story, one alone can be interpreted only at the level of devotion, being almost meaningless on the heroic and human levels, since its climax revolves completely around a supernatural deed performed by Krishna as God. This is the sequence that caps the battle books and puts an end to the heroic and human cycle of revenge, concluding it on an eschatological note of central importance to the epic as a whole; it will be called here the "night-attack sequence," after the book in which it is recounted, the *Sauptikaparvan* (Book X).

The Story

The story of the night-attack sequence goes as follows. Just before his death, Duryodhana has hastily appointed Ashvatthaman to leadership of the completely broken Kaurava army, as its fifth commander in chief (IX.64.38). Ashvatthaman, in any case, has been craving revenge ever since his father, Drona, was slain unfairly by the Pandavas. As general, his endeavor is, with the help of the only other surviving Kaurava warriors, Krpa (his maternal uncle) and Krtavarman, to conduct a night attack on the sleeping camp of the Pandavas, in which all surviving Panchalas and other Pandava partisans are killed (X.8). This Ashvatthaman accomplishes after dedicating himself to Shiva by offering himself as a sacrifice to that god (X.7.50ff.). The Pandava brothers themselves escape the slaughter only because Krishna has gotten them out of the camp;[1] Krishna and Satyaki likewise survive, bringing the Pandava survivors to a total of seven (I.1.158; X.9.47–48). After this action, Ashvatthaman and his two helpers manage to inform Duryodhana of their success, giving him a certain satisfaction before he breathes his last (X.9.46ff.). Yudhishthira, on the other hand, is overwhelmed with grief when he hears of the killing, and utters a lament related to his antiwar statement of V.70, quoted in chapter IIA1 (p. 131): "The others, who were being conquered, conquer; we, who were conquering, have been conquered" (X.10.10), and so forth.

Among those slain in the Pandava camp are the five Draupadeyas, Draupadi's five sons by the Pandava brothers (X.8.50ff.). It is Draupadi who, hearing of the slaughter, first demands that Yudhishthira seek revenge (X.11.14ff.). (He, true to form, has done nothing up to this point but lament.) Draupadi threatens to undertake a *praya* ("going forth") vow (that is, to fast)[2] until revenge is obtained: Ashvatthaman must be slain, and a gem that he has worn on his head since birth (a gem with which he was born) be brought to her, if she is to go on living. She reminds Bhima of his former heroic feats, and he sets out after Ashvatthaman.

Some time later, Krishna, Yudhishthira, and Arjuna, mounted together on Krishna's chariot, follow and catch up with Bhima. They observe as Bhima discovers Ashvatthaman seated by the Ganges River with a group of seers, including Vyasa (X.13.12ff.). At the sight of Bhima and the others, Ashvatthaman calls into being in a reed, "for the annihilation of the Pandavas," the great *brahmashiras* weapon, which he has learned to use from his father (X.13.17ff.).[3] Arjuna, incited by Krishna, calls upon his own *brahmashiras* weapon, also obtained from Drona (see chap. IA),[4] to neutralize Ashvatthaman's weapon (X.14.1ff.).[5]

At this point, Narada and Vyasa appear on the scene to pacify Ashvatthaman and Arjuna (X.14.11ff.).[6] Upon seeing these two great figures, Arjuna calls back his weapon (X.15.1ff.). The narrator, Vaishampayana, states here that none but Arjuna could have accomplished such a feat, not even the gods, including Indra: a great hero, Arjuna was able to recall the *brahmashiras* by virtue of his adherence to his vows, obedience to his teachers, and especially his *brahmacharya* (X.15.5ff.).[7] Ashvatthaman is, however, incapable of recalling his *brahmashiras* weapon. He admits that it was sinful to unloose the weapon, but says he did so in fear of Bhima, who had killed Duryodhana wrongly (X.15.13ff.). Vyasa now demands that Ashvatthaman withdraw the weapon, telling him that he must also relinquish the gem on his head if he wants his life to be spared (X.15.25ff.). The latter Ashvatthaman agrees to do, but he still cannot stop the weapon; the best he can do is divert it from the Paṇdavas by sending it into the wombs of the Pandava women, killing the Pandava heirs rather than the living Pandavas (X.15.31). Krishna, however, promises a revival by his power of the as yet unborn son of Uttarā by Arjuna's dead son Abhimanyu (who will be Arjuna's grandson, Parikshit) as the one remaining heir of the Pandava line (X.16.1ff.). Meanwhile, Krishna condemns the child slayer Ashvatthaman to three thousand years of wandering (X.16.10ff.). Krishna's actual revival of the murdered fetus of Parikshit is described in XIV.65ff.

According to this story, the only way that the continuing chain of revenge in the *Mahabharata* conflict could be ended was by the intervention of Krishna, aided by Arjuna, with some participation of the other "Pancharatra" figures (see chap. IIIA), Narada and Vyasa. Ultimate destruction could be avoided only by way of Krishna's reversal of the human processes of life and death.

The Near Dissolution of the Universe

In part, the night-attack sequence employs the concepts and imagery of the battle books: the humanity of the Kaliyuga superimposed upon a heroic conflict. In particular, Ashvatthaman justifies the night attack on the basis of previously committed Pandava misdeeds, and sees it as a form of policy (X.1.33ff.).[8] Krpa at first disputes the justness of Ashvatthaman's claim, but finally agrees to help, predicting an Indra-like performance on Ashvatthaman's part (X.2, 4). The attack is conducted like a sacrificial act, having much in common with the Khandava Forest burning,[9] but it is, like the war as a whole, a sacrifice of human beings. That only a few survivors remain afterward is very much a Kaliyuga situation, as Yudhishthira's lament, cited above, suggests. Later, when Ashvatthaman sends forth the *brahmashiras*, he does so out of a sense of *apad* (X.13.17). These conceptions are, however, mixed with the devotional imagery of *pralaya*, to which they soon give way almost completely, yielding, in the basest action of the war, a terrible "death-night" (*kalaratri*) (X.8.65, etc.)[10] vision like that of *Gita* XI (see chap. IIIB1).[11]

There is a difference, however. In the *Gita* XI picture of *pralaya*, Krishna himself plays the terrible role of destroyer, emphasis being placed upon his transcendence and identification with fate. In the *pra-*

laya of the night-attack sequence, however, Krishna's beneficent role of preserver and re-creator is emphasized, while the destructive role is Shiva's (through Ashvatthaman). This division of labor reflects the standard mythology that grew up around the concept of *pralaya*[12] and is offered here in a form particularly appropriate for Vishnu devotees: the Shaivic sacrifice that is *pralaya* (see chap. IC) (here, the "sacrifice of war" [see p. 114] gone, under unbearable pressures, out of control) is considered horrible and condemned; later, Vishnu rights it. Pralayic symbolism is emphasized through clear definition of Shiva's role as destroyer here, as nowhere else in the central epic narrative.[13] In the night-attack sequence, Vishnu-Shiva opposition subsumes the god-demon and human oppositions of the heroic and human levels of the *Mahabharata*, and Ashvatthaman, portrayed here as Shiva's representative, becomes Arjuna's chief opponent, in place of the Kauravas with Karna.[14]

The Shaivic role is appropriately Ashvatthaman's. Having all the external heroic traits of beauty and auspicious markings (IX.5.7ff.), and known as a hero,[15] he is nevertheless a peculiar figure, a fighting brahmin, like his father, Drona:[16] in childhood, for example, he distinguished himself among Drona's students "in all the esoteric arts" (I.123.41; see p. 43). He must have been resentful of Arjuna from his earliest days, knowing that his father preferred Arjuna to.him;[17] this resentment intensified after his father's unrighteous slaying. Reflecting Ashvatthaman's fully developed role in the epic, the list of partial incarnations describes him as made up of "portions of Mahādeva [Shiva], Death, Lust, and Fury, which merged into one" (I.61.66–67).[18] Ashvatthaman's human ambiguities and faults are expressed thus at the devotional level.[19]

Ashvatthaman is enabled to act effectively in the night attack by virtue of his devotion to Shiva: as mentioned above, he gains strength by offering himself as a sacrifice to Shiva; afterward his behavior is wildly Shiva-like. The Pandava camp at the time of the night attack is reminiscent of the cremation ground frequented by Shiva; the fire set there by the night attackers resembles that with which Shiva burns the world at the time of *pralaya*. The gem on Ashvatthaman's head is like Shiva's third eye.[20] The wandering to which he is condemned ultimately is Shaivic behavior.

In support of these identifications, the last two chapters of the *Sauptikaparvan* consist of stories of Shiva, narrated by Krishna to Yudhishthira in connection with Krishna's explanation of how Ashvatthaman was able to succeed in the night attack. One story, a version of "Daksha's sacrifice" (see chap. IC) (although Daksha is not mentioned in it by name), has imagery which is connected intimately with that of the night attack, the imagery of sacrifice destroyed (X.18). Here Shiva is portrayed as a malcontent who feels himself slighted by the other gods; these are emotions that closely parallel Ashvatthaman's bitter feeling toward the Pandavas, as depicted throughout the *Sauptikaparvan*. The imagery of this story is that of *pralaya*.

Regarding the eschatological role of the *brahmashiras* weapon, with which Ashvatthaman attempts to complete his destructive work, it is necessary only to state that the epic sometimes views the *brahmashiras* as identical with the *pashupata* weapon (although the night-attack sequence itself does not mention this identification).[21] The name of the *pashupata* weapon indicates its affiliation with Shiva, who himself is Pashupati ("lord of animals"), and the weapon is stated, in III.41.8 and elsewhere, to be the destroyer at the end of an age.[22]

It is possible at this point to present a bit of speculation that, while not essential to this study of Arjuna, would enrich it greatly were it to be accepted. The present author's hypothesis is that the night attack, as recounted in the extant epic, is a tale that was molded by the Pancharatrins to illustrate their own doctrine symbolically: the "night attack" followed by the *brahmashiras* episode represents the "night" (*ratra*) referred to in the compound "Pancharatra." This symbolism would correspond well to the meaning suggested convincingly by Walter G. Neevel, Jr., in the introduction to his book entitled *Yāmuna's Vedānta and Pāñcarātra: Integrating the Classical and the Popular*: that "Pancharatra" refers to the "night of the five," the "five" being the five material elements (earth, air, ether, water, and fire), which disappear at the time of *moksha* or *pralaya*.[23] In the night raid of *Mahabharata* X, the five who are destroyed are the five Draupadeyas (surrogates for the Pandavas)[24] or, alternatively, the Panchalas, whose name contains the element *pancha-* ("five").[25] Ashvatthaman's role here, that of Shiva at *pralaya*, is viewed negatively, from the perspective of the Pancharatrins, Vishnu devotees, whose God opposes Shiva/Ashvatthaman and saves the universe in this sequence.[26]

As pointed out in chapter IA, the enmity between Drona and the Panchalas exists over and above the Kaurava-Pandava hostility in the epic: this is the enmity that Ashvatthaman inherits. It is possible that a cycle of Panchala tales which formed the basis of the *Mahabharata* (see chap. IA) included a story of a night raid featuring some proto-Ashvatthaman,[27] and that the Pancharatrins picked up this tale as an illustration of their doctrines, identifying that proto-Ashvatthaman with Shiva; if so, they could have been attracted to it particularly because the name "Panchala" fit so well into their "five" symbolism. Clearly, the Panchalas remain the major victims of Ashvatthaman's night attack: besides the Draupadeyas (matrilineally Panchalas),[28] Dhrshtadyumna and Shikandin are the most important figures killed, the former, at least, quite predictably so, as Drona's killer, born especially for that purpose (see chaps. IB and IIA3). In fact, all named victims of the night attack are Panchalas.[29] The Pandavas are involved only secondarily in the night-attack story, and it may be hypothesized that it was the Pancharatrins who supplemented this story with the *brahmashiras* episode, starring Arjuna as Krishna's devotee.

Throughout the night-attack sequence, as elsewhere in the epic, but perhaps even more strongly, it is stressed that Arjuna's power derives from his devotion to Krishna. Central in this regard is the story told by Krishna to Yudhishthira in X.12: Ashvatthaman, wandering the world, had once arrived in Dvaraka and asked Krishna for his discus in exchange for the *brahmashiras*. But when Krishna had offered the discus to him, he had been unable to lift it. Ashvatthaman had then admitted that had he obtained the discus, he would have used it to fight against Krishna. Reproving Ashvatthaman, Krishna contrasts Arjuna and several Vrshnis with that extremely evil one: these had never made such a request of him (X.12.25ff.). In X.12.27 he calls Arjuna: "He than whom no other person on earth is dearer to me, to whom I would give anything, even my wives and sons." The contrast between the behavior of Ashvatthaman, who was told even by his father that he would be unrighteous (X.12.9), and Arjuna is implicit elsewhere. Both Arjuna and Ashvatthaman had been warned against indiscriminate use of the *brahmashiras* when they were, at separate times, given this weapon by Drona (Ashvatthaman against Drona's better judgment).[30] The *Sauptikaparvan* notes, thus, that Arjuna set his *brahmashiras* in motion, "having spoken a blessing first for the son of the preceptor [precisely, Ashvatthaman], then at once for himself, and also for all his brothers, having honored the deities and also all the teachers" (X.14.5–6). Unlike

Ashvatthaman, Arjuna shoots on Krishna's order—and only after Ashvatthaman has already shot. It is not surprising, then, that Arjuna is able to withdraw the *brahmashiras* weapon, while Ashvatthaman cannot, although a brahmanic weapon (for such its name and source show it to be) should by rights be handled better by a brahmin than a warrior, especially when that brahmin is the weapons teacher's son. In context, this weapon is devotional in character, unlike Arjuna's other weapons, which may best be understood at the level of heroism; and Arjuna has the devotional power to control it. Toward the end of the *Sauptika* action, the following picture is found:

> The Pandavas, with their enemies slain, having placed Govinda [Krishna] at their head, and also Krishnadvaipayana, and Narada, the great sage, taking the jewel born with Drona's son, hurrying, ran to the wise Draupadi, who had entered into *praya*. [X.16.20–21]

The group portrayed here is the characteristically Pancharatra devotional group, gathered around Krishna.

Arjuna's Grandson Parikshit: The Universe Saved by Devotion

With the help of their God, the devotees just manage to preserve world order at the time of greatest crisis. Or to be more specific, they manage to rescue that very small remnant which Biardeau so rightly points out is necessary to re-create the world after its cyclic destruction.[31] That remnant is Parikshit, Arjuna's grandson and the father of Janamejaya.[32] The pralayic imagery of rebirth from a remnant is probably, as Biardeau indicates, based on the imagery of the funeral sacrifice;[33] here, however, the remnant's survival depends upon God himself—the message being that for humans devotion must inform sacrificial rites (a message identical to that of the *Gita* and the battle scenes, as discussed in chaps. IIIB1 and IIIB2, above). Otherwise there will be nothing left.

Behind the symbolism of Parikshit as remnant surely stands his historical role, as suggested earlier: the *Mahabharata* appears to have been composed largely for the benefit of King Janamejaya (so called), who wished to hear of the glory of his ancestors, and the Parikshit revived by Krishna is, precisely, Janamejaya's father. One is struck by the effort of the extant epic to establish Parikshit's dependence upon Krishna for his very life. The following passage, addressed to Janamejaya, describing Parikshit at the time of his birth (that is, his revival), should be contrasted with the birth stories of heroes quoted in chapter IA (compare Abhimanyu's birth [see chap. IB]), in order to confirm that Parikshit's heroism is connected closely with devotional elements:

> When, O king, the *brahma* [here, the *brahmashiras*] weapon had been drawn back by Krishna, then that dwelling was lit up by your father with his energy. Then all *rakshasas*, having abandoned that house, were destroyed. And there was a voice in the sky, saying: "Good, Keṣhava, good!" And then that blazing weapon went to the Grandfather [Brahma]. Then your father obtained life again, O lord of men, and that child moved according to his power, with all his might. Then, O king, the Bharata women were joyful. And at the command of Govinda they made the brahmins recite. Then all of those women of the lions among the descendants of Bharata, joyful, praised Janardana like people who, having obtained a boat, have crossed to the far shore. Kunti and the daughter of Drupada, Subhadra and also Uttarā, and all the other women of those lions among men were delighted. There *mallas* [wrestlers], *natas* [dancers], *jhallas* [club-fighters], *granthikas* [astrologers], *saukhashayikas* [those who ask if one has slept well], and also throngs of *sutas* and *magadhas* [types of bards] praised Janardana with prayers signifying praise of the Kuru family, O bull among the descendants of Bharata. Uttarā, having arisen with her son at the proper moment, pleased, greeted the descendant of the Yadus [Krishna]. Then he, pleased, gave her in particular much treasure, as did the other tigers among the Vrshnis. And the faithful lord Janardana then gave a name to that father of yours, O great king, speaking thus: "From the fact that this son of Abhimanyu was born when the family had perished [*parikshine kule*], let his name be 'Parikshit.'" Your father grew as time went on, O lord of men, delighting the hearts, O descendant of Bharata, of all the world. [XIV.69.1–11]

It is probable that the devotional emphasis with regard to Parikshit grew specifically out of a historical devotional leaning of the "Parikshit"/"Janamejaya" family, that this was a family of Vishnu devotees;[34] and it is tempting to speculate that they were perhaps members of that very Pancharatra group which has appeared throughout Part III of this study.

The initiatory flavor of Parikshit's revival is striking: is, perhaps, a Pancharatra initiation being reflected here?[35] It is more likely, however, that this family participated in a pre-Pancharatra form of Vaishnavism, and that Pancharatra material entered the epic only later, adhering to the devotional material already there. Surely insofar as Janamejaya is essential to the epic at its earlier stages, the divine Krishna is also essential, since the two are connected intimately through Parikshit.

As if the rather sudden movement from generalized sacrificial to specifically pralayic imagery and from god-demon opposition to Vishnu-Shiva opposition were not enough, an impressive plot twist also serves to underscore the shift in levels of discourse in this sequence: the rightful successors at the heroic level, the children of the rescued Draupadi/Shri, are killed off, as a devotional heir takes their place. But the Draupadeyas have always been such shadowy figures (see chap. IB) that one must wonder whether such a twist has not been anticipated all along.[36] Indeed, not only the night-attack sequence itself, but much of the plot of the extant *Mahabharata* does seem to build up to the episode of the saving of Parikshit. The Vrshnis, the Matsyas, and the Pandavas themselves (particularly Arjuna) represent his ancestry; and an episode such as the year spent incognito in the Matsya kingdom takes on new meaning in this light.[37] In connection with his relationship to Parikshit, Arjuna's devotional affiliation, expressed throughout the epic, is of paramount importance. As Krishna states as part of the act of truth[38] by which he revives Parikshit (XIV.68.18ff.): "As I do not recall ever having quarreled with Vijaya [Arjuna; see Appendix], by that truth may this dead child live" (XIV.68.21).[39] Arjuna's marriage to Subhadra, Krishna's sister (see chap. IB), is seen to be Arjuṇa's most important marriage at the devotional level, not only because it underscores Arjuna's own relationship with Krishna, but also because it establishes Parikshit's blood tie to this God: Krishna was the maternal uncle of Abhimanyu, son of Arjuna and Subhadra and Parikshit's father. Abhimanyu himself is pivotal as a connecting link between the kingly house and its God. As for the Panchalas, so important at the heroic level: at the devotional level, their primary function seems to be to draw their arch-enemy, Ashvatthaman, into the action and set up his conflict with Arjuna, in order to set the devotional tale in motion. On the other hand, certain references to Shiva dispersed throughout the epic point in the direction of a Shiva-possessed Ashvatthaman and deployment of the *pashupata* weapon at the end of the Kurukshetra War: for example, the tale of King Shvetaki, attached to the Khandava episode (see chap. IC), and Arjuna's Book VII journey to Shiva to win the *pashupata* (see, especially, chap. IIA2), reduplicating an aspect of the mountain-man sequence.[40]

With God's help, in the extant epic, the riddles that led to the Kurukshetra War have been solved perfectly; that is, the succession conflict is over permanently: a single descendant of the entire Kuru line has been provided, and the oppositions of the war have been dissolved once and for all. The royal claim of Janamejaya, Parikshit's son, he to whom the epic is being recited, is established absolutely here, on the basis of a devotional relationship with Krishna, who saves world order by saving Parikshit.

At the eschatological turning point, as depicted in the night-attack sequence, Arjuna and his line act as vital participants in cosmic as well as human history. Here resides a new meaning for the heroic statement that the king makes the age, which was seen not to apply at the level of humanity (chap. IIA3): the king must be, above all, a devotee. In this and only this sense does the Kurukshetra War culminate in a Krtayuga:[41] "Where Krishna is, there is *dharma*."

Notes

1. This he has done simply by telling them, at IX.61.35, that they must spend the night out of the camp "for the sake of good fortune."
2. This is the same action as that undertaken earlier by Bhurishravas, Drona, and Chitrangada and Babhruvahana (see chaps. IIA2, IIA3, IIB).
3. That the weapon used by Ashvatthaman is indeed the *brahmashiras* is not actually stated until Vyasa's speech of X.15.19ff. The way has been prepared, however, by the story of Ashvatthaman's acquisition of this weapon, at X.12.4ff.
4. Alternatively, he obtained the weapon from Shiva (see chap. ID); but the night-attack sequence does not mention this fact.
5. Again, the weapon's name is not stated until X.15.19ff., but that it is the *brahmashiras* is implied clearly in the statement that Arjuna learned it from Drona (X.14.2).
6. Vyasa's appearance is redundant, as he was already on the scene as of X.13.13.
7. On Arjuna's *brahmacharya*, see chap. IB.
8. He copies the conduct observed in an owl who kills sleeping crows; this story sounds just like an *arthashastra* parable, but Biardeau also sees in it an image of *pralaya* (see "Conférence," vol. 90, p. 154, etc.).
9. Outstandingly, the setting of fires and the slaying of those fleeing at the gate (X.8.100ff.), as well as the panic of the victims. See further, Scheuer, pp. 318ff.

10. This term, while also occurring elsewhere in the epic, is particularly common in the *Sauptikaparvan*.
11. The chronology works nicely: the war followed by the night attack parallels the *yuga* cycle followed by *pralaya*. Of course, Biardeau, regarding both the war and the night-attack sequence as based on the image of *pralaya*, would not agree with this distinction. To her, the night attack is just a *reprise* and clarification of the war; see "Etudes" IV, p. 209. (She does, however, have an interesting view of the details of the *pralaya* imagery in the night-attack sequence: Bhima as the wind of *pralaya*, Uttarā's womb as the water, etc. ["Etudes" IV, pp. 210ff.]). Similarly, Dumézil seems to view the whole Kurukshetra War as a reflection of the Indo-European eschatological conflict, although, in fact, the night-attack material figures most prominently in his discussion of the matter; see *Mythe et épopée* I, pp. 218ff. Only Hiltebeitel seems to concentrate on the night-attack events (plus the antecedent story of Abhimanyu's death) as particularly eschatological; see *Ritual*, pp. 312ff. (though note his more recent treatment of the war as a whole as pralayic [see chap. IE, n. 21]). Scheuer, although treating the war itself and the night attack quite differently (the war as a sacrifice, the night attack as an image of *pralaya*, as in the present study [see Scheuer, chaps. 8–9]), insists upon continuity between them (p. 336), and is thus led to speak of confusion between sociocosmic and cosmic time (see chap. IIIB1, n. 9), as well as between god-demon "antagonism" and Vishnu-Shiva "polarity," in the epic (pp. 329; 339, n. 65).
12. See Introduction and chap. IC, n. 21.
13. Elsewhere in the narrative, Shiva's role as destroyer is referred to only obliquely; nor is it carried through consistently. Sometimes Shiva, opposing Krishna, is said to be aligned with destructive forces having some Kaurava or anti-Pandava affiliation: e.g., Jarasamdha (II.13.63; II.17.19; II.20.8) and Jayadratha (III.256.25ff.). In the last-mentioned passage, Jayadratha receives a boon from Shiva, which states that he will be able to counter any of the Pandavas except Arjuna; Arjuna, Shiva tells him, cannot be opposed because he has divine Krishna's support. Shishupala, Krishna's enemy (see, especially, chap. IIIB2, n. 33), is said to have been born three-eyed (II.40.1), a trait associated with Shiva. The births of the Kauravas themselves are sometimes said to have taken place only after the propitiation of Shiva (I.103.9; III.240.6); this proves little, however, because propitiation of Shiva is a common expedient for one desiring progeny throughout the epic, and the Kauravas are also said to have been born through a boon from Vyasa (I.107.7ff.). On the other hand, the magic charm that made possible the engendering of the Pandavas (see chap. IA) was a gift to Kunti from Durvasas (I.104.4ff.), who is a portion of Shiva (XIII.145.35; Poona Edition, I, Appendix I, no. 118, lines 73f.; and later texts; Durvasas is also given as a name of Shiva in XII.12.61). Shiva is also involved in the various stories that explain how the multiple marriage of Draupadi came about (see chap. IB) and the birth story of Shikhandin (V.188.7ff.). In many other ways as well, the Pandava side is associated with Shiva; note, especially, the Arjuna-Shiva encounter in the mountain-man sequence (see chap. ID). During this meeting, Shiva gives Arjuna a vision of himself in his divine form (III.40.55 and III.163.40ff.). Here and elsewhere, Arjuna wins the *pashupata* weapon (meanwhile, Ashvattha-

man has the *narayana* weapon, which can be countered only by passive resistance [VII.170.15ff.]). In the battle books, Arjuna is sometimes compared with Shiva (it has, however, been asserted previously that such formulaic comparison proves nothing regarding mythic affiliation), and Shiva is said to precede Arjuna on the battlefield; see chap. IE, especially n. 17, and chap. IIIB2, n. 19. After the war is over, the Pandavas propitiate Shiva to obtain the gold required for their horse sacrifice (XIV.64.1ff.). The preceding summary is thoroughly supported and supplemented by Scheuer, with the proviso that he rejects the Shishupala-Shiva connection (pp. 34, 196f.).

The inconsistency in alignments seems to have a triple cause. At the heroic level there is no Vishnu-Shiva opposition, and thus no reason not to permit the Pandavas to fraternize with Shiva where appropriate; e.g., Arjuna would naturally meet Shiva on a trip to the Himalaya, Shiva's abode. At the devotional level, one finds what Scheuer (p. 79, etc.), following Biardeau ("Etudes" IV, p. 114, etc.), calls Vishnu-Shiva complementarity: Vishnu and Shiva work side by side as (literally and figuratively) preserver and destroyer in the universal cosmic cycles. Such complementarity, Biardeau and Scheuer would argue, serves an important symbolic function in the *Mahabharata*, insofar as *avatara* and king, essential figures in the epic, are thought of as displaying a Shaivic (wild, violent) as well as a tamer Vishnu side; see, especially, Scheuer, pp. 241f. Meanwhile, the epic is interpolated by both Vaishnavas and Shaivas, each group allowing its favorite deity to absorb the deeds of his opponent, taking advantage of the fact that the two are often considered identical anyway (see Introduction). (There are also Shakta [Goddess-oriented] interpolations; see, especially, Poona Edition, IV, Appendix I, no. 4, and VI, Appendix I, no. 1.) One thus finds Narayana praising Shiva at VII.172.63ff., Krishna calling Shiva a manifestation of himself (see chap. IIIB1), etc. No doubt, a single devotional group that had control over part of the epic could mold it at will, and this seems to have occurred in the case of the night-attack sequence. Shiva reveals himself as a force opposing Krishna and the Pandavas here, as he tells Ashvatthaman that he has until now protected the Panchalas for Krishna's sake and to test Ashvatthaman, but that their time has finally run out (X.7.60f.). Scheuer, however, does not find sectarian interpolation to be a particularly helpful explanation (p. 16); cf. Biardeau, "Etudes" IV, p. 114, etc., and Hiltebeitel, "Disguises," p. 159.

14. The following words, spoken by Duryodhana at I.130.16–17, may perhaps be construed as an explanation at the devotional level of the participation of certain elders on the Kaurava side: "Droṇa's son is on my side, and Droṇa will be where his son is, no doubt of that. And Kṛpa Śāradvata will be on the side the three of them can be on together; he'll never desert Droṇa and his sister's son [see chap. IB, n. 4]." Here, then, Ashvatthaman's choice of sides is the deciding factor.
15. Even in the words of Arjuna; see VII.167.25ff.
16. See IV.46.8f. (on Drona and Ashvatthaman); V.164.7f.; IX.5.14.
17. For reference, see chap. IA, n. 85. Note the similarity to Karna's situation: a lost birthright.
18. The same chapter identifies Krpa as an incarnation of the Rudras (v. 71).

19. On Ashvatthaman in the pre-night-attack epic, see further Scheuer, pp. 299ff. Interestingly, Scheuer points to a dramatic hardening of Ashvatthaman's attitude in preparation for the night attack—a point that could be used in support of discontinuity between the war proper and the night-attack sequence (an idea favored by the present study, but not by Scheuer himself [see above, n. 11]).
20. Shiva's third eye is, in fact, mentioned in the night-attack sequence (X.7.8).
21. See III.41.7f. for the identification of *brahmashiras* and *pashupata*.
22. On the other hand, the ultimate nature of the *pashupata* is not always stressed. It is sometimes grouped on lists with other weapons, and both Drona and the Kauravas are said, in such cases, to possess it (VII.163.28; VIII.43.21).
23. Walter G. Neevel, Jr., *Yāmuna's Vedānta and Pāñcarātra: Integrating the Classical and the Popular*, Harvard Dissertations in Religion, 10 (Missoula, Mont.: Scholars Press, 1977), pp. 8ff. The emphasis on the night of the attack as *kalaratri* goes well with this interpretation. Cf. the statement of *Gita* II.69 = *Mahabharata* VI.24.69, implying a total reversal of normal values, or a resolution of opposites: "In what is night for all creatures, one who is restrained is awake. When creatures are awake, that is night for a seeing sage." For a discussion of some other suggestions as to the origin of the name "Pancharatra" in both the traditional texts and modern scholarship, see Jaiswal, pp. 41ff. See also three important articles: J. A. B. van Buitenen, "The Name 'Pañcarātra,'" *History of Religions* 1 (1961–62): 291–99; V. Raghavan, "The Name Pāñcarātra: With an Analysis of the Sanatkumāra-Saṃhitā in Manuscript," *Journal of the American Oriental Society* 85 (1965): 73–79; and H. Daniel Smith, "A Typological Survey of Definitions: The Name 'Pāñcharātra': Utilizing Texts of the Pāñcarātra Saṃhitās," in *Oriental Research Madras: Special Volume Dedicated to H.H. Sri Chandrasekharendra Sarasvati, Sankaracharya of Kanchi Kamakoti Pitha*, ed. V. Raghavan (Madras: Kuppuswami Sastri Research Institute, 1973), pp. 102–17.
24. Indeed, the Pandavas are sometimes compared with the five elements: V.63.2; XII.53.18.
25. It is worth noting here that the *pancharatram* sacrifice of *Shatapatha Brahmana* XIII.6.1.1., etc., often cited in discussions of the etymology of "Pancharatra," is likewise a human sacrifice.
26. It is noteworthy that the "Narayaniya" contains a story of a fight between Rudra and Nara and Narayana, at Daksha's sacrifice, which greatly resembles the confrontation between Ashvatthaman and Arjuna and Krishna in the night-attack sequence; see XII.330.42ff. With regard to the difference between the depiction of *pralaya* in the night-attack sequence and that in the *Gita*, might one suggest that the night-attack sequence reflects the Pancharatra understanding of *pralaya* (popular and mythic), while *Gita* XI reflects the Bhagavata (see chap. IIIB1, especially n. 3) understanding?
27. Cf. the night raid against the Thracians, of *Iliad* X.469ff. A tale of a night raid against the Panchalas would most likely have been the final tale of such a cycle, just as it is the final Panchala tale in the extant epic.
28. That they should be viewed in this manner is emphasized both by their name and by Draupadi's strange marriage.

29. Besides the individually named victims, certain groups mentioned in X.8, Prabhadrakas, Somakas, and Srnjayas, appear also to be Panchalas; see their entries in Søren Sørensen, *An Index to the Names in the Mahābhārata, with Short Explanations and a Concordance to the Bombay and Calcutta Editions and P. C. Roy's Translation* (1904; rpt. Delhi: Motilal Banarsidass, 1978).
30. At I.123.75ff. Drona warns Arjuna not to use the *brahmashiras* on humans: it could burn the world. Shiva warns Arjuna regarding the *brahmashiras/pashupata*, at III.41.15: he must not use it without due consideration. At III.163.49f. Shiva tells Arjuna not to use the *pashupata* against humans: it must only be used against other weapons. Note that Arjuna also promises Indra that he will not use the divine weapons Indra has given him against humans unless his other weapons have been repulsed (III.164.26); cf. Narada's words, at III.172.18ff. Regarding Drona's hesitation and warning to Ashvatthaman, see X.12.6ff.
31. See especially, Biardeau, "Etudes" IV, p. 127.
32. Biardeau, "Etudes" V, p. 162. The idea of a child as remnant is found more than once in the *Mahabharata*: cf. the cases of Parashara (I.167.13ff.) and Aurva (I.169.20ff.).
33. For references, see chap. IC, n. 18.
34. Note the words of Janamejaya's ministers to him in praise of Parikshit: "Janamejaya, your father was friendly to Govinda" (I.45.12).
35. On Pancharatra initiation, see Schrader, pp. 121f.; Jaiswal, pp. 140ff.; and H. D. Smith (citing K. Rangachari), p. 114, n. 35. Note that Krishna is also known elsewhere as a reviver or rescuer of children; see, e.g., *Harivamsha* LXXIX.10ff. and CI ff., where Arjuna is brought into the story (cf. *Bhagavata Purana* X.89.22ff.). Others, however, likewise revive children in the epic; see XII.29.14ff.; XII.149.106ff. More broadly, Parikshit's death and revival provide an example of the hero's threatened childhood (see chap. IA, n. 96).
36. With regard to Panchala dissociation from the devotional level of the *Mahabharata* narrative in the night-attack sequence, it is worth noting that even the earlier books of the epic do not view the Panchalas as particularly talented spiritually; see VII.165.41ff. for an illustration of this point.
37. Also striking, although not emphasized as much as one might expect, is the fact that the Matsya prince Uttara is the first named casualty in the Kurukshetra War (VI.45.38ff.).
38. Regarding acts of truth, see chap. IIA2, n. 18.
39. Other things Krishna swears by here: that he has never lied or turned back in battle (v. 19), that he loves *dharma* and brahmins (v. 20), that he killed Kamsa (see chap. IIA3, n. 31) and Keshin (a demon) righteously (v. 23). In sum (v. 22): "As truth and *dharma* are constantly established in me, so let this dead child, the son of Abhimanyu, live."
40. In addition, aspects of the "Fire in the Lacquer House" (see chap. IA, etc.); see I.131.2; I.134.11.
41. See Introduction and chap. IIA3, n. 87. On Parikshit, thus, bringing Kali(yuga) under control, see *Bhagavata Purana* I.16f.

IIID. THE ASCENT TO HEAVEN, AND CONNECTED EVENTS, II

Yudhishthira's Answer to the Human Condition

This chapter will complete the discussion of the last books of the *Mahabharata*, begun in chapter IIC; as has been usual throughout Part III, its focus will be the epic's attempt to transcend the human weaknesses and ambiguities of its characters and situations. There will be a difference in this chapter, however, which is due to the difference between the ascent-to-heaven sequence and the other portions of the epic discussed in this study. The difference is that the ascent-to-heaven sequence advocates Yudhishthira's answer to the human condition, rather than Arjuna's, that is, the path of knowledge as opposed to the path of devotion. The ascent-to-heaven sequence is the only prolonged portion of the epic narrative with this approach. It has been judged worthwhile to include this sequence in a discussion of Arjuna, since he does take part in it, although by the end his role is a secondary one. The striking point to be considered is his subordination to Yudhishthira here. Also, due to its placement at the end of the epic, the ascent-to-heaven sequence is of particular importance, for it becomes the epic's final statement of its own values.

The difference between knowledge and devotion has already been discussed, in chapter IIIB1, above: knowledge entails a resolution of opposites, and a concomitant acceptance of fate; devotion transforms fate into something positive by way of connection with God. In the *Gita*, it was seen, as throughout most of the *Mahabharata*, "fate" and "God" are not wholly distinguished, and the paths of knowledge and devotion intertwine. Yet in the *Gita* and most of the epic, devotion is the dominant solution, which seems to absorb knowledge. In the ascent-to-heaven sequence as well, there are elements of devotion mixed with elements of knowledge, but here the priorities are reversed: the major point made by the ascent-to-heaven events is that the oppositions of human existence are illusory. This point is made more clearly here than anywhere else in the epic narrative. That is, opposites are established clearly (for what could be more diametrically opposed than heaven and hell?) and then are said to be nothing but illusion. In line with the shift in priorities, a shift in major character takes place. Throughout most of the epic, and even at the start of the ascent-to-heaven sequence, Arjuna is the central and ideal figure, thanks to his relationship with Krishna; but Yudhishthira, the proponent of knowledge, is the central and ideal character of the culminating scenes of the ascent to heaven.

As described in chapter IIC, Yudhishthira loses his brothers on the way to heaven and arrives there alone. Upon his arrival he learns, to his dismay, that his brothers have fallen into hell, while the evil Kauravas appear to have attained heaven. The discussion in Part II explained this reversal as a structural expression of the ambiguity of human morality, but the full explanation offered by the *Svargarohanaparvan* goes further, and really makes sense only at a level above the human: Yudhishthira is told by Indra that his brothers' sojourn in hell and his vision of them there are only products of illusion, imposed upon the Pandavas so that they may expiate the evil deeds they perpetrated in the war; among these, Yudhishthira's lie to Drona is mentioned specifically (XVIII.3.14ff.). Afterward, the epic characters go back into the gods, demons, and other supernatural beings from whom they had originally emerged, as described in the list of partial incarnations, and attain heaven (XVIII.4ff.). One has the impression at the end of the ascent-to-heaven sequence that these figures have done little more than reenter a continuing game of god-demon confrontations, fated to continue eternally; in fact, they never really had emerged from it, except in an illusory manner.[1] Here, then, such human issues as right and wrong, life and death, are resolved completely. With regard to the issue of right versus wrong in particular, the new level makes use of the same structural extremes as were employed in the human version of the story; but now the fact that the good went to hell while the evil went to heaven takes on a totally different significance. Instead of creating a sense of Kaliyuga moral confusion, the reversals point clearly to their own resolution: both heaven and hell are temporary, illusory. The opposites are not mediated in a Lévi-Straussian sense but, rather, treated as ultimately meaningless: dissolved. This is the teaching offered to Yudhishthira in the ascent-to-heaven sequence.

To this teaching, the devotional perspective adds only a little. It is possible, for example, to equate the "illusion" (*maya*) discussed in the sequence with Vishnu's *maya*; but the sequence never suggests doing so: the *maya* is said to be Indra's (XVIII.3.34). Yudhishthira's concern for the dog who is devoted to him (XVII.3.7ff.) could be interpreted as an oblique reference to God's concern for his devotees; but again, this connection is never specified by the epic composers. More important, Yudhishthira finds Arjuna and Krishna together in a devotional relationship in heaven:

> There he saw Govinda endowed with his form as *brahman*, revealed in that likeness seen formerly, shining, with his own form, provided with divine weapons, the discus and so forth, terrible, divine, in their personified forms, being attended by the glorious hero Phalguna. [XVIII.4.2–4]

(The form of Krishna seen here seems to be the same as that seen by Arjuna in *Gita* XI.) The devotional force of this tableau is, however, reduced by reference to its *brahma* nature, as well as by its juxtaposition with the numerous later stanzas that detail the reabsorption of epic characters into their supernatural prototypes (XVIII.5.7ff.).

Note too the sequence's emphasis on the idea that Krishna is bound up in the process of fate: as noted in chapter IIC, fate and curses are cited to account for the destruction of the Vrshnis. An interesting stanza, which views Krishna as being in the power of cyclical time, may be quoted. When in XVII.1 Agni comes to the Pandavas to tell Arjuna to cast off Gandiva, he reminds them: "That jewel among discuses which belonged to noble Krishna has gone and will come back into his hand in time" (XVII.1.38). But the same was said earlier of Arjuna's weapons, when they failed against the Abhiras (thus the devotee is caught up in fate along with his God): "And your weapons, having done what they had to, have gone today as they came. They will come to your hand again when the time is ripe" (XVI.9.35). Here recognition of fate transforms the human meaning of the events, but the further step to devotion is not taken; nor is it taken later in the sequence.

In the ascent-to-heaven sequence, Yudhishthira fulfills the potential inherent in his kingly status as the passive embodiment of *dharma*: as the Pandava most suited to do so, he learns to accept fate. This realization is connected, appropriately, with the sad epic ending describing the deaths of the heroes or, in devotional parlance, the end of the Krishna *avatara*. It seems that the same elements among the epic composers, probably largely brahmanic, who elsewhere made knowledge their primary focus (for example, throughout much of the third part of the *Shantiparvan*, the "Mokshadharma" [XII.168–353]—minus the "Narayaniya")[2] were responsible for the teaching offered here. The importance of this teaching should not be underrated, for it is largely thanks to his role as receptacle for the philosophy of illusion that Yudhishthira has often been considered the "hero" of the *Mahabharata*. In fact, in the person of Yudhishthira, a heroism of knowledge takes its place alongside, and according to some supersedes, the traditional heroism of action and the heroism of devotion depicted in the epic. Thus the Indian aesthetic philosopher Anandavardhana (ninth century A.D.) voiced the opinion of many when he wrote that the central flavor (*rasa*) of the *Mahabharata* is peacefulness (*shanta*),[3] a statement which shows that he regarded the ideal embodied by Yudhishthira, rather than that embodied by Arjuna, to be the primary ideal of the epic.[4] The desirability of that peculiar combination of *dharma* and knowledge which characterizes Yudhishthira (see chap. IIIB1) is indeed the message of a beautiful four-stanza passage which the epic calls the "Bharatasavitri" ("Essence of the *Bharata*")[5] (XVIII.5.51), with the implication that it encapsulates the teaching of the *Mahabharata* as a whole; this passage is found in *Svargarohanaparvan* 5, the last chapter of the epic in its critical version:

> Thousands of mothers and fathers and hundreds of sons and wives experienced in the rounds of existence [*samsareshu*] depart; and others will depart. The thousands of joyous states and hundreds of fearful states day by day affect the confused person, not the wise one. I cry out with uplifted arms, but no one hears me. Profit [*arthah*] and pleasure [*kamah*] come from *dharma*, [so] why is it [*dharma*] not served? One should by no means abandon *dharma* out of desire, fear, or greed, even for the sake of life. *Dharma* is

eternal, but pleasure and pain are not eternal. The soul is eternal, but the cause [of its bondage] is not eternal. [XVIII.5.47–50][6]

The Continuing Importance of Arjuna

It is probable that the ideal represented by Yudhishthira was more important at the later stages of epic development than at the earlier ones, since it seems to have little to do with the instruction to kings that accounts for almost every other major characteristic of the *Mahabharata*. Even in the ascent-to-heaven sequence, the teaching of the illusory nature of worldly existence seems like a late superimposition on the central account of the deaths of the heroes, reversing the outcome of events at the very last moment. Whereas devotion, dominant at most points of the epic, enhances the meaning of heroic action and traditional *dharma*, the teaching of illusion seems to discredit both; even in the ascent-to-heaven sequence it is a teaching offered to a "dead" king, not a living one. Although this argument cannot be defended absolutely, since throughout much of the extant epic the teaching of illusion has been blended neatly with kingly instruction (and such a paragon of kingliness as Janaka of Mithila, mentioned often in the didactic books and elsewhere, does seem to illustrate the benefits accruing to a king through acceptance of a combination of *dharma* and the philosophy of illusion—essentially, the king as *jivanmukta* [see chap. IIIB1]),[7] there can be no doubt that the kingly line descended from the Pandavas (as embodied in Janamejaya) relies primarily upon devotion to Krishna: it is a line that traces its immediate ancestry to Parikshit, whose life was restored by that *avatara*. The ascent-to-heaven sequence itself acknowledges the importance of Parikshit by mentioning his accession to the throne at the time of the Pandavas' retirement (see chap. IIC). If, therefore, the preeminence of Arjuna seems to diminish in the ascent-to-heaven sequence as compared with the remainder of the epic, his importance for succeeding generations is not weakened in the least, for he is still both Parikshit's grandfather and his devotional role model. The death of Krishna, while perhaps affecting the ascent-to-heaven sequence, has little effect on the ideology of the epic as a whole, since Vishnu lives on even if the *avatara* "dies."

A pair of stanzas in the last chapter of the *Svargarohanaparvan* points to the continuing importance for the epic of the values represented by

Arjuna. Mixed in with a statement of the benefits that may be obtained from hearing a recitation of the epic (XVIII.5.35ff.), a statement that has been enlarged in many manuscripts, the stanzas go as follows:

> This history by the name of *Jaya* is to be heard by one desiring well-being, by a king and also by the sons of a king, and also by a pregnant woman. [Hearing it,] one desirous of heaven would obtain heaven, one desirous of victory would obtain victory, a pregnant woman obtains a son or a very fortunate daughter. [XVIII.5.39–40]

It is, first of all, apparent that the heaven being offered here is that of heroes, not the illusory heaven Yudhishthira found. The other benefits promised are worldly benefits, such as a ruler would desire. All the benefits are ones acquired by the Pandavas themselves, through Arjuna, by way of heroism and devotion: heaven, victory, and progeny.

Certain manuscripts substitute *moksham* for *bhutim* ("well-being") in their versions of XVIII.5.39,[8] but the Critical Edition does not support such a change, nor do the parallel stanzas found earlier in the epic (see chap. IE). Here, then, the substitution may be recognized as a late one: those manuscripts that in this way isolate *moksha* as the central ideal of the *Mahabharata* do so because the values associated with Yudhishthira have become dominant in them. But the reading maintained by the critical text appears to be truer to the original intent of the epic, as reflected in the character of Arjuna: to report the story of the establishment of Parikshit's effective kingship on the basis of the religious devotion of his ancestors.

Notes

1. Note, however, that the passage on reabsorption mentions only Yudhishthira explicitly, of all the Pandavas: he enters Dharma (XVIII.5.19). The other Pandavas are traced only as far as the heavens of their respective fathers (or, in Arjuna's case, to Vishnu's heaven), then dropped. It is implied, however, that they went the way of the other epic characters.
2. And in the "Anugita"; see chap. IIIB1, especially n. 23.
3. See *Ānandavardhana's Dhvanyāloka or Theory of Suggestion in Poetry*, trans. K. Krishnamoorthy, Poona Oriental Series, no. 92 (Poona: Oriental Book Agency, 1955), pp. 141ff. (IV.5). See also Sudhisankar Bhattacharyya, *Imagery in the Mahābhārata: Influence on Later Sanskrit Literature* (Calcutta: Sanskrit Pustak Bhandar, 1971), pp. 56ff.; J. P. Sinha, *The Mahābhārata: A Literary Study* (New

Delhi: Meharchand Lachhmandas, 1977), pp. 71ff.; Binod Sarma, *Ethico-Literary Values of the Two Great Epics of India: An Ethical Evaluation of the Mahabharata and the Ramayana*, World's Wisdom Series, no. 13 (New Delhi: Oriental Publishers and Distributers, 1978), chap. 8; Gary A. Tubb, "*Śāntarasa* in the *Mahābhārata*," in *Essays on the Mahābhārata*, ed. Arvind Sharma, *Journal of South Asian Literature* 20 (1985): 141–68.

4. Tubb uniquely argues (pp. 147, 148f.) that the locus of the *Mahabharata*'s *shantarasa* (or the "stable emotion" connected with it, that is, tranquillity, or world-weariness) is not, after all, Yudhishthira, but is, rather (according to Anandavardhana himself, paraphrased by Tubb [p. 156]), "the early glories and the distressing end of the Pāṇḍavas [set] against the unchanging background of God [meaning *brahman*]." On the other hand, Tubb writes (p. 148): "What Yudhiṣṭhira seeks and finds is not the liberated state of one who has passed beyond attachment, but rather the engaging world of a warrior's paradise." Contrast, e.g., J. P. Sinha (pp. 72–73): "To realise the sentiment of quietude in the *Mahābhārata*, the connoisseur, first of all, has to feel like the hero of the *Mahābhārata* who is no other than Yudhiṣṭhira." Obviously, the present study comes out more on the side of Sinha than Tubb on this point. Indeed, it is surprising to see Yudhishthira treated in Tubb's well-documented discussion as a fairly typical warrior type: what, e.g., of his continuous pro-peace stance? Tubb himself offers two disclaimers of sorts, which seem to be of some help here: first, that the ascent-to-heaven sequence does, after all, produce a world-weariness in Yudhishthira (p. 147)—though the statement from p. 148 just quoted undermines this point; second, that the technical difficulties surrounding application of the *rasa* theory to the *Mahabharata* are legion ("We must not expect to find a neat and clear pattern of manipulation of the elements associated with *rasa*, but rather must be attentive to the cumulative effect of less obvious processes" [p. 158]).
5. The "Savitri" or "Gayatri" (*Rg Veda* III.62.10) is a famous prayer to the sun god, which encapsulates Vedic religion; thus the compound "Bharatasavitri" (literally, "Savitri of the *Bharata*").
6. The four aims of life (see chap. IIA3) have tended to inspire controversy as to which depends on which. Cf. the Pandava brothers' discussion of XII.161: here Vidura, who is also present, favors *dharma*; Arjuna supports *artha*; the twins feel that *dharma, artha*, and *kama* are all three important, in that order; Bhima favors *kama*; and Yudhishthira favors *moksha*. On which, see Dumézil, *Mythe et épopée* I, pp. 95f.
7. See, especially, XII.308 (Janaka-Sulabha discourse).
8. These are one Kashmiri and five Devanagari manuscripts, just six of the thirty-six manuscripts collated for the Critical Edition of Book XVIII.

CONCLUSION

Arjuna is a great epic hero who relies upon his bravery and strength to succeed. He is, at the same time, a human being filled with doubts and vulnerability. In addition, however, he plays a third role, which totally reverses the meaning of the other two: he is the religious devotee par excellence, whose success is guaranteed by his devotion to Krishna. In a dialectic, his heroism and humanity play against one another, being resolved by *bhakti* ("devotion"). At the same time, all three levels of his character continue to exist side by side.

Some episodes of the *Mahabharata* illustrate one level best, some another level. In the battle books in particular, all three levels are combined. Arjuna, the best warrior, is fully expected to win the war; yet doubts are expressed. Then, however, one learns that Arjuna really is Nara, and his warrior companion, Krishna, is God; so he cannot possibly lose. But wait! He may lose and be killed! No, he cannot. And so on, back and forth, irregularly. The building up of contradictions and repetitions that one finds here is in part a result of expansion of the text through the centuries on the basis of a loose oral core; in part it seems to be, regarding questions of faith, all too true to life. As has been argued here, however, all three levels of Arjuna's character were probably present from the earliest stages of the *Mahabharata*'s history. Recitation of the epic in "Janamejaya's" court has been offered as a plausible suggestion regarding the manner in which all the levels fit into an early version of the epic text.

Conclusion

In order to understand, in retrospect, what has been discovered in the figure of Arjuna, one may compare him once again with the heroes of some other epics and sagas. These figures, one finds, share some or all of the levels of character that have been noted in Arjuna: Cuchulainn, for example, is primarily "hero";[1] Achilles, Gilgamesh, and Rustam combine the aspects of "hero" and "human"; such figures as Isfandiyar,[2] Jacob, and Roland represent, like Arjuna, a combination of "hero," "human," and "devotee."

Indo-European/Semitic heroism carries within itself the roots of development in the directions both of humanity and of devotionalism. For even the most traditional of epic/saga heroes interacts with the gods, reflects the religious beliefs of the society that tells his story, and is generally himself semidivine. He is, at the same time, semihuman, inviting questions of mortality and morality—for sooner or later traditional heroism (that idealization of joyful, conquering masculinity) will betray its weaknesses vis-à-vis real life. The direction of development for any given heroic figure is determined by the worldview of those who tell his tale. In particular, religious devotion is an outstanding aspect of the hero only where such devotion is an ideal of the society he represents.

In general, the worldview of the storytellers is reflected clearly in the hero they portray. Take, for example, Roland: since he is a product of monotheistic thought, the semidivinity of his heroism is lacking entirely, and he is seen as a human representative of the Christian God in the Christian struggle against the infidels. What is distinctive about Arjuna, on the other hand, is that with regard to him all three levels have been developed fully, without concern for the resulting contradictions. The study of Arjuna presents a unique opportunity to examine the figure of the hero in all its aspects: the development lies in total before the audience, with nothing obliterated by editing, for it seems that the *Mahabharata* has preserved all that its various composers considered worthwhile to say about Arjuna. The eclecticism noted here typifies that often pointed to in Indian thought in general: the same massive and irregular growth that has made an encyclopedic work out of the *Mahabharata* has made of Arjuna an encyclopedic character. Even in India, however, not all heroic figures have developed in the way Arjuna has. In the cases of both Rama Dasharathi in the *Ramayana* and Krishna in the *Mahabharata*, the hero has become a god—and the human element, although present under the surface, is submerged (see chap. IIIA). In this sense, Arjuna is special, for more than any other Indian hero he is both fully human and fully related to divinity. For this very reason, Arjuna typifies the breadth of Indian thought.

Arjuna's multiple character makes him an ideal focal point for the ethical questions that are of central concern to the *Mahabharata* composers. In fact, the need for such a focal point may account in part for the formation of Arjuna's character as we know it today. At the same time, the epic composers' obsession with solving impasses of *dharma* fairly may have contributed to their openness to the devotional solution.

In support of this last suggestion, one may compare the Greek and Roman cases to the Indian. As pointed out in chapter IIA3, the Greek epics show that Greek thought was not so much disturbed by tricky solutions as was Indian thought, as witness the *Mahabharata*. Roman thought, however, was. Maurice B. McNamee writes:

> So highly regarded was intellectual sharpness by the Greeks that they considered it an admirable thing for their heroes to use trickery and deceit to gain their ends. In fact, this attitude prevailed so widely among the Greeks that the Romans came to think that all Greeks were liars. [In partial support of this point, McNamee quotes Virgil's famous words (*Aeneid* II.49): "I fear the Greeks though they come bearing gifts."] For the Romans, who put so much emphasis on social equity, such deceit was hateful, and many of them said so.[3]

Roman ethical sensitivity may account in part for the ultimate success of a monotheistic religion of devotion in the Hellenistic world; recognition of impasses, one may suggest, opened the way for a Christian solution. (The Greeks, meanwhile, although very much caught up in issues of mortality, as the *Iliad* clearly shows,[4] did not move in such a direction.) The Indian case parallels the Roman; or if Hopkins was right in imagining that the Indians approved of deceit originally and condemned it only later (see chap. IIA3), then the Indian case parallels that of the Greeks and the Romans together.

For a society with overriding ethical concerns, a religion of devotion to one supreme God permits transcendence of the impasses of the purely human sphere. The Christian solution and the Krishnaite solution as presented in the *Mahabharata* (which represents, of course, just one aspect of the total Vaishnava—let alone the Hindu—tradition) differ from one another; for in the former the object of devotion is an absolutely ethical figure who is able to atone for the world's sins by means of his own perfection, while in the latter the object of devotion is a trickster god who transforms the meaning of human activity by showing it up as a game. In both cases, however, one finds a similar basic concern with bridging the gap between God and humanity in order to understand human activity at a higher level.

In this respect, the solutions are remarkably similar: Christianity combines human and God in a single figure; Vaishnavism responds with its series of Vishnu incarnations—lately, Krishna. Because, however, Vaishnavas have preferred to emphasize the transcendence of the incarnation rather than his mortal side, the human/heroic figure who stands beside Krishna, the friend who mediates his activity, is of particular importance. This figure is Arjuna. One may say, then, that Arjuna plays a Jesus-like role in the Indian epic context insofar as he unites humanity and divinity; thus it is not surprising that Arjuna and Jesus share a common name: Nara ("man") for Arjuna and the Son of Man for Jesus.[5] Or perhaps one might better say that Nara and Narayana together play a role which, in some respects, parallels that of Jesus in the Christian tradition.[6]

Arjuna is prepared for his intermediary role by the very fact of his semidivine heroism. Jesus' life too reflects many of the usual themes of a heroic biography, for example, the supernatural birth, the initiatory period in the wilderness, and the encounter with, and victory over, death. The same may surely be discovered in many other religious figures who are structural mediators between the divine and the human (saints, prophets, and incarnations), to a greater or less extent.

In any society the figure of the hero represents people's desire to transcend human limitations.[7] The transition from the typical hero of epic and saga to the religious figure is gradual, providing an entire spectrum of roles from which popular thought may choose as its ideal either a hero in the traditional sense or a saint, prophet, or incarnation, depending upon its inclination in a particular place and time. Great spiritual figures, even the most peaceful, the least prone to machismo (for is not religious truth beyond masculine and feminine?), are also (or more so?) "heroes," as the Indian tradition has always recognized. Was not, for example, the founder of Jainism called Mahavira ("great hero")? (The very name "Jaina" is from *jina*, meaning "conqueror"; compare *jaya* in the *Mahabharata*.) The Buddha too was often called "Jina" or "Vira," despite his explicit renunciation of the kingly role.[8] Compare the list of the types of hero, *Mahabharata* XIII.74.22–27, placed at the head of the present study: here traditional and religious heroes are listed side by side. This list is indicative of the breadth of the Indian quest for transcendence and the eclecticism of its discoveries;[9] and Arjuna is all of the heroes on the list. The study of Arjuna presented here may thus provide a model for the study not only of other epic/saga heroes but also of saints, prophets, and incarnations, who are heroes of the "devotional" sort.

Notes

1. Though cf. Heather Stuart, "Cuchulainn and the 'Vater-Sohn Kampf' Motif," *Journal of the Australasian Universities Language and Literature Association* 47 (May 1977): 14ff., on the developed "tragic implications" of Cuchulainn's fight against Ferdia (see chap. IIA1, above).
2. On Isfandiyar as a religious hero representing the ideals of Zoroastrianism, see Marcia E. Maguire, "The *Haft Khvān* of Rustam and Isfandiyâr," in *Studies in Art and Literature of the Near East: In Honor of Richard Ettinghausen*, ed. Peter J. Chelkowski, New York University Near Eastern Round Table, 5 (Salt Lake City: Middle East Center-University of Utah, 1974), pp. 137–47. Isfandiyar's exploits resemble Rustam's, she argues, but have been transformed by their religious dimension.
3. McNamee, p. 48. (Virgil is quoted [slightly wrongly] on p. 50, n. 6.)
4. See Schein, especially chap. 3.
5. An earlier version of the Son of Man bears an even more obvious resemblance to Arjuna; see Daniel 7:13: "And behold, with the clouds of heaven there came one like a son of man. . . ." On this figure, see Frank Moore Cross, *Canaanite Myth and Hebrew Epic: Essays in the History of the Religion of Israel* (Cambridge, Mass.: Harvard University Press, 1973), p. 17, citing the earlier work of J. A. Emerton: "The manlike Being ('like a son of man') who comes to receive kingship is evidently young Ba'l [the Canaanite storm and warrior god] reinterpreted and democratized by the apocalyptist as the Jewish nation."
6. Some of the terminology employed by the *Mahabharata* in its attempt to define the Nara-Narayana relationship (see above, p. 218) resembles, to some extent, the terminology of Christology: one person, two natures.
7. Or to attain the limits and totality of human nature; see, in the Jungian tradition, Erich Neumann, *The Origins and History of Consciousness*, trans. R. F. C. Hull, Bollingen Series, 42 (New York: Pantheon, 1954).

8. One might point, in addition, to the heroic title of the Virashaivas, a modern Hindu group, and other examples. Nor is heroic terminology confined only to the Indian context. In the Jewish tradition, e.g., prophetic and apocalyptic thought culminated in the earliest form of Jewish mysticism, *merkabah* ("chariot") mysticism, which developed the imagery of God's "throne-chariot" presented in Ezekiel 1; see Gershom Scholem, *Major Trends in Jewish Mysticism*, 3rd ed. (New York: Schocken, 1954), second lecture. In the Roman Catholic tradition one finds a large group of warrior saints, and other branches of Christianity likewise know heroic imagery, as witness, e.g., the following lines of a poem by William Blake, which has become a well-known Church of England hymn:

   Bring me my Bow of burning gold:
     Bring me my Arrows of desire:
   Bring me my Spear: O clouds unfold!
     Bring me my Chariot of fire!

   Translated into Sanskrit, these could well be the words of Arjuna.
9. Cf. XII.342.9ff., a strikingly similar list, in this case not of types of hero but, rather, of ways of attaining heaven.

APPENDIX: THE NAMES OF ARJUNA

The purpose of this section will be to discuss the various names of Arjuna found in the *Mahabharata*, insofar as they deepen the understanding of his character aimed at by this study. Søren Sørensen's *An Index to the Names in the Mahābhārata*,[1] on which the following discussion is loosely based, lists nearly seventy separate names of Arjuna, most of which appear in the critical text of the epic, as they did in the earlier Bombay and Calcutta editions, upon which Sørensen based his work.[2] Most of these names are typical oral epithets, formulas of varying length, such as oral poets use to fill out lines of verse as they recite, according to the theory of oral composition.[3] Although all of Arjuna's names express particular aspects of his personality and characteristics, they, like other oral formulas, are not necessarily used where especially appropriate in the story; rather, they are used where metrically suitable, often with little regard for specific meaning (although many times the opposite could be argued).[4] For example, Arjuna is called "Kiritin" ("Diademed One") before he gets his diadem (I.181.18) and "Shvetavahana" ("He of the White Horses") before he gets his horses (I.192.10).[5] Such usage does not, however, create real inconsistencies in the epic portrayal of Arjuna, for the very reason that all aspects of his personality are interdependent, as this study has tried to show. Instead, the use of epithets serves as a constant reminder of Arjuna's depth and scope. In placing the epithets in an appendix, the purpose has been to indicate that they often cut across the tripartite division that has been noted in Arjuna's character, even as they derive from one or another level. The following discussion opens with a list of the more general and less interesting epithets of Arjuna, saving the most striking epithets, those listed in *Mahabharata* IV.39.8, for the conclusion of this appendix. As far as possible, Sanskrit alphabetical order has been adhered to within each cluster of names.

General Epithets

AINDRI, INDRASUTA, INDRATMAJA, PAKASHASANI, MAHENDRATANAYA, VASAVAJA, VASAVANANDANA, VASAVI, SHAKRASUTA, SHAKRASUNU, SHAKRATMAJA, SURASUNU, etc.: Primarily heroic names, all indicating that Arjuna is the son of Indra (Pakashasana, Vasava, Shakra, *sura* ["god"]).

KAURAVA, KAURAVASHRESHTHA, KAURAVEYA, KAURAVYA, PANDAVA, PANDAVEYA, PANDUNANDANA, PAURAVA, BHĀRATA, etc.: Patronymics, referring to Arjuna's heroic descent from Kuru, Pandu, Puru, and Bharata, used of other characters in the epic as well, where appropriate. (For more on the names "Pandava," etc., see under Arjuna, below.)

KUNTIPUTRA, KAUNTEYA, PARTHA: Metronymics, with reference to Arjuna's relationship with Kunti (Prtha), also used for Yudhishthira, Bhima, and Karna on occasion. The name "Prtha," which is related to the words *prthivi* ("earth") and *parthiva* ("prince") and to the name of the archetypical king, Prthu,[6] seems to lend royal overtones to the metronymic based on it, "Partha," which also means "prince" in Sanskrit;[7] thus, perhaps, its exceptionally restricted usage with regard to the unrecognized Karna (just V.143.3 and 12).

TAPATYA: Appears only in the course of Arjuna's conversation with the *gandharva* Chitraratha, in I.160ff. The name is taken as a metronymic from Tapati, second daughter of the sun, viewed as an ancestress of Arjuna. One must see here a reference to Arjuna's heat energy (*tapas* and *tejas*), as discussed in chapters IC ff.; such would certainly be the implication of a stanza such as the following:

> Thus the lady Tapatī, daughter of the Sun, became your ancestress, Pārtha, so that after her you are known as Tāpatya. On Tapatī King Saṃvaraṇa begot Kuru, O greatest of burners [*tapatam*], and hence you are a Tāpatya, Arjuna. [I.163.22–23]

It is possible, too, to see here an attempt to link Arjuna's origins with the Solar Dynasty, in addition to the Lunar Dynasty, with which the Kurus are generally connected.[8] Note that the name is used only for Arjuna, not the other Pandavas or Kauravas.

PRABHANJANASUTANUJA,[9] BHIMASENANUJA, BHIMANUJA: Indications that Arjuna is Bhima's younger brother. That there is no such epithet regarding Arjuna's relationship with Yudhishthira is possibly due only to the length and metrical structure of Yudhishthira's name.

GANDIVADHANVAN, GANDIVABHRT: Heroic epithets, referring to Arjuna as the carrier of his special weapon, the bow Gandiva.

KAPIKETANA, KAPIDHVAJA, KAPIPRAVARA, VANARAKETANA, VANARADHVAJA, VANARAVARYAKETANA, SHAKHAMRGADHVAJA: Names based on Arjuna's possession of a special standard, on which the monkey Hanumat sits, roaring, throughout the war. In fact, each hero is identifiable by his standard, and lists of these may be found in the battle books.[10] Note too how at VIII.63.66ff. Arjuna's monkey actually fights for him in battle, resisted by Karna's *nagakakshya* ("elephant girth") standard. When Arjuna is first given his chariot, at the time of the Khandava Forest burning, it comes equipped with the "monkey banner" (I.216.8), but elsewhere in the epic a half humorous, half deeply serious story, not quite consistent with the earlier statement, tells of how Bhima met Hanumat during the Pandavas' years of exile, and Hanumat promised Bhima that he would sit on Arjuna's standard (III.146.59ff.).[11] Here Bhima is depicted as Hanumat's stepbrother, Vayu being their common father, and the story serves to connect the Pandavas with the cast of characters of the *Ramayana*, for Arjuna's monkey helper is seen to be identical with Rama Dasharathi's. The monkey banner contributes to the animal imagery connected with the Kurukshetra War (see chap. IE), but is, perhaps, more important as a Vaishnava devotional link: Hanumat is known as Rama's ideal devotee, as Arjuna is Krishna's. This monkey is supernatural and disappears at the end of the war (IX.61.12).

KRISHNASARATHI: An epithet that is never found alone but, rather, in connection with other names, indicating that Arjuna has Krishna as his charioteer.

GUDAKESHA: Generally taken as a reference to Arjuna's curly hair (*guda* = "ball"; *kesha* = "hair"), this epithet has been seen in passages describing Arjuna's beauty quoted above (p. 31). The name could also refer to the matted hairstyle of Arjuna as ascetic (or a special warrior style?).[12] "Gudakesha" is sometimes paired with Krishna's epithet "Hrshikesha" (this occurs, for example, in *Gita* I.24 and II.9 = *Mahabharata* VI.23.24 and VI.24.9); here again is the terminology of twinship (see chaps. IC and IIIA).

NARA: Arjuna as human and divine (see, especially, chap. IIIA).

BRHANNADA: The female name taken on by Arjuna while in hiding as a eunuch in Virata's court (IV.2.22ff.). All instances of the name are to be found in Book IV only. Some manuscripts give the name as "Brhannata" or "Brhannala": all three different forms may be found in Otto Böhtlingk and Rudolph Roth, *Sanskrit-Wörterbuch*.[13] The form "Brhannata" could mean "great dancer" (*nata* = "dancer"), which would be appropriate in that Arjuna masquerades as a dance teacher.[14] "Brhannala," on the other hand, suggests a relationship with the character Nala, whose story is told in *Mahabharata* III.50ff. as a parallel to that of the Pandavas—a connection that is supported by Arjuna's own statement as he describes to Yudhishthira the disguise he plans to take on: "In this artful way, not unlike Nala, I shall amuse myself pleasantly, Indra of kings, in Virāṭa's palace" (IV.2.27). The form "Brhannada" seems to mean "large reed," and is difficult to interpret—unless as sexual double-entendre (which would be quite in place in the playful atmosphere of Book IV).[15] Nilakantha understands the reading *brhannala* as a reference to Nara, "Narayana's friend, the first man."[16]

Arjuna's Ten Names and Their Etymology

The most interesting and characteristic epithets of Arjuna are listed together in IV.39.8, where Arjuna enumerates his ten names to the Matsya prince Uttara, in order to prove his identity. All appear frequently throughout the epic. The ten names read as follows:

> . . . arjunah phalguno jishnuh kiriti shvetavahanah/
> bibhatsur vijayah krishnah savyasachi dhanamjayah//

In later stanzas of the chapter, etymologies of the names are offered. The stanzas of etymology read as follows:

> They call me Dhanaṃjaya because I stand in the midst of booty after conquering all the countrysides and plundering their entire wealth. They know me as Vijaya because once I ride out to battle against war-crazed warriors I do not return before I have defeated them. While I fight in battle, white, golden-harnessed horses are yoked to my chariot, therefore I am He of the White Horses [Shvetavahana]. I was born on the roofbeam of the Himālaya under the two constellations of Phālgunī in the firmament, therefore they know me as Phalguna. Once Śakra gave me, when I was fighting the bulls of the Dānavas, a diadem lustrous as the sun for my head, and so they call me the Diademed One [Kiritin]. When I do battle I can in no way perpetrate a loathsome deed, and therefore I am known among Gods and men as the Terrifier [Bibhatsu]. Both my hands are right hands when I draw the Gāṇḍiva, therefore they know me among Gods and men as the Left-handed Archer [Savyasachin]. My coloring [*varnah*] is rare on this four-cornered earth, and I do white deeds, therefore I am known as Arjuna. I am hard to reach, hard to tame, a tamer myself, and the son of the Chastiser of Pāka [Pakashasani; see above], and thus I am famed as Jiṣṇu among Gods and men. My father gave me Kṛṣṇa for my last name, out of love for that little boy of the dazzling black complexion. [IV.39.11–20]

The order of the initial list is followed in the following discussion.

ARJUNA: Like most primary names in the *Mahabharata* (less so—sometimes—the epithets, though many of these are also ancient and quite mysterious), the name "Arjuna" is somewhat opaque. Some progress, however, may be made toward its interpretation. As pointed out in van Buitenen's notes to Book IV of his *Mahabharata* translation, "Arjuna" is given as a "secret name" for Indra in *Shatapatha Brahmana* II.1.2.11.[17] Böhtlingk and Roth also refer to the use of "Arjuna" as a name for Indra, offering as examples *Vajasaneyi Samhita* (*White Yajur Veda*) X.21 and *Shatapatha Brahmana* V.4.3.7 and II.1.2.12 (*sic*). The name is applied to a king in a sacrificial context, specifically, according to White Yajur Vedic practice, at the time of his ritual chariot ride during the royal consecration ceremony: "Now Indra is called Arguna, which is his mystic name; and this (king) is Indra for a twofold reason, namely because he is a Kshatriya and because he is a Sacrificer: therefore he says, 'the unharmed Arguna' [calling himself that]."[18] One may speculate that the origin of this usage goes back to the Vedic meaning of *arjuna* as "white" or "shining,"[19] which comes into relationship with Indra as storm god because lightning is associated with the storm: the thunderbolt is described as *arjuna* in *Rg Veda* III.44.5. As Indra's son, Arjuna has inherited this name and the associated brightness; note statements such as the following: "We have seen him girt, like a monsoon cloud bright with lightning" (*Mahabharata* V.55.4) (this despite the fact that Arjuna is also described as "dark" [see chaps. IA and IIIA, and below]). On the Vedic character Kutsa, whose patronymic is "Arjuneya," see chapter IIA3, n. 22; and on the comparison of the Pandava Arjuna with Arjuna Kartavirya, see, especially, chapter IA.[20]

It is not surprising that a name signifying "white" should have attached itself to Arjuna, since this color has extremely positive connotations throughout the *Mahabharata*. A quotation such as the following, from Karna's description to Krishna of a dream he had before the war, suggests a connection between the color white and victory:

> I had a dream in which I saw Yudhiṣṭhira and his brothers ascend to a thousand-pillared palace, Acyuta [Krishna]. All wore white turbans and white robes, and I saw that they all had beautiful stools. . . . In the Dhārtarāṣṭra's armies too I saw three white-turbaned men, Janārdana Keśava—know who they are: Aśvatthāman, Kṛpa, and Kṛtavarman Sātvata. All other kings wore red turbans, Mādhava. [V.141.27–28, 38–39]

Here the white-turbaned warriors are those who will survive the war, the red-turbaned ones, those who will be killed. Elsewhere, white umbrellas are a frequent symbol of kingship[21] or a gift to be given to brahmins.[22] White is also associated, as in the etymology from IV.39 quoted above, with purity, and in classificatory schemes is correlated with those entities considered to be highest and purest; it is said, for example, to be the color of the brahmin class (XII.181.5)[23] and of Vishnu in the Krtayuga (III.148.16; III.187.31),[24] and is aligned with the *sattva guna* (the quality of goodness in nature) (XII.291.42ff.).[25] In sum, white is considered the highest color, as indicated in a passage discussing the "six colors of souls" (XII.271.33ff.), at XII.271.34: "But white is the best, spotless, free from grief, free from fatigue." The White Island, with its white inhabitants, is the domain of Narayana (see chap. IIIA).[26] Arjuna's explanation of his name in terms of his *varna* in the etymology points to such conceptions, as well as to Arjuna's brightness.[27] The various implications of the color white give it meaning at both the heroic and the devotional levels.

In this connection, it is important to point out that the name "Pandu" (from which comes the patronymic "Pandava") also means "white."[28] Pandu, it is said, was born pale because his mother turned pale at the sight of his father, Vyasa (I.100.15ff.). To some, the name "Whites" has seemed to identify the Pandavas as an organization rather than a family.[29] Whether the names "Arjuna" and "Pandava" have any connection is a question that, to the present author's knowledge, has not been answered satisfactorily.

PHALGUNA: *Shatapatha Brahmana* II.1.2.11, in suggesting the time when the new moon is in the (double) lunar mansion of Phalguni as one of the appropriate periods for a householder to set up his sacred fires, draws a connection between Phalguni, the god Indra, and the name "Arjuna":

> He may also set up his fires under the Phalgunîs. They, the Phalgunîs, are Indra's asterism, and even correspond to him in name; for indeed Indra is called Arguna, this being his mystic name; and they (the Phalgunîs) are also called Argunîs. Hence he overtly calls them Phalgunîs, for who dares to use his (the god's) mystic name? Moreover, the sacrificer himself is Indra, so that he in that case sets up his fires under his own asterism. Indra is the deity of the sacrifice. . . .

In view of this passage, then, Arjuna's relationship with Indra and the sacrifice itself could account for the *Mahabharata* IV.39 assertion that he was born under Phalguni. The connection of Phalguni with Indra is not, however, constant.[30] According to *Taittiriya Brahmana* I.8.4.1f., the month of Phalguna (that is, when the full moon is in Phalguni), at the end of the cool season, was the traditional period of ritual "conquest of the world" for the Kuru-Panchala people;[31] thus the name "Phalguna" could be a heroic reference to Arjuna as sacrificer and conqueror. One thing is certain: as Phalguna is also the borderline of springtime (the festival of Holi [see chap. ID] being in this month), this name of Arjuna has powerful overtones of fertility and auspiciousness.[32]

JISHNU: In his notes to Book IV, van Buitenen follows Nilakantha's gloss of this name ("jayashilah") by translating it as "in the habit of conquering"; he adds that Jishnu is also an epithet of Indra.[33] The name, however, is not applied to Indra in the *Mahabharata*, but is applied a few times to Vishnu,[34] thus undergoing a transposition from heroic to devotional. William Dwight Whitney's *Sanskrit Grammar*,[35] paragraph 1194a, translates *jishnu* as "victorious," bringing it close to the meaning of "Jaya" and "Vijaya" (see below). "Jishnu" is a name that is, in sound, complementary to the name of Vishnu, a point utilized by the epic composers, as, for example, in III.45.20.[36]

Kiritin, Kiritabhrt, Kiritamalin, Kiritavat: These names refer to Arjuna as the diadem (crown) wearer. The diadem in question was given to Arjuna by Indra when Arjuna defeated various groups of demons for his father (see chap. ID), as related in Book III (III.165.13; III.171.5).[37] Arjuna's diadem is knocked off twice during the war: once by the warrior Bhagadatta (Arjuna retrieves it immediately) (VII.28.12f.) and a second time by an arrow shot by Karna (VIII.66.11).[38]

The diadem is of course a kingly (in terms of the present study, heroic) attribute, and XIII.40.29 indicates that a diadem, along with his thunderbolt, was seen as an attribute of Indra as well.[39] That Arjuna's diadem was originally made for Indra is stated at VIII.66.13. On the other hand, some devotional connections may be implied here, in that Vishnu also wears a diadem (*Gita* XI.17, 46 = *Mahabharata* VI.33.17, 46). With Arjuna's bejeweled (VIII.66.13ff.) diadem, contrast Ashvatthaman's inborn jewel (see chap. IIIC).

Shvetavahana, Shvetavaha, Shvetahaya, Shvetashva: This cluster of names describes Arjuna as the one with white horses. The most striking point to be made here is that the various parts of the epic are not in agreement as to where Arjuna got the horses. One may point to a number of Indo-European epic/saga heroes who are characterized by their ownership of a particular horse or horses: for example, Achilles, Cuchulainn, Rustam;[40] Krishna himself has special chariot horses, and the various participants in the Kurukshetra War have horses of characteristic colors,[41] but none are nearly so important for identifying the figure as Arjuna's are for him. Special horses and a chariot are characteristic of Indra from Vedic times onward, and it may be through him that this feature passed over to Arjuna; Indra's horses are, however, tawny, not white.[42]

Why then specifically white horses? Over and above the general significance of the color white, discussed under Arjuna, above, the particular connection of the color with horses may be noted. Uchchaihshravas, the great horse produced at the churning of the ocean,[43] is explicitly white (I.16.34),[44] but a black tail is produced for him, apparently by fraud (I.18ff.); elsewhere in the epic, the story of Galava is predicated upon the desirability of white horses with one black ear each (V.104.26ff.).[45] Regarding pure white horses, one may refer to the horse to be ridden by the Messianic future incarnation of Vishnu, Kalki, according to late Hindu mythology (although this horse is not mentioned in the account of Kalki in the epic);[46] compare the horse of Revelation 19:12 or, for example, that of the Christian St. George (an extension, to be sure, of the typical medieval knight on a white horse). Jan Gonda explains such a horse as the sun steed, which is a royal symbol,[47] but by way of the connection with Kalki a devotional aspect may also be discerned. Finally, one may point to the title of the *Shvetashvatara Upanishad*, as an indication of the importance of this symbol in Hindu thought.[48]

The various sources from which Arjuna is said to have obtained his steeds at different points in the epic are as follows: from Varuna, when that god, under the instructions of Agni, gave Arjuna a chariot and some weapons just prior to the Khandava Forest burning (I.216.5ff.); from the *gandharva* Chitraratha (V.55.12);[49] and, it seems, from Krishna himself (XIII.143.24), this last being the devotional source. Note that even after Arjuna's chariot is consumed, horses and all, at the end of the war, by the delayed effect of fiery weapons (IX.61.13f.), Arjuna is still said to ride "on a chariot with the brilliance of the sun, yoked with divine white horses" (XV.30.11).[50] Although perhaps more striking, the inconsistencies found here generally parallel those surrounding Arjuna's receipt of his other accoutrements: here are characteristic possessions of Arjuna, the stories of their acquisition and other chronologically significant points being added only as an afterthought.

That the horses, like the monkey Hanumat on the standard, are viewed as animal helpers of Arjuna, such as appear in many folkloric parallels, is strikingly apparent in the passage from VIII.63 cited above, under Kapiketana, where in v. 70 the horses as well as the standards of Arjuna and Karna seem to take up the battle before it is taken up by their respective masters.

BIBHATSU: Although the *Mahabharata*'s own etymology (seconded by Nilakantha) interprets this name in a favorable sense, it is generally explained by modern scholars as meaning "disgusting," derived as it probably is from the desiderative of the root *badh* ("repel").[51] It thus would refer to Arjuna in his Bhima-like aspect, as a wild and violent warrior. Possibly, however, the name originated at a time before the unpleasant meaning had attached itself to the word; it would thus have meant simply "repeller";[52] van Buitenen translates, "Terrifier." Biardeau, however, prefers an interpretation of the name that would emphasize the *répugnance* Arjuna himself feels: repugnance for certain warlike acts required of him (for example, the killing of Bhishma), which he nevertheless goes on to perform in the interest of desireless action.[53]

VIJAYA, JAYA: Meaning "victory," these names of Arjuna are rich in significance, coming as they do out of the pure *kshatriya* tradition, which puts such emphasis on victory in battle. These two are heroic names, in line with the heroic level of *Mahabharata* interpretation presented in this study. As noted above (chap. IE, etc.), the epic itself is known as *Jaya*, and *jaya* is a benefit that is supposed to accrue to one who hears it recited. Because the meaning of "Vijaya" and "Jaya" is quite straightforward, one need draw no special conclusions from the fact that these names are applied elsewhere in the epic to others besides Arjuna: that Indra's bow and Karna's are both called "Vijaya" (V.155.5 and VIII.22.44), as is Shiva's trident (III.221.10), that "Jaya" is a snake name (V.101.16, etc.), or, for that matter, that "Vijaya" and "Jaya" both are found on lists of names of the sons of Dhrtarashtra (VII.24.43, etc.).[54]

Yet there is more to the names "Vijaya" and "Jaya." When the Pandavas go into hiding in Virata's city, they assume the following secret names, given to them by Yudhishthira: "Jaya, Jayanta, Vijaya, Jayatsena, and Jayadbala" (IV.5.30),[55] of which the middle one is Arjuna's, as the list in IV.39 confirms. Perhaps of greater significance is the fact that both "Vijaya" and "Jaya" are names applied to the gods Vishnu and Shiva,[56] and that, as noted throughout Part III of this study, victory is said at the level of devotion to rest directly upon God. That *jaya* refers to spiritual as well as physical victory is evidenced by the fact that it is sometimes (for instance, by Nilakantha himself) applied as a name to a variety of devotional texts.[57] *Jayakhyasamhita* ("Text Called *Jaya*") is a major Pancharatra work.

Because of the wide usage of the names "Vijaya" and "Jaya," they lend themselves to punning: note in particular Dhrtarashtra's litany recited to Samjaya in I.1.102–55; listing the events of the epic story one after another, he says again and again (more than fifty times) that after this event took place "tada nashamse vijayaya . . . " ("then . . . I lost hope of victory"). "Vijaya" was, of course, on the other side. Compare too those stanzas where *jaya* is said to be automatically where *dharma* is, Krishna is, or Krishna and Arjuna are (see chaps. IA, IE, and IIIB2).

KRISHNA: A devotional epithet, deriving from Arjuna's relationship with Krishna, it generally occurs in the phrase "the two Krishnas" (see chaps. IC and IIIA), and is rarely found referring to Arjuna alone outside of IV.39.[58] The meaning of Krishna's name is "black," and the black Vishnu of the Kaliyuga mentioned twice in the epic (III.148.32f. and III.187.31) must be he. The name is also applied to Vyasa (Krishna-dvaipayana)[59] and Draupadi (Krishnā),[60] and why three figures share it has been considered by Hiltebeitel.[61] In general, the names "Krishna" and "Arjuna" may be viewed as complementary, since they mean, respectively, "black" and "white":[62] the completeness of the pair is stressed. Black-white complementarity is rather common throughout the epic, for example, in the image of the threads of past and present, night and day being woven by two women observed by the brahmin Uttanka in the world of the *nagas* (I.3.147ff.), or the dark and light paths mentioned in the *Gita* (*Gita* VIII.24ff. = *Mahabharata* VI.30.24ff.); note too the black and white horses mentioned under Shvetavahana, above. One notes that a similar complementarity to that between Krishna and Arjuna exists between Krishna and his brother Baladeva, for it is said:

> God Hari [Krishna] had plucked two hairs of his head;
> One hair was white, the other was black.
> These hairs then went into the Yadu women,
> Into Rohiṇī and Devakī.
> The one of them became Baladeva,
> The other, the black one, Keśava. [I.189.31][63]

With regard to the application of the name "Krishna" to Arjuna, van Buitenen's translation of IV.39.20 has already been quoted: "My father gave me Kṛṣṇa for my last name, out of love for that little boy of the dazzling black complexion." (The "little boy" referred to here is Krishna as a child, a figure of great popularity in the *Harivamsha* [a Purana of sorts, appended to the *Mahabharata*], the Puranas [proper], and later materials, but little utilized by the *Mahabharata* itself.) Although van Buitenen's translation is correct, and agrees with Nilakantha's gloss, it does not emphasize sufficiently that the original Sanskrit is not ignoring the Krishna-Arjuna/black-white complementarity, but seems to be aware of the anomaly of applying a name meaning "black" to Arjuna. The Sanskrit compound that van Buitenen translates as "of the dazzling black complexion" reads *krishnavadatasya,* which really means "of black and whiteness" or "of shining blackness," *avadata* having a meaning that appears to be very close to the meaning of the word *arjuna*. Note in this connection that, as pointed out previously (chap. IIIA), Krishna and Arjuna share darkness of complexion. It is most striking to see the heroic imagery of Arjuna as shining and bright yet darkly handsome come together with the devotional imagery, in which Arjuna takes on the dark coloration of his God.[64]

SAVYASACHIN: This epithet, implying ambidexterity (*savya* = "left"), is strictly heroic, referring to Arjuna's great skill with the bow, which he can shoot with either his left or his right hand, as pointed out in chapter IE.[65]

DHANAMJAYA: This is another of Arjuna's *kshatriya*-oriented names, connected with victory: it means "wealth winner."[66] Also the name of a snake (I.31.5, etc.), it likewise becomes a name of Vishnu, drawing to itself a devotional connotation (XIII.135.83). Originally, however, the name would surely have had to do with that wealth winning which is the major task of a king, enabling him to run his kingdom successfully, that is, in traditional terms, to hold large sacrifices. Such a task is performed, for example, by the Pandavas just prior to Yudhishthira's horse sacrifice, when they rediscover the wealth left over from a sacrifice of King Marutta, to use for their own purposes (XIV.62ff.). Arjuna's most significant wealth winning in the eyes of the *Mahabharata* as a whole seems to be that which he engages in during the "conquest of the world" before Yudhishthira's royal consecration; here Arjuna conquers the northern direction, which is referred to specifically as the direction protected by Dhanada ("God of Riches" = Kubera) (II.24.1). The "conquest of the world" is undoubtedly what the text is referring to when it states that it was Arjuna who won Yudhishthira his kingdom (III.142.16ff., etc.) or, more strikingly, that he won the kingdom for the Kurus (V.88.31)—for of course the kingdom that Duryodhana took over was as already enlarged by the Pandavas.

Notes

1. For reference, see chap. IIIC, n. 29.
2. All have been checked, and all those listed in this appendix actually appear in the critical text.
3. See Lord, pp. 30ff.
4. See, e.g., below, n. 65.
5. Van Buitenen's translation of these names is not always consistent. At the stanzas cited, he translates, specifically, "the diademed Pāṇḍava" and "Arjuna of the white stallions." The simpler translations offered here are borrowed from van Buitenen's translation of IV.39.11–20 (see p. 281).
6. On Prthu, see chap. IIIA, n. 13.
7. Note too the *partha* oblations of the royal consecration and other sacrifices (*Shatapatha Brahmana* V.3.5.4ff.; IX.3.4.6f.). Their name is said to be derived from the name of King Prthu.
8. For references, see chap. IB, n. 39.
9. Literally, "younger brother of the wind's son."
10. See, e.g., VII.80.2ff. On Duryodhana's standard, see chap. IE, n. 42.
11. Note the parody of Arjuna's *Gita* XI vision in the vision of himself given by Hanumat to Bhima, in III.149.
12. See, e.g., the definition provided by Monier Monier-Williams in his *Sanskrit-English Dictionary* (Oxford: Clarendon Press, 1872): "Whose hair forms tufts or matted locks. . . . " The epithet, Monier-Williams points out, can also refer to Shiva. On the matted hair of Nara and Narayana, see chap. IIIA, n. 17.
13. For reference, see chap. IIB, n. 10.
14. Might one see here an oblique reference to Shiva as Nataraja? Cf. chap. ID, n. 40.
15. For a further suggestion, see Hiltebeitel, "Disguises," p. 160.
16. Nilakantha on IV.2.27 = Critical Edition IV.2.22. Hiltebeitel takes this line of interpretation one step further, interpreting the suggested etymology "*bṛhad-nara* ('great man')" as a reference to Shiva as Mahapurusha ("great Purusha" [see chap. IIIA, n. 8], who is androgynous); see "Disguises," pp. 156f., and "One Chariot," pp. 25f. Cf., e.g., Biardeau ("Conférence," vol. 82, p. 91) on *bṛhad-nara*'s relationship to some feminine counterparts of Vishnu. Indeed, here we are beyond "Vishnu" and "Shiva," in the realm of the impersonal Absolute; but as far as the original meaning goes, if there ever was a form "Brhannara," it seems just as likely to have been a more mundane play on masculinity and femininity, in connection with Arjuna's eunuch disguise. In any case, such a playful name as this is would

easily have become a fair target for religious interpretations such as Nilakantha's, Hiltebeitel's, and Biardeau's.

17. Van Buitenen, *Mahābhārata*, III, 536.
18. *Shatapatha Brahmana* V.4.3.7. (Quoted [as is the passage on p. 283] from Julius Eggeling, trans., *Satapatha-Brâhmana according to the Text of the Mâdhyandina School*, the Sacred Books of the East, vols. 12, 26, 41, 43, 44 [Oxford: Clarendon Press, 1882–1900].)
19. Böhtlingk and Roth; Manfred Mayrhofer, *Kurzgefasstes etymologisches Wörterbuch des Altindischen*, 3 vols. (Heidelberg: Carl Winter, 1956–76). Traditionally, however, the name "Arjuna" has been derived from the verbal root *rj*, meaning (Monier-Williams) "to go; to stand or be firm; to obtain, acquire; to be strong or healthy . . ."; see Nilakantha's commentary on IV.44.20 = Critical Edition IV.39.18. Nilakantha tenuously connects this derivation with the etymology offered in IV.39.18, by understanding the word *samah* (in the phrase *durlabhah samah* ["rare"]) in that stanza to mean *rjuh* ("straight," "upright"); *samatvat*, he then says, is one of the sources of Arjuna's name.
20. See further, Biardeau, "Kārtavīrya," pp. 295ff.
21. See the scene of XII.38.32ff., where, entering the city of Hastinapura triumphantly after the war, Yudhishthira rides a white chariot yoked with white oxen. As Bhima drives, Arjuna holds a white umbrella over Yudhishthira's head and the twins fan him with white fans.
22. E.g., in XIII.98.18f.
23. The same stanza states that the color of *kshatriyas* is red, of *vaishyas* yellow, of *shudras* black.
24. In both chapters cited, all of Vishnu's colors for the four declining ages are given: white, red, yellow, black; or white, yellow, red, black.
25. According to the Samkhya philosophy (see chap. IA, n. 61), there are three *gunas*. The other two, *rajas* ("passion") and *tamas* ("darkness"), are associated with the colors red and black.
26. On the whiteness of the inhabitants, see XII.323.24ff. Narayana himself is also thought of as white; see, e.g., XII.335.57ff., where he is said to be white as he lies on the waters.
27. Nilakantha (commentary on IV.44.20 = Critical Edition IV.39.18), however, refers only to the latter meaning of *varna*: "*Varna* is radiance."
28. Though cf. Biardeau's derivation of the name, mentioned in chap. ID, n. 41. Jain, on the other hand, suggests (pp. 290ff.) the derivation of "Pandava" from the word *panchadevas* ("five gods"), an intriguing suggestion at more than one level, but one without linguistic support.
29. Held (pp. 297ff.) sees the Pandavas as a phratry specializing in initiation, named for a color, in a classificatory scheme including other phratries. In fact, the color white is often associated with initiation; see Eliade, *Rites and Symbols*, pp. 37, 44.
30. See Eggeling, note to II.1.2.11.
31. See Johannes Cornelis Heesterman, *The Ancient Indian Royal Consecration: The Rājasūya Described according to the Yajus Texts and Annotated* (The Hague: Mouton, 1957), p. 211.

32. Cf. the posited etymological relationship between the word "hero" and Greek *hōrē* ("season," "springtime"); see Schein, p. 69 (citing Walter Pötscher).
33. Van Buitenen, *Mahābhārata*, III, 536. Böhtlingk and Roth offer a few references for this usage.
34. Strikingly, in V.68.13.
35. William Dwight Whitney, *Sanskrit Grammar: Including Both the Classical Language, and the Older Dialects, of Veda and Brahmana*, 2nd ed. (Cambridge, Mass.: Harvard University Press, 1889).
36. Cf. "Krishna and Jishnu" (see chap. IIIB2, n. 19).
37. See also VIII.66.14.
38. This event is part of the story of Ashvasena, mentioned above (chap. IE, etc.). The diadem is hit after Krishna pushes Arjuna's chariot down to save him (see chap. IIIB2, n. 30).
39. See also II.7.5.
40. On some horses in epic and saga, see Bowra, *Heroic Poetry*, pp. 157ff.
41. See V.55.12ff.; VII.22.2ff.
42. This was true from Vedic times (Macdonell, p. 55) and still provides epithets for Indra in the epic (I.181.16, etc.).
43. See chap. IC, especially n. 13.
44. In the same stanza, Shri, also produced at the churning, is described as *panduravasini*, which van Buitenen translates as "clothed in white robes."
45. See also III.115.12ff. Any connection with the sort of horse considered desirable for the horse sacrifice (see Dumont, pp. 22f., and Kane, II, 1230)?
46. See Margaret Stutley and James Stutley, *A Dictionary of Hinduism: Its Mythology, Folklore and Development 1500* B.C.–A.D. *1500* (London: Routledge and Kegan Paul, 1977), p. 138. The main account of Kalki in the epic is at III.188.89ff.
47. Gonda, *Kingship*, p. 38.
48. Although "Shvetashvatara" in this context is derived from a person's name; see *Shvetashvatara Upanishad* VI.23.
49. It is stated here that the horses are one hundred in number and, by a special boon, will never diminish, even if some are killed. Cf. I.158.45f., which states that the *gandharva* Chitraratha gave supernatural horses to all the Pandavas; these, however, were not specifically white but, rather, could take on any color (v. 51). II.24f. mentions that Arjuna won horses (including *gandharva* horses) as tribute in the "conquest of the world," but these were not white.
50. Part of a list of conveyances used by the Pandavas in their visit to the retired king Dhrtarashtra.
51. Böhtlingk and Roth, etc.
52. Professor Ingalls's suggestion.
53. Biardeau, "Conférence," vol. 84, p. 184; vol. 85, p. 165; etc.
54. Neither of these names appears, however, on the full list of Dhrtarashtra's sons at I.108.2ff.
55. Jayanta is a son of Indra (see p. 64).
56. Vishnu as Vijaya: XIII.135.29. Vishnu as Jaya: XIII.135.67. Shiva as Vijaya: XIII.17.50. Shiva as Jaya: Poona Edition, XII, Appendix I, no. 28, line 329.

57. See Lévi, "*Tato jayam*," p. 14.
58. One example of such an occurrence has, however, been quoted on p. 144.
59. See chap. IIIA, n. 33, etc.
60. See pp. 167 and 179, and chaps. IIB, n. 11, and IIIB2, n. 2.
61. Hiltebeitel, *Ritual*, pp. 60ff., where his suggestions are as follows: all three may be signs of the Kaliyuga; some or all of them may reflect popular deities; all may be viewed as mediators (black being a structural mediator between red and white); all may be united as a trifunctional group. See further, Hiltebeitel, "Two Kṛṣṇas, Three Kṛṣṇas, Four Kṛṣṇas, More Kṛṣṇas: Dark Interactions in the *Mahābhārata*," in A. Sharma, pp. 71–77.
62. Gonda suggests that such complementarity may be traced back to the *Ṛg Veda*; see *Aspects*, p. 159 (the reference is to *Ṛg Veda* VI.9.1).
63. See also IX.59.10.
64. See further, Barbara Babcock-Abrahams, " 'A Tolerated Margin of Mess': The Trickster and His Tales Reconsidered," *Journal of the Folklore Institute* (Indiana University) 11 (1975): 160: "In keeping with their creative/destructive dualism, tricksters tend to be ambiguously situated between life and death, and good and evil, as is summed up in the combined black and white symbolism frequently associated with them."
65. What seems to be an interesting play on this idea occurs when Ekalavya's competition with Arjuna results in his losing his right thumb so that he can no longer shoot well (see chap. IA, n. 92). Arjuna is, pointedly, called "Savyasachin" in this episode (I.123.29). It must further be noted that Hiltebeitel sees again in this epithet a possible connection with Shiva as male and female, in that it indicates that Arjuna "shoots equally well with the left (female) or right (male) hand" ("One Chariot," p. 25). Certainly the implication of ambidexterity here is a marvelous resolver of opposites.
66. Van Buitenen translates "winner of booty"; see his *Mahābhārata*, III, 536.

BIBLIOGRAPHY

Mahabharata Texts and Commentary, Sanskrit and English

Buitenen, J. A. B. van, trans. and ed. *The Bhagavadgītā in the Mahābhārata: Text and Translation*. Chicago: University of Chicago Press, 1981.

———. *The Mahābhārata*, Books I–V. 3 vols. Chicago: University of Chicago Press, 1973–78.

Dutt, Manmatha Nath. *A Prose English Translation of the Mahabharata*. 18 books. Calcutta: Elysium Press, 1895–1905.

Edgerton, Franklin, trans. and interp. *The Bhagavad Gītā*. 1944; rpt. Cambridge, Mass.: Harvard University Press, 1972.

[Ganguli, Kisari Mohan], trans. *The Mahabharata of Krishna-Dwaipayana Vyasa*. Pub. and distrib. Pratap Chandra Roy. 2nd ed. 12 vols. Calcutta: Oriental Publishing Co., n.d.

Kinjawadekar, Ramchandrashastri, ed. *The Mahābhāratam with the Bharata Bhawadeepa Commentary of Nīlkaṇṭha*. 2nd ed. 6 vols. New Delhi: Oriental Books Reprint Corporation, 1979.

Mahābhārata with the commentary *Bhāratabhāvadīpa* of Nīlakaṇṭha. 18 books. Bombay: Gaṇpat Kṛṣṇājī, 1885–88.

Radhakrishnan, Sarvepalli. *The Bhagavadgītā: With an Introductory Essay. Sanskrit Text. English Translation and Notes*. 1948; rpt. New York: Harper Torchbooks, 1973.

Sargeant, Winthrop, trans. *The Bhagavad Gītā*. Ed. Christopher Chapple. Rev. ed. SUNY Series in Cultural Perspectives. Albany: State University of New York Press, 1984.

Sukthankar, Vishnu S., S. K. Belvalkar, P. L. Vaidya, et al., eds. *Mahābhārata*. (Critical Edition) 19 vols. plus 6 vols. of indexes. Poona: Bhandarkar Oriental Research Institute, 1933–72.

Zaehner, R. C. *The Bhagavad-Gītā: With a Commentary Based on the Original Sources*. Oxford: Clarendon Press, 1969.

Other Works

Alexander, Michael, trans. *Beowulf*. Harmondsworth: Penguin, 1973.

Algeo, John. "The Black God and the White Prince: Names of Krishna and Arjuna in the Bhagavad Gita." *Names* 28 (1980): 141–51.

Autran, Charles. *L'Epopée indoue: Etude de l'arrière-fonds ethnographique et religieux*. Paris: Les Editions Denoël, 1946.

Babcock-Abrahams, Barbara. " 'A Tolerated Margin of Mess': The Trickster and His Tales Reconsidered." *Journal of the Folklore Institute* (Indiana University) 11 (1975): 147–86.

Bascom, William. "The Myth-Ritual Theory." *Journal of American Folklore* 70 (1957): 103–14.

Belvalkar, S. K. "Saṁjaya's 'Eye Divine.' " *Annals of the Bhandarkar Oriental Research Institute* 27 (1946): 310–31.

———. "Some Interesting Problems in Mahābhārata Text Transmission: Problem #3." *Annals of the Bhandarkar Oriental Research Institute* 26 (1945): 106–19.

Bergaigne, Abel. *La Religion védique d'après les hymes du Rig-Veda*. 3 vols. Paris: F. Vieweg, 1878–83.

Berreman, Gerald D. *Hindus of the Himalayas*. Berkeley: University of California Press, 1963.

———. "Pahari Polyandry: A Comparison." *American Anthropologist* 64 (1962): 60–75.

Betai, R. S. "Vissada of Arjuna and Duryodhana at the Critical Juncture—A Comparison." *Journal of the Gujarat Research Society* 27 (1965): 326–30.

Bhandarkar, R. G. *Vaiṣṇavism, Śaivism and Minor Religious Systems*. 1913; rpt. Varanasi: Indological Book House, 1965.

Bhat, G. K. "The Problem of the Mahābhārata Plays of Bhāsa." *Annals of the Bhandarkar Oriental Research Institute* 35 (1954): 73–83.

Bhatt, G. H. "The Draupadīvastraharaṇa Episode: An Interpolation in the Mahābhārata." *Journal of Oriental Research* (Madras) 18 (1948–49): 170–78.

Bhattacharya, N. N. "The King and the Dice: A Study in the Rituals of the Rājasūya." *Journal of the Oriental Institute* (Baroda) 23 (1973–74): 288–307.

Bhattacharyya, Sudhisankar. *Imagery in the Mahābhārata: Influence on Later Sanskrit Literature.* Calcutta: Sanskrit Pustak Bhandar, 1971.

Biardeau, Madeleine. "Brahmanes et poitiers." *Annuaire de l'Ecole Pratique des Hautes Etudes, v[e] Section (Sciences Religieuses)* 79 (1971–72): 31–55.

———. "Conférence de Mlle. Madeleine Biardeau." *Annuaire de l'Ecole Pratique des Hautes Etudes, v[e] Section (Sciences Religieuses)* 73 (1965–66): 72–76; 77 (1969–70): 168–73; 78 (1970–71): 151–61; 79 (1971–72): 139–47; 80–81 (1973–74): 121–41; 82 (1974–75): 89–101; 83 (1975–76): 103–11; 84 (1976–77): 165–86; 85 (1977–78): 135–67; 86 (1977–78): 143–53; 87 (1978–79): 145–70; 88 (1979–80): 167–82; 89 (1980–81): 221–50; 90 (1981–82): 145–55; 91 (1982–83): 153–73.

———. *Cosmogonies purāṇiques.* Vol. I of *Etudes de mythologie hindoue.* Publications de l'Ecole Française d'Extrême-Orient, vol. 128. Paris: Ecole Française d'Extrême Orient, 1981.

———. "Etudes de mythologie hindoue," I–V. *Bulletin de l'Ecole Française d'Extrême-Orient* 54 (1968): 19–45; 55 (1969): 59–105; 58 (1971): 17–89; 63 (1976): 111–263; 65 (1978): 87–238.

———. "Mythe épique et hindouisme d'aujourd'hui." *Indologica Taurinensia* 5 (1977): 43–53.

———. "The Salvation of the King in the *Mahābhārata.*" *Contributions to Indian Sociology*, NS 15 (1981): 75–97.

———. "Some More Considerations about Textual Criticism." *Purāṇa* 10 (1968): 115–23.

———. "The Story of Arjuna Kārtavīrya without Reconstruction." *Purāṇa* 12 (1970): 286–303.

Biardeau, Madeleine, and Charles Malamoud. *Le Sacrifice dans l'Inde ancienne.* Bibliothèque de l'Ecole des Hautes Etudes, Section des Sciences Religieuses, vol. 79. Paris: Presses Universitaires de France, 1976.

Blake, William. *The Poetical Works of William Blake.* Ed. John Sampson. London: Humphrey Milford-Oxford University Press, 1914.

Bloomfield, Maurice. "Contributions to the Interpretation of the Veda," I: "The Story of Indra and Namuci." *Journal of the American Oriental Society* 15 (1893): 143–63.

———, trans. *Hymns from the Atharva-Veda together with Extracts from the Ritual Books and the Commentaries.* The Sacred Books of the East, vol. 42. Oxford: Clarendon Press, 1897.

Böhtlingk, Otto, and Rudolph Roth. *Sanskrit-Wörterbuch.* 7 vols. St. Petersburg: Buchdruckerei der Kaiserlichen Akademie der Wissenschaften, 1855–75.

Bosch, F. D. K. *The Golden Germ: An Introduction to Indian Symbolism.* The Hague: Mouton, 1960.

Bowra, Cecil Maurice. *Heroic Poetry.* London: Macmillan, 1952.

———. *The Meaning of a Heroic Age.* Thirty-seventh Earl Grey Memorial Lecture Delivered at Kings College, Newcastle upon Tyne. Newcastle upon Tyne: Andrew Reid, 1957.

Brown, Norman O. *Hermes the Thief: The Evolution of a Myth.* 1947; rpt. New York: Vintage-Random House, 1969.

Brown, W. Norman. "Duty as Truth in Ancient India." *Proceedings of the American Philosophical Society* 116 (1972): 252–68.

Bühler, Georg, trans. *The Laws of Manu.* The Sacred Books of the East, vol. 25. 1886; rpt. New York: Dover, 1969.

Buitenen, J. A. B. van. "The Name 'Pañcarātra.'" *History of Religions* 1 (1961–62): 291–99.

———. "On the Structure of the Sabhāparvan of the Mahābhārata." In *India Maior: Congratulatory Volume Presented to J. Gonda.* Ed. J. Ensink and P. Gaeffke. Leiden: Brill, 1972; pp. 68–84.

Caland, W. *Das Jaiminīya-Brāhmaṇa in Auswahl: Text, Übersetzung, Indices.* Verhandelingen der Koninklijke Akademie van Wetenschappen te Amsterdam, Afdeeling Letterkunde, Part 1, NS Part 19, no. 4. 1919; rpt. Wiesbaden: M. Sändig, 1970.

———, trans. *Pañcaviṃśa-Brāhmaṇa: The Brāhmaṇa of Twenty-Five Chapters.* Calcutta: Asiatic Society of Bengal, 1931.

Campbell, Joseph. *The Hero with a Thousand Faces.* 2nd ed. Bollingen Series, 17. Princeton: Princeton University Press, 1968.

Carman, John Braisted. *The Theology of Rāmānuja: An Essay in Interreligious Understanding.* New Haven: Yale University Press, 1974.

Chadwick, H. Munro. *The Heroic Age.* Cambridge, Eng.: Cambridge University Press, 1912.

Chadwick, H. Munro, and N. Kershaw Chadwick. *The Growth of Literature.* 3 vols. 1932–40; rpt. Cambridge, Eng.: Cambridge University Press, 1968.

Chaudhuri, J. B. "The Wife in the Vedic Ritual." *Indian Historical Quarterly* 16 (1940): 70–98.

Clark, Walter Eugene. "Śākadvīpa and Śvetadvīpa." *Journal of the American Oriental Society* 39 (1919): 209–42.

Coldstream, J. N. "Hero Cults in the Age of Homer." *Journal of Hellenic Studies* 96 (1976): 8–17.

Coomaraswamy, Ananda K. "Angel and Titan: An Essay in Vedic Ontology." *Journal of the American Oriental Society* 55 (1935): 373–419.

———. "On the Loathly Bride." In *Selected Papers: Traditional Art and Symbolism*. Vol. I of *Coomaraswamy*. Ed. Roger Lipsey. Bollingen Series, 89. Princeton: Princeton University Press, 1977; pp. 353–74.

Cowell, Edward Byles. *The Jātaka or Stories of the Buddha's Former Births*. Vol. V. 1905; rpt. Delhi: Cosmo Publications, 1978.

Crooke, W. *The Popular Religion and Folk-lore of Northern India*. 2nd ed. 2 vols. 1896; rpt. Delhi: Munshiram Manoharlal, 1968.

Cross, Frank Moore. *Canaanite Myth and Hebrew Epic: Essays in the History of the Religion of Israel*. Cambridge, Mass.: Harvard University Press, 1973.

Dahlmann, Joseph. *Das Mahābhārata als Epos und Rechtsbuch: Ein Problem aus Altindiens Cultur- und Literaturgeschichte*. Berlin: Felix L. Dames, 1895.

———. *Genesis des Mahābhārata*. Vol. I of *Mahābhārata-Studien: Abhandlungen zur altindischen Literatur und Culturkunde*. Berlin: Felix L. Dames, 1899.

Dandekar, R. N. "The Mahābhārata: Origin and Growth." *University of Ceylon Review* 12 (1954): 65–85.

Dange, Sadashiv Ambadas. "Aspects of War from the Ṛgveda." *Journal of Indian History* 44 (1966): 125–38.

———. *Legends in the Mahābhārata*. Delhi: Motilal Banarsidass, 1969.

———. "The Pāndava Riddle (Birth and Marriage in a New Light)." *Journal of the University of Bombay*, NS 26, no. 2 (1957): 159–76.

Darmesteter, M. J. "Points de contact entre le Mahâbhârata et le Shâh-Nâmah." *Journal Asiatique*, 8th series, 10 (1887): 38–75.

Dasgupta, Kalyan Kumar. "The Ārjunāyanas: An Ancient Indian Tribe." *Journal of the Oriental Institute* (Baroda) 20 (1970–71): 431–41.

Dasgupta, Surendranath. *A History of Indian Philosophy*. 5 vols. Cambridge, Eng.: Cambridge University Press, 1922–55.

Date, Govind Tryambak. *The Art of War in Ancient India*. London: Humphrey Milford-Oxford University Press, 1929.

Davids, Thomas William Rhys. *The Questions of King Milinda*. The Sacred Books of the East, vols. 35 and 36. Oxford: Clarendon Press, 1890 and 1894.

De, Sushil Kumar. "A Note on Pañca-Kāla in Connection with Pañcarātra." *Journal of the Royal Asiatic Society of Great Britain and Ireland* (1931): 415–18.

———. "Sects and Sectarian Worship in the Mahabharata." *Our Heritage* 1 (1953): 1–29.

De, Sushil Kumar, et al., eds. *The Cultural Heritage of India*. Vol. II. 2nd ed. Calcutta: Ramakrishna Mission Institute of Culture, 1962.

Delcourt, Marie. "The Legend of Sarpedon and the Saga of the Archer." *History of Religions* 2 (1962–63): 33–51.

De Nicolás, Antonio T. *Avatāra: The Humanization of Philosophy through the Bhagavad Gītā*. New York: Nicolas Hays, 1976.

Devasthali, G. V. *Religion and Mythology of the Brāhmaṇas with Particular Reference to the Śatapatha-Brāhmaṇa*. Bhau Vishnu Ashtekar Vedic Research Series, vol. 1. Poona: University of Poona, 1965.

Dhar, M. M. Lachhmi. "The Myth of the Five Husbands of Draupadī." In *Woolner Commemoration Volume*. Ed. Mohammad Shafi. Mehar Chand Lachhman Das Sanskrit and Prakrit Series, vol. 8. Lahore: Mehar Chand Lachhman Das, 1940; pp. 311–16.

Dikshitar, V. R. Ramachandra. *The Purana Index*. 3 vols. Madras: University of Madras, 1951–55.

———. *War in Ancient India*. Madras: Macmillan, 1948.

"Dinkar," Ram Dhari Singh. *The Sun Charioteer*. Trans. Ram Dayal Munda, David Nelson, and Paul Staneslow. Shoreview, Minn.: Nagari Press, 1971.

Divanji, P. C. "Authorship and Date of the Bhārata Epic and the Bhagavadgītā." *Journal of the Ganganatha Jha Research Institute* 4 (1946–47): 113–24.

———. "Bhagavadgītā and Aṣṭādhyāyī." *Annals of the Bhandarkar Oriental Research Institute* 30 (1949): 263–76.

Dorson, Richard M., ed. *Folklore and Folklife: An Introduction*. Chicago: University of Chicago Press, 1972.

———, ed. *Folklore and Traditional History*. Studies in Folklore, 1. 1971; rpt. The Hague: Mouton, 1973.

Drekmeier, Charles. *Kingship and Community in Early India*. Stanford: Stanford University Press, 1962.

Dumézil, Georges. *The Destiny of a King*. Trans. Alf Hiltelbeitel. Chicago: University of Chicago Press, 1973.

———. *The Destiny of the Warrior*. Trans. Alf Hiltebeitel. Chicago: University of Chicago Press, 1970.

———. "Karṇa et les Pāṇḍava." *Orientalia Suecana* 3 (1954): 60–66.

———. "Les pas de Kṛṣṇa et l'exploit d'Arjuna." *Orientalia Suecana* 5 (1956): 183–88.

———. *Mythe et épopée [I]: L'idéologie des trois fonctions dans les épopées des peuples indo-européens*. Paris: Gallimard, 1968.

———. *Mythe et épopée [II]: Types épiques indo-européens: Un héros, un sorcier, un roi*. Paris: Gallimard, 1971.

Dumont, P. E. *L'Aśvamedha: Description du sacrifice solennel du cheval dans le culte védique d'après les textes du Yajurveda blanc*. Paris: Paul Geuthner, 1927.

Dundes, Alan, ed. *The Study of Folklore*. Englewood Cliffs, N.J.: Prentice-Hall, 1965.

Dutt, Manmatha Nath, trans. *A Prose English Translation of Harivamsha*. Calcutta: Elysium Press, 1897.

Eggeling, Julius, trans. *Satapatha-Brâhmana according to the Text of the Mâdhyandina School*. The Sacred Books of the East, vols. 12, 26, 41, 43, 44. Oxford: Clarendon Press, 1882–1900.

Eliade, Mircea. *The Myth of the Eternal Return or Cosmos and History*. Trans. Willard R. Trask. Bollingen Series, 46. 1954; rpt. Princeton: Princeton University Press, 1974.

———. *Rites and Symbols of Initiation: The Mysteries of Birth and Rebirth*. Trans. Willard R. Trask. New York: Harper Colophon Books, 1975.

———. *Shamanism: Archaic Techniques of Ecstasy*. Trans. Willard R. Trask. Bollingen Series, 76. New York: Pantheon, 1964.

Evelyn-White, Hugh G., trans. *Hesiod, the Homeric Hymns and Homerica*. Loeb Classical Library, no. 57. 1914; rpt. Cambridge, Mass.: Harvard University Press; London: W. Heinemann, 1936.

Falk, Nancy E. "Wilderness and Kingship in Ancient South Asia." *History of Religions* 13 (1973–74): 1–15.

Farnell, Lewis Richard. *Greek Hero Cults and Ideas of Immortality: The Gifford Lectures Delivered in the University of St. Andrews in the Year 1920*. Oxford: Clarendon Press, 1921.

Farquhar, J. N. *An Outline of the Religious Literature of India*. 1920; rpt. Delhi: Motilal Banarsidass, 1967.

Finnegan, Ruth. *Oral Poetry: Its Nature, Significance and Social Context*. Cambridge, Eng.: Cambridge University Press, 1977.

Fitzgerald, James L. "The Great Epic of India and the Emergence of 'Hinduism': The *Mahābhārata* as a Religious Paradigm." Inaugural Lecture, Department of Religious Studies, University of Tennessee, Knoxville, 25 February 1980. Mimeographed.

Fleet, J. F. "The Kaliyuga Era of B.C. 3102." *Journal of the Royal Asiatic Society of Great Britain and Ireland* (1911): 479–96, 675–98.

Fontenrose, Joseph. *Python: A Study of Delphic Myth and Its Origins*. Berkeley: University of California Press, 1959.

Frazer, Sir James George, trans., *Apollodorus: The Library*. Loeb Classical Library, nos. 121–22. 1921; rpt. Cambridge, Mass.: Harvard University Press; London: W. Heinemann, 1939 and 1946.

Frye, Northrop. *Anatomy of Criticism: Four Essays*. Princeton: Princeton University Press, 1957.

Gangoly, O. C. "Indra-Cult versus Kṛṣṇa-Cult." *Journal of the Ganganatha Jha Research Institute* 7 (1949–50): 1–27.

Gehrts, Heino. *Mahābhārata: Das Geschehen und seine Bedeutung.* Abhandlungen zur Kunst-, Musik- und Literaturwissenschaft, vol. 178. Bonn: Bouvier, 1975.

Geldner, Karl Friedrich. *Der Rig-Veda: Aus dem Sanskrit ins Deutsche übersetzt und mit einem laufenden Kommentar versehen.* Harvard Oriental Series, vols. 33–36. (4th vol. is *Namen- und Sachregister zur Übersetzung . . .*, by Johannes Nobel.) Cambridge, Mass.: Harvard University Press, 1951–57.

Gennep, Arnold van. *The Rites of Passage.* Trans. Monika B. Vizedom and Gabrielle L. Caffee. Chicago: Phoenix-University of Chicago Press, 1960.

Ghose, Aurobindo. *Essays on the Gita.* Sri Aurobindo International Centre of Education Collection, vol. 8. 1922; rpt. Pondicherry: Sri Aurobindo Ashram, 1966.

———. *Vyasa and Valmiki.* 1956; rpt. Pondicherry: Sri Aurobindo Ashram, 1964.

Ghosh, Juthika. *Epic Sources of Sanskrit Literature.* Calcutta Sanskrit College Research Series, no. 23. Calcutta: Sanskrit College, 1963.

Ghoshal, Upendra Nath. *A History of Indian Political Ideas: The Ancient Period and the Period of Transition to the Middle Ages.* London: Oxford University Press, 1959.

———. "On Some Recent Interpretations of the Mahābhārata Theories of Kingship." *Indian Historical Quarterly* 31 (1955): 323–29.

———. *Studies in Indian History and Culture.* 2nd ed. Bombay: Orient Longmans, 1965.

Goldman, Robert P. "Fathers, Sons and Gurus: Oedipal Conflict in the Sanskrit Epics." *Journal of Indian Philosophy* 6 (September–December 1978): 325–92.

———. *Gods, Priests, and Warriors: The Bhṛgus of the Mahābhārata.* Studies in Oriental Culture, Columbia University, no. 12. New York: Columbia University Press, 1977.

Gonda, Jan. *Ancient Indian Kingship from the Religious Point of View.* Leiden: Brill, 1966.

———. *Aspects of Early Viṣṇuism.* 2nd ed. Delhi: Motilal Banarsidass, 1969.

———. *Change and Continuity in Indian Religion.* Disputationes Rheno-Trajectinae, 9. The Hague: Mouton, 1965.

———. "Dumézil's Tripartite Ideology: Some Critical Observations." In *Symposium: The Achievement of Georges Dumézil. Journal of Asian Studies* 34 (1974–75): 139–49.

———. "The Vedic Mitra and the Epic Dharma." *Journal of the Royal Asiatic Society of Great Britain and Ireland* (1971): 120–33.

———. *Viṣṇuism and Śivaism: A Comparison* (Jordan Lectures, 1969). London: Athlone Press-University of London, 1970.

Goswami, C. L., trans. *Srīmad Bhāgavata Mahāpurāṇa* (with Sanskrit text and English translation). 2 vols. Gorakhpur: Motilal Jalan at the Gita Press, 1971.

Govindacarya Swamin, A. "The Pancaratras or Bhagavat-Sastra." *Journal of the Royal Asiatic Society of Great Britain and Ireland* (1911): 835–61.

Griffith, Ralph T. H. *The Hymns of the Ṛgveda: Translated with a Popular Commentary*. Ed. J. L. Shastri. New rev. ed. Delhi: Motilal Banarsidass, 1973.

Grintser, Pavel A. *Drevneindiiskii epos: genezis i tipologiia*. Moscow: Nauka, 1974.

Gupta, S. P., and K. S. Ramachandran, eds. *Mahābhārata: Myth and Reality: Differing Views*. Delhi: Agam Prakashan, 1976.

Guthrie, W. K. C. *The Greeks and Their Gods*. Boston: Beacon Press, 1951.

Hamilton, Edith, and Huntington Cairns, eds. *The Collected Dialogues of Plato including the Letters*. Bollingen Series, 71. New York: Pantheon-Random House, 1961.

Hawley, John Stratton. *Krishna, the Butter Thief*. Princeton: Princeton University Press, 1983.

Hazra, R. C. "The Aśvamedha, the Common Source of Origin of the Purāṇa Pañca-Lakṣaṇa and the Mahābhārata." *Annals of the Bhandarkar Oriental Research Institute* 36 (1955): 190–203.

Heesterman, Johannes Cornelis. *The Ancient Indian Royal Consecration: The Rājasūya Described according to the Yajus Texts and Annotated*. The Hague: Mouton, 1957.

Heidel, Alexander. *The Babylonian Genesis: The Story of Creation*. 2nd ed. 1951; rpt. Chicago: Phoenix-University of Chicago Press, 1963.

———. *The Gilgamesh Epic and Old Testament Parallels*. 2nd ed. 1949; rpt. Chicago: Phoenix-University of Chicago Press, 1963.

Held, Gerrit Jan. *The Mahābhārata: An Ethnological Study*. London: Kegan Paul, Trench, Trubner and Co.; Amsterdam: Uitgeversmaatschappij Holland, 1935.

Herbert, Jean. *La Mythologie hindoue: Son message*. 2nd ed. Spiritualités Vivants, Série Hindouisme. Paris: Albin Michel, 1980.

Hiltebeitel, Alf. "Brothers, Friends, and Charioteers: Parallel Episodes in the Irish and Indian Epics." In *Homage to Georges Dumézil*. Ed. Edgar C. Polomé. *Journal of Indo-European Studies*, Monograph no. 3. Washington D.C.: *Journal of Indo-European Studies*, Institute for the Study of Man, 1982; pp. 85–111.

———. "The Burning of the Forest Myth." In *Hinduism: New Essays in the History of Religions.* Ed. Bardwell L. Smith. Studies in the History of Religions (Supplements to *Numen*), 33. Leiden: Brill, 1976; pp. 208–24.

———. "Draupadī's Garments." *Indo-Iranian Journal* 22 (1980): 97–112.

———. "Dumézil and Indian Studies." In *Symposium: The Achievement of Georges Dumézil. Journal of Asian Studies* 34 (1974–75): 129–37.

———. *Mythologies: From Gingee to Kurukṣetra.* Vol. I of *The Cult of Draupadī.* Chicago: University of Chicago Press, 1988.

———. Review of *Mahābhārata: Das Geschehen und seine Bedeutung,* by Heino Gehrts. *Erasmus* 29 (1977): columns 86–91.

———. *The Ritual of Battle: Krishna in the Mahābhārata.* Ithaca: Cornell University Press, 1976.

———. "Śiva, the Goddess, and the Disguises of the Pāṇḍavas and Draupadī." *History of Religions* 20 (1980–81): 147–74.

———. "Toward a Coherent Study of Hinduism." *Religious Studies Review* 9 (1983): 205–12.

———. "The Two Kṛṣṇas on One Chariot: Upaniṣadic Imagery and Epic Mythology." *History of Religions* 24 (1984–85): 1–26.

The Holy Bible, Revised Standard Version.

Holtzmann, Adolf (elder). *Indische Sagen.* 2 vols. Stuttgart: Adolph Krabbe, 1854.

Holtzmann, Adolf (younger). *Arjuna: Ein Beitrag zur Reconstruction des Mahābhārata.* Strassburg: Karl J. Trübner, 1879.

———. *Zur Geschichte und Kritik des Mahābhārata.* Vol. I of *Das Mahābhārata und seine Teile.* Kiel: C. F. Haeseler, 1892.

Hopkins, E. Washburn. "The Bhārata and the Great Bhārata." *American Journal of Philology* 19 (1898): 1–24.

———. "The Divinity of Kings." *Journal of the American Oriental Society* 51 (1931): 309–16.

———. *Epic Mythology.* 1915; rpt. Delhi: Motilal Banarsidass, 1974.

———. "The Epic Use of Bhagavat and Bhakti." *Journal of the Royal Asiatic Society of Great Britain and Ireland* (1911): 727–38.

———. *The Great Epic of India: Its Character and Origin.* New York: Scribner, 1901.

———. "Indra as God of Fertility." *Journal of the American Oriental Society* 36 (1916): 242–68.

———. "The Oath in Hindu Epic Literature." *Journal of the American Oriental Society* 52 (1932): 316–37.

———. "The Social and Military Position of the Ruling Caste in Ancient India, as Represented by the Sanskrit Epic." *Journal of the American Oriental Society* 13 (1889): 57–376.

Huizinga, Johan. *Homo Ludens: A Study of the Play-Element in Culture*. 1950; rpt. Boston: Beacon Press, 1955.

Hume, Robert Ernest. *The Thirteen Principle Upanishads Translated from the Sanskrit with an Outline of the Philosophy of the Upanishads*. 2nd ed. London: Oxford University Press, 1931.

Humphries, Rolfe, trans. *Ovid: Metamorphoses*. Bloomington: Indiana University Press, 1955.

Hyman, Stanley Edgar. "The Ritual View of Myth and the Mythic." *Journal of American Folklore* 68 (1955): 462–72.

Ingalls, Daniel H. H. "Authority and Law in Ancient India." In *Authority and Law in the Ancient Orient*. Supplement to the *Journal of the American Oriental Society*, 17. Baltimore: American Oriental Society, 1954; pp. 34–45.

Jacobi, Hermann. *Mahābhārata: Inhaltsangabe, Index und Concordanz der Calcuttaer und Bombayer Ausgaben*. Bonn: Friedrich Cohen, 1903.

———. Review of *Das Mahābhārata als Epos und Rechtsbuch*, by Joseph Dahlmann. *Göttingische gelehrte Anzeigen unter der Aufsicht der Königlichen Gesellschaft der Wissenschaften* (1896): 67–78.

Jain, Ram Chandra. *Jaya: The Original Nucleus of Mahabharata*. Delhi: Agam Kala Prakashan, 1979.

Jaiswal, Suvira. *The Origin and Development of Vaiṣṇavism (Vaiṣṇavism from 200* B.C. *to* A.D. *500)*. Delhi: Munshiram Manoharlal, 1967.

Jauhari; Manorama. *Politics and Ethics in Ancient India: A Study Based on the Mahābhārata*. Varanasi: Bharatiya Vidya Prakashan, 1968.

Johnsen, Gösta. "Varuṇa and Dhṛtarāṣṭra." *Indo-Iranian Journal* 9 (1965–66): 245–65.

Jolly, J., ed. *Mânava Dharma-Śâstra: The Code of Manu*. London: Trübner and Co., 1887.

Jones, Clifford R., and Betty True Jones. *Kathakali: An Introduction to the Dance-Drama of Kerala*. San Francisco: American Society for Eastern Arts; New York: Theatre Arts Books, 1970.

Jong, J. W. de. "Recent Russian Publications on the Indian Epic." *Adyar Library Bulletin* 39 (1975): 1–42.

———. Review of *The Mahābhārata*, vol. III, trans. J. A. B. van Buitenen. *Indo-Iranian Journal* 22 (1980): 58–62.

Kane, Pandurang Vaman. *History of Dharmaśāstra (Ancient and Mediaeval Religious and Civil Law)*. 2nd ed. Government Oriental Series, Class B, no. 6. 5 vols. in 8. Poona: Bhandarkar Oriental Research Institute, 1968–77.

Karmarkar, A. P. "Dr. V. S. Sukthankar's Theory of the Bhṛguisation of the Original Bhārata and the Light It Throws on the Dravidian Problem." *Annals of the Bhandarkar Oriental Research Institute* 20 (1938–39): 21–24.

Karve, Irawati. *Yugānta: The End of an Epoch.* Poona: Deshmukh Prakashan, 1969.

Kashalikar, M. J. "The Origin of the Pāṇḍavas (as Related in the Mahābhārata . . . and Some Later Jain Works, and Its Sociological Implications)." *Journal of the Oriental Institute* (Baroda) 16 (1966–67): 349–59.

Kātre, S. L. "Avatāras of God." *Allahabad University Studies*, Arts and Sciences 10 (1934): 37–130.

Katre, S. M. "Dharmopaniṣad in Mahābhārata." *Journal of the Ganganatha Jha Research Institute* 1 (1943–44): 118–22.

Katz (Arabagian), Ruth. "Cattle Raiding and Bride Stealing: The Goddess in Indo-European Heroic Literature." *Religion* 14 (1984): 107–42.

———. "Human and Divine Time in the Bhagavadgītā." *Journal of Studies in the Bhagavadgītā* 1 (1981): 100–12.

Keith, Arthur Berriedale, trans. *Rigveda Brahmanas: The Aitareya and Kauṣītaki Brāhmaṇas of the Rigveda.* Harvard Oriental Series, 25. 1920; rpt. Delhi: Motilal Banarsidass, 1971.

Keny, Liladhar B. "The Image of Nārāyaṇa." *Annals of the Bhandarkar Oriental Research Institute* 29 (1948): 213–26.

———. "The Origin of Nārāyaṇa." *Annals of the Bhandarkar Oriental Research Institute* 23 (1942): 250–56.

Kerényi, Károly. *The Heroes of the Greeks.* Trans. H. J. Rose. London: Thames and Hudson, 1959.

Khan, Benjamin. *The Concept of Dharma in Valmiki Ramayana.* Delhi: Munshiram Manoharlal, 1965.

Kinsella, Thomas, trans. *The Tain: Translated from the Irish Epic Tain Bo Cuailnge.* London: Oxford University Press, 1969.

Kinsley, David R. *The Sword and the Flute: Kālī and Kṛṣṇa, Dark Visions of the Terrible and the Sublime in Hindu Mythology.* Berkeley: University of California Press, 1975.

Kirk, G. S. *Myth: Its Meaning and Functions in Ancient and Other Cultures.* London: Cambridge University Press; Berkeley: University of California Press, 1970.

Klaes, Norbert. *Conscience and Consciousness: Ethical Problems of Mahabharata.* Bangalore: Dharmaram College, 1975.

Klapp, Orrin E. "The Clever Hero." *Journal of American Folklore* 67 (1954): 21–34.

Knipe, David M. "The Heroic Theft: Myths from Ṛgveda IV and the Ancient Near East." *History of Religions* 6 (1966–67): 328–60.

———. "One Fire, Three Fires, Five Fires: Vedic Symbols in Transition." *History of Religions* 12 (1972–73): 28–41.

Kosambi, D. D. "The Autochthonous Element in the Mahābhārata." *Journal of the American Oriental Society* 84 (1964): 31–44.

Kraatz, Gisela. *Vers und Prosa: Entstehungstheorien zum deutschen und indischen Heldenepos*. Munich: Steinbauer und Rau, 1961.

Krishnamoorthy, K., trans. *Ānandavardhana's Dhvanyāloka or Theory of Suggestion in Poetry*. Poona Oriental Series, no. 92. Poona: Oriental Book Agency, 1955.

Kurtkoti, Dr. [Shri Shankaracharya]. "Influence of the Mahābhārata on Hindu Social Life." *Annals of the Bhandarkar Oriental Research Institute* 19 (1937–38): 1–9.

Lal, P. *An Annotated Mahabharata Bibliography*. Calcutta: Writers Workshop, 1967.

Lattimore, Richmond, trans. *The Iliad of Homer*. Chicago: University of Chicago Press, 1951.

———, trans. *The Odyssey of Homer*. New York: Harper and Row, 1967.

Leach, Edmund. *Claude Lévi-Strauss*. New York: Viking, 1970.

Lévi, Sylvain. *La Doctrine du sacrifice dans les Brâhmaṇas*. 2nd ed. Bibliothèque de l'Ecole des Hautes Etudes, Section des Sciences Religieuses, vol. 73. Paris: Presses Universitaires de France, 1966.

———. *"Tato jayam udirayet."* Trans. L. G. Khare. *Annals of the Bhandarkar Institute* 1 (1918–19): 13–20.

Levy, Gertrude Rachel. *The Sword from the Rock: An Investigation into the Origins of Epic Literature and the Development of the Hero*. New York: Grove Press, 1953.

Lincoln, Bruce. *Priests, Warriors and Cattle: A Study in the Ecology of Religions*. Berkeley: University of California Press, 1981.

Littleton, C. Scott. *The New Comparative Mythology: An Anthropological Assessment of the Theories of Georges Dumézil*. Rev. ed. Berkeley: University of California Press, 1973.

Long, J. Bruce. *The Mahābhārata: A Select Annotated Bibliography*. South Asia Occasional Papers and Theses. Ithaca: South Asia Program-Cornell University, 1974.

Lord, Albert B. *The Singer of Tales*. Harvard Studies in Comparative Literature, 24. Cambridge, Mass.: Harvard University Press, 1960.

Lüders, Heinrich. *Das Würfelspiel im alten Indien*. Abhandlungen der Königlichen Gesellschaft der Wissenschaften zu Göttingen, Philologisch-Historische Klasse, NS vol. 19, no. 2. Berlin: Weidmannsche Buchhandlung, 1907.

Ludwig, Alfred. *Über das Verhältnis des mythischen Elementes zu der historischen Grundlage des Mahâbhârata*. Abhandlungen, 6th Series, vol. 12, Classe für Philosophie, Geschichte und Philologie, no. 5. Prague: Verlag der königlichen böhmischen Gesellschaft der Wissenschaften, 1884.

Macdonell, Arthur Anthony. *Vedic Mythology*. 1898; rpt. Delhi: Motilal Banarsidass, 1974.

Macdonell, Arthur Anthony, and Arthur Berriedale Keith. *Vedic Index of Names and Subjects*. 2 vols. London: John Murray, 1912.

McNamee, Maurice B. *Honor and the Epic Hero: A Study of the Shifting Concept of Magnanimity in Philosophy and Epic Poetry*. New York: Holt, Rinehart and Winston, 1960.

Maguire, Marcia E. "The *Haft Khvān* of Rustam and Isfandiyār." In *Studies in Art and Literature of the Near East: In Honor of Richard Ettinghausen*. Ed. Peter J. Chelkowski. New York University Near Eastern Round Table, 5. Salt Lake City: Middle East Center-University of Utah, 1974; pp.137–47.

Majumdar, D. N. *Himalayan Polyandry: Structure, Functioning and Cultural Change: A Field Study of Jaunsar-Bawar*. New York: Asia Publishing House, 1960.

Malory, Thomas. *Le Morte d'Arthur*. Ed. Janet Cowen. 2 vols. Harmondsworth: Penguin, 1969.

Mani, Vettam. *Purāṇic Encyclopaedia: A Comprehensive Dictionary with Special Reference to the Epic and Purāṇic Literature*. Trans. P. Rajaram Menon et al. Delhi: Motilal Banarsidass, 1975.

Matsubara, Mitsunori. "The Early Pāñcarātra with Special Reference to the Ahirbudhnya Saṃhitā." Dissertation, Harvard 1972.

Mayrhofer, Manfred. *Kurzgefasstes etymologisches Wörterbuch des Altindischen. (A Concise Etymological Sanskrit Dictionary.)* 3 vols. Heidelberg: Carl Winter, 1956–76.

Mazumdar, B. C. "Mahābhārata (Ādiparva, ch. 94)." *Journal of the Royal Asiatic Society of Great Britain and Ireland* (1906): 225–26.

Mehta, J. M., et al., eds. *The Vālmīki-Rāmāyaṇa: Critically Edited for the First Time*. 7 vols. Baroda: Oriental Institute, 1960–75.

Meyer, Johann Jakob. *Sexual Life in Ancient India: A Study in the Comparative History of Indian Culture*. Delhi: Motilal Banarsidass, 1971.

———. *Trilogie altindischer Mächte und Feste der Vegetation: Ein Beitrag zur vergleichenden Religions- und Kulturgeschichte, Fest- und Volkskunde*. Zurich: Max Niehans, 1937; Part III.

Monier-Williams, Monier. *A Sanskrit-English Dictionary Etymologically Arranged with Special Reference to Latin, Gothic, German, Anglo-Saxon and other Cognate Indo-European Languages*. Oxford: Clarendon Press, 1872. (1899 edition also consulted; rpt. Delhi: Motilal Banarsidass, 1979.)

———. *Indian Epic Poetry: Being the Substance of Lectures Recently Given at Oxford: With a Full Analysis of the Rámáyaṇa and of the Leading Story of the Mahá-Bhárata*. London: Williams and Norgate, 1863.

Muir, John. "Notes on the Lax Observance of Caste Rules and Other Features of Social and Religious Life in Ancient India." *Indian Antiquary* 6 (1877): 251–64.

———. "On the Question Whether Polyandry Ever Existed in Northern Hindustân." *Indian Antiquary* 6 (1877): 315–17.

Mullick, Promatha Nath. *The Mahabharata as It Was, Is, and Ever Shall Be: A Critical Study*. Calcutta: For Author, by Pioneer Press (Allahabad), 1934.

Nagaraja Rao, M. S. *Kirātārjunīyam in Indian Art (with Special Reference to Karnataka)*. Delhi: Agam Kala Prakashan, 1979.

Nagy, Gregory. *The Best of the Achaeans: Concepts of the Hero in Archaic Greek Poetry*. Baltimore: Johns Hopkins University Press, 1979.

———. "On the Death of Sarpedon." In *Approaches to Homer*. Ed. Carl A. Rubino and Cynthia W. Shelmerdine. Austin: University of Texas Press, 1983; pp.189–217.

Narasimhan, Chakravarthi V. *The Mahābhārata: An English Version Based on Selected Verses*. Records of Civilization: Sources and Studies, 71. New York: Columbia University Press, 1965.

Neevel, Walter G., Jr. *Yāmuna's Vedānta and Pāñcarātra: Integrating the Classical and the Popular*. Harvard Dissertations in Religion, 10. Missoula, Mont.: Scholars Press, 1977.

Neumann, Erich. *The Origins and History of Consciousness*. Trans. R. F. C. Hull. Bollingen Series, 42. New York: Pantheon, 1954.

Nock, Arthur Darby. "The Cult of Heroes." *Harvard Theological Review* 37 (1944): 141–74.

Norman, H. C. "The Kalki Avatāra of Viṣṇu." *Transactions of the Third International Congress for the History of Religions*. 2 vols. Oxford: Clarendon Press, 1908. II, 85–89.

Oertel, Hans. "Contributions from the Jāiminīya Brāhmaṇa to the History of the Brāhmaṇa Literature," III: "Indrasya kilbiṣāṇi." *Journal of the American Oriental Society* 19, no. 2 (1898): 118–25.

O'Flaherty, Wendy Doniger. *Asceticism and Eroticism in the Mythology of Śiva*. London: Oxford University Press, 1973.

———. "The Clash between Relative and Absolute Duty: The Dharma of Demons." In *The Concept of Duty in South Asia*. Ed. Wendy Doniger O'Flaherty and J. Duncan M. Derrett. [Columbia, Mo.]: South Asia Books, 1978; pp. 96–106.

———. *Hindu Myths: A Sourcebook Translated from the Sanskrit*. Harmondsworth: Penguin, 1975.

———. *The Origins of Evil in Hindu Mythology*. Berkeley: University of California Press, 1976.

———. Review of *The Mahābhārata*, vols. I–II, trans. J. A. B. van Buitenen. *Religious Studies Review* 4 (1978): 19–28.

Oldenberg, Hermann. *Das Mahabharata: Seine Entstehung, sein Inhalt, seine Form*. Göttingen: Vandehoeck und Ruprecht, 1922.

Pargiter, F. Eden. *Ancient Indian Historical Tradition*. London: Humphrey Milford-Oxford University Press, 1922.

———. trans. *The Mārkaṇḍeya Purāṇa*. 1904; rpt. Delhi: Indological Book House, 1969.

———. "The Nations of India at the Battle between the Pandavas and Kauravas." *Journal of the Royal Asiatic Society* (1908): 309–36 (with discussion surrounding this paper by George A. Grierson and A. Berriedale Keith, pp. 602–7, 831–44, 1138–43).

Parrinder, Geoffrey. *Avatar and Incarnation: The Wilde Lectures in Natural and Comparative Religion in the University of Oxford*. London: Faber and Faber, 1970.

Pisàni, Vittore. "The Rise of the Mahābhārata." In *Volume of Eastern and Indian Studies Presented to Professor F. W. Thomas C.I.E. on his 72nd birthday 21st March 1939*. Ed. S. M. Katre and P. K. Gode. *New Indian Antiquary*, Extra Series, 1. Bombay: Karnatak Publishing House, 1939; pp. 166–76.

Propp, Vladimir. *Morphology of the Folktale*. Trans. Laurence Scott. 2nd ed. Revised by Louis A. Wagner. American Folklore Society Bibliographical and Special Series, vol. 9. Indiana University Research Center in Anthropology, Folklore, and Linguistics, 10. Austin: University of Texas Press, 1968.

Przyluski, J. "Le Prologue-cadre des *Mille et une Nuits* et le thème du svayaṃvara." *Journal Asiatique* 205 (1924): 101–37.

Puhvel, Jaan, ed. *Myth and Law among the Indo-Europeans: Studies in Indo-European Comparative Mythology*. Publications of the UCLA Center for the Study of Comparative Folklore and Mythology, 1. Berkeley: University of California Press, 1970.

———. "Transposition of Myth to Saga in Indo-European Epic Narrative." In *Antiquitates Indogermanicae: Studien zur indogermanischen Altertumskunde und zur Sprach- und Kulturgeschichte der indogermanischen Völker: Gedenkschrift für Hermann Güntert zur 25. Wiederkehr seines Todestages am 23. April 1973*. Ed. Manfred Mayrhofer et al. Innsbruck: Innsbrucker Beiträge zur Sprachwissenschaft, 1974; pp.175–84.

Pusalker, A. D. *Studies in the Epics and Puranas*. Bhavan's Book University, no. 36. Bombay: Bharatiya Vidya Bhavan, 1963.

Radin, Paul. *The Trickster: A Study in American Indian Mythology*. With commentaries by Karl Kerényi and C. G. Jung. Introductory essay by Stanley Diamond. New York: Schocken, 1972.

Raghavan, V. "The Name Pāñcarātra: With an Analysis of the Sanatkumāra-Saṃhitā in Manuscript." *Journal of the American Oriental Society* 85 (1965): 73–79.

Raglan, FitzRoy Richard Somerset. *The Hero: A Study in Tradition, Myth, and Drama*. 1949; rpt. Westport, Conn.: Greenwood Press, 1975.

Rajagopalachari, Chakravarti. *Mahabharata*. 13th ed. Bombay: Bharatiya Vidya Bhavan, 1974.

Ramachandran, T. N. "Aśvamedha Site Near Kalsi." *Journal of Oriental Research* (Madras) 21 (1951–52): 1–31.

———. "Fresh Light on the Deogarh Relief of Nara-Nārāyaṇa." *Indian Historical Quarterly* 27 (1951): 191–96.

———. "The *Kirātārjunīyam* or 'Arjuna's Penance' in Indian Art." *Journal of the Indian Society of Oriental Art* 18 (1950–51): 1–110.

Rangachari, K. *The Sri Vaishnava Brahmans. Bulletin of the Madras Government Museum*, NS–General Section 2, Pt. 2 (1931): 1–158.

Rank, Otto. *The Myth of the Birth of the Hero and Other Writings*. Ed. Philip Freund. New York: Vintage-Random House, 1959.

Rapson, E. J., ed. *The Cambridge History of India*. Vol. I. New York: Macmillan, 1922.

Raychaudhuri, Hemchandra. *Political History of Ancient India*. 3rd ed. Calcutta: University of Calcutta, 1932.

Rees, Alwyn, and Brinley Rees. *Celtic Heritage: Ancient Tradition in Ireland and Wales*. London: Thames and Hudson, 1961.

Rice, Edward P. *The Mahabharata: An Analysis and Index*. London: Humphrey Milford-Oxford University Press, 1934.

Rohde, Erwin. *Psyche: The Cult of Souls and Belief in Immortality among the Greeks*. Trans. W. B. Hillis (from 8th ed.). London: Routledge and Kegan Paul, 1950.

Rose, H. J. *A Handbook of Greek Mythology: Including Its Extension to Rome*. 6th ed. London: Methuen, 1958.

Roy, Brajdeo Prasad. *Political Ideas and Institutions in the Mahābhārata (Based on Poona Critical Edition)*. Calcutta: Punthi Pustak, 1975.

Ruben, Walter. "The Adventures of Indian Epic Heroes in the Forest." *Our Heritage* 8 (1960): 65–68.

———. *Krishna: Konkordanz und Kommentar der Motive seines Heldenlebens.* Istanbul: Istanbuler Schriften, 1944.

Sandesara, Upendraray J. "Interpretation of the Word *Jaya* in the First Verse of the Mahābhārata." *Journal of the Oriental Institute* (Baroda) 7 (1957–58): 262–64.

Sarma, Binod. *Ethico-Literary Values of the Two Great Epics of India: An Ethical Evaluation of the Mahabharata and the Ramayana.* World's Wisdom Series, no. 13. New Delhi: Oriental Publishers and Distributors, 1978.

Sayers, Dorothy L., trans. *The Song of Roland.* Harmondsworth: Penguin, 1937.

Schein, Seth L. *The Mortal Hero: An Introduction to Homer's Iliad.* Berkeley: University of California Press, 1984.

Scheuer, Jacques. *Śiva dans le Mahābhārata.* Bibliotheque de l'Ecole des Hautes Etudes, Section des Sciences Religieuses, vol. 84. Paris: Presses Universitaires de France, 1982.

Schmitt, Rüdiger. *Dichtung und Dichtersprache in indogermanischer Zeit.* Wiesbaden: Otto Harrassowitz, 1967.

———. "Indogermanische Dichtersprache. Eine Skizze." In *Indogermanische Dichtersprache.* Ed. Rüdiger Schmitt. Wege der Forschung, vol. 165. Darmstadt: Wissenschaftliche Buchgesellschaft, 1968; pp. 334–43.

Scholem, Gershom. *Major Trends in Jewish Mysticism.* 3rd ed. New York: Schocken, 1954.

Schrader, F. Otto. *Introduction to the Pāñcarātra and the Ahirbudhnya Saṃhitā.* Madras: Adyar Library, 1916.

Sen, Chitrabhanu. *A Dictionary of the Vedic Rituals: Based on the Śrauta and Gṛhya Sūtras.* Delhi: Concept Publishing, 1978.

Sharma, Arvind, ed. *Essays on the Mahābhārata. Journal of South Asian Literature* 20 (1985): 1–168.

Sharma, Ram Karan. *Elements of Poetry in the Mahābhārata.* University of California Publications in Classical Philology, vol. 20. Berkeley: University of California Press, 1964.

Shastri, Hari Prasad, trans. *The Ramayana of Valmiki.* 3rd ed. 3 vols. London: Shanti Sadan, 1976.

Shetterly, Indira Viswanathan. "Recurrence and Structure in Sanskrit Literary Epic: A Study of Bhāravi's *Kirātārjunīya.*" Dissertation, Harvard 1976.

Sidhanta, N. K. *The Heroic Age of India: A Comparative Study.* London: Kegan Paul, Trench, Trubner and Co.; New York: Alfred A. Knopf, 1929.

Simson, Georg von. "Die Einschaltung der *Bhagavadgītā* im *Bhīṣmaparvan* des *Mahābhārata.*" *Indo-Iranian Journal* 11 (1968–69): 159–74.

Singer, Milton, ed. *Krishna: Myths, Rites, and Attitudes.* Chicago: Phoenix-University of Chicago Press, 1968.

Sinha, J. P. *The Mahābhārata: A Literary Study*. New Delhi: Meharchand Lachhmandas, 1977.

Sinha, N. K. P. *Political Ideas and Ideals in the Mahabharata: A Study of the First Two Parvans*. New Delhi: Oriental Publishers and Distributors, 1976.

Sircar, D. C., ed. *The Bhārata War and Purāṇic Genealogies*. Calcutta: University of Calcutta, 1969.

Smith, H. Daniel. "A Typological Survey of Definitions: The Name 'Pāñcarātra': Utilizing Texts of the Pāñcarātra Saṃhitās." In *Oriental Research Madras: Special Volume Dedicated to H.H. Sri Chandrasekharendra Sarasvati, Sankaracharya of Kanchi Kamakoti Pitha*. Ed. V. Raghavan. Madras: Kuppuswami Sastri Research Institute, 1973; pp. 102–17.

Smith, John D. "Old Indian: The Two Sanskrit Epics." In *The Traditions*. Vol. I of *Traditions of Heroic and Epic Poetry*. Ed. A. T. Hatto. Publications of the Modern Humanities Research Association, vol. 9. London: Modern Humanities Research Association, 1980.

———. "The Singer or the Song? A Reassessment of Lord's 'Oral Theory.' " *Man*, NS 12 (1977): 141–53.

Smith, Mary Carroll. "The Core of India's Great Epic." Dissertation, Harvard 1972.

———. "The Mahābhārata's Core." *Journal of the American Oriental Society* 95 (1975): 479–82.

Sørensen, Søren. *An Index to the Names in the Mahābhārata, with Short Explanations and a Concordance to the Bombay and Calcutta Editions and P. C. Roy's Translation*. 1904; rpt. Delhi: Motilal Banarsidass, 1978.

Spellman, John W. "The Symbolic Significance of the Number Twelve in Ancient India." *Journal of Asian Studies* 22 (1962–63): 79–88.

Stevenson, Robert Walter. "Historical Change in Scriptural Interpretation: A Comparative Study of Classical and Contemporary Commentaries on the Bhagavadgītā." Dissertation, Harvard 1975.

Strauss, Otto. *Ethische Probleme aus dem "Mahābhārata."* Florence: Tipografia Galileiana, 1912.

Stuart, Heather. "Cuchulainn and the 'Vater-Sohn Kampf' Motif." *Journal of the Australasian Universities Language and Literature Association* 47 (May 1977): 5–17.

Stutley, Margaret, and James Stutley. *A Dictionary of Hinduism: Its Mythology, Folklore and Development 1500* B.C.–A.D. *1500*. London: Routledge and Kegan Paul, 1977.

Subramanian, M. V. *The Mahabharata Story: Vyasa and Variations*. Madras: Higginbothams, 1967.

Sukthankar, Vishnu Sitaram. *Critical Studies in the Mahābhārata*. Vol. I of *Sukthankar Memorial Edition*. Ed. P. K. Gode. Bombay: Karnatak Publishing House, 1944.

———. *On the Meaning of the Mahābhārata*. Society's Monograph, no. 4. Bombay: Asiatic Society of Bombay, 1957.

Tadapatrikar, S. N. "The Kṛṣṇa Problem." *Annals of the Bhandarkar Oriental Research Institute* 10 (1929–30): 269–344.

Tagare, Ganesh Vasudeo, trans. *The Bhāgavata-Purāṇa*. Ancient Indian Tradition and Mythology, vols. 7–11. Delhi: Motilal Banarsidass, 1976–78.

Taylor, Archer. "The Biographical Pattern in Traditional Narrative." *Journal of the Folklore Institute* 1 (1964): 114–29.

Thadani, N. V. *The Mystery of the Mahabharata*. 5 vols. Karachi: Bharat Publishing House, 1931–35.

Thompson, Stith. *Motif-Index of Folk Literature: A Classification of Narrative Elements in Folktales, Ballads, Myths, Fables, Mediaeval Romances, Exempla, Fabliaux, Jest-Books and Local Legends*. Rev. ed. 6 vols. Bloomington: Indiana University Press, 1955–58.

———. *The Oral Tales of India*. Indiana University Publications Folklore Series, no. 10. Bloomington: Indiana University Press, 1958.

Trautmann, Thomas R. *Dravidian Kinship*. Cambridge Studies in Social Anthropology, 36. Cambridge, Eng.: Cambridge University Press, 1981.

Turner, Victor. *The Forest of Symbols: Aspects of Ndembu Ritual*. Ithaca: Cornell University Press, 1967.

Ulbricht, H. *Wayang Purwa: Shadows of the Past*. Kuala Lumpur: Oxford University Press, 1970.

Vaidya, Chintaman Vinayak. *Epic India or India as Described in the Mahabharata and Ramayana*. Bombay: Mrs. R. A. Sagoon, 1907.

———. *The Mahābhārata: A Criticism*. Delhi: Mehar Chand Lachhman Das, 1966.

Vaidya, Parashuram Laksman, ed. *The Harivaṃśa: Being the Khila or Supplement to the Mahābhārata*. (Critical Edition) 2 vols. Poona: Bhandarkar Oriental Research Institute, 1969 and 1971.

Van Nooten, Barend A. *The Mahābhārata Attributed to Kṛṣṇa Dvaipāyana Vyāsa*. New York: Twayne, 1971.

Venkat Rao, Vedula. *The Message of the Maha Bharata*. Visakhapatnam: S. G. Sambandan, 1976.

Vogel, Jean Philippe. *Indian Serpent-Lore or the Nagas in Hindu Legend and Art*. London: Probsthain, 1926.

Vora, Dhairyabala P. *Evolution of Morals in the Epics (Mahābhārata and Rāmāyaṇa)*. Bombay: Popular Book Depot, 1959.

Vreese, K. de. "The Game of Dice in Ancient India (The Vibhītaka Game)." In *Orientalia Neerlandica: A Volume of Oriental Studies Published under the Auspices of the Netherlands' Oriental Society (Oostersch Genootschap in Nederland) on the Occasion of the Twenty-fifth Anniversary of Its Foundation (May 8th 1945)*. Leiden: Sijthoff, 1948; pp. 349–62.

Vries, Jan de. *Heroic Song and Heroic Legend*. Trans. B. J. Timmer. London: Oxford University Press, 1963.

Ward, Donald. *The Divine Twins: An Indo-European Myth in Germanic Tradition*. Folklore Studies, 19. Berkeley: University of California Press, 1968.

———. "On the Poets and Poetry of the Indo-Europeans." *Journal of Indo-European Studies* 1 (1973): 127–44.

Warner, Arthur George, and Edmond Warner, trans. *The Sháhnáma of Firdausí*. 9 vols. London: Kegan Paul, Trench, Trübner and Co., 1905–25.

Weller, Hermann. "Who Were the Bhriguids?" *Annals of the Bhandarkar Oriental Research Institute* 18 (1936–37): 296–302.

Whitman, Cedric H. *Homer and the Heroic Tradition*. 1958; rpt. New York: Norton, 1965.

Whitney, William Dwight. *Sanskrit Grammar: Including Both the Classical Language, and the Older Dialects, of Veda and Brahmana*. 2nd ed. Cambridge, Mass.: Harvard University Press, 1889.

Winternitz, Moriz. *A History of Indian Literature*. Vol. I. Trans. S. Ketkar. 2nd ed. 1927; rpt. New Delhi: Oriental Books Reprint Corporation, 1972.

———. "Notes on the Mahābhārata, with Special Reference to Dahlmann's 'Mahābhārata.'" *Journal of the Royal Asiatic Society of Great Britain and Ireland* (1897): 713–59.

———. "The Serpent Sacrifice Mentioned in the Mahābhārata." *Journal of the Bombay Branch of the Royal Asiatic Society*, NS 2 (1926): 74–91.

Woolner, A. C., and Lakshman Sarup, trans. *Thirteen Trivandrum Plays Attributed to Bhāsa*. Panjab University Oriental Publications, no. 13. 2 vols. London: Humphrey Milford-Oxford University Press, 1930 and 1931.

Yu, Anthony C., ed. *Parnassus Revisited: Modern Critical Essays on the Epic Tradition*. Chicago: American Library Association, 1973.

Zaehner, R. C. *Hinduism*. 1962; rpt. London: Oxford University Press, 1971.

AUTHORS INDEX

Authors Index

Authors Index

SUBJECT INDEX

(Primary entries in Sanskrit are given in simplified transliteration, followed by standard transliteration in parentheses. To avoid unnecessary complications, a simple *-s* has been appended to standard transliteration of plurals.)

Subject Index

Subject Index

Subject Index

Subject Index

Subject Index

Subject Index

Subject Index